The BIBLICAL TRUTH ABOUT AMERICA'S DEATH PENALTY

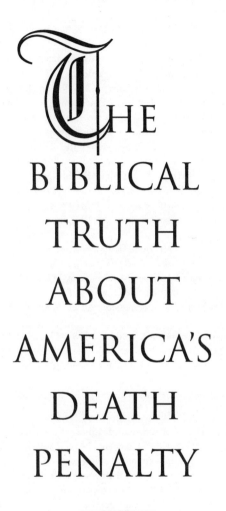

THE BIBLICAL TRUTH ABOUT AMERICA'S DEATH PENALTY

DALE S. RECINELLA

NORTHEASTERN UNIVERSITY PRESS
BOSTON

✳ 55149559

NORTHEASTERN UNIVERSITY PRESS

Copyright 2004 by Dale S. Recinella

Excerpts from Sydney E. Ahlstrom,
A Religious History of the American People,
© 1972 Yale University Press.
Reprinted with permission. All rights reserved.

Excerpts from *The Code of Maimonides*
(Book Fourteen): The Book of Judges,
trans. Rabbi Abraham M. Hershman, D.D., D.H.L.,
© 1949 Yale University Press.
Reprinted with permission. All rights reserved.

Scripture verses taken from the HOLY BIBLE, NEW INTERNATIONAL VERSION.
Copyright © 1973, 1978, 1984 International Bible Society. Used by permission of
Zondervan Bible Publishers. (Signified by NIV.)

Library of Congress Cataloging-in-Publication Data

Recinella, Dale S., 1951–
The biblical truth about America's death penalty / Dale S. Recinella.
p.   cm.
Includes bibliographical references and index.
ISBN 1–55553–633–6 (hardcover : alk. paper)—
ISBN 1–55553–632–8 (pbk. : alk. paper)
1. Capital punishment—Biblical teaching.   2. Capital punishment—
United States.   I. Title.
BS680.C3R43   ~~2005~~ 2004
261.8'3366'0973—dc22   2004006714

Designed by Steve Kress

Composed in Weiss by Coghill Composition
in Richmond, Virginia.
Printed and bound by Maple Press in York, Pennsylvania.
The paper is Maple Tradebook, an acid-free sheet.

MANUFACTURED IN THE UNITED STATES OF AMERICA
08 07 06 05 04   5 4 3 2 1

TO

Murray Bodo, Susan Ward Recinella, and Michael Foley,
each blessed by God with the eyes to see what is not yet visible

For I desire goodness, not sacrifice;
Obedience to God, rather than burnt offerings.
—TANAKH

For I desired mercy, and not sacrifice;
And the knowledge of God more than burnt offerings.
—AUTHORIZED (KING JAMES) VERSION

For I desire mercy, not sacrifice,
And acknowledgement of God rather than burnt offerings.
—NEW INTERNATIONAL VERSION

Hosea 6:6

———◦◦◦———

But go ye and learn what that meaneth,
I WILL HAVE MERCY, AND NOT SACRIFICE.
—AUTHORIZED (KING JAMES) VERSION

But go and learn what this means:
"I desire mercy, not sacrifice."
—NEW INTERNATIONAL VERSION

Matthew 9:13

CONTENTS

PART TWO

WHAT DOES BIBLICAL TRUTH TELL US ABOUT THE REQUIRED
PROCEDURES AND THE PLIGHT OF THE FAMILIES OF THE VICTIMS?

TABLES

PREFACE

No one is more surprised than I that a book about the death penalty is being typed by my fingers. Twenty, fifteen, even ten years ago, I would have given it longer odds than winning the Florida lottery. Consequently, it is only fair to allow readers to glimpse the unexpected but real twists and turns of life that nudged me—rather thrust me—to the point of this compilation.

During the autumn days of 1975, in my second year at Notre Dame Law School, I obtained a part-time position as a law clerk for a small criminal law firm that held the public defender contract in Benton Harbor on the Michigan side of the border. In and of itself, the job was not noteworthy. Yet, on a personal front, as my first brush with law-related employment, it seemed like the most significant job in the world.

My initial assignment was to interview a new client at the jail. He was being held pending arraignment on kidnapping, auto theft, and concealed weapons charges. My brisk steps to the jail attested to the officiousness and enthusiasm of a green law clerk about to take his first plunge into noble waters, saving the downtrodden from certain drowning in the deep pool of society's evils. My enthusiasm waned when the guards stationed me in front of a steel-barred cell door and told me that the huge naked man, grunting and rocking on his haunches against the rear corner of the cell, was my new client. I had seen *Counsellor at Law* and *To Kill a Mockingbird*. None of the clients had looked like this guy.

Clearing my throat, I forced the pitch of my voice down an octave below normal and started out strong. It wasn't to last. Any remnant of officiousness and enthusiasm that had survived the introductions was smashed when my client let out a shriek and lunged from the rear corner to the door of the cell in a single bound. Before I could blink, he grabbed my tie through the cell door and began vigorously yanking on it—hammering me repeatedly against the metal bars.

By the time the guards were able to cut off my tie by maneuvering scissors between the bars of the door and my bruised ribs, I had sustained an injured throat and lines of significant purple welts that crisscrossed in a surreal pattern from my forehead to my knees. I looked like I had come out the worst in a fight with a giant waffle iron. The gray-uniformed jailers valiantly feigned sympathy while choking back tears and stifling peals of laughter. My wife, a seasoned nurse at a local hospital who had disapproved of the job in the first place, was far less inclined to feign anything. She simply opined that I now sported the most geometrically precise bruises she had ever seen.

The next day found me completing two new imperatives. First, I drove to the five-and-ten and purchased a dark blue clip-on tie. Then I visited the law school placement office and deleted all poverty and criminal law jobs from my prospects. I would finish out my current employment in Benton Harbor. But there would be no new interviews for me except with multinational companies and prestigious commercial and financial law firms. The downtrodden would not tread on me again. They were on their own!

That was my last brush with criminal law or the criminal justice system for almost twenty years. Many laypeople assume that every lawyer knows about all the various fields of law. That may have been true in the days of the general practitioner when the small-town lawyer handled everything from wills to contracts to felonies. Modern law is practiced much differently in America. For the most part, American law is a system of specialties. Long gone are the days of one-stop shopping for lawyers. My career had turned toward project finance, negotiations, documentation, approving legal opinions. In twenty years, I had never been in a court in the role of litigation counsel. My arenas were the conference rooms, the capital markets, and the closing tables.

Through continuing legal education courses and bar conferences, I knew in general about the developments in criminal law, even about the resurgence of the death penalty. I was vaguely aware that the death penalty was constitutional if applied fairly and that it was reserved for the most heinous crimes. I always assumed that everything was working as it should. I could not have imagined otherwise. Politically, I supported the death penalty.

"Why not?" I would respond to queries of my position. "What else are we supposed to do with those people?"

From a faith standpoint, I was equally satisfied. After all, the death penalty is scriptural. God said, "Eye for eye; tooth for tooth; life for life." I was convinced and comfortable about it. I did not seek any answers about the death penalty because I did not have any questions.

Then in 1995, a lawyer friend asked me to help with a death penalty brief on behalf of a murderer. He would be the attorney of record and would finalize and sign the brief. He just needed help with the research and some of the initial drafting. I was reluctant. It had been twenty years since the last time I had prepared a criminal law brief. Not only that, but almost all the constitutional and state law regarding capital punishment in America had happened after I graduated from law school in December 1976.[1] My friend, however, was insistent.

I started reading the law review articles and ultimately actual cases. This was far from enjoyable. American death penalty cases are heavy on facts. That is because in our country, whether someone can be given the death penalty depends on the answers to fact-driven questions. Was the crime especially cruel and heinous? Was torture involved? Did the murderer go out of his way to make the victim suffer excruciating pain? To paraphrase the words of the Florida Supreme Court, was it a conscienceless or pitiless crime that was unnecessarily torturous to the victim?[2]

To the uninitiated, the very language of death penalty case law, rules, and statutes is bizarre and unreal. In an effort to deal competently with judgment unto physical death, the courts struggle with whether a particular crime is a "normal" murder or a "heinous" murder. Horrible crimes against people's children, wives, husbands, parents, and grandparents are all discussed in terms of what is a normal horrible crime and what is an atrocious horrible crime. A strange twist in all of it is that defendants who have committed horrible crimes can *seem* to be exonerated if not deemed worthy of the death sentence.

As I poured through the cases, an inner voice kept asking, "What if that had been *my* daughter? *My* son? *My* wife? *My* parents?" I frequently had to pause in the middle of reading a case because I felt physically ill.

"Anybody who wants to argue abolition based solely upon secular humanism or liberal political principles has missed the point,"
I said to myself. "For the most part, the inmates sitting on death
row have killed people—usually in horrible and torturous ways.
Based on their crimes, many of them make my first client of
twenty years ago seem noble by comparison. Their cases do not
stir the cockles of my human heart to mercy. Their crimes do not
call forth pity or forgiveness or compassion from me." My emo-
tions tended to agree with U.S. Supreme Court justice Antonin
Scalia: "[Death by lethal injection] looks pretty desirable next to
. . . the case of the 11-year-old girl raped by four men and then
killed by stuffing her panties down her throat. . . . How enviable
a quiet death by lethal injection compared with that!"[3] Justice
Scalia was simply putting words to the revulsion I felt in my gut.

Even though my feelings about capital punishment seemed
clear and very black-and-white, a parallel experience was occurring during the research and preparation of that brief. It became
apparent that I had no idea what was actually going on in my
country, or even in my own state, with respect to the death penalty.

I was astounded to discover that we are in the grips of a tremendous conflict between the death penalty system we believe
we should have and the system that actually exists. Most of us
believe there can be a model system that works as it should. That
ideal system is the concept we support with scripture. Yet, I was
beginning to wonder if the system we actually have is anything
like the one we hope for. A question began to form: other than
the fact that people are executed, does our system bear any re-
semblance to the one we defend with scriptural quotes?

Such a crisis would be more than just a clash of fantasy and
reality. It would pose legal quandaries of constitutional dimension
as well as an ethical and social tear in the cloth of our culture. As
the realities of the actual death penalty in America were becoming clearer to me, I realized that our American death penalty system could be creating unbridgeable chasms between who we say
we are as a people and what our actions say about who we are as
a people.

I learned that the constitutional conflicts center primarily on
two issues. The first is that the constitutional requirements that

have governed death penalty law in this country for the last twenty-seven years demand that the legal procedures be *specific enough* to prevent arbitrary application. In other words, proportionality requires that crimes of similar heinousness receive similar punishment.[4] That seems reasonable enough.

The Constitution also requires that the legal procedures be *flexible enough* to allow for consideration of all relevant factors.[5] This second requirement is driven by the need for each person and each set of facts to be fully considered. That also seems reasonable.

If I had been a U.S. Supreme Court justice in 1976, I probably would have taken great comfort that these two standards would ensure a fair and constitutional death penalty process. The concerns for specificity and for flexibility are vital constitutional issues in the relationship between our government and the individual. Common sense and reason dictate that both must be accomplished. That is the problem. In the context of the death penalty, these requirements clash head-on.

I discovered that after twenty years on the high wire of this balancing act between the specific and the flexible, at least one U.S. Supreme Court justice who had been a longtime death penalty proponent declared it a mission impossible: "Experience has taught us that the constitutional goal of eliminating arbitrariness and discrimination from the administration of the death penalty can never be achieved without compromising an equally essential component of fundamental fairness—individualized sentencing. . . . The death penalty must be imposed 'fairly, and with reasonable consistency, or not at all.'"[6] (citations omitted)

He noted that the U.S. Supreme Court had retreated from that constitutional standard, abdicating its constitutional role.[7] Finally, he concluded that we could only have the death penalty if we are willing to give up our constitutional safeguards:

> For more than 20 years I have endeavored—indeed, I have struggled—along with a majority of this Court, to develop procedural and substantive rules that would lend more than the mere appearance of fairness to the death penalty endeavor. . . . I feel morally and intellectually obligated simply to concede that the death penalty experiment has failed. . . . [N]o combi-

nation of procedural rules or substantive regulations ever can
save the death penalty from its inherent constitutional deficiencies. The basic question—does the system accurately and
consistently determine which defendants *deserve* to die?—
cannot be answered in the affirmative. . . . The problem is that
the inevitability of factual, legal, and moral error gives us a
system that we know must wrongly kill some defendants, a
system that fails to deliver the fair, consistent, and reliable sentences of death required by the Constitution.[8] (citations
omitted)

A different approach might be to just junk one of the two
constitutional standards. That is the method adopted by Justice
Scalia, who announced that he would no longer require death
sentence procedures to take individualized factors into account.[9]
Under this approach, the sentencing court would only look at the
specifics of the crime committed. The downside of this simplified
process is that the Constitution becomes a blind eye that sees
not.[10] Thus, we have executed the mentally retarded,[11] minors,[12]
and even those who have new evidence establishing their innocence.[13]

I had no idea that all of this had been going on with the death
penalty during the twenty years after I graduated from law school.
When I asked other lawyers who were not involved in death penalty law, I found out that most of them had no awareness of it
either. The nonlawyers (laypeople) I questioned were clueless as
well. Two decades of endless media and political sound bites
about the death penalty, and nobody but the specialists knew
anything about the reality.

Unfortunately, I soon learned that the reality was worse than
just the constitutional conflicts over specificity and flexibility.
Even among equally horrible crimes, the death penalty is not
meted out with equanimity. The *vengeance of the people* is quite selective. The statistics show that race matters when the punishment
is death.

The most comprehensive study ever done (in Georgia) showed
that blacks who kill whites are twenty-two times more likely to
get a death sentence than blacks who kill blacks and seven times
more likely than whites who kill blacks.[14] In my home state the

situation is very similar.[15] All studies done since 1972 indicate that race plays a major factor in determining who gets the death penalty in Florida. A study from 1991 showed that since capital punishment was begun in Florida as a territory in 1769, Florida had never executed a white person for a crime against a black victim.[16] As of this writing, that is still true.

Our national record is equally appalling. An analysis of the records of the most comprehensive archive of government executions in the United States over its entire history[17] showed that of the 15,978 cases recorded up to 1989, only 30 were for crimes by whites against blacks.[18]

The evidence that we are unable to structure a death penalty system that is not racially biased is overwhelming.[19] Notwithstanding, our U.S. Supreme Court (in a five-to-four majority) has thrown up its hands and departed from its consistent approach in every other area of constitutional law.[20] Despite overwhelming evidence of systemic racial injustice, the Court allows the killing by executions to continue.

When the rough draft of the death penalty brief was finally finished, I delivered it to my friend. In honoring my commitment to help him with his project, I found that my legal comfort level with the death penalty had been shattered. At the time, however, I did not expect to deal with the issue anymore. I was done with the death penalty. It was time to pack and move the family overseas.

In the summer of 1996, I had accepted a position in the Rome, Italy, office of an international American law firm. While my wife and I were living in Rome with our three youngest children, we would also be studying theology. It was a transition point between my legal career and a second career in lay ministry. The death penalty would be six thousand miles behind us. At least that is what I thought. But no such luck.

Within a few months, the American death penalty was in the headlines in Rome.[21] A Virginia man, Joseph O'Dell, was pleading for DNA testing of the evidence in his murder and rape conviction. Pope John Paul II had made a plea for clemency in his case, especially in light of the significant doubts about O'Dell's guilt.[22] In reviewing the case in 1991, three U.S. Supreme Court justices had said they had doubts about O'Dell's guilt and whether he should have been allowed to represent himself. Without the blood evidence, there was little linking O'Dell to the crime. In September 1996, the Fourth Circuit of the U.S. Court of Appeals reinstated his death sentence and upheld his conviction. Then the U.S. Supreme Court refused to review O'Dell's claims of innocence. O'Dell asked the state to conduct DNA tests on other pieces of evidence to demonstrate his innocence, but he was refused. O'Dell was executed on July 23, 1997.

At the time of the headlines about the papal appeal, I was working as a lawyer at a conservative international corporate law office in Rome and was also teaching in an MBA program full of conservative middle managers from multinational corporations and financial institutions. The milieu in America had left me with the impression that all good conservatives favored the death penalty and only bleeding heart liberals opposed it. I was totally unprepared for the onslaught of conservative disgust:

> "How can America perpetuate such an abomination?"
> "It is barbaric!"
> "Even if he is guilty, how can a modern democratic government kill its own citizens?"
> "Does America feel shame at being grouped with Iran and Iraq and China on human rights?"
> "I have always admired America and wanted to be American. Not anymore."

These speakers were not wide-eyed liberals dancing in the streets in tie-dyed shirts. These were not anticorporate communist sympathizers. These were three-piece-suited, club-tie-wearing corporate lawyers, managers, and bankers who daily handled billions of dollars in responsibilities in the global economy. The notion that all good law and order conservatives support the death penalty was clearly an American myth.

It was not the only American myth about the death penalty that I had lugged across the ocean. Within weeks I learned about another American misconception of the death penalty. An associate of the law firm had written her doctoral thesis for law school in Italy on the death penalty. Because she was Jewish, she had taken an entire year to return to Israel and research the practices of the ancient Hebrews concerning the death penalty under the Torah, the scriptures that are also the first five books of the Christian Bible. She was happy to share her research results with me. I was flabbergasted.

In short, she suggested that we Christians who are quoting "eye for eye . . . life for life" as blanket God-support for America's death penalty system may have no idea what the biblical death penalty actually was. The ancient Hebrews, who originally received those divine revelations and structured their laws and society under them, might be shocked at our practices.

By the time our family returned to the United States at the beginning of 1998, I was ready to start from scratch in trying to understand what is real and what is myth in the American death penalty fantasy. Still, I probably would not have ever thought of writing a book about it. Another twist was still coming.

In relocating back to the United States from Rome, we headed for a rural, almost antebellum town of four thousand people, just west of Jacksonville and three miles from the Georgia border. We were bound for the heart of Dixie. We moved to the Deep South of extreme north Florida in August 1998. That is where I would assist the pastor of a small rural Catholic church with pastoral responsibility for the 360-some men on Florida's death row and the 2,300 men in solitary and psychiatric solitary confinement at the state prisons in Raiford and Starke—fifteen miles from our front door. I was ministering on Florida's death row three weeks after we moved to our new home.

Suddenly, after all the other experiences outlined earlier, I found myself standing at the cell doors of Florida's death row, ministering to the very men that my state was holding to kill.

The mentally ill and mentally retarded on death row? I had read about them. Now I knew their names.

Those on death row claiming innocence? Here they were—my state of Florida had found more innocent people on death row than any other state in America.

The disproportionate numbers of death row inmates based on indigence and race? Now I could count them.

The inhumane conditions of heat and deprivation? No more guesswork. It was all right in my face, several days a week.

It was just a matter of time before one of these men asked me to be his spiritual adviser and his witness for his execution. From just three feet away I looked on as my state of Florida killed him.

Through all of this, I continued to hear hundreds, maybe thousands, of Christian brothers and sisters quoting verses from Torah/ Pentateuch, the biblical death penalty, as God's mandate for the American system of capital punishment. In fact, I have found almost no Americans who support the American death penalty without referring to those Hebrew scriptures. That is how I came, in a personal way, to the point of seeking answers to a battery of questions:

What was the biblical death penalty?
Who was executed under the biblical death penalty?
How was it carried out and why was it imposed?
How does the American death penalty compare with the standards of the biblical death penalty?
Can we really justify the American death penalty based upon biblical truth?

These are the steps that led me to the task of this work, a mission to assemble the facts that describe what we are really doing with capital punishment in America and evaluate that squarely in the light of biblical truth.

This book is a compilation of many important facts ascertained through the research and scholarship of others concerning the biblical and American death penalties. Those facts are interwoven with a narration of my own search and of what I have learned. This work is divided into two main parts based upon the most prominent questions posed by biblical truth in addressing the particulars of the American death penalty. Part 1 is What Does Biblical Truth Tell Us about Who Is Deserving of Death and the Authority to Kill? Part 2 is What Does Biblical Truth Tell Us about the Required Procedures and the Plight of the Families of the Victims?

The answer to each of these questions is summarized at the conclusion of that section and a proposed faith response for persons of biblical faith is presented. For the sake of correctness and clarity, the first five books of the Bible—whether Hebrew or Christian—are the crucial books addressed in this work. As noted earlier, the Hebrew Bible calls these books Torah. The Christian terminology for the first five books is Pentateuch. Consequently, throughout this work the phrase Torah/Pentateuch is used to designate the combined books: Genesis, Exodus, Leviticus, Numbers, and Deuteronomy.

Several aspects of the presentation made in this book are a direct result of my experiences with audiences to oral presentations of the subject. Frequently, upon hearing the particular requirements of biblical truth with respect to capital punishment, I have been asked, "Is it possible that those words are in your translation of the Bible but not in the translation that I use?" or, "Is it possible that the old Hebrew scriptures said something different from what the modern Christian translations say?"

When it comes to the death penalty, the English translation of the Hebrew Masoretic Texts, the Authorized (King James) Version, and the New International Version may have slightly different wording, but they all yield the same conclusions. To close this door of doubt, throughout this work all three such English renditions of the Hebrew scriptures are quoted in parallel, and both of the latter renditions of the Christian scriptures are quoted in parallel.

Frequently in this work, Talmud is referenced as a source for the practices necessary to meet the standards required and the spirit of the provisions set forth in the Torah/Pentateuch. It is important for readers to understand that these Talmudic references are a record, a compilation over time, of the practices employed under the biblical death penalty in order to ensure compliance with the restrictions on the death penalty set forth in the scriptures. To comprehend the full impact of the severe scriptural limitations imposed on the death penalty, we must deal with the standards of biblical truth as they were understood when the biblical death penalty was in practice.

To facilitate readers' understanding of how such practices are biblical, this work does trace the direct link between the scriptural restrictions and their incorporation into the practices of the biblical death penalty. In some instances, such as the derivation of courts with authority to kill, this step-by-step development can seem tedious. Yet, I have concluded that providing these links to the sources in scripture is crucial to avoid misleading readers into the impression that the Talmudic cites simply record various men's freewheeling opinions. Nothing could be further from the truth. To the contrary, they are deliberate and time-tested attempts to interpret and give gravity to every single word of the relevant scriptures. Although the steps may seem labored, no shorthand explanation would suffice.

Readers may note that in several passages quoted from Talmud, various rabbis are mentioned. Those named are the giants of Talmudic biblical scholarship, best understood by Christians as analogous to the Christian Early Fathers. Consequently, their opinions, rendered upon the scriptural demands in the context of specific human factual situations, are given great weight.

In-depth studies of the actual particulars of the American death penalty are relatively recent. Professional studies by law schools and other organizations are being performed. Even at this time, however, to accumulate the detailed facts of what takes place in a particular state, or nationwide with respect to a particular issue, one must rely upon investigative reports provided by major newspapers. Several newspaper investigative reports are cited in this work. I have selected them based upon satisfaction that the studies were broad enough and in-depth enough to accurately reflect the true state of affairs being presented. For example, one study picked all such cases nationwide over a particular time period; another studied every death penalty case in the particular state over the time period. Readers, however, have a right to independently come to their own conclusion. To facilitate that process, the URLs for each of the investigative reports are included in the notes citing those reports.

Finally, each of us writes best when we write about that which is most familiar to us. Consequently, even though this work makes an effort to address the facts of the American death penalty nationwide, I have placed special emphasis upon specific matters in Florida, my home state. This focus is further justified by Florida's historical role as the bellweather state for the American death penalty.

I hope the material in this book will be as challenging and illuminating to you as compiling it has been to me. Join me now as we search for the answers revealed by the biblical truth about the American death penalty.

ACKNOWLEDGMENTS

Readers will quickly note that I have taken the position of a tour guide, a narrator of sorts who leads the way through myriad compilations of facts and studies, all established and produced by others. Hence, it should be no surprise that the acknowledgments necessary to honor others' works are lengthy. The main task of this book is to establish what biblical truth has to tell us about the American death penalty. Part of this effort involves reconstructing the substantive laws and procedural rules of the biblical death penalty under the Torah/Pentateuch and Talmud. We must then compare those biblically based standards with the American death penalty today. Consequently, the acknowledgments to the works of others incorporated herein fall into two main categories: those dealing with biblical and Bible-related sources, and those establishing the facts of the American death penalty.

As for biblical and Bible-related sources, I am especially indebted to the excellent rendition of Talmud published by the Mesorah Heritage Foundation as the ArtScroll Series, Schottenstein Edition: *Talmud Bavli*. The Talmud presented is the Vilna, the most significant version of Talmud historically. The English translations of this edition are easy to understand and exceptionally well cross-referenced and annotated to commentaries by various schools of different periods. The editors and publishers of this excellent resource indicate their hope that the renewed interest in Talmud among the new generation of Jewish faith will benefit from this work. There is also a blossoming interest among Christians who desire understanding of the Jewish roots of our faith. Every religious library should possess the Schottenstein edition of Talmud. Each page brings life to the biblical texts at deeper levels than we normally encounter. This marvelous multivolume work was a tremendous benefit to my efforts at reconstructing the standards of the biblical death penalty.

It is said that Talmud is an ocean. Standing in the wings of the Isser and Rae Price Library of Judaica at the University of Florida,

I was confronted by dozens of bookcases filled with such oceans. My sincere gratitude belongs to Mr. Robert Singerman, university librarian of the University of Florida Judaica Library, and his staff, who ably served as my lifeguards to ensure that I did not drown in the ocean of Talmud. Their patience and excitement both enhanced this effort and kept me close to the shores of proper understanding.

Regarding the facts of the American death penalty, I found myself turning again and again to the outstanding studies and reports produced by the Death Penalty Information Center (DPIC) in Washington, D.C. The DPIC is a nonprofit organization serving the media and the public with analysis and information on issues concerning capital punishment through in-depth reports, press releases, briefings for journalists, and resource material for those working on this issue. The DPIC is widely quoted and consulted by all those concerned with the American death penalty. Richard C. Dieter, an attorney and the executive director of the DPIC, has authored all of the DPIC reports quoted and referenced in this book. I am in very good company in relying upon the well-reputed work of the DPIC. Recently, a federal judge relied upon certain reports of the DPIC, explaining his comfort in doing so as follows: the DPIC's information is based on "reasonably strict and objective standards in listing and describing the data and summaries that appear on its website." That has been my experience as well.

Above and beyond the need for accurate statistical information, an effort of this kind requires the enfleshed stories of the real people and real cases behind the numbers. If one thinks of the statistics as telling the "play-by-play," then it is the details of the anecdotal accounts that provide the "color." In the areas critical to the work of this book, no one does that better than attorney Stephen B. Bright. The organization that he heads, the Southern Center for Human Rights (SCHR) is a nonprofit, public interest legal project to enforce the constitutional protections against "cruel and unusual punishment." The SCHR challenges discrimination against people of color, the poor, and the disadvantaged in the criminal justice and corrections systems of the South, raises public awareness of these issues, and works with community groups and individuals to improve the criminal justice and corrections systems and develop constructive, humane, and nonviolent solutions to crime.

Mr. Bright, who has taught courses on criminal law, capital punishment, prisoners' rights, and international human rights at Yale, Harvard, Georgetown, Emory, Northeastern, Florida State, and St. Mary's law schools, has authored, or is the lead author, of all the SCHR reports that are quoted and referenced in this book.

Finally, I must express gratitude to all those who reviewed copies of the initial manuscript and provided such valuable feedback as to subjects and treatment. So many friends and professionals pulled oars on this duty that it's not possible to mention them all; however, special mention must be made of the over-the-top assistance provided by Rabbi W. Jack Romberg and librarian Robert Singerman of the University of Florida Judaica Library; law professors Tahirih V. Lee, Charles E. Rice and Jay Tidmarsh; attorneys Stephen Bright, Lee Chotas, Vernon Davids, Richard Dieter, Stephen Hanlon, Thomas Horkan, Thomas Lang, Steven Mindlin, and Gregory C. Smith; friends John Corwin, Russ Eanes, Linda Fuller, Gail Hollenbeck, Michael McCarron, Charles Moore, Bill and Shirley Poore, and William Tierney; retired theology professor and former seminary president, Rev. Dr. Luder Whitlock; Robert Link and Revs. James Francis Stafford, Victor Galeone, John J. Snyder, Joseph Maniangat, Jose Maniyangat and Marcus Hepburn, whose friendship and counsel have provided invaluable assistance in my work; and my wife and partner in ministry, Susan Recinella.

Special thanks also go to Shirley and Dana for countless hours over the fax machine, and to Marian McDanield and Becky McKee, who in the spring of 2000 initiated the written version of this project by providing me, unsolicited, with a typed transcript of my oral presentations; and to all the staff at Northeastern University Press, especially my editors, Sarah Rowley and Emily McKeigue, and marketing director Jill Bahcall, without whose assistance and guidance this work would have remained only an oral presentation.

So many others have done the tremendous work that was necessary to make this effort possible. I can only hope that my inclusion of their research, investigations, reports, and analysis will serve as my statement of gratitude for their invaluable contribution to this attempt to synthesize the standards of biblical truth with the legal, statistical, historical, economic, sociological, and political facts that compose the reality called the American death penalty.

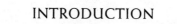

INTRODUCTION

Chapter One

─────

TRENDS IN THE AMERICAN DEATH PENALTY

Some dramatic changes in public perception of the American death penalty have taken place in the last decade. In 1994 80 percent of Americans favored capital punishment, but by May 2001, that level of support had dropped to 65 percent.[1] An ABC News poll from April 2001 found that 51 percent of Americans supported a nationwide moratorium on the death penalty.[2] More recently, a May 2002 Gallup poll showed that when Americans are given the sentencing alternative of life in prison without the possibility of parole, only 52 percent of Americans support the death penalty. Even so, 82 percent of respondents oppose the death penalty for the mentally retarded, 73 percent oppose it for those who are mentally ill, and 69 percent of Americans oppose capital punishment for juvenile offenders.[3]

A revealing poll at the state level in New Jersey mirrors this change in the American climate.[4] As recently as 1999, state polls had shown that only 37 percent of New Jersey residents preferred life imprisonment to execution as the penalty for murder. Now, just three years later, in a poll that asked New Jersey residents to choose between executions and life imprisonment without possibility of parole, 48 percent of New Jersey residents support a life sentence, while only 36 percent support capital punishment. The poll also reflects that support for the death penalty has dropped considerably in the state: two-thirds (66 percent) of New Jersey residents now support a moratorium on the death penalty.

Such changes in the public opinion polls on the American death penalty coincide with trends in the statistics concerning death sentences and executions. The number of persons sentenced to death in America during the year 2000 was only 214, a 20 percent decline from the prior year.[5] That number has continued to drop, with only 139 death sentences handed down in the United States in the year 2003, "a 53 percent drop from the average of 296 death sentences per year between 1994 and 2000[6] and a 56 percent drop from the "modern day peak of 319 in 1996."[7]

Juries in fifteen of the last sixteen federal capital trials have declined to impose the death penalty, despite a more aggressive pursuit of this punishment by the Justice Department. Legal experts believe that overreaching by prosecutors and some jurors' growing unease with the death penalty may account for the trend.[8] Federal capital juries have rejected the death penalty for twenty of the last twenty-one defendants who have completed trial and thirty-eight of the last forty-three since the year 2000.[9] In Florida, often called the "belt buckle of the death penalty belt," only twenty-two first-time[10] death sentences were handed down in the year 2000 and fifteen in 2001.[11] This continues a downward trend that began in 1996. From 1986 through 1995, Florida averaged 39.9 death sentences per year. That number dropped to an average of 22.4 for the years 1996 through 2000.

The number of actual executions per year is also decreasing. In 1999, there were ninety-eight executions in the United States.[12] This made 1999 the highest year for executions since capital punishment resumed in America in 1976. During the ensuing year the number of executions declined by 13 percent to eighty-five, making 2000 the second highest year for executions since 1976. In 2001, that number still dropped another 22 percent to sixty-six. Executions in 2002 rose slightly to seventy-one, but declined to sixty-five during 2003.[13] The net result is that from 1999 to 2003 the number of annual U.S. executions dropped from ninety-eight to sixty-five, a falloff of 33.7 percent.

The population of America's death rows has peaked and begun to decline, a significant turn from the steady population increase that occurred over the past twenty-five years.[14] The number of death row inmates in the United States as of January 1, 2004 was 3,503 down 223 (6 percent) from 3,726 on January 1, 2001.

Although the secular statistics appear to show that America has turned a corner in its use of the death penalty, there is much more to the story. Capital punishment in America is not just a legal or political reality; it is also a religious phenomenon encompassing matters of belief, faith, and morals. That is where one finds the most strident and, in some cases, strengthening support for the American death penalty.

It is not unusual for prosecutors to quote the Hebrew scriptures to juries in their arguments for death sentences in capital cases. In the last fifteen years, almost one hundred reported appeals of court decisions in death penalty cases have involved legal challenges by the defendant based on the grounds that the prosecutor used religious remarks to support leveling a death sentence.[15] There is no indication that the instances of this practice are decreasing.

The most popular scripture quotes to be used by prosecutors are those involving vengeance as justice. Eight reported appellate cases involved quotations of "eye for an eye." The verse from Exodus 21:12, "He that smiteth a man, so that he die, shall surely be put to death," appears in nine such cases. The so-called Rule of Blood in Genesis 9:6, "[Who] so sheddeth a man's blood, by man shall his blood be shed," was used by prosecutors in eight other appealed decisions. Finally, six appealed cases involved a quotation from Numbers 35:16, "[T]he murderer shall [surely] be put to death." Other arguments usually involve statements that support the government's right to take life, either by analogy to Noah or based on an interpretation of Romans 13.

Those familiar with American death penalty practice know that religion and interpretation of scripture are surprisingly common issues in the courtroom. One prominent American academic and theological commentator on the death penalty has written that his interest in applying his knowledge to the death penalty arose when a North Carolina public defender asked him to be an expert witness, to testify before the jury in a capital case as to whether the Bible mandates capital punishment.[16] This is just the tip of the iceberg.

> Religious arguments, however, are particularly powerful and are likely to resonate with most jurors. Prosecutors often draw support from the Bible for imposing the death penalty. The average juror, and even the legal system, holds the Bible sacrosanct and accords it great weight in influencing behavior. Yet, because they cannot ascertain the arguments' actual influence on jurors, judges often justify excusing biblical references by characterizing the references as innocuous.
>   . . . Religions generally, and Christianity and Judaism in particular, provide moral principles to guide their adherents' actions, and the jurors in a capital sentencing face "the ultimate moral decision." Furthermore, the propriety of death as a form of punishment engenders a debate fraught with religious arguments, with principles and beliefs coming from authoritative religious texts.[17] (citations omitted)

The use by prosecutors of religious authority in death penalty cases is particularly popular in the Bible Belt.

> Assertions that biblical law supports the legality of the American death penalty arise most frequently in arguments of prosecuting attorneys to juries in capital cases. The North Carolina Supreme Court recently upheld as proper the following admonition to the jury by a prosecutor: "Well the Bible . . . says an eye for an eye and a tooth for a tooth. The law is clear." The prosecutor had made this statement during his closing argument in a capital case. . . .
>   . . . [A]n Alabama prosecutor . . . made the following argument during a sentencing hearing: "Our Legislature, you know we are governed by the laws of [God] and man. And I'll submit to you the laws of [God.] He believed in capital punishment and you will find it many times in the Bible." The reviewing court did not find this to be reversible error, rationalizing that the prosecutor was merely telling the jurors that they should not refuse to impose the death penalty because of religious feelings.[18] (citations omitted; bracketed language mine)

Critical to the bulwark of support for the death penalty in America is the religious phenomenon called the Bible Belt. While the Bible Belt is generally evangelical and fundamental in religious disposition, provincial and culturally conservative in nature, it also is historic in origin and geographic in scope, and has profound political implications for the nation. It is not possible to understand the American death penalty without comprehending the role of the American Bible Belt, which has evolved from the pre–Civil War slaveholding states. Scripture was used to defend the institution of slavery and—in some cases—even the specific slavery of blacks. (The nature of those scriptural arguments and the parallels between them and the modern-day scriptural arguments given to support capital punishment will be examined in chapter 9.)

Suffice it to say that the support in the southern states for the peculiar institution of slavery was not made in spite of the Christian churches. It was made on the backbone and with the support of the Christian churches. Although the Baptist and Methodist churches made up between 90 and 95 percent of church membership in the southern states,[19] it seems that all the Christian churches in the South sought to make some sort of an accommodation with slavery.[20] Richard Furman, an outstanding Baptist minister and a significant church leader in the early nineteenth-century southern states,[21] provided an elaborate scriptural defense of slavery that was "adopted by the South Carolina Baptist Association in 1822," and a Roman Catholic bishop also defended the institution in 1844.[22]

The major evangelical churches, including Presbyterian,[23] Methodist,[24] and Baptist,[25] split along the geographic boundaries of North and South, which were also the religious-political boundaries of abolition and slavery.

In May 1845, the Southern Baptist Convention was established in Augusta, Georgia. Thus was born the precursor to the modern American reality known as the Bible Belt. As a person who has lived in the Deep South of extreme north Florida since 1986 (except for a short time in Rome, Italy), I can attest that the southern understanding of the Bible Belt consists of the regions whose largest religious affiliation is Baptist. That is virtually synonymous with the states and territories of the Old Confederacy and the slave-owning border states, as shown in Table 1.1.

Table 1.1

American Bible Belt States: Status in the Civil War

State	Status
Alabama	Confederate state
Arkansas	Confederate state
Florida	Confederate state
Georgia	Confederate state
Kentucky	Border state[a]
Louisiana	Confederate state
Mississippi	Confederate state
Missouri	Border state
North Carolina	Confederate state
Oklahoma	Territory-supported Confederacy[b]
Tennessee	Confederate state
Texas	Confederate state
South Carolina	Confederate state
Virginia	Confederate state
West Virginia	Border state

Sources: "Regional Distribution of Major Denominations," Newsweek, March 4, 2002, 46;
   Microsoft Encarta Encyclopedia (2000), s.v. "Nation Divided" and "Slavery in the United
   States."
[a]The border states had divided loyalties internally; although slavery was practiced within
   their respective jurisdictions, the border states did not secede with the Confederacy.
[b]Oklahoma was a slaveholding Indian Territory at the time of the Civil War and did not
   achieve statehood until the twentieth century. The Five Civilized Tribes, the key Native
   American populations in the Indian Territory, allied with the Confederacy.

With 16 million members and 42,000 congregations, the
Southern Baptist Convention is now the largest Christian non-
Catholic denomination in America. It is the second largest religious denomination in the United States and is the largest in the
Bible Belt. The Southern Baptist Convention exerts a tremendous
influence on the thinking and beliefs of many of the smaller fundamentalist and evangelical denominations in the Bible Belt, even
though such groups are not formally affiliated with the convention.

The largely fundamentalist and evangelical church communities of the Bible belt believe that the death penalty is mandated

by the Hebrew scriptures, is not prohibited by the Gospels, and seems supported by the Epistles in the Christian scriptures.[26]

> Evangelical Protestants, in particular, are committed to what one scholar calls "biblicism": looking to the Bible for direct, specific answers to current ethical or social questions such as the death penalty. . . .
> Bible-oriented supporters of the death penalty tend to start with the passage in the book of Genesis where immediately after the Flood, God covenants with Noah and describes to him how human society will be reconstituted, stating among other things, that "[w]hosoever sheds the blood of Man, in Man shall his blood be shed; for in the image of God He made Man." [Gen. 9:6] . . . Bible-oriented proponents of the death penalty then go on to say that "[n]othing in the teachings of Jesus or the apostles contradicts this sanctioning" of capital punishment. They point, for example, to the passage in the 13th chapter of Paul's [L]etter to the Romans, which endorses human government as the instrument of God's "wrath" against offenders and speaks of government wielding the "sword," [Rom. 13:4] both of which the proponents say refer specifically to the use of death as punishment."[27] (scripture citations added)

Virtually undiscussed in modern American religious circles is the fact that such an approach to scripture exactly parallels the approach used in the Bible Belt to justify slavery in the eighteen hundreds. We will investigate this issue in more detail in chapter 9.

The Bible Belt churches are relatively unaffected by the secular statistics and studies that have influenced much of the rest of the country on the death penalty. Their position is that secular reporting of the problems with the American death penalty has no bearing on God's will as reflected in God's word. As opposed to moving away from the death penalty like the rest of Americans, conservative evangelical Christians in the Bible Belt are digging in to defend the veracity of the Bible by defending the American death penalty. "In the summer of 2000, even as other conservatives voiced their doubts, the increasingly fundamentalist Southern Baptist Convention explicitly endorsed capital punishment for the first time."[28]

This religious fervor is significant. The death penalty, as practiced in America today, is a Bible Belt phenomenon. Almost 90
percent of executions in America during the last five years have
taken place in the Bible Belt (see table 1.2).

Table 1.2
American Executions in the Bible Belt (1999–2003)

Year	Executions	Executions in Bible Belt	Percentage in Bible Belt
1999	98	81[a]	83%
2000	85	80[b]	94%
2001	66	55[c]	83%
2002	71	67[d]	94%
2003	65	59[e]	90%
Five-year total	385	342	88.8%

[a]Bible Belt executions (1999): Tex. 35, Okla. 6, Va. 14, Fla. 1, Mo. 9, Ala. 2, Ark. 4, N.C.
4, S.C. 4, La. 1 and Ky. 1: total of 81.
[b]Bible Belt executions (2000): Tex. 40, Okla. 11, Va. 8, Fla. 6, Mo. 5, Ala. 4, Ark. 2, N.C.
1, S.C. 1, La. 1 and Tenn. 1: total of 80.
[c]Bible Belt executions (2001): Tex. 17, Okla. 18, Va. 2, Fla. 1, Mo. 7, Ark. 1, N.C. 5, Ga.
4: total of 55.
[d]Bible Belt executions (2002): Tex. 33, Okla. 7, Mo. 6, Va. 4, Ga. 4, Fla. 3, S.C. 3, Ala. 2,
N.C. 2, Miss. 2, La. 1: total of 67.
[e]Bible Belt executions (2003): Tex. 24, Okla. 14, Va. 2, Fla. 3, Mo. 2, Ark. 1, N.C. 7, Ga.
3, Ala. 3: total of 59.

Over 80 percent of the twenty-two executions that have taken
place in 2004 have been in the Bible Belt.[29] Moreover, the Bible
Belt has hosted all twenty-two of the juvenile executions[30] that
have taken place in America since 1976.[31] See table 1.3.

The impact of this Bible Belt phenomenon extends to the rest
of the country. The quotes of "eye for an eye" and "life for a life"
have become a part of the American culture. For example, in a
recent death penalty case in Colorado, the appeals court discovered that jurors had written biblical passages on note cards and
taken them into deliberations. The passages written on the cards,
which included Leviticus 24:20, "fracture for fracture, eye for eye,
tooth for tooth, as he has caused disfigurement of a man, so shall
it be done to him," were used to persuade other jurors to impose
a death sentence.[32]

Table 1.3
U.S. Executions for Crimes Committed as a Juvenile (1976–2003)

State	Executions
Texas	13
Virginia	3
Georgia	1
Missouri	1
Louisiana	1
Oklahoma	2
South Carolina	1
Total	22

Even outside the confines of fundamentalist and evangelical Christianity, biblical Christians of other denominations and other people of biblical faith frequently quote these scripture texts as a basis for religious support for the American death penalty. Under this wave of religiously generated political pressure, several northern states that had abandoned the death penalty earlier in the twentieth century have reinstated it. For example, in 1995 the death penalty was reinstated in New York: "In the white-hot debates surrounding this issue, the Bible often was cited to support reimposition of the death penalty. A state Assemblyman argued: 'We as a society, we as a state, we as a nation have the right to seek retribution against those who commit heinous crimes. This tradition can be found as far back as our Bible.'"[33] (citations omitted)

Throughout the Bible Belt and the other states affected by its approach to the Bible, the religious notion that the American death penalty is mandated by God's word has become, to use the words of T. Richard Snyder from *The Protestant Ethic and the Spirit of Punishment*, "part of the air we breathe, a silent or hidden part of the culture" that flows from "certain religious beliefs being taken for granted."[34]

Some possible explanations for this phenomenon can be found in various studies of Christian belief at large. For example, Christians believe that Jesus Christ "atoned" for our sins. As will be discussed in more detail in chapters 7 and 8, the actual understanding of the mechanics of that atonement have varied over time and still vary among different Christians. Christians in the Bible Belt strongly lean toward the sacrificial and penal substitutionary models of the atonement. This tends to result in a view of Jesus' crucifixion that has been stripped of the horror of humanly inflicted death and the actual criminal charges that provided the Romans with legal authority to execute him. The danger in this model is that the event can become completely spiritualized in a way that removes almost all its possible meaning in dealing with capital punishment today.[35] The small remnant of meaning that survives this total spiritualization is a divine sanction for retributive justice.

The penal substitutionary model of atonement is one of a range of atonement theories that are grouped in the category of "satisfaction models." Satisfaction models of atonement postulate that God has required and accepted the death of his son as the only possible satisfaction for the seriousness of human sin. This presupposes a definition of justice that requires infliction of harm equal to the harm done. Thus, the satisfaction models of atonement can yield a biblical interpretation that makes sense out of human sacrifice for human killing.

Beyond the disconnect between the historical facts and events of Jesus' death and the historical facts and events of capital punishment today, some theologians fear that a satisfaction model of atonement can create a great risk of biblical faith without personal ethics. This is especially the case where personal salvation is offered devoid of any requirement to live a "transformed life under the rule of God."[36] Such is the case in those belief systems where salvation by atonement follows a legalistic formula without any regard to transformation. Anyone who has spent significant time in prison ministry knows that this formula is especially popular behind bars because it requires no changes in the behavior of the new Christian. The post-incarceration consequences of such a personally inexpensive salvation without transformation, which Dietrich Bonhoeffer would have labeled as "cheap grace,"[37] has made many Americans skeptical of the phenomenon pejoratively referred to as "getting jailhouse religion."

Regarding capital punishment, the combination of satisfaction atonement with the social ethos of American rugged individualism can result in a biblical faith that speaks only to "me and God" and leaves all others to fend for themselves. The grace of redemption can be relegated solely to a means for filling the hole left by personal sin, (i.e., satisfaction) but providing nothing for the outpouring of love to others who are suffering outside the margins of society or the law.[38] To the contrary, any notion of community or corporate complicity in others' pitiful condition is abrogated. Their plight is attributed solely to their lack of worthiness and their sinfulness, thus deservingly so, together with any consequences,[39] even execution. In this fashion, the atmosphere of the moral values formed within our so-called American Protestant ethic shores up the moral foundations of the death penalty.

As a person who has lived in the Bible Belt for almost twenty years, I can testify that the overwhelming majority of people in the Deep South are deeply religious, good-hearted people who earnestly desire to put God's will first in their life. The critical inquiry is the question "What is being taught as God's will from the pulpits?" Almost none of the rank and file of biblical faith in the Bible Belt have engaged the analysis outlined earlier. All they know are the selected scripture quotes that are constantly repeated to justify the conclusions of biblical support for the death penalty, conclusions that have not been thoroughly analyzed or explained.

On their face, the oft-touted Bible quotes can seem to overcome any opposition. After all is said and done, there is a death penalty in the Bible. No one can argue that there is not. Yet, the question one rarely hears mentioned is this: are the Bible quotes really being applied properly in the context of the American death penalty? This and many other extremely important questions seem to go unasked. Unasked questions remain unanswered.

Because of its pervasive presence and significant leadership throughout the Bible Belt and its clear enunciation of the basis for Christian biblical support of the American death penalty, the Southern Baptist Convention's statements on the death penalty are crucial to our inquiries. For example, the year 2000 Southern Baptist Convention Resolution on Capital Punishment passed in Orlando, Florida, in June 2000 (which is reproduced in its entirety in appendix C and which I refer to in this book as Resolution No. 5) looks to the Noahic blessing in Genesis 9:6 to validate

God's will that capital punishment be applied for murder and to Romans 13:4 to support the conclusion that civil magistrates are God's agents to carry out executions.

The first thing we note about Resolution No. 5 is that there is not a single citation to the Gospels. The logic of the statement seems uncomfortably similar to the approach of biblical arguments that supported slavery in the nineteenth century, which basically went as follows. The practice of slavery existed in the Hebrew scriptures, the practice of slavery was not explicitly condemned in the Gospels, and it is possible to interpret the Epistles of Paul in support of the practice of slavery. The modern logic of Resolution No. 5 seems to be saying that the death penalty is mandated by the Hebrew scriptures, is not expressly prohibited by the Gospels, and is arguably supported by a particular way of interpreting Paul's Epistle to the Romans.

Consequently, the most obvious unasked question is: How does the scriptural analysis that results in supporting capital punishment differ from the method of analysis used in the Bible Belt of 1845, which determined that slavery is God's will for society?

Another unasked question is: How is the scriptural analysis of Resolution No. 5 different from that used by Bible Belt scripture theologians of the eighteen hundreds who held that the Noahic curse of Ham in Genesis 9 validated God's will that blacks should be enslaved by whites?

> [T]his text has for centuries provided divine justification for the enslavement of black Africans. . . . As an American proslavery writer, J. J. Flourney, declared in 1838: "The blacks were originally designed to vassalage [slavery] by the Patriarch Noah. . . ."
>
> [I]t was a notion that went back, at least, to the year 1700, when the Puritan Samuel Sewall published one of the earliest antislavery tracts and argued against the idea that "these Blackamores are the Posterity of Cham [sic], and therefore are under the Curse of Slavery."[40]

If the basic analytic approach to scripture used for supporting capital punishment today is the same as the one that was used for slavery, how can the analysis on slavery have been so wrong and the same analysis on capital punishment be right?

Resolution No. 5 explicitly recognizes that scripture requires proof that a person is guilty before punishment is administered. It also acknowledges that this is a daunting task in the face of the perils of our human and, therefore, imperfect criminal justice systems. The unasked questions are: What about the biblical command of Exodus 23:7, which absolutely forbids the execution of the innocent, thereby setting a biblical standard of absolute certainty of guilt? Where in scripture does it say that proof beyond a reasonable doubt is sufficient for execution of the innocent? Where is the support from scripture that dictates going forward with capital punishment even if the system is imperfect and slays the innocent? When did negative scriptural commands become nonbinding on people of biblical faith?

Resolution No. 5 rightly concedes that scripture requires all people to be treated equally under the law. The unasked questions are: Where is our biblical authority to take human life by execution when the system is so biased against the poor that finding a rich person on death row is like finding a needle in a haystack? Where is our biblical authority to take human life by execution when the system is so biased against those of diminished capacity that they are overrepresented on death row by multiples of their proportion of the general population? Where is our biblical authority to take human life by execution when the system is so biased racially that our own U.S. Supreme Court has thrown up its hands and given up on trying to make the American death penalty blind to color? When did scriptural mandate become diluted to merely wishful thinking on God's part?

Does the American death penalty in practice come anywhere close to the standard of proof espoused by Resolution No. 5, let alone the stricter biblical standard of absolute certainty? As we will see in the course of this book, it does not satisfy either one.

Above and beyond such concerns, for Christians of biblical faith there is the nagging problem that the words and deeds of Jesus Christ seem to fly in the face of retaliatory violence. What about the refusal by Jesus to endorse execution of the woman caught in adultery John 8:1–11? What about His words in that passage, which call into question the ability of broken flesh to judge other broken flesh unto death? The unasked question is: Does capital punishment performed at the hands of Christians contravene the spirit of Jesus Christ?

Moreover, the modern purpose of the scripture quotations being touted in courts, in legislative assemblies, on talk shows, and in our homes is not to justify the executions performed by the Sanhedrin three millennia ago. The scriptures are being quoted to support what is being done in America today. That application appears to form a part of the concerns that have moved the Christian Life Commission of the Baptist General Convention of Texas, an independent Baptist organization, to call for a moratorium on the death penalty in Texas.[41]

The concerns of the Christian Life Commission and the unasked questions set out earlier are imperative for the Bible-believing person of faith. They also beg a penultimate question: Can the American death penalty really be supported based upon the biblical truth of scripture? That reveals an even more basic unasked question: What is really in the Bible about the death penalty?

There was a time more than two millennia ago when the scripture verses in Torah/Pentateuch set the standards for the law of the land. What does the biblical truth of those standards tell us about the American death penalty today? Is America's fervent religious support for its death penalty standing solidly upon biblical truth or standing in spite of it?

The purpose of this book is to ask those unasked questions and to search for their answers. America restarted the death penalty machinery in 1976, almost twenty-eight years ago. It is time to sift through that experience and measure ourselves against the standards of biblical truth.

Chapter Two

TORAH AND TALMUD

What is the biblical death penalty? Is it an abstract concept without any earthly reality? Or does it have actual standards that we can study and compare ourselves to?

The biblical death penalty was actually utilized within the human condition back in the days when the scriptures of Torah/Pentateuch, the first five books of the Bible, were the law of the land. That means we can identify the standards of the substance and procedures of the biblical death penalty and measure our modern activities against them.

That is the basis of this search, the premise that the biblical death penalty is not an esoteric concept whose use is confined to heady discussion in the ivory towers of theological academies. Rather, the biblical death penalty has specific standards as to substance and procedures. Those standards are formed by biblical truth, which is accessible to us through the scriptures of Torah/Pentateuch and through Talmud, our source for the practices necessary to meet the requirements and spirit of the provisions set forth in Torah/Pentateuch.

We are approaching these Talmudic references as a record, a

compilation over time, of the standards required of the biblical death penalty in order to ensure compliance with the restrictions on the death penalty set forth in the scriptures. This allows us to engage the full impact of the severe scriptural limitations imposed on the death penalty. Our approach in addressing Torah and Talmud is not the same as a merely secular approach. For the person who approaches this matter without a faith perspective, the laws of the ancient Hebrews can seem somewhat typical of ancient Near East legal codes. The ancient Near East had no shortage of law codes. Some of the ancient legal codes that have been discovered are the Sumerian laws of Lipit-Ishtar and the Akkadian laws of Eshnunna (1900–1850 B.C.), the Code of Hammurabi (1728–1686 B.C.), the Hittite laws (1600–1200 B.C.), the Assyrian laws (1400–1100 B.C.), and some of the neo-Babylonian laws (600 B.C.).[1]

According to scripture, Moses, who lived in the thirteenth century B.C., received the law of the ancient Hebrews from God on Mount Sinai. The origin of Torah is God. While there are some similarities between certain provisions of the Hebrew law and elements of the other ancient laws of the Near East, for people of biblical faith this divine source is a distinction that allows the Hebrew law a status all its own. The other legal codes were sourced in man.

King Hammurabi wrote his code. The other rulers did likewise. Not only did their laws not come from the gods, but also in some cases the earthly rulers purported to bind the gods themselves. In Rome and Greece, the laws were the products of human beings.[2] Even in our own modern Western societies, the law of the land is a creature of the state and thus subject to the whims of the state.

This is not the case with the ancient Hebrew law. In the eyes of Christians and Jews, Torah is completely and uniquely different. The source of Torah is God. "The laws were given by God to Moses on Sinai. For his part, Moses gave them to Israel and wrote them down (Deut. 31:9). We find the direct act of God writing only in the tradition of the stone tablets (Exod. 32:16; Deut. 9:10 and elsewhere). We have divine law transmitted by a human figure in the distant past."[3]

Torah means law.[4] In the speech of the common person living in biblical times, it meant, quite literally, "instructions given by a mother (Prov. 1:8; 6:20; cf. 31:26) and a father (4:1f.) to their children to instruct them in matters of living and to warn them about morally dangerous situations."5 In current common usage by Christians, Torah refers to the first five books of the Bible, namely Genesis, Exodus, Leviticus, Numbers, and Deuteronomy. These books of the Bible are also called the Pentateuch, from the Greek word *pentateuchos,* meaning a book of five volumes. This is considered to be the written law given by God to the Hebrews. I refer to the five books collectively in this work as Torah/Pentateuch.

Yet there is more to the story. Orthodox Judaism holds that Moses received more than just the written law on Mount Sinai. It holds that when Moses came down the mountain, the Ten Commandments were in his hands and the oral law, equally given to him by God, was in his head. "The words of the Law would be transmitted from teacher to student in an eternal chain of generations. According to this view, the Written and Oral Law must be read together."6

The primary purpose of oral law was to maintain the understanding of scripture across the generations. "The basic task of the oral law, therefore, was to transmit the meaning of words."7 As values and customs changed over the ages, it was the oral law that maintained the meaning of scriptural words and described activities that had fallen out of common usage. Oral law also determined the scope of critical commands—e.g., what is the meaning of "labor" (Exod. 20:10) for purposes of the Sabbath? What is the meaning of "booths" as used in Leviticus 23:42?8

Finally, scripture frequently acknowledges the existence of oral law by referring briefly to matters that are assumed to exist outside of scripture. For example, the scriptures require a man to grant his wife a "bill of divorce" when he divorces her.9 What is a bill of divorce? What must it include? What must it not include? All these matters are assumed by scripture to be elaborated outside the written law. In fact they were well covered by the oral law.

For purposes of our inquiry, we need not delve into the issue of whether the oral law meets a Christian understanding of divine revelation. Our concern is different: namely, to identify the standards of the substance and procedures of the biblical death penalty and measure our modern activities against them. Most of the substance and procedures are contained right in the scripture verses of Torah/Pentateuch. The rest have been transmitted as part of the oral law, which has been written down and is called Talmud. The provisions that we will be addressing in Talmud have to do with the standards of substance and procedures necessary to comply with the very strict limitations on the death penalty contained in the scriptures of Torah/Pentateuch. Consequently, those standards are a potent barometer of biblical truth in measuring our own American death penalty system.

If we look at the history of the Torah/Pentateuch, we can better understand the Jewish belief of God handing down to Moses both the written law and the oral law, followed by the transmission of both to successive generations: "In the First Temple era we already find mention of *tofsei* Torah (those learned in Torah), people who engaged in study and interpretation of the law. At the beginning of the Second Temple era, when Ezra the Scribe read aloud to the people from the Torah (445 B.C.) a group of Levites would stand at his side in order to expound the full significance of the text."[10]

The Jewish Bible was canonized by the Knesset Gedolah (Great Assembly) in the period 539–332 B.C.

> The members of the Great Assembly actually collected holy writings, decided which books would be canonized in the Bible, which chapters of each book should be selected, and gave the Bible its definitive form and style. The completion of the Bible, one of the greatest projects of the Great Assembly, also marked the beginning of the reign of the oral law.[11] . . . It was these scribes who evolved the basic methods of . . . learning and deriving *halakhah* [law] from the biblical texts themselves."[12] (bracketed language mine)

Ultimately, in order to preserve the oral law for future generations, it became necessary to compile it in written form. Some authors believe that the destruction of Jerusalem and the temple by the Romans in the first century A.D. played a significant role in this development. The written collection of the nuts and bolts of the oral law given to Moses on Mount Sinai was completed about A.D. 200. It is called the Mishnah. This compilation is what lawyers would refer to as "black letter law."

The second phase of this multicentury work was the compilation in written form of the commentary and debates of the sages concerning the black letter law. This commentary and reflection, similar in some ways to a Bible commentary on scripture, took another three hundred years to complete. It is called the Gemara. The Mishnah and Gemara together make up the Talmud.

Talmud literally means "teaching."[13] It can refer, in common English usage, to either of two compilations: the Jerusalem (Palestinian) Talmud (Talmud Yerushalmi) or the Babylonian Talmud (Talmud Bavli). For historical and geographic reasons, the Babylonian Talmud is the more complete and is the predominant Talmud in use in Western societies.[14] The Babylonian Talmud consists of over sixty volumes with in excess of five thousand pages.

In the twelfth century, a Jewish scholar, Moses Maimonides, produced a comprehensive work that sorted and codified the entire oral law. This compilation is known as the Mishneh Torah.

We will focus on the standards for substantive and procedural laws concerning the biblical death penalty found in Torah and Talmud. In cases where such laws are also reflected in the Mishneh Torah, quotes from the Mishneh Torah may be provided as well.[15] All references to Talmud mean the Babylonian Talmud unless otherwise indicated. All Talmud references are to Mishnah, the black letter law, unless otherwise indicated.

Christians have incorporated the Decalogue (the Ten Commandments) of the Torah into our consciousness. In some quarters we even continue to quote the "eye for an eye" of Torah as a support for certain substantive laws, e.g., the death penalty. Yet our selections have been arbitrary compared with the whole of the written law.[16] We have not adopted the scriptural precepts prohibiting interest on loans or profit from the poor. Nor have we incorporated into our legal system the reconciliation and restorative justice principles of Torah. We have certainly not employed the severe restrictions in Torah as to application and procedures of the biblical death penalty.[17]

As sporadic as our use of Torah has been, we have virtually ignored the Talmud, leaving much of the relevant criminal procedures of the Mishnah far away from any analysis of our modern criminal procedures. This is especially true in the case of the death penalty.

Some background in the legal system of biblical times will be helpful in understanding the procedural laws of biblical days. The Talmud deals with both of the areas we would think of as civil and criminal law. It also addresses the structure of the courts. "The command to appoint judges and establish courts is mentioned in Deuteronomy 16:18."[18] The court system for civil cases consisted of three forums: "The highest level was a court of three ordained judges. . . . Below it was the court of three laymen (*hedyotot*). . . . Of equal standing with the three lay judges was the court consisting of a single ordained judge who, in certain cases, was empowered to pass judgment alone."[19]

The references to ordained judges refer to *semikhah* (in modern Judaism, *semikhah* is considered to be the parallel to ordination), "an ancient ceremony of transmitting judicial authority from rabbi to disciple. The chain of authority extended from the ordination of Joshua by Moses through the generations to the beginning of the Middle Ages."[20] The courts established for the hearing of capital cases were a whole different matter:

> Capital offenses were tried by a specially composed court of twenty-three judges, known as the *Sanhedri Ketana* (Small Sanhedrin). Not only were the judges all ordained, but other strict criteria had to be observed. Since there were standing instructions to courts to refrain, insofar as possible, from passing the death sentence, it was customary to remove from the bench any man who was believed to be incapable of maintaining an impartial attitude toward the defendant.[21]

The ultimate authority, the Great Sanhedrin, which consisted of seventy-one members, was housed in the temple and appointed the members of the Small Sanhedrins.[22]

In the civil law area, that law dealing with monetary damages, Talmud addressed business dealings (including purchase and sale and risk of loss), labor law, contract law, bills and notes, fraudulent and backdated documents, negligence, bailment and leases, nuisance, estate and inheritance, and even the responsibilities of and to those who serve the public, e.g., innkeepers. An astounding aspect of Talmudic law is that theft of money and property are dealt with as matters of civil law (monetary damages and/or fines) not as matters of criminal law (physical punishment).[23]

Criminal procedural law for the biblical death penalty contained numerous restrictions that are set forth in the scriptures of Torah/Pentateuch and in Talmud, e.g., there must be at least two witnesses whose testimony agrees on virtually every detail in all material respects,[24] confessions of the accused are of no validity or effect, circumstantial evidence is not allowed, premeditation has to be proven by establishing that the accused was warned right before the act that he was about to commit a capital crime,[25] and conviction requires a majority of two votes by the judges but release requires only a majority of one.[26] Furthermore, those subject to capital punishment under the biblical death penalty were evaluated by the strict standards of criminal intent. "Thus, there were categories of people who were exempt from criminal punishment: minors, the mentally unstable, and the mentally retarded; so too, certain actions committed under duress were exempt."[27]

Moreover, the substantive law of the biblical death penalty excluded many factual situations from consideration as a capital crime. Some of these same factual situations are significant factors in the burgeoning of America's death rows today. For example, let us consider the concept of felony murder. Put simply, under the American doctrine of felony murder, any person who willingly participates in the commission of a felony is liable for the murder of anyone killed during the commission of that felony. This includes liability for persons shot by a codefendant, persons killed by accident, even persons shot by law enforcement officers responding to the crime. It also means that any accomplice to the commission of the crime has the same level of liability as the person who actually pulled the trigger or did the stabbing.

Even if we can understand the rationale behind the felony murder rule, we might be shocked at the bizarre results when triggermen are out walking free because they cut a deal to turn state's evidence against their own accomplices, not infrequently mentally retarded accomplices who were recruited to drive or serve as lookouts and are now on death row. The critical question of our search, however, is not whether the death penalty as punishment for felony murder is reasonable or even effective. Our question is whether it meets biblical standards. How does the doctrine of felony murder in America's death penalty measure up under the scrutiny of biblical truth?

The answer to this question is not even ambiguous. There is no room for disagreement. The concept of felony murder in the American death penalty cannot be supported based upon biblical truth. The scriptures in Torah/Pentateuch and the provisions of Talmud also exclude from the death penalty the intentional killing of an unintended person,[28] the intentional killing by indirect means,[29] reckless homicide[30] and the liability of any accomplice.[31] There may still be punishment, but under the standards of the biblical death penalty, the punishment is not death.

Needless to say, with all the restrictions we have already mentioned, it became very difficult to impose the biblical death penalty.

The double-barreled solution that was worked out by the Jewish religious leaders (1) found inherent authority in the monarchy to establish courts outside the confines of divine revelation, and (2) found exigency jurisdiction to punish criminals who used the procedural safeguards as a foil.[32]

The concept of exigency jurisdiction is best understood by analogy to a current situation in the United States: special tribunals have been established to judge foreign terrorists outside the normal constitutional protections afforded to U.S. citizens. That is an exigency solution to the limitations of the Constitution. The Jewish religious leaders did the same thing to avoid the restrictions of the biblical death penalty.

We are not interested in the question of whether exigency jurisdiction was reasonable or unreasonable. The only important facts for purposes of this work are that exigency jurisdiction was political, extra-biblical, extra-Torah, and extra-Talmud. In other words, exigency jurisdiction for capital cases was outside the scope of the biblical death penalty. It was a political solution, not a matter based upon divine revelation. This will be discussed further in chapter 9.

Consequently, in our effort to gauge the American death penalty under biblical truth, we do not make reference to the post-Talmudic Jewish courts, especially those of the Middle Ages in Europe. They dispensed with the requirements of Torah/Pentateuch and Talmud in order to achieve politically valued executions. Although such endeavors may more closely parallel our situation in America today, those courts were not adhering to the standards of the biblical death penalty procedures and they were not biblical courts.

The scriptures of the Torah/Pentateuch and the procedures in Talmud required to fulfill those scriptures are our sources for the standards of biblical truth about the death penalty.

THEONOMY, ETHICS, AND THE ISSUES OF CIVIL, MORAL, AND CULTIC LAW

At this point we must address the issue of theonomy, a branch of Protestant evangelicalism that "take[s] the Pentateuchal texts as external and immutable mandates of God, just as much in force for obedient Christians of modern secular society as they are presumed to have been for ancient Israelites."[33] This book is not an argument for a theonomist incarnation of the biblical death penalty.[34] Quite to the contrary, I believe that careful scrutiny of the biblical texts reveals the fallacies of such an endeavor.

For example, as noted in chapter 1, Genesis 9:6 is quoted as biblical support for God's mandate of the death penalty. This claim of support can become very dicey, very quickly under even mild scrutiny. While the passage clearly stands for the proposition that human life is sacred, any attempt to turn the verse into a biblical law mandating capital punishment as God's will must deal with the other portions of the same scripture: Is God forbidding the consumption of rare roast beef by modern Americans? (Gen. 9:4) Is God mandating that any animal that kills a human must be executed? (Gen 9:5) At least one source indicates that a pig and a horse may have been tried for murder in the Middle Ages based on that scripture verse.[35] Such is not one of my goals.

The purpose of this book is to evaluate the "claimed biblical support" for the American death penalty against the standards of biblical truth revealed in the scriptures and in the requirements of Talmud deemed necessary to satisfy those scriptures. Having dispelled any notion that we are arguing for theonomy, how, then, do we reconcile the mission of this work with the classic notions of deriving ethics, standards of moral behavior, from the Hebrew scriptures?

Most people of biblical faith know very little about the extensive and complex rules for deriving ethics from scripture. For the average pew-sitting believer, ethics would be an esoteric science reserved to the confines of rabbinical schools, seminaries, and universities. At least among Christians of biblical faith, part of the reason for this state of affairs may be the wide variance among Christian ethicists as to the ethical requirements derived from scripture. All quote scripture as their source, but few reach the same conclusions on specifics.[36]

The most generally accepted approach among Christian ethicists appears to be the classification of the scriptural demands and prohibitions of Torah/Pentateuch into three broad categories: moral law, civil law, and ceremonial (or cultic) law. This categorization originates in the third century, being "partly perceived by Origen, given clear shape by Calvin, [and] enshrined for Anglicans . . . in the Thirty-nine Articles of Religion and for the Reformed tradition in the Westminster Confession of Faith."[37] As explained to me by a retired evangelical seminary faculty member, moral laws continue to be binding, cultic laws are not, and civil laws may be binding depending upon the similarities and dissimilarities between the contemporary society and the society of Israel in that time and place. Some scholars believe that the three-category method has outlived its usefulness; however, there are strong arguments on both sides.

Most important for our purpose is the notion that, as opposed to looking only for moral laws, which are typically limited to the Decalogue, "there is a breadth of moral *principles* that inform the whole core and meaning of the Torah."[38] (italics in original) For the purposes of this book, those moral principles are the standards revealed by biblical truth about the required procedures and substantive law of the biblical death penalty. Those moral principles are the biblical standards that inform the whole core and meaning of the biblical death penalty.

The biblical death penalty did not exist in a vacuum, standing alone, justified by its own merits as a punishment appropriate and dictated by God. The biblical death penalty existed within an entire matrix of biblical moral principles and structures, as widely gauged as ordination, covenant, worship, idolatry, sacrifice, atonement, etc. We dare not manifest the arrogance of claiming biblical support and divine sanction for the specific acts we are carrying out under the American death penalty without, at the very least, first holding ourselves up to the measure of those biblical moral principles. Those are the standards of biblical truth that we will identify and measure ourselves against in the course of this book.

Now we are ready to delve into that matrix of biblical moral principles and structures, the scriptures and the procedures necessary to fulfill them. In doing so, we will discover what the standards of biblical truth reveal about our American death penalty.

Chapter Three

A POINT OF BEGINNING

BEYOND PLATITUDES

We are seeking after two distinct realities. The first are the standards of the biblical death penalty as it actually existed in the scriptures of Torah/Pentateuch and the provisions of Talmud necessary to fulfill those scriptures. The other is the American death penalty as it actually exists and functions today in our nation. Where does such a search begin? The facts about the American death penalty are not as obvious as one might expect. Much of the information we need has never been presented to us in the media. Why is this so?

One of the reasons we have not heard many of the facts about the death penalty in the American media is a phenomenon I call "football-style reporting." In this currently popular genre, most news events are reduced to a "who's winning" rendition. No matter how complex the reality behind the story, the reporting jams everything into one of two contrived sides. Then one of the artificial sides is declared to be winning. An extreme example of this approach occurred a few years ago in our local Jacksonville newspaper in Florida. The headline of an editorial on the death penalty read, "CAPITAL PUNISHMENT: Killers lead—4,000–12."[1] The report

compared the number of murders in Florida over a two-year period (4,000) to the number of executed murderers over the same
period (12). It then declared that the murderers were winning.

While few newspapers would be so blatant with their football-
style reporting of the news, subtler versions of this approach are
pervasive in our media. The most popular American versions pit
left against right, big government against small government, and
liberals against conservatives. In the context of the death penalty,
the sides are cast as "those who are tough on crime" versus "bleeding hearts and criminal coddlers."

Because football-style reporting does not allow for any gray
areas needing discussion, American death penalty reporting has
traditionally painted all those who support the current version
of the death penalty as "supporting victims of crime" and labeled
all those who raise any questions about the punishment or the
process as "uncaring about victims or about crime." That is it.
Everything is forced through this two-dimensional prism. After
masticating the complexities into a formless pulp that can be
divided into two meaningless but well-defined halves, the reporter then declares which side is winning. We have been given
few if any of the actual facts that paint a realistic picture of
the complex and multifaceted issues behind the death penalty in
America today.

In the last few years we have started to hear about the failures
and the problems of the death penalty. A procession of inmates
has been released from death rows across America. About a dozen
were freed because DNA evidence proved that they were innocent. Others have been released after establishing state misconduct and significant evidence of their innocence.

The media have finally started to move out of football-style
reporting, beyond platitudes and into the facts. That is a real
blessing. Until recently, I had never heard many of the facts about
the American death penalty. Even though I was a lawyer and a
partner in some well-respected and prestigious law firms, I did
not know a thing about how capital punishment really worked in
America or how it really worked in Florida.

To answer our questions, we must look behind the tired and
simplistic descriptions of America's death penalty. We cannot
work from the shorthand sound bites. We must examine the full

reality of our death penalty in America. But where do we start? What is our "point of beginning"?

There are many possible points of beginning. Secular humanists, philosophers, sociologists, political ideologues, and others will all have pet points of beginning. Yet, for those of us who are seeking a point of beginning anchored in God's revelation and in our biblical faith, our point of beginning is in the scriptures of the Torah/Pentateuch and in the practices, as recorded in Talmud, that were necessary to fulfill the strict limitations of those scriptures.

The books of the Torah/Pentateuch are more than just scriptures. Both Christians and Jews refer to them as "God's law" because they contain the Mosaic law, the keystone of Jewish faith and a cornerstone of our Judeo-Christian ethics and morality. The concept of "law" is crucial to our search. First and foremost, the issue of the death penalty involves law.

What is law? The answer is not simple. In *Webster's*, the definition of the word "law" is one of the longest entries in the dictionary. A portion of it reads as follows: "A binding custom or practice of a community; a rule of conduct or action prescribed or formally recognized as binding or enforced by a controlling authority . . . the revelation of the will of God set forth in the Old Testament . . . the first part of the Hebrew scriptures: Pentateuch."[2]

All law must have two essential components. One part of the law describes the *whats*: identifying what is forbidden, what is allowed, what is required, and what is the punishment for breaking the law. Lawyers refer to this part of the law as the *substantive law*.

The other aspect of law identifies the *hows*: specifying how one is to be arrested, how one is to be determined guilty or innocent, and how the prescribed punishment is to be carried out. This portion of the law is called *procedural law*.

Our American death penalty system is primarily a regimen of procedural laws governing the process by which one is found to be deserving of death. This system of procedures is built on the foundation of a legal premise in substantive law. That premise is the conclusion that certain crimes deserve death.

For many years Christians supporting the American death penalty system, myself included, have been liberally quoting scriptures from the Torah/Pentateuch, especially the Mosaic law contained in the books of Leviticus, Exodus, and Deuteronomy, to support our position. In reality, however, did we ever think to compare our substantive and procedural laws with the requirements of those scriptures and the actual practices necessary to fulfill their limitations? I had never taken the time to do that and had never met any other Christian who had taken the time to do so. How can any of us speak competently when we quote God's law to support our laws without even having compared the two?

This amazing oversight amounts to claiming support for the outcome, executions, without any analysis of why execution should be applied or how a sentence of execution should be arrived at. In its barest form, this stance is tantamount to saying, "The death penalty is in the Bible. So it does not matter why or how America does the death penalty as long as we do it." Of course that is so simplistic as to be absurd.

Based on the revelations of biblical truth, nothing could be further from the truth. *Why* we impose the death penalty and *how* we carry out the death penalty both seem to matter a great deal from a biblical standpoint. For example, the execution of the innocent is strictly prohibited, the role of execution as an atoning sacrifice is abundantly clear, etc. The list goes on.

Thanks to the preliminary information provided to me by the young lawyer in Italy, I found my way to the Isser and Rae Price Library of Judaica at the University of Florida, where I would learn the particular moral principles applicable to the biblical death penalty and structure a comparison to our American death penalty. The comparison amazed me.

Yet, I stumbled upon even more basic questions. For example, I had always heard that the scriptures of Torah/Pentateuch mandate the death penalty. Therefore, I assumed that all Jewish people who take the Torah seriously must be pro–death penalty. That assumption is quite wrong.

In December 1999, the National Jewish Catholic Consultation joined with representatives of a Christian denomination to issue a joint statement that contained the following: "A Sanhedrin that puts one person to death once in seven years is called destructive. Rabbi Eliezer ben Azariah says: Or even once in seventy years. Rabbi Tarfon and Rabbi Akiba say: Had we been the Sanhedrin, none would ever have been put to death"[3] Mishnah Makkot 1:10

[second century C.E.]). The rabbis went on to quote another spokesperson for the Jewish community who said it this way:

> In biblical times, capital punishment was a search for justice when justice seemed impossible to reach. As the rabbis did years ago when they considered the use of the death penalty, let us take the time to ask ourselves some relevant questions. Is justice reached when we are taking the chance of killing an innocent person? Is justice reached when we are discriminating against minorities in our death sentences? "See that justice is done," the prophet Zechariah proclaims. If justice is not done by legalizing the death penalty—and it is not—human decency and biblical values that stress the sanctity of life require that we put an end to this grisly march of legalized death.[4]

All this is not to say that there is not a split of opinion in the modern U.S. Jewish community about the death penalty. Many American Jews favor the death penalty. That is a far cry, however, from stating that the Hebrew scriptures mandate the death penalty. Why had I never heard that the Hebrew scriptures might not demand life for a life? I could not help but wonder how many other Christians were aware of this.

Even more startling was the discovery that this was no secret. For example, in 1972, when the U.S. Supreme Court struck down the existing death penalty statutes in America, the question before our country was whether our society's standard of decency had matured to the point that capital punishment was no longer acceptable.

Within four years, thirty-five states had passed new death penalty statutes. My state of Florida was the first state to pass a new death sentence statute (within six months).[5] At the conclusion of a hectic three-day special legislative session, Florida enacted "a complicated legal contraption for weighing shades of evil."[6]

In Florida, two versions of the death penalty statute were put to a vote in the state legislature. Only one person out of the entire Florida legislature voted against both proposed death penalty statutes. (Nobody else voted against one version, and two people voted against the other—for political reasons.) That sole nay vote, which was in the Florida senate (thirty-nine to one), was freshman senator Jack Gordon. He voted against both proposed death penalty statutes for religious reasons. Jack Gordon is not a Christian. He is Jewish—and his religious reason for opposing the death penalty was based upon his religious interpretation of the very same Hebrew scriptures that the Christians quote to support the death penalty. In his words, "From a Jewish theological perspective, [capital punishment] is not something you should be for. . . . Even though there's an eye for an eye and a tooth for a tooth in the Bible, the history of Jewish jurisprudence, Talmudically, is that if the court sentences . . . someone to death more frequently than every sixty or seventy years, then they're supposed to get a new court."[7]

In evaluating such poignant commentaries, we dare not rely on the oft-repeated hearsay about what the Mosaic law says. Jews both for and against the death penalty have the Mosaic law in their scriptures. This means that the answers to our questions of substantive death penalty law might require going further back in biblical time, before the Mosaic law.

Our point of beginning in the search for what biblical truth reveals about our American death penalty has been pushed back even further than anticipated. After pausing for a moment to reflect upon the crucial scriptures in the Mosaic law, we must turn back to Genesis, all the way back to the very beginning.

Part One

WHAT DOES BIBLICAL TRUTH TELL US ABOUT
WHO IS DESERVING OF DEATH AND THE
AUTHORITY TO KILL?

Chapter Four

THE MOSAIC LAW

FROM MOSES TO JESUS; FROM CAIN TO LAMECH

Our search begins with the divinely revealed truth of the Mosaic law. The specific Hebrew scriptures typically quoted by Christians in support of the death penalty appear in two different books of the Torah/Pentateuch. Evangelicals frequently use the 1611 Authorized (King James) Version (AV). Protestants also use the New International Version (NIV). The pivotal scriptures cited in this work will be quoted from both translations in parallel, and for those that appear in the Hebrew scriptures as well, they will be quoted from the Tanakh (TNK).

> But if other damage ensues, the penalty shall be life for life, eye for eye, tooth for tooth, hand for hand, foot for foot, burn for burn, wound for wound, bruise for bruise.   Exod. 21:23–25 TNK

> And if any mischief follow, then thou shalt give life for life, eye for eye, tooth for tooth, hand for hand, foot for foot, burning for burning, wound for wound, stripe for stripe.   Exod. 21:23–25 AV

But if there is serious injury, you are to take life for life, eye for eye, tooth for tooth, hand for hand, foot for foot, burn for burn, wound for wound, bruise for bruise. Exod. 21:23–25 NIV

If anyone kills any human being, he shall be put to death. . . . If anyone maims his fellow, as he has done so shall it be done to him: fracture for fracture, eye for eye, tooth for tooth. The injury he inflicted on another shall be inflicted on him . . . one who kills a human being shall be put to death. Lev. 24:17, 19–21 TNK

And he that killeth any man shall surely be put to death. . . . And if a man cause a blemish in his neighbour; as he hath done, so shall it be done to him; breach for breach, eye for eye, tooth for tooth; as he hath caused a blemish in a man, so shall it be done to him again. . . . [A]nd he that killeth a man, he shall be put to death. Lev. 24:17, 19–21 AV

If anyone takes the life of a human being, he must be put to death. . . . If anyone injures his neighbor, whatever he has done must be done to him: fracture for fracture, eye for eye, tooth for tooth. As he has injured the other, so he is to be injured. . . . [W]hoever kills a man must be put to death. Lev. 24:17, 19–21 NIV

Nor must you show pity: life for life, eye for eye, tooth for tooth, hand for hand, foot for foot. Deut. 19:21 TNK

And thine eye shall not pity; but life shall go for life, eye for eye, tooth for tooth, hand for hand, foot for foot. Deut. 19:21 AV

Show no pity: life for life, eye for eye, tooth for tooth, hand for hand, foot for foot. Deut. 19:21 NIV

It is absolutely clear from the referenced scriptures that the Mosaic law is describing a retributive system of punishment. Furthermore, this retributive punishment is enacted as retaliatory violence directly proportional to the harm caused. Whatever the injury that has been suffered by the victim, that identical injury is to be inflicted on the perpetrator by the community.[1] Without any other analysis, a critical issue jumps forth from the scriptural texts. If we are seeking to support a death penalty based on compliance with this biblical standard, does not consistency require the parallel retaliatory violence for lesser offenses?

In other words, if we exact time in prison for the crimes of blinding someone, maiming someone, burning someone, or punching someone in the mouth, how can we then claim the endorsement of a biblical mandate for applying proportional violence in kind to only the most grievous offense, killing? Is this an inconsistency that we can explain or justify based upon scripture? Or is our failure to insist upon reciprocal maiming based upon the fact that it seems barbaric to have our government maim its citizens in the name of criminal justice? Is it any less barbaric for a government to kill its own citizens?

Yet, the problems posed by those questions are small compared with the next one. Those of us who are Christians of biblical faith accept both the Hebrew scriptures and the Christian scriptures, also called the New Testament, as God's divine revelation. Having said that, even the most minimal amount of scripture analysis brings us to a puzzling question: Do the Christian scriptures contradict the Hebrew scriptures? More specifically, do the words of Jesus Christ overrule the Mosaic law?

THE ETERNAL BUT

Two series of statements by Jesus, as recorded in the Gospel of Matthew, bear directly on this issue. The first statement appears to settle the issue:

> Think not that I am come to destroy the law, or the prophets: I am not come to destroy, but to fulfill. Mt. 5:17 AV

> Do not think that I have come to abolish the Law or the Prophets; I have not come to abolish them but to fulfill them. Mt. 5:17 NIV

Without more, the matter appears decided. Whatever is in the Mosaic law still applies. We should be able to end our inquiry right here.

But no such luck. The problem is that we cannot ignore what

Jesus says directly on point just a few verses later. He literally speaks about the very scriptures we quote as "eye for eye." We must deal with the following text:

> Ye have heard that it hath been said, AN EYE FOR AN EYE, AND A TOOTH FOR A TOOTH: But I say unto you, That ye resist not evil: but whosoever shall smite thee on thy right cheek, turn to him the other also. And if any man will sue thee at the law, and take away thy coat, let him have thy cloak also. Mt. 5:38–40 AV

> You have heard that it was said, "Eye for eye, and tooth for tooth." But I tell you, Do not resist an evil person. If someone strikes you on the right cheek, turn to him the other also. And if someone wants to sue you and take your tunic, let him have your cloak as well. Mt. 5:38–40 NIV

This text throws our search into a quandary. We could choose to just ignore these words of Jesus, but that would leave our results devoid of biblical basis. This is no ancillary clause. These texts refer explicitly to the Mosaic law of justice through infliction of proportional retaliatory violence, also called the law of tit for tat or *lex talionis*. At first glance, it sounds like Jesus is overruling the law and the prophets. However, that cannot be true because in verse 17 of this same chapter of Matthew's Gospel (quoted earlier), Jesus disclaims that.

This conundrum was so perplexing that I coined it "the eternal *but*": "You have heard it said . . . *but*, I tell you. . . ." How can the second clause of such a phrase not overrule the first clause? These two phrases sound inconsistent. Is Jesus wrong? Was Moses wrong? Is the Bible contradicting itself?

To my amazement, I found out that these scriptural phrases are not inconsistent. There is an answer, an answer that pulls the biblical verses into total and consistent alignment. That answer is rooted in understanding the world of the Bible back to its beginning.

That is where we must go next: Genesis, chapter 4, and the world at the very beginning of the Bible.

FROM CAIN TO LAMECH

Our exploration for the solution to this biblical puzzle of "the eternal *but*" starts with Cain in the book of Genesis. We all know that Cain commits the first homicide recorded in human history. The Bible tells us that Cain kills his brother Abel. (Gen. 4:8). Yet, God does not execute Cain. Instead, Cain is sent into exile and becomes a fugitive and a vagabond upon the earth. We begin the next phase of our search with the dialogue between God and Cain:

Cain said to the LORD, "My punishment is too great to bear! Since You have banished me this day from the soil, and I must avoid Your presence and become a restless wanderer on earth—anyone who meets me may kill me!" The LORD said to him, "I promise, if anyone kills Cain, sevenfold vengeance shall be taken on him." And the LORD put a mark on Cain, lest anyone who met him should kill him. Gen. 4:13–15 TNK

And Cain said unto the LORD, My punishment is greater than I can bear. Behold, thou hast driven me out this day from the face of the earth; and from thy face shall I be hid; and I shall be a fugitive and a vagabond in the earth; and it shall come to pass, that every one that findeth me shall slay me. And the LORD said unto him, Therefore whosoever slayeth Cain, vengeance shall be taken on him sevenfold. And the LORD set a mark upon Cain, lest any finding him should kill him. Gen. 4:13–15 AV

Cain said to the LORD, "My punishment is more than I can bear. Today you are driving me from the land, and I will be hidden from your presence; I will be a restless wanderer on the earth and whoever finds me will kill me." But the LORD said to him, "Not so; if anyone kills Cain, he will suffer vengeance seven times over." Then the LORD put a mark on Cain so that no one who found him would kill him. Gen. 4:13–15 NIV

These passages contain phenomenal information. First we must look at the concept of exile. Exile is banishment from one's country or home. Exile can occur in many ways. In biblical times, the world was sparsely populated, and everybody who was part of a group lived closely in one place. Those who became offenders were banished from that place and sent out into the wilderness. If the society was a walled city, the offenders were put outside the walls. This kept the offenders away from the innocent and law-abiding people who were following the rules. Such was the application of exile in biblical times.

In the last few hundred years, the places where we are living have become large settlements of hundreds of thousands, even millions of people. The law-abiding citizens no longer have the option of sending offenders out into a wilderness. In modern times people are sent into exile by incarcerating them in isolated places with walls around them. Biblically speaking, to be sent into prison in the year 2004 in America serves the same purpose as being exiled thousands of years ago: separation from society at large.

In the passages quoted from Genesis earlier, God deals with Cain by exile and not by vengeance. In fact God prohibits vengeance against Cain. Cain is banished and ultimately settles in the land of Nod. Cain fears that he will be a fugitive and a vagabond, meaning essentially that he would be left to move from place to place without a fixed home, residing in places for only a short duration.

Cain's lament over his banishment sounds similar to the attributes of modern imprisonment. One could hardly pick better words than "fugitive" and "vagabond" to describe the itinerant, rootless life of prison where men are constantly moving from one facility to another, never at home, never carrying more than a small box of property. Some of them must even work harder to conceal the nature of their crimes out of fear of violence from fellow inmates in the prison.

Cast in modern terms, Cain's lot easily parallels life in prison without possibility of parole. The major difference is that Cain will be allowed to marry, father children, and raise and support a family. In fact, scripture tells us that he even built a city. (Gen. 4:17).

The biblical account continues to unfold with the descendants of Cain. His son Enoch fathers Irad, who fathers Mehujael, who fathers Methusael, who fathers Lamech. Lamech, who takes two wives, contributes the next major piece to our understanding from scripture. The world has changed in the five generations that have elapsed since Cain. A new system, the law of the clan, has taken hold. The Bible, in reporting Lamech's words to his wives, Adah and Zillah, records the extent of this social and legal development toward escalating retaliatory violence:

> And Lamech said to his wives, "Adah and Zillah, hear my voice; O wives of Lamech, give ear to my speech. I have slain a man for wounding me, And a lad for bruising me. If Cain is avenged sevenfold, Then Lamech seventy-sevenfold." Gen. 4:23–24 TNK

> And Lamech said unto his wives, Adah and Zillah, Hear my voice; ye wives of Lamech, hearken unto my speech: for I have slain a man to my wounding, and a young man to my hurt. If Cain shall be avenged sevenfold, truly Lamech seventy and seven fold. Gen. 4:23–24 AV

> Lamech said to his wives: "Adah and Zillah, listen to me; wives of Lamech, hear my words. I have killed a man for wounding me, a young man for injuring me. If Cain is avenged seven times, then Lamech seventy-seven times." Gen. 4:23–24 NIV

In verse 15, we are told that if Cain is killed by anyone, the vengeance on the person that perpetrates that homicide will be seven times. Then, just five generations and eight lines later, in verses 23–24, we hear that Lamech is to be avenged seventy-seven times, that he exacts death for a bruise. What is happening here?

THE LAW OF THE CLAN

The answer is both simple and well understood. It is the law of the clan, which has already spun out of control. The world has taken on escalating retaliatory violence through family and clan vengeance as the law of the land. This is not necessarily chaos. It is a social structure based upon escalating retaliation intended as a means to control violence against one's kin.[2] As a legal and social structure, the law of the clan attempts to preserve order as follows:

Assume there is Clan A and Clan B. If Clan B burns one woman in Clan A, Clan A must burn twenty women in Clan B.
If Clan B knocks out the eye of one person in Clan A, Clan A must blind thirty people in Clan B.
If Clan B knocks out the tooth of one person in Clan A, Clan A must hit forty people in Clan B in the mouth.
If Clan B kills one person in Clan A, Clan A is committed to killing ten people in Clan B.

We can observe in the case of Lamech that he has already exceeded escalating retaliatory vengeance in kind and has escalated the nature of the injuries. Rather than bruise ten young men, he has inflicted a far more grievous injury on the one who wronged him. Thus, a young man is killed for just bruising Lamech.

These are the means and the methods of the law of the clan, the social structure and legal system to control violence. It is not intended to perpetrate violence, but rather to preserve order by the threat of escalating retaliatory violence.

This structure should be familiar to modern America. It is "mutual assured destruction" with primitive technology. It is exactly the logic of our nuclear weapons policies through the 1960s, 1970s, and 1980s: if Clan B shoots so much as one nuclear missile at our Clan A, we will unload 6,000 warheads on Clan B. It was not the intention of this policy to have a nuclear war. Rather it was to prevent nuclear war. If anybody launched the first missile, both sides were assured of total destruction. That is the law of the clan with updated technology.

In our modern age, we have thus far escaped the horror of unleashing escalating nuclear retaliatory violence. This was not the case in the early days of the Bible. The law of the clan did not always deliver peace back in the days before Moses. In the pre–Mosaic law period, "families were responsible for seeking the human sacrifice that would atone for a serious crime committed against one of its members. This system led to an unregulated cycle of violence, in which families could be trapped into continuous deadly conflict with each other."[3]

Moreover, something even subtler has occurred between the time of Cain and the time of Lamech. The change is easy to miss. Yet it is crucial to understanding how escalating retaliatory violence by man makes its entry into the Bible.

God originally tells Cain that if anyone kills him, Cain will be avenged seven times. We might jump to the conclusion that God is mandating human vengeance as a way to control people's murderous tendencies. But we must look closer.

God says this in response to Cain who said: "And it shall come to pass, that every one that findeth me shall slay me" (Gen. 4:14). Cain knows he has killed his brother who was a good and innocent man. Cain knows that everyone in the whole world who finds him shall slay him.

This creates a dilemma. If everyone in the whole world would seek to slay Cain, who in the whole world would there be to avenge the murder of Cain seven times? It is so subtle we could easily miss it. Scripture reports that no one wants Cain to live. Cain knows that everyone will slay him. So who is left to avenge Cain's execution sevenfold?

The point is that everyone minus everyone equals no one. Based on scripture, there is no one in the whole world to avenge the murder of Cain. Yet God has promised that the murder of Cain will be avenged sevenfold. The only person who can be standing ready to avenge the murder of Cain is God himself.

The movement from Cain to Lamech is not just a movement from sevenfold to seventy-sevenfold vengeance. It is also a drastic change from vengeance by God to vengeance by man. This is not a small shift. This is monumental.

Scripture tells us that vengeance belongs to the Lord:

Dearly beloved, avenge not yourselves, but rather give place unto wrath: for it is written: VENGEANCE IS MINE, I WILL REPAY, saith the Lord. . . . Be not overcome of evil, but overcome evil with good. Rom. 12:19, 21 AV

Do not take revenge, my friends, but leave room for God's wrath, for it is written: "It is mine to avenge; I will repay," says

the Lord. . . . Do not be overcome by evil, but overcome evil
with good. Rom. 12:19, 21 NIV

Lamech tells us that vengeance is his, a ruthless vengeance that
kills for a bruise.

This is the landscape against which God speaks in the scripture
verses most often quoted by Christians to support the death penalty—the eye for an eye and life for life of the Mosaic law.

Chapter Five

LIFE FOR LIFE AND THE RULE OF BLOOD

MANDATE OR LAW OF LIMITATION?

We have seen the possible discordance between the content of Matthew 5:17 on the one hand and of Matthew 5:38–40 on the other. If the Mosaic law is mandating "life for life," then these two sayings of Jesus are inconsistent and mutually exclusive. On the other hand, given the reality of the law of the clan in the world before the Mosaic law, a different understanding is possible that reconciles these sayings and leaves God and his word both consistent.

The Mosaic law is indeed more than just a law. It is endowed with a covenant that defines the people of God and their relationship with him. It is also a system of law. The statutes of the Mosaic law are legal statutes. Every lawyer knows the difference between a law that mandates behavior and a law that provides a legal limit to behavior. The latter is called a "law of limitation."

A law of limitation is every bit as much a law as one that mandates an activity. It is simply a law that is understood as providing a limit to the legality of an action. Let us look at some examples in modern terms.

An instance of a law that mandates an activity would be the

statutes that require me to obtain a registration and license plate for my vehicle. I must do this. No matter how many vehicles I own, I must do it for every single one. This is a law requiring specific behavior. Another example is the mandatory seat belt law. I must wear my seat belt when I am in a moving vehicle. It does not matter if I'm driving a hundred miles or just to the corner store. This is a mandated activity.

The speed limit on a road is a law of limitation. It sets the maximum speed that I am legally allowed to travel. Any speed up to that limit is allowed and is legal.

When we apply this distinction between laws of mandate and laws of limitation to the "eye for an eye" statutes of the Mosaic law, an amazing consistency between the words of Jesus in Matthew 5:17, 38–40 and the Mosaic law of the Hebrew scriptures comes into relief. If the setting immediately preceding the handing down of the Mosaic law was a blank slate—in other words, nobody was taking anybody's life as vengeance for killing someone—we might argue vigorously that the legal statutes of "eye for an eye, life for a life" must be mandates. God must have been ordering proportional retaliatory violence as God's revealed will.

Yet, as described in the preceding chapter, we know that just the opposite was the case. God did not need to mandate killing in order for people to kill as punishment for murder. The Bible reveals that the law of the clan, escalating retaliatory violence by man, was already firmly rooted in the world as early as Lamech.

Against this backdrop, it is obvious that God is intervening through the Mosaic law with a divine revelation of his will, a revelation that limits the retaliatory violence of the law of the clan, limiting escalating retaliatory violence to only proportional retaliatory violence. With this understanding we can see that the Mosaic law was meant to be a limitation that reduced violence. "Old Testament scholars have long recognized that the Mosaic Law was meant to be a limitation on violence rather than an endorsement of it."[1]

For example, for those living at the time of Moses, people well aware of the law of the clan, Leviticus 24:17–20 would be understood as follows (inserted language expressing the limitations inherent in the biblical-historical context is underlined):

If anyone kills any human being, he <u>alone</u> shall be put to death. . . . If anyone maims his fellow, as he has done so shall it be <u>the limit of what is</u> done to him: <u>not more than a</u> fracture for fracture, <u>not more than an</u> eye for eye, <u>not more than a</u> tooth for tooth. The injury he inflicted on another shall be inflicted on him <u>and not more</u>.   Lev. 24:17–20 TNK

And he that killeth any man, <u>he alone</u> shall surely be put to death. . . . And if a man cause a blemish in his neighbor; as he hath done so shall it be <u>the limit of what is</u> done to him; <u>not more than a</u> breach for breach, <u>not more than an</u> eye for eye, <u>not more than a</u> tooth for tooth; as he hath caused a blemish in a man, <u>and not more</u>, so shall it be done to him again.   Lev. 24:17–20 AV

If anyone takes the life of a human being, he <u>alone</u> must be put to death . . . <u>not more than a</u> life for life. If anyone injures his neighbor, whatever he has done must be <u>the limit of what is</u> done to him: <u>not more than a</u> fracture for fracture, <u>not more than an</u> eye for eye, <u>not more than a</u> tooth for tooth. As he has injured the other, <u>and not more</u> so, he is to be injured.   Lev. 24:17–20 NIV

This understanding of the Mosaic law's "eye for eye; life for life" as a law of limitation unveils an incredible struggle in the scriptures. God begins by ordaining that his vengeance protects Cain from violence. Vengeance by man sneaks in through Lamech, five generations after Cain. Lamech employs escalating retaliatory violence by man, the law of the clan. He proclaims that he is avenged seventy-seven times by his own hand. Unless God intervenes, in the world after Lamech escalating retaliatory human violence will be the norm.

BIBLICAL REVELATION OF GOD'S RESPONSE TO HUMAN VIOLENCE

We are surrounded by modern and historical examples of human retaliatory violence. In modern America, this law of the clan is referred to as the "law of the streets." The relevant question for us

is whether God desires human vengeance or, instead, God re-
serves vengeance unto himself. The scriptures support the latter.

In the limitations of the Mosaic law, Moses undoes Lamech
and brings the people closer to where God started by limiting
human vengeance to one life for one life. That may have been
the best Moses could do in the face of the people's hardness of
heart, even though God wanted and revealed something different.

This portion of the Mosaic law may not have been God's perfect will. Rather, this may be another example where God's permissive will is in contrast to his divine will. Such was surely the
case with polygamy and with the appointment of kings. God's
will is monogamy, and he warned his people against the treacher-
ies and burdens of appointing kings over themselves. Yet, polygamy, which first appears in the Bible through Lamech (Gen. 4:23),
persisted in biblical times with such critical biblical heroes as
Abraham, Jacob, David, and Solomon. And God's people appointed kings to rule over them (1 Sam. 8:6–22).

Another example of the conflict between God's permissive will
and his divine will takes place right in the Mosaic law. It is the
issue of divorce. We can look to the biblical revelation with respect to divorce as a parallel to God's revelation on the subject of
human vengeance.

In the beginning God made man and wife inseparable. God
opposed divorce. Moses had to allow divorce in the Mosaic law
because the people could not accept God's complete will. The
Pharisees of Jesus' time try to assert that the practical compromise
struck by Moses is God's will. Jesus will not allow it. Instead, he
takes us back to where God started:

> Moses because of the hardness of your hearts suffered you to
> put away your wives; but from the beginning it was not so. Mt.
> 19:8 AV

> Moses permitted you to divorce your wives because your
> hearts were hard. But it was not this way from the beginning.
> Mt. 19:8 NIV

The same is true with "life for life."

In the beginning God proclaimed that his vengeance protected

Cain. God opposed human vengeance. After Lamech's legacy of human retaliatory violence, Moses had to allow the people at least one life in human vengeance for murder. Finally, Jesus takes us back to where God started (Mt. 5:38–40), and the Christian scriptures remind us to return good for evil because vengeance is only the Lord's. (Rom. 12:19, 21).

When the "eye for an eye, life for a life" of the Mosaic law is properly understood in its biblical-historical context, we see that capital punishment may not have been God's ideal. Rather, the death penalty may have been allowed in limited form in the Mosaic law because of the people's hardness of heart. Furthermore, this "law of limitation" in the Mosaic law would drastically reduce the violence described by Lamech, requiring both similarity in kind and proportionality of the violence in amount.

For the Christian, Jesus completes the perfection of God's revelation of his will. Jesus speaks his clarification with the combination of the verses in Matthew 5:17 and 38–40.

In summary, the "eye for an eye, life for a life" of the Mosaic law introduces a drastic change in human affairs. The change, however, is by way of a law of limitation on human retaliatory violence. Because this is a law of limitation, Jesus can admonish us not to engage in any retaliatory violence at all, not take a tooth, an eye, a limb, or a life. He can do this without overruling the law and the prophets. He is simply making clear where God has been directing us all along.

The biblical progression of this revelation can be presented graphically as follows:

God Shows Us His Approach by How God Deals with Cain:
Prohibiting Retaliatory Violence by Man (Gen. 4:15)

Lamech Moves to the Law of the Clan:
Escalating Retaliatory Violence by Man (Gen. 4:23–24)

Moses Moves the People Back toward Where God Started:
Allowing Only Limited Retaliatory Violence by Man (Exod. 21:23–25; Lev. 24:17, 19–21; Deut. 19:21)

Jesus Christ Returns Us to the Place Where God Started:
Prohibiting Retaliatory Violence by Man (Mt. 5:17, 38–40)

A test of this revelatory progression is to determine if God has acted consistently with it. We know God did not slay Cain for killing Abel. Rather God allowed Cain to go into exile. But what about the Noahide law, the rule of blood contained in Genesis 9:6?

THE NOAHIDE LAW: THE RULE OF BLOOD

The question of the rule of blood is an especially important one with respect to the American death penalty. The Bible Belt in America's South overlaps with the death penalty belt. Anyone who does not think that American support for the death penalty is critically connected to Americans' understanding of the scriptures in Torah/Pentateuch just hasn't been paying attention. As we have seen, it is not unusual for Bible Belt prosecutors to quote the Hebrew scriptures to juries in their arguments for death sentences in capital cases.

As a person who lives in the Deep South Bible Belt, in the state called the belt buckle of the death penalty belt,[2] I have seen numerous Christian billboards, placards, and pamphlets supporting the death penalty. Almost all of them feature the verse from Genesis 9:6. This is also called the rule of blood.

> Whoever sheds the blood of man, By man shall his blood be shed; For in His image Did God make man. Gen. 9:6 TNK

> Whoso sheddeth man's blood, by man shall his blood be shed; for in the image of God made he man. Gen. 9:6 AV

> Whoever sheds the blood of man, by man shall his blood be shed; for in the image of God has God made man. Gen. 9:6 NIV

This passage is included in God's blessing of Noah and his family (Gen. 9:1–7).

As discussed earlier, the law of the clan had held sway in the world for generations before Noah. After the Flood, God blessed Noah and his family. In doing so, God spoke certain words that, some believe, were to govern the affairs of the life of all people on earth—precepts that governed Hebrews and non-Hebrews alike. These are called the Noahide law.

There are many different ways to analyze this particular set of verses in God's blessing of Noah. Some scripture scholars point out that the style of the text is in poetic form, "typical of Hebrew wisdom literature" and "biblical laws were never written in poetic form."[3] Persons of biblical faith who rely upon Talmud consider these verses as only a portion of the law binding upon all the world.

> *The seven commandments [given] to Noah's descendants:* Seven universal laws binding on all mankind. They are: (1) The prohibition against idolatry. (2) The prohibition against murder. (3) The prohibition against incest and adultery. (4) The prohibition against robbery. (5) The prohibition against blasphemy. (6) The prohibition against eating flesh torn from a living animal. (7) The obligation to establish courts of law. . . . Some authorities have compiled more extensive lists comprising up to thirty commandments. However, the death penalty applies only to the seven listed.[4] (italics in original; bracketed language mine)

They locate the rest of the verses throughout other passages of scripture.

Christians of biblical faith in the Bible Belt generally hold that the Noahide law governed the entire world, descendants of Abraham and everyone else, until the Mosaic law was handed down on Mount Sinai. From that point on, they believe, the Jews became subject to the Mosaic law and the rest of the world continued under the Noahide law. Even so, their interpretation of the application of Genesis 9:6 to capital punishment, however, is limited to first-degree murder. There is no basis for this limitation in the text itself, which, by a plain reading, seems to cover all taking of human life.[5] If interpreted as binding law from God mandating capital punishment, the plain words of the text would include accidents, negligent homicide, even self-defense. I have never seen an explanation of the basis for this nonbiblical selectivity on any of the placards or billboards that quote Genesis 9:6 as God's mandate for executions.

Also, as mentioned in chapter 2, Christians claiming that Genesis 9:6 is God's mandate for capital punishment have not explained why other portions of the blessing do not also continue to be binding, e.g., the prohibition on consumption of rare meat (Gen. 9:4) or the mandate that any animal that kills a human must be executed (Gen. 9:5).

The rule of blood scripture verse in the Noahide law describes human retaliatory violence. For those who believe it is a command, the critical issue concerning this passage is whether it describes God's perfect will or only temporarily allows for man's stubborn adherence to vengeance. In other words, for those who interpret Genesis 9:6 as law, is this provision a stopgap, a temporary means of forcing men "into relatively peaceful relationships through the threat of death"?[6] This issue under the Noahide law is similar to the one discussed earlier with respect to the Mosaic law. The retaliatory human violence of killing those who have taken human life may not have been God's perfect will. Rather, this may be another example where God's permissive will contrasts with his divine will.

What does God want? Where do we look for guidance?

A possible source of understanding would be God's own conduct with respect to a prominent first-degree premeditated murderer after the blessing of Noah's family but before the handing down of the Mosaic law.

If the rule of blood in Genesis 9:6 is indeed God's perfect will, then it is God's desire that anyone who kills another human being must be executed. God would apply this penalty uniformly because God is infinitely just. Consequently, a prominent first-degree premeditated murderer after the blessing of Noah's family but before the handing down of the Mosaic law would have to be executed. So, we can look for guidance to the very next prominent murderer who appears in scripture after Genesis 9:6 to see how God deals with him.

What does the Bible report as God's punishment for the most significant and prominent first-degree murderer under the Noahide law, the rule of blood?

The first prominent figure that commits premeditated first-degree murder in the Bible after Genesis 9:6 is none other than Moses.

Some time after that, when Moses had grown up, he went out to his kinsfolk and witnessed their labors. He saw an Egyptian beating a Hebrew, one of his kinsmen. He turned this way and that and, seeing no one about, he struck down the Egyptian and hid him in the sand. Exod. 2:11–12 TNK

And it came to pass in those days, when Moses was grown, that he went out unto his brethren, and looked on their burdens: and he spied an Egyptian smiting an Hebrew, one of his brethren. And he looked this way and that way, and when he saw that there was no man, he slew the Egyptian, and hid him in the sand. Exod. 2:11–12 AV

One day, after Moses had grown up, he went out to where his own people were and watched them at their hard labor. He saw an Egyptian beating a Hebrew, one of his own people. Glancing this way and that and seeing no one, he killed the Egyptian and hid him in the sand. Exod. 2:11–12 NIV

These scriptures tell us quite clearly that Moses looked this way and that to make sure nobody was watching. To qualify for first-degree premeditated murder under Florida law, one only needs the briefest amount of time for reflection—e.g., the time it takes to put a bullet in a gun.[7] Looking this way and that to make sure no one saw the murder qualifies for premeditated first-degree murder.

Under Florida law, Moses has committed premeditated first-degree murder. He is eligible for the death penalty if there is at least one aggravating circumstance. In fact there are several. First, under the laws of Egypt, there was no legal or moral justification for Moses' act of freeing the Hebrew slave and killing the Egyptian slave master. That is enough to merit Florida's death row.[8]

The Egyptian that he has killed appears to have been acting in his official capacity as a slave master. That would also put Moses on Florida's death row.[9] Or Moses may have intended to allow the Hebrew slave to go free. That means the killing also occurred in the commission of a felony. Either one of those factors is enough for Moses to qualify for Florida's death row.[10]

Moreover, the scriptures tell us that Moses took affirmative steps to hide the evidence of his crime. He not only freed the slave from his lawful employment and then killed the Egyptian to escape punishment, but he also hid the body in the sand.[11] That totals at least four aggravators. Only one is needed. Moses is on Florida's death row.

If Genesis 9:6 is God's perfect will that everyone in the world who intentionally kills a human being is to be killed by a human being, Moses is finished. Pharaoh certainly wants Moses to be executed.

When Pharaoh learned of the matter, he sought to kill Moses. Exod. 2:15 TNK

Now when Pharaoh heard this thing, he sought to slay Moses. Exod. 2:15 AV

When Pharoah heard of this, he tried to kill Moses. Exod. 2:15 NIV

The execution of Moses would have been the rule of blood in action. The governing authority of the country where the crime occurred was even willing to carry out the execution on God's behalf. Yet, that is not what happens.

Instead God allows Moses to go into exile and live in Midian. God is totally consistent here. He allows the same consequence to Moses that he allowed to Cain: exile. In our time and language, we have a name for modern exile: prison.

The conclusion is clear. The rule of blood scripture verse in the Noahide law describes human retaliatory violence. Yet, this passage does not describe God's perfect will because it does not describe what God does with Cain or with Moses. Rather, this may be another example where God's permissive will is in contrast to his divine will. It only temporarily allows for man's stubborn adherence to vengeance. In this respect, the rule of blood under the Noahide law (Gen. 9:6) is similar to the Mosaic law (Exod. 21:23–25; Lev. 24:17, 19–21; Deut. 19:21). The killing of those who have taken human life, human retaliatory violence, is not God's perfect will.

We are left to conclude that the scriptures in Torah/Pentateuch, including the Mosaic law, certainly mention capital punishment but they may not mandate executions. In fact, God's divine will may have been thwarted in the Mosaic law by the hardness of the people's hearts, similar to what happened with God's divine will about polygamy, kings, and marriage and divorce.

Our search for the biblical truth about America's death penalty is still only beginning. We turn now to the question of who deserved to die under those scriptures in the Mosaic law.

Chapter Six

WHO DESERVES DEATH?

TORAH, THE AMERICAN COLONIES, AND MODERN AMERICA

The list of death-qualified infractions under the Mosaic law must be gleaned from three different books of the Hebrew scriptures: Exodus, Leviticus, and Deuteronomy. The codes in these three books are not identical. There have been several ways of grouping and categorizing the death-qualified crimes under the Mosaic law. For example:

There are differing interpretations with respect to the exact number of crimes for which the Torah imposes a death sentence. Hyman E. Goldin sets the number at thirty-six, and places these crimes into the following six categories: (1) eighteen moral abuses, arising out of illegal sexual relations, including adultery, "unnatural sexual relations," and incest; (2) twelve violations of religious laws, including blasphemy, idolatry, profanation of the Sabbath, and witchcraft; (3) three crimes against parents; (4) murder; (5) kidnapping and selling into slavery; and (6) the case of the rebellious elder. George Horowitz lists a total of eighteen offenses: idolatry, apostasy, blasphemy, sorcery and witchcraft, sacrifice of children, labor on the Sabbath, false evidence in capital cases, insubordination to a priest of [God] or a judge, murder, kidnapping, rape of a betrothed woman, striking a parent, disloyalty to a parent, adultery, incest, sodomy, bestiality, and licentiousness of a priest's daughter.[1] (citations omitted; bracketed language mine)

CAPITAL OFFENSES UNDER TORAH

Here is a partial list (illustrative but not by any means exhaustive) of the most prominent offenses that qualified for the death penalty under Mosaic law.

Murder

He who fatally strikes a man shall be put to death. Exod. 21:12 et seq. TNK

He that smiteth a man, so that he die, shall be surely put to death. Exod. 21:12 et seq. AV

Anyone who strikes a man and kills him shall surely be put to death. Exod. 21:12 et seq. NIV

Adultery

If a man is found lying with another man's wife, both of them—the man and the woman with whom he lay—shall die. . . . In the case of a virgin who is engaged to a man—if a man comes upon her in town and lies with her, you shall take the two of them out to the gate of that town and stone them to death. Deut. 22:22–24 TNK

If a man be found lying with a woman married to an husband, then they shall both of them die, both the man that lay with the woman, and the woman. . . . If a damsel that is a virgin be betrothed unto an husband, and a man find her in the city, and lie with her: then ye shall bring them both out unto the gate of that city, and ye shall stone them with stones that they die. Deut. 22:22–24 AV

If a man is found sleeping with another man's wife, both the man who slept with her and the woman must die. . . . If a man happens to meet in a town a virgin pledged to be married and he sleeps with her, you shall take both of them to the gate of that town and stone them to death . . . Deut. 22:22–24 NIV

Rape of an Engaged Woman

But if the man comes upon the engaged girl in the open country, and the man lies with her by force, only the man who lay with her shall die.   Deut. 22:25 TNK

But if a man find a betrothed damsel in the field, and the man force her, and lie with her: then the man only that lay with her shall die.   Deut. 22:25 AV

But if out in the country a man happens to meet a girl pledged to be married and rapes her, only the man who has done this shall die.   Deut. 22:25 NIV

Kidnapping

He who kidnaps a man—whether he has sold him or is still holding him—shall be put to death.   Exod. 21:16 TNK

And he that stealeth a man, and selleth him, or if he be found in his hand, he shall surely be put to death.   Exod. 21:16 AV

Anyone who kidnaps another and either sells him or still has him when he is caught must be put to death.   Exod. 21:16 NIV

Fornication by a Woman

A man marries a woman and cohabits with her. Then he takes an aversion to her and makes up charges against her and defames her, saying, "I married this woman; but when I approached her, I found that she was not a virgin." In such a case, the girl's father and mother shall produce the evidence of the girl's virginity before the elders of the town at the gate. And the girl's father shall say to the elders, ". . . But here is the

evidence of my daughter's virginity!" And they shall spread out the cloth before the elders of the town. The elders of that town shall then take the man and flog him. . . . But if the charge proves true, the girl was found not to have been a virgin, then the girl shall be brought out to the entrance of her father's house, and the men of her town shall stone her to death.
Deut. 22:13–21 TNK

If any man take a wife, and go in unto her, and hate her, and give occasions of speech against her, and bring up an evil name upon her, and say, I took this woman, and when I came to her, I found her not a maid: then shall the father of the damsel, and her mother, take and bring forth the tokens of the damsel's virginity unto the elders of the city in the gate: and the damsel's father shall say unto the elders . . . these are the tokens of my daughter's virginity. And they shall spread the cloth before the elders of the city. And the elders of the city shall take that man and chastise him. . . . But if this thing be true, and the tokens of virginity be not found for the damsel: then they shall bring out the damsel to the door of her father's house, and the men of her city shall stone her with stones that she die.
Deut. 22:13–21 AV

If a man takes a wife and, after lying with her, dislikes her and slanders her and gives her a bad name, saying, "I married this woman, but when I approached her, I did not find proof of her virginity," then the girl's father and mother shall bring proof that she was a virgin to the town elders at the gate. The girl's father shall say to the elders, ". . . here is the proof of my daughter's virginity." Then her parents shall display the cloth before the elders of the town, and the elders shall take the man and punish him. . . . If, however, the charge is true and no proof of the girl's virginity can be found, she shall be brought to the door of her father's house and there the men of her town shall stone her to death.   Deut. 22:13–21 NIV

Cursing One's Parents

He who insults his father or his mother shall be put to death.   Exod. 21:17 TNK

And he that curseth his father, or his mother, shall surely be put to death. Exod. 21:17 AV

Anyone who curses his father or mother must be put to death. Exod. 21:17 NIV

Incest

If a man lies with his father's wife, it is the nakedness of his father that he has uncovered; the two shall be put to death. . . . If a man lies with his daughter-in-law, both of them shall be put to death. Lev. 20:11–12 TNK

And the man that lieth with his father's wife hath uncovered his father's nakedness: both of them shall surely be put to death. . . . And if a man lie with his daughter-in-law, both of them shall surely be put to death. Lev. 20:11–12 AV

If a man sleeps with his father's wife, he has dishonored his father. Both the man and the woman must be put to death. . . . If a man sleeps with his daughter-in-law, both of them must be put to death. Lev. 20:11–12 NIV

Buggery (Sex with Animals)

If a man has carnal relations with a beast, he shall be put to death; and you shall kill the beast. If a woman approaches any beast to mate with it, you shall kill the woman and the beast; they shall be put to death. . . .
Lev. 20:15–16 TNK

And if a man lie with a beast, he shall surely be put to death: and ye shall slay the beast. And if a woman approach unto any beast, and lie down thereto, thou shalt kill the woman, and the beast: they shall surely be put to death. . . . Lev. 20:15–16 AV

If a man has sexual relations with an animal, he must be put to death and you must kill the animal. If a woman approaches an animal to have sexual relations with it, kill both the woman and the animal. They must be put to death. . . . Lev. 20:15–16 NIV

Sorcery

> A man or a woman who has a ghost or a familiar spirit shall be put to death; they shall be pelted with stones. Lev. 20: 27 TNK

> A man also or woman that hath a familiar spirit, or that is a wizard, shall surely be put to death: they shall stone them with stones. Lev. 20:27 AV

> A man or woman who is a medium or spiritist among you must be put to death. You are to stone them. Lev. 20:27 NIV

Idolatry

> If there is found among you . . . a man or woman who has affronted the LORD . . . turning to the worship of other gods . . . you shall take the man or the woman who did that wicked thing out to the public place, and you shall stone them, man or woman, to death. Deut. 17:2–5 TNK

> If there be found among you . . . man or woman, that . . . hath gone and served other gods . . . then shalt thou bring forth that man or that woman, which have committed that wicked thing, unto thy gates . . . and shalt stone them with stones, till they die. Deut. 17:2–5 AV

> If a man or woman living among you . . . has worshipped other gods . . . take the man or woman who has done this evil deed to your city gate and stone that person to death. Deut. 17:2–5 NIV

False Witness in a Capital Case

> And the magistrates shall make a thorough investigation. If the man who testified is a false witness, if he has testified falsely against his fellow, you shall do to him as he schemed to do to his fellow. . . . Nor must you show pity: life for life, eye for eye, tooth for tooth, hand for hand, foot for foot.
> Deut. 19:18–21 TNK

And the judges shall make diligent inquisition: and, behold, if the witness be a false witness, and hath testified falsely against his brother; then shall ye do unto him, as he had thought to have done unto his brother. . . . And thine eye shall not pity; but life shall go for life, eye for eye, tooth for tooth, hand for hand, foot for foot.   Deut. 19:18–21 AV

The judges must make a thorough investigation, and if the witness proves to be a liar, giving false testimony against his brother, then do to him as he intended to do to his brother. . . . Show no pity: life for life, eye for eye, tooth for tooth, hand for hand, foot for foot.   Deut. 19:18–21 NIV

Prophecy in the Name of Other Gods and False Prophecy

But any prophet who presumes to speak in My name an oracle that I did not command him to utter, or who speaks in the name of other gods—that prophet shall die.   Deut. 18:20 TNK

But the prophet, which shall presume to speak a word in my name, which I have not commanded him to speak, or that shall speak in the name of other gods, even that prophet shall die. Deut. 18:20 AV

But a prophet who presumes to speak in my name anything I have not commanded him to say, or a prophet who speaks in the name of other gods, must be put to death.   Deut. 18:20 NIV

Rebelliousness on the Part of a Son

If a man has a wayward and defiant son, who does not heed his father or mother and does not obey them even after they discipline him, his father and mother shall take hold of him and bring him out to the elders of his town at the public place of his community. They shall say to the elders of his town, "This son of ours is disloyal and defiant; he does not heed us. He is a glutton and a drunkard." Thereupon the men of his town shall stone him to death.   Deut. 21:18–21 TNK

If a man have a stubborn and rebellious son, which will not obey the voice of his father, or the voice of his mother, and that, when the have chastened him, will not hearken unto them: then shall his father and his mother lay hold on him, and bring him out unto the elders of this city, and unto the gate of his place; and they shall say unto the elders of his city, This our son is stubborn and rebellious, he will not obey our voice; he is a glutton and a drunkard. And all the men of his city shall stone him with stones, that he die. Deut. 21:18–21 AV

If a man has a stubborn and rebellious son who does not obey his father and mother and will not listen to them when they discipline him, his father and mother shall take hold of him and bring him to the elders at the gate of his town. They shall say to the elders, "This son of ours is stubborn and rebellious. He will not obey us. He is a profligate and a drunkard." Then all the men of his town shall stone him to death. Deut. 21:18–21 NIV

Work on the Sabbath

Six days may work be done, but on the seventh day there shall be a sabbath of complete rest, holy to the LORD; whoever does work on the sabbath day shall be put to death. Exod. 31:15 TNK

[W]hosoever doeth any work in the sabbath day, he shall surely be put to death. Exod. 31:15 AV

Whoever does any work on the Sabbath day must be put to death. Exod. 31:15 NIV

APPLICATION OF CAPITAL PUNISHMENT UNDER TORAH

It should be no surprise that, as time went on, this massive body of capital crimes was subject to much interpretation and even limitation. The rabbis frequently went to great lengths to interpret limitations in the application of these capital crimes. For example, S. Mendelsohn, the scholar of Hebrew criminal jurisprudence, tells us that the offense of cursing one's parent was only punishable by death if one took the name of God in doing so;[2] and a death sentence for rebelliousness in fact required violation of filial duty, so as to make the son a "prodigal son."[3] The important point for our purposes, however, is to realize that those charged with enforcing the biblical death penalty under the scriptures of Torah/Pentateuch and the rules of Talmud were constantly finding that God intended for the death penalty to be extremely limited in its application. So limited as to be almost impossible to use.[4] This is completely different from the impression created by some religious death penalty proponents.

Why would the biblical death penalty be so limited in application? One logical answer can by deduced just from the laundry list of death-eligible offenses: if everyone who is worthy of death is killed, who will be left? The echoes of that question may speak loudly to us today. First we must bridge the gap from the time of the ancient Hebrews until our present day.

THE MOSAIC LAW IN THE AMERICAN COLONIES

Many Americans may not realize how extensively the Mosaic law has shaped our criminal statues. In the original northeastern American colonies, much of the scriptural list of capital crimes from Torah/Pentateuch was incorporated into law by statute. Without going as far back as England (which, although more civilized than the rest of Europe at the time, had more than two hundred capital crimes on the books by the eighteen hundreds),[5] it is safe to say that the original capital offenses written into law in our New England colonies were quoted from the scriptures complete with the chapter and verse cites.[6]

For example, in 1665 New York, striking one's parents was a capital crime and in 1647 Massachusetts, the death penalty covered witchcraft, adultery, cursing one's parents, and being a rebellious son.[7] Furthermore, capital punishment was applied to religious crimes, such as wrongly believing. In the Massachusetts colony, the death penalty was applied to Anabaptists, Quakers, and Jesuits.[8] In some cases, the incorporation of the scriptural law into the secular colonial statutes went so far as to include the penalties requiring execution of the offending animal (as well as the defendant). In his classic research work, *Crime and Punishment in American History*, Lawrence M. Friedman cites specific examples of this phenomenon:

> Thomas Granger, of Plymouth, a boy of sixteen or seventeen, was indicted in 1642 for buggery "with a mare, a cow, two goats, five sheep, two calves, and a turkey." Granger confessed and was required to identify the sheep he had buggered, in a kind of lineup. The animals were killed, then Granger himself was executed.[9]

> The offending animal was a "deodand," that is, a chattel that caused a human death, and could be punished or forfeited along with the offending human. Under a law of New Hampshire, for example, the death penalty was prescribed for every man or woman "that shall have Carnal Copulation with any Beast or brute Creature," and the "Beast shall be slain and burned."[10]

Between that time and the 1970s, the U.S. Supreme Court has gradually disallowed various punishments under our U.S. Constitution. As a result, in modern America we would not allow punishments such as disemboweling, beheading, drawing and quartering,[11] burning at the stake, crucifixion, breaking on the wheel, or the like.[12]

Interestingly, our U.S. Supreme Court has continued to hold that the death penalty itself is not inherently unconstitutional. Instead the Court pronounced that the constitutional standard for acceptable punishment was not a historic one, but rather an evolving standard of decency marked by the progress of a maturing society. While this standard does not quote the scriptures or the Talmud, it certainly benefits from the historical process revealed in scripture and Talmud.

For example, as God's people mature in faith through history, they become monogamous instead of polygamous. Women become persons instead of property. And, as we have seen in the preceding chapters, the escalating human retaliatory violence of Lamech yields to the limited retaliatory violence of the Mosaic law. Finally, for Christians of biblical faith, Jesus Christ brings us back to the original intent of God, evidenced by his dealing with Cain, that there be no retaliatory violence by man at all. It is only logical that we would also mature in our understanding of acceptable punishments.

The biblical death penalty provided four modes of capital punishment: stoning, burning, decapitation, and strangulation. In the opinion of the rabbis, stoning was the severest and strangulation was the mildest.[13] The numerous other punishments contained in the Mosaic law were incorporated into our American history through customs and mores just as effectively as the death penalty was included in the penal statutes of the American colonies. Through the course of our history and development as a society, we have had to reevaluate those punishments as well.

MOSAIC LAW AND MODERN AMERICA

Based upon our American jurisprudence to date, our society has evolved to the point where cutting a person's tongue out,[14] stoning,[15] burning people alive,[16] beating the evil out of children,[17] public executions and exile in the form of expatriation,[18] all punishments prescribed in the scriptures, no longer meet the evolving standard of decency marked by the progress of our maturing society. As we assess modern America in light of the effort to support capital punishment based on the Mosaic law, clearly there are some serious inconsistencies in our appraisal of punishments.

At a deeper level, there are also significant issues of intellectual honesty when we clamor "life for life" but reject the balance of the lex talionis, the law of tit for tat. (Exod. 21:23–25). For example, why are we not requiring fracture for fracture? Eye for eye? Tooth for tooth? Hand for hand? Foot for foot? What is our scriptural foundation for insisting that God mandates the punishment in part of a scripture verse but does not really care about the punishments listed in the rest of the same verse?

Finally, we have total inconsistency with the biblical death penalty based upon our selectivity of capital offenses. What about capital punishment for the following:

Adultery—Different studies quote America's rate of adultery as high as 50 to 70 percent.

Fornication by a single woman—Studies indicate that as many as two-thirds of single women in America are engaging in premarital sex.

Sorcery—What about tarot cards, palm reading, and the like?

False witness in a capital case—What about prosecutorial misconduct or less than honest detectives?

Prophecy in the name of other gods—In Deuteronomy 17:2–5, this proscription refers to the sun, the moon, and the other heavenly objects. What about our modern-day practice of writing and reading horoscopes?

False prophecy—Will we start executing the hotline psychics who get it wrong?

Cursing one's parents—Have not most of us done this at least once in our thoughts?

Rebelliousness on the part of a son—How many American men would survive this test?

Idolatry—In the Epistles, Paul called "greed" a form of idolatry (Col. 3:5). Today, between lotteries and huge jury verdicts, some say greed is a national pastime.

Work on the Sabbath—Under the biblical death penalty, this included all commercial activities.[19] What about owners of restaurants and stores, the people that work there and those of us who shop there—all on Sunday/Sabbath?

Who picked murder as the only item off the list that God really mandates for execution? What is our scriptural foundation for insisting that God mandates execution for murder but wasn't really serious about the rest? How can we arbitrarily pick one item out of so many and then call it God's ordained will?

Even more profound is the realization that if we used the whole list from the Mosaic law to select Americans deserving of execution, who in America would not be executed? If we used the whole list from the Mosaic law, who in America would not have daughters, nieces, or granddaughters executed? If we used the whole list from the Mosaic law, who in America would not have sons, nephews, or grandsons executed? If we used the whole list from the Mosaic law, who in America would not have coworkers, friends from church, or members of their home community executed? Who in America would be left to pull the switch?

These are the questions that bring us to our next point in understanding of the biblical truth about America's death penalty.

Chapter Seven

A CHRISTIAN CONUNDRUM UNDER MOSAIC LAW

ATONEMENT BY SACRIFICE VERSUS RECONCILIATION BY GRACE

In every society, the criminal code, the accepted list of offenses and punishments, serves multiple purposes. One of those purposes is determination of culpability and application of appropriate punishment. Another purpose, perhaps just as important, is the establishment of the values of the community.

The biblical death penalty in Mosaic law was no exception. It served the parallel functions of stating that the enumerated offenses were so destructive to the life of the community that such infractions were deserving of death. Consequently, the identification of the death penalty with certain enumerated offenses served the purpose of setting a community standard that those offenses were the worst crimes against God and the community. Yet, literal enforcement of the ultimate price for so many proscriptions could decimate the populace.

Language has many uses. Law codes are not automatically to be understood literally as simple mirrors of practice. One function of the juridical death threat was to get people's attention, to lay down a solemn warning, to alert all to the extreme seriousness of certain misdeeds. The [teaching] function of the law is accomplished by the texts themselves. . . . If they were ever implemented literally, however, the streets of the community would run red with blood, the populace would be slaughtered by its own courts.[1]

The actual practice of the ancient Hebrews strongly supports this understanding of the practical purpose of the death penalty in the Mosaic law. The Talmud shows that "notwithstanding the severity attributed to the Pharisees, they rendered the execution of a death sentence all but impossible."[2]

The Mishnah records an anonymous view that considered a court that passed the death penalty even once in seven years to be overly zealous; in the opinion of R. Eleazar b. Azariah this could be said of even once in every seventy years. Yet a third, much quoted view, attributed to the tannaim R. Tarfon and R. Akiva, was so opposed to the death penalty that, in their words, "had we been members of the Sanhedrin, no one would ever have been executed."[3]

This parallel role of the biblical death penalty is also evident in the history of our own criminal jurisprudence. Although our codification of the Mosaic law prescribed execution, the colonial communities in the North allowed the death penalty to serve as a statement of the severity of the offense while moving away from the practice of execution. This was the case, for example, with sexual crimes: "Apparently the colonists had misgivings about executing adulterers. . . . After the mid–17th century, there were no more executions for adultery; after 1673, executions for buggery, too, came to an end in New England."[4] This also appears to have occurred with respect to crimes of rebelliousness and incorrigibility in children.

Some of the other capital laws were also all bark and no bite. Under the *Laws and Liberties of Massachusetts* (1648), a "stubborn or REBELLIOUS SON" sixteen or over "which will not obey the voice of his Father, or the voice of his Mother" and instead lived in "sundry notorious crimes" was to be put to death. (Apparently a daughter so rebellious was unthinkable.) Cursing or smiting a natural father or mother was also a capital offense. But nobody, it seems, was ever put to death for these crimes.[5]

The fact that the death penalty was not applied in a case does not render the criminal statute futile. The statute still speaks loudly and clearly to the fact that the related offense is of such severity that it merits death.

What seems to have dropped out of our American effort to fashion and support a death penalty based upon the Bible is the understanding that executions should not be based merely on whether or not the perpetrator is deserving of death. Based upon the lists in the Mosaic law, virtually everyone is deserving of death, including anyone who kills another with premeditation. This is especially so in the opinion of the victim's loved ones. Yet based upon the biblical truth about the death penalty, asking only if the crime is worthy of death is the wrong question. If that were the right test, we would still be executing adulterers, single women who have given up their virginity, and clerks who work at discount stores on Sundays.

Perhaps this is why the practices of the ancient Hebrews under the scriptures of Torah/Pentateuch went to such great lengths to find reasons that excused the death penalty. Such excuses went so far as to place a burden on the community to ensure that the offender, who was assumed to be unwitting, was properly advised in the moment that he should cease his death-eligible activity.[6]

In the same way that asking only if the crime is worthy of death frames the wrong question, so too there are wrong questions about the redemptive power of executions. Questions about redemption may have been answered by the biblical death penalty for the ancient Hebrews, but Christians have already answered those issues in other ways.

THE DEATH PENALTY AS REDEMPTION FOR THE OFFENDER

A fundamental concept of the biblical death penalty under the Mosaic law is the atoning power of the sacrificial offering made through the execution of the offender. "The Torah teaches that if [a person] himself killed another, it does not suffice for him to pay money (*kofer*, ransom) as atonement; only through being put to death does he atone for his sin."[7] (bracketed language in original) The biblical death penalty holds that the execution is for the benefit of the accused and provides atonement between the sinner and God.[8] "Notwithstanding the high regard for man, the cherished value of every unique individual, and the great love that we have for every individual made in the image of God, even those condemned to death . . . nonetheless an evil man cannot be permitted to remain alive, for by his death he gains atonement, even as he is removed from life."[9] (ellipsis in original)

In other words, the Mosaic law incorporates a sin code. For some sins, one sacrifices a bird, for others a bull. For the most serious sins, one sacrifices oneself. Execution of the offender is seen as a redemptive sacrifice. "[The condemned is to say] 'Let my death be an atonement for all my sins.'"[10] (bracketed language mine)

Atonement by one's sacrificial death is evidenced in the actual procedures for execution under the biblical death penalty.

When he is about ten cubits from the place of execution, he is told to make a confession, for it is incumbent on all who are condemned to death to make confession. Everyone who does so has a portion in the world to come. If he knows not how to confess, he is instructed: "Say, 'May my death be an expiation for all my sins.'" Even if he knows that the evidence on which he is convicted is false, he uses this form of confession.[11]

This understanding and belief under the biblical death penalty was based on the scriptural recounting of the execution of Achan by Joshua:

When the Jewish nation began their conquest of the Land of Israel and destroyed the city of Jericho, Joshua decreed that they were forbidden to take any of its spoils. Achan transgressed this prohibition by taking valuables from the city, and he was sentenced to death for this.[12] (Josh. ch. 7)

For so we find concerning Achan, that Joshua said to him before he was executed: *"My son, please give honor [to Hashem],*

God of Israel, and give a confession to Him." And then—Scripture states: *And Achan answered Joshua and said: "In truth I have sinned [against Hashem, God of Israel], and thus and thus, etc. [have I done]."*[13] Now, from where do we know that the confession [of Achan] brought him atonement? For subsequently, it is stated: *Joshua said to Achan: "Why have you ruined us? God will ruin you on this day."*[14] This implies: On *this* day you are ruined, but in the World to Come, you will not be ruined.[15]

Joshua's emphasizing that Achan would be ruined *on this day* implies that after this day was over [i.e., after his execution] the stain of his actions would be lifted, and he would attain his share in the World to Come.[16] (bracketed language and italics in originals)

For the Bible-believing Christian, the quoted scripture passage (Josh. 7:25) is surpassed by the words of Jesus Christ to the good thief while hanging on the cross. Jesus Christ is being executed under Roman authority by crucifixion. Simultaneously, there are two criminals also being executed. The "good thief" confesses his guilt and then makes a profession of faith in Jesus Christ. Jesus responds:

> And he said unto Jesus, Lord, remember me when thou comest into thy kingdom. And Jesus said unto him, Verily I say unto thee, today shalt thou be with me in paradise. Lk. 23:42–43 AV

> Then he said, "Jesus, remember me when you come into your kingdom." Jesus answered him, "I tell you the truth, today you will be with me in paradise." Lk. 23:42–43 NIV

Jesus has explicitly undone redemption and atonement via execution. Unlike Achan, who must be "ruined today by God" (executed) so that he may have a portion tomorrow in the world to come, Jesus proclaims that there is no need to ruin the good thief "today." Through the merits of Jesus Christ, the good thief, who has confessed and professed, will receive his portion *today*, now. The destruction of the good thief by execution is no longer relevant to atonement. For the Bible-believing Christian, the lesson of Joshua and Achan has been surpassed by the fulfillment of the promise through the atonement by Jesus Christ.

CHRISTIAN CONCEPTS OF THE ATONEMENT

Atonement literally describes a state of restored unity. The concept is frequently driven home by segmenting the word into its three parts: at-one-ment. Virtually all Christians of biblical faith would agree that Jesus Christ has atoned for our sin. The amazing aspect of this concept, however, is that Christians have not agreed on the mechanics of *how* Jesus Christ atoned for our sin. They do not agree now, and they have not agreed across the centuries since the crucifixion of Jesus.

The multimillennial dialogue on this subject, referred to in theological circles as "soteriology" could be very discomforting for the average American Christian sitting in the pew. The *Wycliffe Dictionary of Theology*, which does an admirable job of recounting the historical development of our concepts of atonement,[17] reveals the extent to which such concepts have been shaped by cultural experiences over time.

For example, the notion of a person or a people being captured and enslaved by an enemy power was a pervasive part of the human experience during the times of early Christianity. Consequently, the Christian scriptures were understood to describe a transaction where Satan had taken man hostage and was holding man for ransom. The price of ransom was so great that only God himself could pay it. Thus, Christ paid the price of ransom with his life, setting men free.[18] This is referred to as the *Christus Victor* or Christ Victorious model. Modern Christians find this description particularly difficult because the ransom was understood to have been paid to Satan.

Some of the early great writers of Christianity also struggled with the "payment of ransom to the devil" concept. In the fourth century, a new explanation arose which explained that God had tricked Satan by taking on human flesh to disguise himself. When Satan attacked Christ, the devil "took the bait" like a fish biting a hook, and God won our freedom and the devil's.[19]

Augustine continued with the "baited hook" theory, even to the point of describing "the cross as a mousetrap baited with the Savior's blood."[20] He took an additional step, however, by speaking of the atonement in terms of satisfaction, through Christ's death, of God's justice, a development in theology that paralleled "the vocabulary of Western Christendom."[21] Augustine also interjected the notion that Christ could have utilized means other than his death to achieve atonement. Perhaps this reflects an aspect of the discussion from the Byzantine portion of Christianity, where the understanding of Christ's atonement focused upon his roles as "Victor," "Conqueror," "Revealer," "Benefactor," "Physician," "Victim," and "Reconciler."[22]

It took almost a thousand years for Christianity to fully incorporate a satisfaction model and experience a massive revision in atonement theology. This came courtesy of St. Anselm of Canterbury (1033–1109) in his landmark work, *Cur Deus Homo (Why Did God Become Man?)*, which recast the atonement from a ransom model to a satisfaction model, focusing upon the infinite satisfaction that must be paid *to* God in order to restore the infraction of sin against God's infinite honor.[23] A modern commentator astutely points out that Anselm's concept of satisfaction was based in the feudal culture of his time, a reflection of the shame/honor/loyalty system of the Middle Ages that had nothing to do with our modern Anglo-Saxon notions of guilt and punishment.[24]

The Anglo-Saxon culture began to inform our understanding of the atonement during the Reformation period. Martin Luther (1483–1546) characterized the atonement as a "propitiatory sacrifice" that serves to placate "both the law and the wrath of God," thus giving "priority to God's justice rather than his love."[25] Finally, John Calvin (1509–1564) crystallized the "Protestant doctrine," contending that "not divine honor but divine justice must be satisfied."[26] The term for this analysis is "expiation" because it covers the guilt for sin and the penalty due.[27] This model is mirrored by Anglo-Saxon legal concepts, which focus upon innocence, guilt, and punishment rather than honor, shame, and loyalty.

As one of the key Protestant theologians in nineteenth-century America, Charles Hodges (1797–1878) refined the final tenets of the theological premise that God's perfect justice "renders it necessary that the righteous be rewarded and the wicked be punished."[28] This is a major theme of the classic American Protestant ethic that nurtures the spirit of punishment described by T. Richard Snyder[29] and coexists with the environment of retributive justice.[30] It also happens to fit like a hand in a glove with the prevalent American acceptance of the penal substitution model of atonement.[31] Thus cast, the atonement becomes a penal and substitutionary satisfaction wherein Jesus substitutes himself for us sinners in order to take the hits from the Father, licks that should have been our punishment and must be imposed as a necessary precondition to God's forgiveness.

Other understandings of the atonement have also been offered. Some theologians have focused upon the love of God, finding in the crucifixion so powerful a statement of that love that humanity is set free from the bondage of sin and death through the moral influence of God's hand. Others have taken the entirety of Christ's life, which culminates in the ultimate spiritual reality of God's victory over evil, and characterized the atonement as a biblical narrative of Christ Victorious.[32] The latter comports well with the faith expressed in the popular piety of some Christians who pray "through Our Lord and Savior, Jesus Christ, who by his life, death and resurrection, purchased for us the rewards of eternal life."

The variety of understandings about atonement can be numbing. No one has definitively synthesized them all. At least some authors have explained the various models as the result of Paul's effort in scripture to employ a wide range of metaphors to describe the many facets of a spiritual reality—the legal model (justification), the transactional model (redemption), the relationship model (reconciliation), the worship model (sacrifice), and the spiritual battleground model (triumph over evil).[33]

The scope of this book does not allow for a relative weighing of the merits and shortcomings of each model or of many lesser-known explanations among theologians today. We are able to say, however, that regardless of one's understanding of the mechanics of atonement, Christians of biblical faith should all be clear on at least one point: For those who accept Jesus Christ as their Lord and Savior, execution is no longer a means of atonement between the offender and God. For Christians of biblical faith, as scripture confirms, atonement between the offender and God has been accomplished and completed by Jesus Christ (2 Cor. 5:18; Rom. 5:10). For Bible-believing Christians, no additional redemptive sacrifice is necessary or proper or even possible. Biblical truth reveals that the biblical death penalty serves the redemptive purpose of atonement. For the Christian, that job was completed by Jesus Christ. This is a major problem for any Bible-based death penalty carried out at the hands of Christians.

THE DEATH PENALTY AS REDEMPTION FOR THE COMMUNITY

The biblical death penalty also treats the execution of the offender as a redemptive sacrifice for the community. For example, the execution of the blasphemer is treated as parallel to the burning of the sacrificial bull because both the person and the sacrificial bull are to be removed, to a place outside the camp, where there is preparation (in the case of the person, for execution; in the case of the bull, for burning of the carcass) for purposes of atonement for the offender and the community.[34] As noted by the Gemara, this similarity has to do with atonement and not with the ritualistic requirements of a mitzvah.[35]

This understanding of redemption for the community is also based upon the scriptures in Torah/Pentateuch. The execution of the offender brings about atonement for the land itself, for the entire community.

> You shall not pollute the land in which you live; for blood pollutes the land, and the land can have no expiation for blood that is shed on it, except by the blood of him who shed it. Num. 35:33 TNK

> So ye shall not pollute the land wherein ye are: for blood it defileth the land: and the land cannot be cleansed of the blood that is shed therein, but by the blood of him that shed it. Num. 35:33 AV

> Bloodshed pollutes the land, and atonement cannot be made for the land on which blood has been shed, except by the blood of the one who shed it. Num. 35:33 NIV

For Christians of biblical faith, the atonement of Jesus Christ has reconciled us once and for all to each other as well as to God. All things have been reconciled to God through the atoning actions of Jesus Christ (Col. 1:20–22).

THE CHRISTIAN CONUNDRUM

The Christian scriptures are clear. We've been reconciled to each other and to God, all things have been reconciled to God, all through Jesus Christ. There is no more reconciling or atoning to do. For Bible-believing Christians, no additional redemptive sacrifice is necessary or proper or even possible. Biblical truth reveals that when Christians engage in executions, our own stated beliefs strip our pretenses of every biblical justification, exposing the motives of naked vengeance. When Bible-believing Christians take hold of the reins of the death penalty, we face a dilemma of biblical proportions.

As Christians we dare not support capital punishment based upon its atoning, redemptive powers under the sin code of the Mosaic law. To do so is to renounce by our actions the efficacy of Jesus Christ's saving acts. How do we quote the scriptures from Torah/Pentateuch that support executions but disregard the portion of those same scriptures that explain the saving and redemptive justification for the executions? As Christians, are we saved by grace or by executions?

Furthermore, based on the scriptural lists of death-eligible offenses under the biblical death penalty, virtually the entire community should be lining up for lethal injection. This reality does comport with our Christian theology—that the wages of sin are death and that anyone who says he does not sin is a liar. Christians believe that we are all deserving of death; that is why we all need a Savior. When we pick one crime off the scriptural list of capital offenses and wheel in the gurney only for the sinners who have broken *that* law, our scripture-based theology falls apart. If *all* are deserving of death, where is our scriptural support for claiming that only a particular person *really* deserves death?

Can we only hold the threads of biblical support for our American death penalty together by placing blinders on our eyes, by simultaneously reading highly selective portions of biblical texts while ignoring huge portions of these same texts? Surely this is not how God intended for us to read scripture. There is a death penalty in scripture, but based on the revelations of biblical truth, is it anything like our American death penalty? So far, it does not seem to be.

We must conclude that our American death penalty may not be supportable based upon biblical truth. For Christians of biblical faith, that is sobering at best and terrifying at worst.

Chapter Eight

AUTHORITY TO KILL

THE SANHEDRIN

As we saw in chapters 4 and 5, the biblical accounts reveal that God led his people from the escalating retaliatory vengeance of Lamech, the law of the clan, and to the partway step of severely restricted human retaliation of the law of Moses (though, for Christians, this was an intermediate stop on the way to the nonretaliatory revelations of Jesus). God knew that a society could not bear such a change unless a just and accessible system was put in place to redress the grievances of all citizens against each other. Such a system must provide justice for one's grievances regardless of the respective wealth or social status of the parties. It must also serve this function for both grievances over money and those over personal injury and death.

How do we know that God knew this? Because in the scriptures that are called the Noahide law, God prepares his people and the entire world to live a new way, by mandating the creation of a system of judicial courts.[1] This is fleshed out in the scriptures of Torah/Pentateuch.

You shall appoint magistrates and officials for your tribes, in all the settlements that the LORD your God is giving you, and they shall govern the people with due justice.   Deut. 16:18 TNK

Judges and officers shalt thou make thee in all thy gates, which the LORD thy God giveth thee, throughout thy tribes: and they shall judge the people with just judgment.   Deut. 16:18 AV

Appoint judges and officials for each of your tribes in every town the LORD your God is giving you, and they shall judge the people fairly.   Deut. 16:18 NIV

This biblical source actually incorporates two explicit commands: the establishment of courts, and the obligation to administer the courts with justice, in a fair and impartial manner. The biblical death penalty was only to be administered under a court system fashioned upon this scriptural foundation.

What is such a court system? Talmud provides the answer in detail. The derivation of the court structure under Talmud easily could be misunderstood as merely men's ideas if the reader is not exposed to the in-depth analysis of scripture that results in the rules. While a detailed rendition of all such analysis is beyond our scope, we will look at a portion of it in order to grasp the extent to which the Talmudic results are for the purpose of fulfilling the scriptural mandates in Torah/Pentateuch.

THE SANHEDRIN

The critical components of this judicial system are the Supreme Court, called the Great Sanhedrin, and the local courts, each called a Small Sanhedrin. "The Great Sanhedrin was composed of seventy-one judges, and a lesser one was composed of twenty-three judges."[2] "Capital cases are judged by a court of twenty-three judges."[3]

Under the biblical death penalty, nothing was left to chance, not even the numbers of judges designated to each of the courts. Every component of the judicial system had to be rooted in scripture. Sometimes this required meticulously working through biblical passages in a search for revealed truth. The rules for consistent application of these exegetical techniques were well established and spanned numerous centuries.[4] The first scripture verses we address in this process are the following:

> Then the LORD said to Moses, "Gather for Me seventy of Israel's elders of whom you have experience as elders and officers of the people, and bring them to the Tent of Meeting and let them take their place there with you. I will come down and speak with you there." Num. 11:16–17 TNK

> And the LORD said unto Moses, Gather unto me seventy men of the elders of Israel, whom thou knowest to be the elders of the people, and officers over them; and bring them unto the tabernacle of the congregation, that they may stand there with thee. And I will come down and talk with thee there. Num. 11:16–17 AV

> The LORD said to Moses: "Bring me seventy of Israel's elders who are known to you as leaders and officials among the people. Have them come to the Tent of Meeting, that they may stand there with you. I will come down and speak with you there." Num. 11:16–17 NIV

This scriptural mandate is the basis for the Great Sanhedrin, the Supreme Court under biblical law. "[T]here is established a Supreme Court holding sessions in the sanctuary. This is styled 'the Great Sanhedrin' and consists of seventy-one elders, as it is said: *Gather unto Me seventy men of the elders of Israel* (Num. 11:16), with Moses at their head, as it is said *that they may stand there with thee (ibid.)*, thus making a tribunal of seventy-one."[5] (italics in originals)

THE BIBLICAL CIRCUIT COURTS

What about all the far-flung towns throughout the region? How will they be brought into compliance with revealed biblical truth? Every town has a gate. The gate is the center of commerce and activity. Again, scripture provides the answer:

Hate evil and love good, And establish justice in the gate; Perhaps the LORD, the God of Hosts, Will be gracious to the remnant of Joseph.   Amos 5:15 TNK

Hate the evil, and love the good, and establish judgment in the gate: it may be that the LORD God of hosts will be gracious unto the remnant of Joseph.   Amos 5:15 AV

Hate evil, love good; maintain justice in the courts. Perhaps the LORD God Almighty will have mercy on the remnant of Joseph.   Amos 5:15 NIV

The phrase *in the gate* refers to adversaries in litigation. In biblical times, law courts functioned in the open area near the main city gate. This scriptural mandate to *establish justice*, in other words to set up courts, is the basis for the circuit court system under biblical law. "Moreover, in each town with a population of one hundred and twenty and upward there is set up a Small Sanhedrin, meeting at the gate of the town, as it is said: *And establish justice in the gate.*"[6] (Amos 5:15) (italics in original)

How was the number 120 arrived at as the minimum population for a town to qualify for a Small Sanhedrin? First, keep in mind that only adult males are counted. Women and children are not counted. Then, the number of men necessary to fill out a legal trial and to carry on the other requirements of God's law in the town are counted:

The community must be large enough to supply twenty-three men, making up the Sanhedrin; three rows of disciples, each comprising twenty-three; ten men of leisure to attend services at the Synagogue; two clerks; two court attendants; two litigants; two witnesses; two to refute the witnesses; two to rebut the refuters; two collectors of charity; one more in addition to the two collectors to constitute a commission of three for the distribution of charity; an expert surgeon; a scribe; and a schoolteacher. Hence the total population must be (at least) one hundred and twenty.[7]

Although provision was made for three judge courts and solo judge magistrates for particular monetary decisions, a court of twenty-three must preside over capital cases. "How many are to make up the Small Sanhedrin? Twenty-three. The most learned among them is the presiding judge; the others are seated in the form of a semicircular threshing floor, so that the presiding judge is able to see them all."[8]

The requirement for a minimum of twenty-three judges in a capital case is derived from the following scripture verses dealing with decisions between murder and manslaughter:

The assembly shall decide between the slayer and the blood-avenger. The assembly shall protect the manslayer from the blood-avenger. Num. 35:24–25 TNK

Then the congregation shall judge between the slayer and the revenger of blood according to these judgments: And the congregation shall deliver the slayer out of the hands of the revenger of blood. Num. 35:24–25 AV

[T]he assembly must judge between him and the avenger of blood according to these regulations. The assembly must protect the one accused of murder from the avenger of blood. Num. 35:24–25 NIV

The key word from the Hebrew of these verses is *congregation* (translated in more recent English editions as "assembly"). That is the basis for the ensuing literal application of the verse to the Small Sanhedrin. "As it is stated: *And the congregation shall judge . . . and the congregation shall save.* This teaches that the [S]anhedrin contains a congregation that judges, i.e., argues to convict, and a congregation that saves, i.e., argues to acquit. Since each congregation represents ten judges (as the Mishnah will soon demonstrate), we now have twenty judges."[9] (italics in original; emphasis added)

The Talmud then proceeds to explain the scriptural derivation of the fact that the word "congregation" as used in the Hebrew scriptures means "ten": "And from where is it derived that a congregation is composed of at least ten people? For it is stated concerning the twelve spies sent to Eretz Yisrael; *Until when, this evil 'congregation.'* And Joshua and Caleb are excluded from their number.[10] Thus, the term 'congregation' refers to a group of at least ten people."[11] (italics in original; emphasis added)

Having established the scriptural basis for a congregation to contain at least ten people, the Mishnah then explains the scriptural basis for arriving at a number of twenty-three: "And from where is it derived that we are to add another three judges? From the implication of that which is stated: *Do not follow a majority to harm,*[12] i.e., to convict, I may already infer that I should follow (the majority) to benefit, i.e., to acquit."[13] (italics in original; emphasis added)

A general rule of scriptural interpretation is that scripture is never redundant. Because scripture wastes no words, if a verse appears to repeat what has already been said or implied, a deeper or additional truth is being revealed.

If so, why is it stated further in the very same verse: *According to the majority (the matter) shall be decided?* This cannot mean that we are to follow the majority to acquit, since this is already implied in the earlier part of the verse. Rather, this latter part of the verse must indeed refer to following the majority to convict and it teaches: Not like your tilting in favor of the majority to acquit shall be your tilting in favor of the majority to convict. Rather, your tilting in favor of the majority to acquit can be based on a single-vote majority, whereas your tilting in favor of the majority to convict must be based on at least a two-vote majority.[14] (italics in original; emphasis added)

Thus, in order to allow for two congregations of at least ten votes and the possibility of a two-vote majority, a minimum of twenty-two judges is required. This is an even number, which could result in a tie. Hence, to avoid ties, one more is added. "[S]ince it is unacceptable for a court to consist of an even number of judges, a third judge is added, bringing the total to twenty-three."[15]

BIBLICAL VOTE COUNTING AMONG JUDGES

In terms of the judges' voting, the rules are clearly in favor of the defendant. They can be summarized as follows:[16]

If the voting judges vote twenty-three to zero, unanimously, for his conviction, he is acquitted. There must be at least one vote for his acquittal in order for him to be found guilty.

If the vote is twelve to eleven in favor of acquittal, he is acquitted.

If the vote is twelve to eleven for conviction or if even one judge is undecided (whether eleven to eleven with one abstention or twenty-two to zero with one abstention), two judges are added and the abstaining judge is treated as null.

From that point on, each time there is a vote and the judges fail to acquit by one or to convict by two, two more judges are added until the tribunal reaches the number of seventy-one.

At that point, if thirty-six are for acquittal and thirty-five are for conviction, the defendant is released. If thirty-six are for conviction and thrity-five are for acquittal, the two sides continue to argue until either a vote is changed or the presiding judge declares an impasse. An impasse results in acquittal.

A judge who has voted for acquittal cannot reverse his decision. A judge who has voted for conviction can always reverse himself and determine to vote for acquittal.[17]

BIBLICAL JUDICIAL AUTHORITY FOR CAPITAL CASES

The next major requirement for judges in capital cases (and others) is the manifestation of individual authority to serve as a judge through the process of ordination by laying on of hands: "No one is qualified to act as a judge, whether of the Great or a Small Sanhedrin or even of a court-of-three, unless he has been ordained by one who has himself been ordained. Moses, our teacher, ordained Joshua by laying his hands upon him, as it is said: *And he laid his hands upon him, and gave him a charge.*"[18] (Num. 27:23) (italics in original) The corporate element of authority is vested in the court itself: "The Divine Presence dwells in the midst of any competent Jewish tribunal. Therefore, it behooves the judges to sit in court enwrapped (in fringed robes) in a state of fear and reverence and in a serious frame of mind. . . . They should concentrate their minds on matters of Torah and wisdom."[19]

This authority is not derived from the mere act of convening a

Small Sanhedrin of ordained judges. It is a derivative authority that only is extant during periods when the Great Sanhedrin is housed in the holy place of the temple. "Capital charges are tried only while the Temple is in existence, provided that the Supreme Court meets in the Hall of Hewn Stones in the sanctuary."[20]

Consequently, even if the Great Sanhedrin is in existence, the authority to hear death penalty cases, and the derivative authority for inferior courts to do so, only exists if the Great Sanhedrin is housed at the temple. If the Great Sanhedrin is expelled from or exiled from the temple, the biblically based death penalty ceases to operate. "Forty years prior to the destruction of the Second Temple, the right of Israel to try capital cases ceased, for, though the sanctuary still existed, the Sanhedrin was exiled and no longer held sessions in the place assigned to it in the sanctuary."[21]

BIBLICAL REQUIREMENTS AND THE AMERICAN COURT SYSTEM

For those seeking to support the American death penalty on a biblical basis, these limitations are formidable.

First, we do not have a system of ordained judges and none of our courts are structured on the basis of the biblical court system.

Second, vote counting in American appellate and supreme courts does not follow the mandated procedures.

Many U.S. Supreme Court death penalty cases have been decided by a five-to-four vote, including decisions to sustain a death sentence. If an appeals court rules three to three or four to four because a justice abstains or is ill, the lower court sentence of death is sustained and enforced.

Finally, and this is perhaps most critical of all, as repugnant as it may seem to some of us, it is offensive to our U.S. Constitution to state or imply that the presence of the God revealed in the Holy Bible resides among our justices.

The judges and attorneys in an American courtroom may sit by half-listening while we swear before our personal God to "tell the truth, the whole truth, and nothing but the truth." The screams of objections will be deafening, however, if we assert that the God to whom we swear is exclusively, for all purposes of the trial and for everyone present, the God revealed by the Holy Bible.

For those of us who are people of biblical faith, the God of the Bible is sovereign. For those of us who are Christians of biblical faith, the God revealed in the Holy Bible is triune, was enfleshed incarnate in the person of Jesus Christ, and is the source of all truth through the power and person of the Holy Spirit. In either case, we can take that God with us into the courtroom if we choose, but we must keep him to ourselves. No American court is allowed to acknowledge his power, presence, dominion, or sovereignty. No American court is allowed to pay him homage.[22]

Under the biblical death penalty, the commitment of the judges to Torah and the ordination by laying on of hands, the court's physical and spiritual connection to the temple, and the presence of *the one, true God* in and through sovereign jurisdiction over the court are all essential to the ability of the court to judge in God's stead in capital cases. No one can even argue with a straight face that those conditions are met in an American courtroom. There is simply no way to squeeze the American court system into the confines of the biblically required courts under the biblical death penalty. It cannot be done.

CALVARY AND THE END OF CAPITAL PUNISHMENT UNDER THE BIBLE

For the many Christians in the Bible Belt and around the United States who accept the penal substitutionary model of the atonement, it is a foundational belief that Jesus Christ, through his sacrifice on Calvary, offered the perfect and final atonement, once and for all, for all persons, all times, and all places. This final sacrifice took place on Calvary in approximately A.D. 30. It is also clear that the biblical death penalty could not proceed without the Great Sanhedrin sitting in the temple. Yet, "*[f]orty years prior to the destruction of the Second Temple, the right of Israel to try capital cases ceased, for, though the sanctuary still existed, the Sanhedrin was exiled and no longer held sessions in the place assigned to it in the sanctuary.*"[23] (italics mine)

The second temple was destroyed in A.D. 70.[24] Forty years before the destruction of the second temple is A.D. 30. That is the same time that Jesus died on Calvary. This is not a small matter. What we are realizing here is that biblically based capital punishment ceased to function at the same time that Jesus Christ died on the cross on Calvary.

For every Bible-believing Christian who accepts the penal substitutionary model of the atonement, this means that the sin offering of biblical capital punishment ceased at the same time that the eternal sacrifice of God's Son was offered for all on Calvary. Does any Bible-believing Christian dare to call this a coincidence?

For Bible-believing Christians who accept other models of the atonement, the fact that biblically based capital punishment ceased to function at the same time that Jesus Christ died on the cross on Calvary speaks a loud confirmation to their conclusions that the state-sponsored killing of a human being adds nothing to God's honor, yields no increase to God's victory over evil, and fails to magnify in any way the compelling moral force of God's love for us.

Our conclusion is not ambiguous. Biblical truth reveals that the American death penalty cannot be conducted under the judicial authority behind the biblical death penalty.

Chapter Nine

AUTHORITY TO KILL

EXTRA-BIBLICAL COURTS AND ROMANS 13

For many of us who are Bible-believing Christians, the revelations of biblical truth at the end of chapter 8 will serve to answer our questions about the American death penalty. For purposes of completing our search, however, we must proceed to exhaust all options as to a biblical justification for capital punishment in our time. We can phrase the next question in this process as follows: Is there biblical authority for a death penalty that does not meet the requirements of the biblical death penalty, i.e., an extra-biblical death penalty?

This portion of the quest is bifurcated: we have two possible sources of biblical authority—the Hebrew scriptures or the Christian scriptures.

IS THERE AUTHORITY IN THE HEBREW SCRIPTURES
FOR AN EXTRA-BIBLICAL DEATH PENALTY?

The problem of finding biblical authority in the Hebrew scriptures for an extra-biblical death penalty is not unique to Christians in twenty-first-century America. Throughout the Middle Ages and beyond, the rabbis wrestled with the question of capital punishment in a post–second temple world. We can learn a great deal from their struggle. The key question repeatedly starts from the point that there is no biblical death penalty without the Great Sanhedrin. This is a constant whether the setting is medieval Europe or the Knesset in the modern state of Israel. "Ever since the Sanhedrin . . . there were attempts to implement the death penalty. While those who made these attempts recognized that they were going beyond the biblical warrant for the death penalty, they believed that doing so could be justified by other considerations of Jewish law."[1]

The two "other considerations of Jewish law" are (1) the inherent right in the power of kings and (2) the necessity of exigency situations. In this regard, the rabbis were falling back upon the evolved solutions from a prior time. As we have seen, it was very difficult for the biblical courts to impose the biblical death penalty because of all the restrictions that applied. This problem was being faced as early as the second temple period, which ran from 515 B.C. to A.D. 70.

As discussed in chapter 2, the double-barreled solution that was worked out by the Jewish religious leaders (1) found inherent authority in the monarchy to establish courts outside the confines of divine revelation and (2) found exigency jurisdiction to punish criminals who used the procedural safeguards as a foil.[2] Those two approaches have dominated post–second temple period efforts to revive a death penalty.

THE POWERS OF KINGS

The inherent right in the powers of kings is strictly limited to the Davidic line: "Maimonides implies that the power . . . derives not from Gentile permission or the popular will but from the fact that he is a descendant of the Davidic dynasty. As Maimonides puts it, it is not his wisdom that counts but his lineage."[3]

America is a post-Enlightenment democracy. We do not have any king, let alone a king whose lineage follows the Davidic line. Furthermore, there is no feasible way to place this authority in a non-king government in America. The rabbinical arguments in favor of allowing the will of the people in a modern democracy to give such kingly power to someone outside the Davidic line are premised "on the assumption that those wielding the power would demonstrate complete fealty to the Torah and its commandments."[4] In America's multicultural, religiously pluralistic society, the odds that the country would become a Jewish state are not even a remote possibility.

Finally, even if we could find a way to install the Davidic lineage in the American system, without the Great Sanhedrin sitting in the temple, there is no authority for any form of the death penalty except decapitation: "The court is empowered to inflict four modes of death: stoning, burning, slaying by the sword, and strangulation.[5] . . . The State, however, has no right to employ any mode of execution other than by the sword."[6]

Decapitation is prohibited as an unconstitutional punishment under the U.S. Constitution. Consequently, even if we were able to meet the requirements of Davidic lineage and total fealty to Torah, we could not employ biblically supportable capital punishment, beheading, under our American Constitution.

This means we must look to the Hebrew scriptures for support of the second alternative, extra-biblical capital punishment in exigency situations.

EXIGENCY COURTS

The rabbis generally recognized a right to employ the death penalty outside the confines of the biblical death penalty based upon the duty to protect the Torah. In the context of the diaspora, the dispersion of the Jews after the destruction of Jerusalem, this frequently required application to the immediate concerns of Jewish populations in the midst of Christian cities and towns, especially in Europe. The protection of Torah included protecting the Jews against informers to the Christians and protecting the reputation of God's chosen people.

For example, it was considered a scandal to have Jews executed by Gentile courts. Moreover, if Jews took responsibility for determining and handling the executions, the numbers executed would probably be less than if Gentiles decided who should die. Thus, exigency conditions were proclaimed justified: "Catholic courts would have executed many more Jews had Jewish courts not assumed responsibility for such cases; furthermore, it was necessary 'to execute those guilty of capital crimes according to our own laws.'"[7] Protecting the image and reputation of God's chosen people was also of paramount concern: "[There is capital punishment authority in] *any* contemporary [Jewish] court, especially where Gentile authorities are involved, lest the Jews be ridiculed and God's name desecrated."[8] (bracketed language mine)

The protection of Torah or of God's reputation through protecting the reputation of God's chosen people is not even cognizable under the American Constitution. This solution of the rabbis offers us no assistance.

IS THERE AUTHORITY IN THE CHRISTIAN SCRIPTURES FOR AN EXTRA-BIBLICAL DEATH PENALTY?

It is telling that as we comb the Christian scriptures for explicit support of the American death penalty, we come out of the four Gospels with absolutely nothing supportive. The same result obtained with respect to the historical efforts to use scripture to defend slavery. Perhaps that is why the historical attempts to support slavery and the modern efforts to support the American death penalty from the Christian scriptures have both turned to the Epistles of Paul. Let us first look at the favorite source for modern biblical support of the American death penalty: Paul's Letter to the Romans.

ROMANS 13

The Apostle Paul is writing between A.D. 55 and 60 to the church in Rome. Paul speaks in his letter of both Jews and Gentiles, thus raising the possibility that although the church in Rome probably started within the large Jewish community, by this time there have been many Gentile converts.

This is critical because for Paul and other Roman citizens, capital punishment involved death by the sword, the most dignified and least horrible form of capital punishment. For the Jewish and slave members of the Roman church, however, capital punishment at the hands of Rome would mean crucifixion.

Paul is also a well-educated Jew and he knows that of the four types of capital punishment allowed under the biblical death penalty, beheading by the sword is the only one allowed to the state. "Four modes of execution were given over to the court, but to the civil regime was given over only death by the sword alone."[9] Against this backdrop we read the following scripture verse:

> For rulers are not a terror to good works, but to the evil. Wilt thou then not be afraid of the power? Do that which is good, and thou shalt have praise of the same: For he is the minister of God to thee for good. But if thou do that which is evil, be afraid; for he beareth not the sword in vain: for he is the minister of God, a revenger to execute wrath upon him that doeth evil.   Rom. 13:3–4 AV

> For rulers hold no terror for those who do right, but for those who do wrong. Do you want to be free from fear of the one in authority? Then do what is right and he will commend you. For he is God's servant to do you good. But if you do wrong, be afraid, for he does not bear the sword for nothing. He is God's servant, an agent of wrath to bring punishment on the wrongdoer.   Rom. 13:3–4 NIV

My experience in Bible Belt dialogues concerning these verses confirms that the literal words of the English translations are critical to many Christians' support for the death penalty. Members of church audiences have frequently asked, "Why did God use the word *execute* if he didn't mean capital punishment?" That is where our analysis must begin.

The two most significant words in these passages, vis-à-vis scriptural support for the death penalty, are *sword* and *execute*. If government bears the *sword* as God's minister to *execute* offenders, it certainly sounds like we have a scriptural endorsement for secular capital punishment outside the context of the biblical death penalty.

We begin by looking at the meaning of the word *sword*. In fact there are distinctly different Greek words that we translate into English as *sword*. In a culture that is familiar with different metal slashing instruments, the words in Greek convey realities as different as *pistol* or *rifle*. For us moderns of the ammo age, they are all just *swords*. That was not the case in Paul's time.

After referring to *A Concise Dictionary of the Words in the Greek New Testament* by James Strong, we can see that[10]

MACHAIRA: means a short sword worn on the belt, in King James English we would say a *dirk;* in modern English, a *dagger.* This is not the instrument used for decapitation, the form of capital punishment by sword in Paul's day.[11] This word is used as a symbol or metaphor for the authority of the courts to inflict punishment. We know that such punishments could include fines, prison, flogging, etc.

RHOMPHAIA: means a saber, a long and broad cutlass. This is the instrument used for decapitation, the form of capital punishment by sword in Paul's day.

The word that is used in the original Greek scriptures of Romans 13:4 is *Machaira*. That does not seem to make any sense standing in a sentence with the word *execute*. Why would Paul use the word for dagger if he were talking about capital punishment? Should not he have used the word for a broadsword? We need to do a word search.

By referring to *The Complete Word Study New Testament with Greek Parallel (King James Version)*,[12] we find verse 4 of chapter 13 of Romans at page 532. The word *execute* is in italics, just like it is in the text of the Authorized (King James) Version of the Bible. This means that the word *execute* is not in the original Greek scriptures. The word *execute* has been inserted by the translator to fill in a verb that is required for the sentence to make sense in English. The Greek original does not have this verb. The English translation does.

The other Christian translation of the Bible referenced in this work has also filled in a verb. The NIV inserts the word *bring*. We can see that the usage of the word *execute* in the AV does not mean capital punishment. It means *to carry out, to perform, to apply*. This is the same usage we make in modern English when we talk about *executing a football play.* The announcer on *Monday Night Football* may shake his head and say "sloppy execution" when the running back stumbles and fumbles, or "brilliant execution" when a timing pass hits the outstretched hands of a wide receiver one foot into the end zone. No one has been decapitated. No one has been killed. *Execute* can simply mean the act of getting something done, completing a task, fulfilling a duty.

Now the verse Romans 13:4 makes complete sense. A synonym would be:

But if thou do that which is evil, be afraid; for he beareth not the power of judicial punishment in vain: for he is the minister of God, a revenger to carry out wrath upon him that doeth evil.

When we properly understand Romans 13:4, based on the usage of the actual Greek words in the earliest scriptures, it is clear that the verse contains no mandate for capital punishment. It does support the power of judicial authority to impose punishment upon malefactors. Our prisons are full of felons who are experiencing judicially imposed punishment without being subject to the death penalty. There is no need to impose capital punishment in order to be faithful to the proper understanding of Romans 13:4.

Based upon the word study approach, biblical truth reveals that we do not have scriptural-based authority (in the Christian scriptures) for an extra-biblical death penalty.

THE DISTRESSING PARALLELS BETWEEN CLAIMED BIBLICAL SUPPORT FOR SLAVERY AND FOR CAPITAL PUNISHMENT IN AMERICA

An uncanny parallel exists between the foregoing analysis and some of the alleged biblical support for slavery that existed in nineteenth-century America. The foundation of both uses of the Pauline Epistles is an assumption that Paul is a proponent of the status quo, i.e., advocating that Christians support what is considered normal and customary in the host culture and under their particular social and legal environment. In America's nineteenth-century Bible Belt, that created a presumption of support for slavery that was defended by the following logic: the practice of slavery existed in the *Hebrew* scriptures, the practice of slavery was not explicitly condemned in the Gospels, and it is possible to interpret the Epistles of Paul (out of context) in support of the practice of slavery. This approach resulted in an "[e]vangelical slaveholding ethic" that made appeals to Christian slave owners, not for abolition, but rather for adherence to biblical standards in the conduct of their slave ownership.[13]

The graphic Christian litmus test, "Is slavery consistent with the spirit of Jesus Christ?" appears to have gone unasked.

The following quotes are from *A Consuming Fire: The Fall of the Confederacy in the Mind of the White Christian South*, a history of the religious psychology behind the Civil War and its aftermath. This work by renowned American historian Eugene Genovese was published in 1998 by the University of Georgia Press and documents how far Christians can be misled by such a deficient analysis:

> In 1861 Southern Christians marched to war behind their Lord of Hosts, convinced that He blessed their struggle to uphold a scripturally sanctioned slavery and their right to national self-determination. The Episcopal Church in Virginia responded to the Yankee invasion by declaring the War "a Revolution, ecclesiastical as well as civil." The Methodist Reverend R. N. Sledd of Petersburg, Virginia, spoke for leading men in all denominations when he credited the South with fighting a religious war for the "cause of Christ, the interests of religion. . . ."
>
> Virtually all Southern spokesmen, clerical and lay, readily acknowledged that the South was fighting to uphold slavery. . . . As the Reverend J. S. Lamar of the Christian Church put it: Northerners and Southerners differ "as radically and as rigidly as . . . [a]bolitionism differs from the Bible."
>
> Southerners grounded the proslavery argument in an appeal to Scripture and denounced abolitionists as infidels who were abandoning the plain words of the Bible. The Southern divines, relying on the Word, forged a strong scriptural case. They cited the Old Testament to show that the Israelites, including Abraham and other favored patriarchs, held slaves without

drawing God's censure. They cited the New Testament to demonstrate that neither Jesus nor the apostles ever preached against slavery and that, while Jesus drove the money changers from the temple, He never drove slaveholders from His church. Although most divines turned to the Noahic curse to provide a racial justification for the specific enslavement of blacks, the basic religious argument, abstractly considered, had nothing to do with race.[14]

The modern logic of biblically based support for the American death penalty follows the same tack as the biblical logic for defending slavery: the death penalty is present in the Hebrew scriptures, is not expressly prohibited by the Gospels, and is arguably supported by a particular way of interpreting Paul's Epistle to the Romans (out of context). Some Christian death penalty proponents have gone so far as to argue that Jesus drove the money changers from the temple, but he did not stop his own execution under Pilate, thereby verifying Jesus' approval of capital punishment.

The logic of the Bible Belt's proslavery biblical arguments has been resurrected with new verses to defend the death penalty.

Even the word study approach outlined earlier had parallels in the days of slavery (e.g., 1 Corinthians 7:21).[15] The translation problem was that the Greek phrasing of that verse *implied* a direct object that could have been either *slavery* or *freedom*. In the days of Christian-supported slavery in America, the Greek words were translated into English as Paul directing those who were slaves to remain slaves, even if they had an opportunity to become free, and to use their slavery to serve God. In other words, the assumption that Paul supported slavery was read into the passage, thereby resulting in an interpretation that Paul supported slavery.

Modern translations are based on the sound premise that no one is called by God to be enslaved to another human being. The implied object is properly understood to be *freedom*, resulting in a translation that directs those who were originally slaves, but have an opportunity to become freedmen, to use their newfound freedom to serve God.

The cultural assumptions that the reader brings to the Epistles of Paul can result in the erroneous conclusion that Paul supports the status quo of those very same cultural assumptions. Paul's Epistles were quoted in the southern states to show God's support for enslavement of blacks by whites. Romans 13:1 was used in Germany to "stifle Christian opposition to Nazi policies."[16] Romans 13 verses 1–7 were "quoted to defend apartheid" in South Africa.[17] Now the same verses are being quoted to drape American capital punishment with God's purported blessing.

The problem, in a nutshell, seems to result from two failures. The first is a deficiency in approach. The Epistles of Paul in general do not offer much in the way of incontrovertible concrete ethical content unless read through the lens of the Gospels. Even on matters for which the Gospels do not offer explicit commands or prohibitions, the spirit of the words, deeds, life, death, and resurrection of Jesus Christ speaks volumes. Therefore, any analysis that begins with the assumption that the Gospels have nothing to say on the subject is probably overly legalistic and headed for trouble in interpreting Paul's words without any Gospel foundation.

The second is the failure to place Paul's words in the context of the specific issues to which he was responding. When dealt with abstractly as a cosmic theology of church and state, the pragmatic verses in Romans 13:1–7 can be misconstrued into anointing even the most horrendous governmental abuses with divine accolade.[18] Modern insights into the historical context of those verses, especially when read for consistency with the balance of the letter, suggest that Paul's goal may have been to discourage trouble in the streets (largely over then hot issues between Roman Jews and Roman Christians) by stressing mutual compassion and the upholding of the common good.[19] Moreover, the modern reader must keep in mind that the early church was looking to the imminent return of Christ, and therefore many social issues simply were deemed transitory and not addressed.[20]

During the first few centuries of Christianity, those verses from Romans fell from the lips of Christian martyrs, not the lips of executioners.[21] It should not surprise anyone that reading those verses as though Paul were a slave master in 1845 or an American political candidate in 2004 would drastically and erroneously alter their meaning. That was true with American slavery in the eighteen hundreds, and it is true in the twenty-first century with American capital punishment.

The answers we are revealing are difficult and uncomfortable. Many of us have never heard about the Christian biblical support for slavery or how the political splitting of America in the great secession was almost an afterthought to the splitting of the great religious denominations in disagreement over what God's word said about slavery. Yet we must be aware of our history in order to avoid the pitfalls of donning the same mistakes in different garb. The approach to scripture that was so far wrong on the issue of slavery has little chance of being right on the issue of capital punishment.

The last question we must address with respect to the authority to kill is whether this power is implicit in the scriptures of the biblical death penalty. That is our next step.

Chapter Ten

AUTHORITY TO KILL

BIBLICAL DETERRENCE

In the last few years, more and more Christians, especially in the Bible Belt, are espousing support for the American death penalty based on the argument of deterrence. Is deterrence a biblical basis for support of the American death penalty? Scripture does speak of deterrence, and it is an essential element of the standards revealed by the biblical death penalty.

> All the people will hear and be afraid and will not act presumptuously again.   Deut. 17:13 TNK

> And all the people shall hear, and fear, and do no more presumptuously.   Deut. 17:13 AV

> All the people will hear and be afraid, and will not be contemptuous again.   Deut. 17:13 NIV

> Others will hear and be afraid, and such evil things will not again be done in your midst.   Deut. 19:20 TNK

> And those which remain shall hear, and fear, and shall henceforth commit no more any such evil among you.   Deut. 19:20 AV

The rest of the people will hear of this and be afraid, and never again will such an evil thing be done among you.   Deut. 19:20 NIV

Thus you will sweep out evil from your midst; all Israel will hear and be afraid.   Deut. 21:21 TNK

So shalt thou put evil away from among you; and all Israel shall hear, and fear.   Deut. 21:21 AV

You must purge the evil from among you. All Israel will hear of it and be afraid.   Deut. 21:21 NIV

Ten years ago, arguments supporting American capital punishment based on deterrence asserted that executions keep other criminals from killing. As we will see in a moment, the actual studies do not support that conclusion. Perhaps that is the reason why pro–death penalty politicians and pro–death penalty editorials have started enunciating a new definition of deterrence, namely, *the man who is executed will never kill again.* That may well be an interesting philosophical, sociological, or even political position. The argument, however, has no bearing in scripture.

BIBLICAL DETERRENCE

The deterrence required of the biblical death penalty is an effect on the society at large. The use of the words "and all the people shall hear and fear and do no more presumptuously" in several places where the Torah deals with the death penalty implies a deterrent value.[1] Even more telling is the fact that biblical deterrence is not a justification for the death penalty; rather it is a limitation upon it. "Implicit in the views opposed to the implementation of capital punishment is the recognition of the fact, recorded in the Talmud, that when faced with an increased rate of homicide, far from further implementing the death penalty, the Sanhedrin deliberately chose to suspend it as a judicial response to 'the needs of the hour.'"[2]

The Great Sanhedrin had the inherent authority to declare a moratorium on the biblical death penalty worldwide simply by vacating their chamber in the temple. All other types of cases would continue undisrupted.

There is no reason why [noncapital criminal] cases may be judged only when the Great Sanhedrin is located in the Chamber of Hewn Stone. Capital cases, on the other hand, may not be judged in any lesser court unless the Great Sanhedrin is functioning in its normal location. This is derived from the verse . . . that states (Deut. 17:8) *You shall arise and go up to the place,* which indicates that the Sanhedrin's presence in the Holy Temple determines whether capital punishment is imposed.[3] (italics in original; bracketed language mine)

Based upon the scriptural limitation of deterrence in the biblical death penalty, the Great Sanhedrin had a duty to vacate the temple (placing themselves in exile) when executions failed to show a deterrent effect on capital crimes in the society at large. And the Sanhedrin knew to discontinue use of the death penalty if the deterrent effect was not working.[4]

DETERRENCE UNDER THE AMERICAN DEATH PENALTY

The American death penalty is not a deterrent to homicide or violent crime. This is a surprising fact to many of us who have been inundated with media and political sound bites indicating the opposite. We might be even more astounded to learn that several justices on our U.S. Supreme Court had acknowledged over a quarter century ago that there is no correlation between capital punishment and deterrence of crime.[5] "[E]vidence that executions do not deter crime *is* conclusive."[6] (emphasis in original) In fact, there is demographic evidence:

Some studies show an increase in homicides immediately after publicized executions, although as yet the evidence of such "brutalization" is inconclusive.[7]

As well as social analysis:

No matter how ultimate the death penalty as a solution may seem, or how rarely it is employed, its official existence or acceptance in the law symbolizes the fact that it is permissible—even desirable—to resolve issues by murder; it is only necessary to define the criteria for justification.[8]

And psychiatric basis:

> But I am convinced that there is an even more specific way in which the death penalty breeds murder. It becomes more than a symbol. It becomes a promise, a contract, a covenant between society and certain (by no means rare) warped mentalities who are moved to kill as part of a self-destructive urge. These murders are discovered by the psychiatric examiner to be, consciously or unconsciously, an attempt to commit suicide by committing homicide. It only works if the perpetrator believes he will be executed for his crime. I believe this to be a significant reason for the tendency to find proportionally more homicides in death penalty states than in those without it.[9] (citations omitted)

That suggests capital punishment can foster homicide, even though public executions are forbidden in the United States by state laws. (There is serious doubt as to whether public executions could be sustained today under the Eighth Amendment to the U.S. Constitution.) This is called the "brutalization effect," which recognizes that the killing of offenders by government fosters the consciousness of killing as a solution to problems. "The abolition of the death penalty in Canada in 1976 has not led to increased homicide rates. Statistics Canada reports that the number of homicides in Canada in 2001 (554) was 23% lower than the number of homicides in 1975 (721), the year before the death penalty was abolished. Canada currently sentences those convicted of murder to life sentences with parole eligibility."[10] Four new studies of deterrence (published from 1997 to 1999) throw further doubt on the existence of any deterrent effect from sentencing people to death or executing people for homicide. The studies do find support for a brutalization effect.[11]

On the Front Line: Law Enforcement Views on the Death Penalty reports on the opinions of the chiefs of police of our American cities. In short, they recognize that the death penalty is a political football and not a deterrent to violent crime.[12] The following summarizes and quotes some of the salient points from the report.

In January 1995, Peter D. Hart Research Associates conducted a national opinion poll of randomly selected police chiefs in the United States. In that poll, the chiefs had the opportunity to express what they believe really works in fighting crime and where the death penalty fits in their priorities as leaders in the law enforcement field.

The Hart poll found the following:

1. Police chiefs rank the death penalty last as a way of reducing violent crime, placing it behind curbing drug abuse, more police officers on the streets, lowering the technical barriers to prosecution, longer sentences, and a better economy with more jobs.
2. The death penalty was rated the least cost-effective method for controlling crime.
3. Insufficient use of the death penalty is not considered a major problem by the majority of police chiefs.
4. Strengthening families and neighborhoods, punishing criminals swiftly and surely, controlling illegal drugs, and gun control are considered much more important than the death penalty.
5. Although a majority of the police chiefs support the death penalty in the abstract, when given a choice between the sentence of life without parole plus restitution versus the death penalty, barely half of the chiefs support capital punishment.
6. Police chiefs do not believe that the death penalty significantly reduces the number of homicides.
7. Police chiefs do not believe that murderers think about the range of possible punishments.
8. Debates about the death penalty distract Congress and state legislatures from focusing on real solutions to crime.

In sum, while many police chiefs support the death penalty philosophically, a strong majority does not believe that it is an effective law enforcement tool in practice, "because most people do not think about the death penalty before they commit a violent or capital crime."[13] They simply do not believe it is a deterrent to crime.

Law enforcement officers were asked: "What, in your opinion, works in the battle against crime?" This question was approached from a variety of directions. Police were first given an open-ended opportunity to state the areas that would have the biggest impact on reducing violent crime in their jurisdiction. Their answers:

1. sentencing reform, including truth in sentencing, elimination of parole, and stiffer sentences was the most often cited area of reform (33 percent of respondents);
2. other areas of emphasis included the development of family values and parenting skills (23 percent)
3. education (15 percent); and
4. more police (13 percent).

The death penalty was mentioned by fewer than 2 percent of the chiefs and ranked below twenty-five other areas of concern.

Police chiefs are demonstrably less supportive of solutions like the death penalty, which merely sound tough but produce little return for the large amount of money invested.

> Recently, attention has focused on one form of punishment: the death penalty. . . .
> . . . [W]e share the belief that other law enforcement priorities are far more important and urgent than capital punishment. The death penalty absorbs an inordinate portion of the financial resources and valuable time of the criminal justice system. . . .
> In many communities, the public would be better served by measures such as the hiring of additional police officers, the implementation of community policing, drug interdiction programs, early childhood intervention programs, weapons control programs, speedier trials, or better funded probation and parole departments. . . . The death penalty may fascinate the media and the public, but it is truly peripheral to our efforts to make this society safer.[14]

Some in law enforcement are totally opposed to capital punishment. Others support it in theory. But few would give it the high priority accorded it in political campaigns and in legislative agendas designed mostly for sound bites and illusory quick fixes, and to stir up votes. "The death penalty does little to prevent crime. It is fear of apprehension and the likely prospect of swift and certain punishment that provides the largest deterrent to crime."[15]

Some professionals are honest enough to state unequivocally that none of this is news. It has been known in the business for a long time. "Take it from someone who has spent a career in Federal and state law enforcement. . . . The death penalty actually hinders the fight against crime."[16]

Actual statistics from the FBI continue to bear out the fact that the American death penalty is not a deterrent: Since the death penalty was reinstated, over 80 percent of all executions have occurred in the South; the Northeast has accounted for less than 1 percent of the executions. The FBI *Uniform Crime Report* for 2001[17] showed that in calendar year 2000, the national murder rate decreased 3.1 percent from 1999, with the smallest decline in the South (the region with the highest murder rate, 6.8 victims per 100,000, compared with 5.1 in the West and Midwest, and 4.0 in the Northeast).

This trend has continued through 2001 and 2002. According to data released in October 2002, as part of the FBI's *Uniform Crime Report* for 2001, the South again had the highest murder rate of the four U.S. regions. The report noted that the Texas crime rate rose 4 percent in 2001, nearly five times the national average, and the state posted a 7.6 percent increase in homicides. At the same time, the total number of executions in Texas was more than three times that of any other state in the nation. The Northeast, the region with the lowest murder rate, had no executions in 2001.[18] According to the FBI's *Preliminary Uniform Crime Report* for 2002, the murder rate in the South *increased* by 2.1 percent while the murder rate in the Northeast *decreased* by almost 5 percent.[19]

The same failure of deterrence is evidenced in the FBI's statistics concerning felonious killings of police officers. According to statistics from the FBI's *Uniform Crime Report*, regions of the country that use the death penalty the *least* are the safest for police officers. Police are *most* in danger in the South. From 1989 to 1998, 292 law enforcement officers were feloniously killed in the South, 125 in the West, 121 in the Midwest, and 80 in the Northeast, the region with the fewest executions—less than 1 percent.[20]

Also, the statistics continue to show that states without the death penalty have a better record on homicide rates. A survey by the *New York Times* found that states without the death penalty have lower homicide rates than states with the death penalty. During the last twenty years, the homicide rate in states with the death penalty has been 48 to 101 percent higher than in states without the death penalty. "'I think Michigan made a wise decision 150 years ago,' said the state's governor, John Engler, a Republican, referring to the state's abolition of the death penalty in 1846. 'We're pretty proud of the fact that we don't have the death penalty.'"[21]

The facts and our conclusions are obvious. First, biblical truth, revealed through the scriptures in Torah/Pentateuch concerning deterrence and the rules of Talmud to give them effect, indicates that the death penalty should cease when it is no longer a deterrent to capital crimes in the society at large. Second, the American death penalty is not a deterrent to capital crime.

We must conclude, therefore, that biblical truth reveals no support for any implied authority to kill through the American death penalty based upon biblical deterrence.

Chapter Eleven

SUMMARY OF PART ONE

We are searching for the revelations of biblical truth about America's death penalty. Thus far our scope has been the questions "Who deserves death?" and "Who has authority to kill?"

We have looked at Noahide laws, Mosaic laws, Talmudic laws, English laws, and American laws. We have studied the differences between Greek and English with respect to swords; analyzed the rabbinical basis for kings of David's lineage wielding the sword, and exigency courts protecting the Torah and God's reputation. We have even addressed the biblical concept of deterrence and compared it with the realities of modern America.

The biblical truth of the scriptures in Torah/Pentateuch and the provisions of Talmud that fulfill the limitations of those scriptures reveal that the American death penalty is completely at odds with its supposedly biblical support. Furthermore, with the constitutional requirements that apply to capital punishment in America, it is not clear that the differences could, or even should, be resolved.

With respect to the issue of who is deserving of death, we have confronted an overwhelming list of culpability. Do we really want to engage the biblical list? Do we really desire execution for our teenage daughters and Sunday/Sabbath shoppers? Are we prepared to begin execution of all those whose religious beliefs differ from our own?

Are we ready to levy the ultimate penalty for committing adultery; for being greedy or inciting greed in others; for playing with tarot cards or engaging in palm reading; for prosecutorial misconduct and other false witness in a capital case; for writing, printing, or reading horoscopes; for bad predictions by psychics; for cursing one's parents; or for being a rebellious son?

Are we ready to slaughter most of our people? Of course not.

Then what is our scriptural basis for picking one offense off the biblical list and claiming that God wasn't really serious about the other thirty-some capital offenses on his list? Or does our disparate treatment of the offense of murder indicate that we have misunderstood the point of God's list?

Do we really believe that God has mandated the *lex talionis*, the law of tit for tat, which is the biblical basis of "life for life"? If we do believe this, why haven't we clamored to replace personal injury lawsuits and prison terms with reciprocal maiming, "fracture for fracture, eye for eye, tooth for tooth, hand for hand, and foot for foot"? What is our scriptural basis for insisting that God meant it literally when he said "life for life," but he was only humoring us with the rest of the scripture verse? Or does our disparate treatment of "life for life" indicate we have misunderstood the point of the whole scripture verse?

Biblical truth reveals even deeper troubles for those of us who are Bible-believing Christians. It is not at all clear from a nonselective reading of scripture that God desires the death penalty, especially if one accepts the teachings of Jesus Christ. This is not based on the premise that Jesus overrules the Mosaic law. Rather Jesus affirms the Mosaic law and appears to put us back on track with God's intention from the very beginning, as evidenced by God's own dealings with the murderer Cain and confirmed in his dealings with the murderer Moses: no human retaliatory violence.

For those seeking to support the American death penalty on a biblical basis, biblical truth reveals that the requirements for court structure, judicial ordination, vote-counting procedures, physical connection to the temple, and unqualified allegiance to Torah and the God of the Bible are insurmountable for America's secular governance. No one can even argue with a straight face that those conditions are met in an American courtroom. There is simply no way to squeeze the American court system into the confines of the biblically required courts. It cannot be done.

America's death penalty also fails to satisfy the requisites for biblical support of an extra-biblical death penalty. America is a post-Enlightenment democracy. We do not have any king, let alone a king whose lineage follows the Davidic line. Furthermore, there is no feasible way to place this authority in a non-king government in America. Even if we could, decapitation—the sole permissible form of execution biblically allowed at the hands of a sovereign—is prohibited as an unconstitutional punishment under the U.S. Constitution. Do we want to bring back monarchies and the guillotine?

There is also no support available on the basis of exigency courts because the protection of Torah or of God's reputation through protecting the reputation of God's chosen people is not even cognizable under the American Constitution. This solution of the rabbis in the Middle Ages offers us no assistance.

Nor do the Christian scriptures save us. When we properly understand Romans 13:4, based on the usage of the actual Greek words in the earliest scriptures, it is clear that the verse contains no mandate for capital punishment. It does support the power of judicial authority to impose punishment for malefactors. That is the purpose of our elaborate American prison system.

The American death penalty is not a deterrent to homicide or violent crime. Even if we had a biblical basis for operating the death penalty, the biblical truth of Torah/Pentateuch and the rules of Talmud that fulfill the scriptures demands that executions cease when the death penalty is not a deterrent to capital crimes in the society at large.

Most profoundly troubling of all for Christians of biblical faith is the truth that the biblical death penalty defies the final atonement accomplished by Jesus Christ. The purpose of capital punishment under Torah/Pentateuch was redemptive. The sacrificial offering of the offender brought atonement, redemption, to the offender and to the community, thus achieving reconciliation for both.

How can any Bible-believing Christian participate in this? Was the atonement by Jesus Christ sufficient for all people, all times, all places or not? What part of redemption did Christ leave undone that must be completed by human sacrifice? Why are Christians quoting scripture to support the sacrificial redemptive offering of human lives?

Finally, as Americans of biblical faith, we must be profoundly disturbed by the parallels between the scriptural arguments offered to support slavery in the eighteen hundreds and the scriptural arguments being offered in our time to support capital punishment. The logic of the Bible Belt's proslavery biblical arguments has been resurrected with new verses to defend the death penalty. The approach to scripture that was so far wrong on the issue of slavery has little chance of being right on the issue of capital punishment.

Our conclusions are not ambiguous. These are hardly nominal matters. Some of them slice to the core of Christian belief. Many Bible-believing Christians may find it impossible to continue to support a death penalty that is based on sacrificial atonement. Others may feel it is not possible to support any death penalty that is so far at variance from the substantive provisions of biblical truth.

For myself, as a Bible-believing Christian, the most jarring revelation of biblical truth is that in A.D. 30, forty years before the destruction of the second temple, biblically based capital punishment ceased at the same time that Jesus died on Calvary and has never resumed anywhere in the world to this day. For the Bible-believing Christian, this means that the sin offering of biblical capital punishment ceased at the same time that Jesus consummated his atonement. That is a confirmation in temporal history of the congruity of God's word through the Hebrew scriptures and the Christian scriptures. In the face of this historical reality, how can we claim to be reviving God's death penalty of the Bible in American form? Are we trying to undo Calvary?

My personal faith conclusion is that there is no possible way to support the American death penalty based upon biblical truth. If I do support it, I will be standing solely on my secular legal right to naked vengeance. Yet, as a Bible-believing Christian, vengeance is not available to me. That is only God's prerogative.

Consequently, since I cannot support the American death penalty based upon biblical truth, then I cannot support the American death penalty at all. My faith position is that the American death penalty should be abolished.

What, then, are we to do with those who have killed? That is the subject of chapter 22.

Other people of biblical faith may conclude that abolition is not appropriate. Even so, they will want to explore what the standards of biblical truth reveal about procedures of the American death penalty. That is what the balance of this book is about.

Those of us who believe that biblical truth demands abolition of the American death penalty may wish to formalize our belief. A form of resolution for this purpose is shown in appendix A.

Regardless of our faith position at this point in our search, we all now turn our eyes to the revelations of the standards of biblical truth about the procedures of the American death penalty.

Part Two

WHAT DOES BIBLICAL TRUTH TELL US ABOUT
THE REQUIRED PROCEDURES AND THE PLIGHT
OF THE FAMILIES OF THE VICTIMS?

Chapter Twelve

AN INNOCENT PERSON YOU SHALL NOT SLAY

WITNESSES PERMITTED

Of all the concerns evidenced by the procedures under the biblical death penalty, none is more pronounced than the fear of executing the innocent. This primary focus drives most of the restrictions and required steps in the process. The source of the overriding mandate to avoid killing those who are not guilty is the Bible itself.

> Keep far from a false charge; do not bring death on those who are innocent and in the right. Exod. 23:7 TNK

> Keep thee far from a false matter; and the innocent and righteous slay thou not. Exod. 23:7 AV

> Have nothing to do with a false charge and do not put an innocent or honest person to death. Exod. 23:7 NIV

The nature of permissible evidence, the statements and questions that judges are required to make and to ask, the penalties for lying in a capital case, even the requirements of character for a judge to sit in a capital case all flow from the scriptural mandate to avoid the execution of an innocent man.

In biblical times a death penalty case started with the identification of witnesses. For the most part, this is true today as well. What were the legal requirements for witnesses in death penalty cases under the standards of biblical truth?

First and foremost, the witness must be of impeccable character with nothing to gain from his testimony. This was accomplished by listing numerous undesirable characteristics that prohibited one from serving as a witness in a capital case. For example, if a person is of ill repute, poor moral character, a robber, an extortionist, or suspect in any money matters, he cannot be a witness.[1] That includes anyone who gambles, who is a usurer (lends money at interest) or races pigeons (it being understood that this was done for wagering purposes), and anyone who transacts business in the produce of the Sabbath year.[2] Also excluded from witnesses were herdsmen (because they dishonestly allow cattle to graze on land that belongs to others), tax collectors, and farmers of the revenue.[3] The application of this principle went so far as to prohibit a proper witness from testifying with an unqualified witness. This prohibition was based on scripture:

> Transgressors are ineligible as witnesses by biblical law, for it is said *Put not thy hand with the wicked to be an unrighteous witness* (Exod. 23:1). The traditional interpretation of this injunction is: "Accept not the wicked as a witness." Aye, if a competent witness knows that his fellow witness is a transgressor, but the judges do not know it, he is forbidden to join with him, even if the evidence is true, for by thus associating with him, the latter's testimony is accepted and the religiously competent man is in league with the wicked. It is hardly necessary to state that if the eligible witness knows that the other is a false witness, he is forbidden to give evidence, as it is said: *Put not thy hand with the wicked.*[4] (italics in original)

Second, anyone with something to gain from his testimony or with a special relationship to the accused is disallowed as a witness: "Any evidence from which the witness may derive benefit is inadmissible, for it is as though he would testify in his own behalf."[5] This prohibition applies broadly enough to even prevent testimony by anyone who stands to inherit from the estate of the accused.[6] No one with any possibility of gain is allowed to testify.

Children are not allowed to testify against a parent, and a father cannot testify against a child. Both friends and enemies of the accused are disqualified as witnesses as well.[7]

These are the relatives who are disqualified: One's brother, his father's brother, his mother's brother, his sister's husband, his father's sister's husband, and his mother's sister's husband; and his mother's husband, his father-in-law and his brother-in-law; all these are disqualified—they, their sons and their sons-in-law. And his stepson alone is disqualified, but not the stepson's son or son-in-law. . . .

One's close friend and one's enemy are also disqualified to judge or testify about him. What is considered a "close friend" or "enemy"? "A friend" is one's groomsman; "an enemy" is anyone with whom he did not speak for three days out of enmity.[8]

Why were so many persons, who could conceivably have meaningful testimony, excluded as witnesses? Simply because the biblical truth of Torah/Pentateuch and the provisions of Talmud necessary to fulfill those scriptures were the standards to be met: "The disqualification by Scripture of kinsmen from testifying concerning one another is not to be accounted for on the presumption that they love one another, for one may not testify either for or against a relative. The disqualification is a biblical decree."[9]

Third, the biblical death penalty is rigorous in the requirement for multiple witnesses who agree in every material respect on all essential facts: "For lo, the Torah has said, On the testimony of two witnesses or three witnesses shall he that is to die be put to death."[10] (Deut. 17:6)

The reference to Deuteronomy 17:6 deals with capital punishment for idolatry. The scriptures referring to murder are equally clear about the mandate for multiple witnesses in order to avoid executing the innocent.

A single witness may not validate against a person any guilt or blame for any offense that may be committed; a case can be

> valid only on the testimony of two witnesses or more. Deut.
> 19:15 TNK

> One witness shall not rise up against a man for any iniquity, or
> for any sin, in any sin that he sinneth: at the mouth of two
> witnesses, or at the mouth of three witnesses, shall the matter
> be established. Deut. 19:15 AV

> One witness is not enough to convict a man accused of any
> crime or offense he may have committed. A matter must be
> established by the testimony of two or three witnesses. Deut.
> 19:15 NIV

This is repeated with respect to murder:

> If anyone kills a person, the manslayer may be executed only
> on the evidence of witnesses; the testimony of a single witness
> against a person shall not suffice for a sentence of death.
> Num. 35:30 TNK

> Whoso killeth any person, the murderer shall be put to death
> by the mouth of witnesses: but one witness shall not testify
> against any person to cause him to die. Num. 35:30 AV

> Anyone who kills a person is to be put to death as a murderer
> only on the testimony of witnesses. But no one is to be put to
> death on the testimony of only one witness. Num. 35:30 NIV

The biblical death penalty requires that the testimony agree on
all essential facts:

> The testimony of these witnesses was also required to be un-
> controverted as to any fact. If there was any discrepancy be-
> tween their testimony it was excluded. The Sanhedrin . . .
> separately interrogated the witnesses, and then questioned
> them concerning the most minute details of the crime. If they
> contradicted each other as to any fact whatsoever, their testi-
> mony was excluded. The pervasiveness and intensity of the
> Sanhedrin's questioning was illustrated by [the fact that one
> court] interrogated witnesses about the number of figs growing

on the tree underneath which the crime was committed.[11] (citations omitted)

Finally, confessions are prohibited as evidence: "[N]o one may testify as to himself."[12] "[If he said, 'I have something to say] in favor of my own conviction,' they emphatically shut him up."[13] (bracketed language in original)

Rabbi Adel Steinsaltz explains this faith-based prohibition against confessions:

> The basic assumption in *halakhah* is that a man does not belong only to himself; just as he has no right to cause physical harm to others, so he has no right to inflict injury on himself. [Therefore] the confession of the defendant had no legal validity and should not be taken into consideration. This rule . . . served courts for centuries as a powerful weapon against attempts to extract confessions by force or persuasion. Not only can no man be forced to incriminate himself through his own testimony, but self-incrimination has no significance and is unacceptable as evidence in court.[14]

The biblical death penalty also prohibits confessions because of fear of attempts to commit suicide by execution, a phenomenon that is only starting to be recognized in modern America.

> For it is possible that he was confused in mind when he made the confession. Perhaps he was one of those who are in misery, bitter in soul, who long for death, thrust the sword into their bellies or cast themselves down from the roofs. Perhaps this was the reason that prompted him to confess to a crime he had not committed, in order that he might be put to death. To sum up this matter, the principle that no man is to be declared guilty on his own admission is a divine decree.[15]

Having identified three very fundamental principles of the biblical death penalty, our search requires us to measure the American death penalty against this standard. How do the witness requirements of the American death penalty stack up against the standards of the biblical death penalty?

A Florida gentleman and person of faith who has been an American lawyer for over fifty years summarized this aspect of the American death penalty as follows:

> The people sentenced to death are not the worst offenders, but the dumber ones, the slower ones, and those with the least effective lawyers. An article in the *American Bar Journal* advised lawyers whose clients were accused of involvement with others in a murder to run not walk to the prosecutor's office and make a deal. It said that the first one to make a deal will be free in a few years, while the others will get the death penalty.[16]

The first thing we can say with absolute certainty is that the American death penalty does not even pretend to adhere to the standards for witnesses under the biblical death penalty. The biblical death penalty excluded anyone of questionable repute and anyone with anything to gain from his testimony. Yet the use of jailhouse informants, codefendants, and other inherently unreliable witnesses, as well as the prosecutions of defendants based upon circumstantial evidence or upon testimony of a single such witness, are not unusual in America[17] or in Florida and have accounted for scores of wrongful convictions.[18]

Although the American ideal for testimony in capital cases is that only *reliable* bargained-for testimony would be allowed after full disclosure of the witness's conflict of interest to the judge and the jury, the actual practice in America is that even inherently unreliable bargained-for testimony is used by the prosecution. Both the ideal and the practice fall far short of the biblical standard, which would strictly prohibit any bargained-for testimony in a capital case.

Under the biblical death penalty, the utmost concern was avoiding the execution of an innocent person. Under our American death penalty, the utmost concern appears to be securing convictions, even if the testimony for the state is unreliable and is obtained through trading favors. While achieving a high level of convictions can certainly sound like a laudable goal from a secular standpoint, the change in focus from biblical principles can be disastrous.

Testimony for deals is an arrangement whereby those who are under the custody, control, or supervision of the state (incarceration, parole, or probation) or are about to be charged by the state (usually for drugs, prostitution, etc.) agree to testify for the state in exchange for a deal in their own case. The deals range widely: dropping charges against the witness; reducing time in prison for the witness; even helping out the witness's boyfriend by dropping his charges. In such cases, the state is bartering for testimony. Bartering for testimony has no basis in the Bible and flies in the face of the standards revealed by biblical truth.

The biblical death penalty asks: Are we absolutely certain that the testimony is being given solely because it is true? There is no biblical basis for admitting testimony just because it is a good deal for the witness and will help the prosecutor obtain a conviction.

In too many cases the state's star witness has been the person who came running to the police and fingered the defendant. Far too often, after the defendant has been convicted and placed on death row, evidence comes to light showing that the state's star witness was the one who actually did the killing. For example, in the case of James Richardson, a Florida man wrongly convicted in the poisoning deaths of his seven children, certain evidence undermining the state's case surfaced only after being stolen from a prosecutor's office by a man dating the prosecutor's secretary. The state's star witness was a baby-sitter who fingered Richardson for poisoning his children in order to collect insurance money. On her deathbed in a nursing home, the sitter confessed to having committed the murders herself. Then it came out that the police and prosecution knew all along that there were no life insurance policies on the children. Richardson was set free in 1989 after serving twenty-one years on Florida's death row.[19] Under the biblical death penalty, this could not have happened.

As bad as things can get when a solo witness runs to the state to make a deal, things can get even worse when the state goes shopping for a witness, looking for someone to cut a deal. William Kelley was sent to Florida's death row twenty-two years ago for a thirty-five-year-old murder. According to reports in the *Miami Herald*, the former county prosecutor had told the jury that the state's star witness had nothing to gain by his testimony. In fact, the state's witness had cut a multistate deal to be released of charges in exchange for his testimony in Florida. The state's star witness had actually been convicted of the murder in a previous trial, but was released when his lover, the deceased victim's widow, admitted that she lied on the stand. He then fingered the new defendant and testified against him at trial on the state's behalf. In response to rigorous questioning from the federal judge, the former prosecutor answered: "It was never my intention to lie. But maybe the way the words came out is not how they should have come out."[20]

The death row inmate's twenty-three-year fight for a new trial, which is discussed further in chapter 15, is still pending before the federal appeals court.

Under the revealed truth of Torah/Pentateuch and the provisions of Talmud necessary to fulfill those scriptures, no such witness would have ever been allowed to testify in the first place.

TESTIMONY BY JAILHOUSE SNITCHES

This problem of testimony in capital cases from witnesses with an incentive to please the state is not unique to Florida. Recently, in a rare study of the use of jailhouse informants, circumstantial evidence, and confessions (all techniques prohibited under the biblical death penalty), a series of articles published in the *Chicago Tribune*[21] found that many of the 285 death penalty cases since capital punishment was reinstated in Illinois (1977) are plagued by the same circumstances that have been shown to have put thirteen innocent men on death row in Illinois.[22] (Since that time, four more persons have come off Illinois' death row exonerated because of concerns that they are innocent.) The following quotes from the report are chilling:

Even prosecutors acknowledge that jailhouse informants are among the least reliable of witnesses. Yet in Illinois, at least 46 inmates have been sent to death row in cases where prosecutors used a jailhouse informant, according to a *Tribune* investigation that examined the 285 death-penalty cases since capital punishment was reinstated in 1977.

In about half of those 46 cases, the informant played a significant role in the conviction. Often, prosecutors put jailhouse informants on the witness stand in cases where the evidence of guilt was flimsy or during sentencing to demonize a defendant with inflammatory accounts of the crime.

Prosecutors tried to use jailhouse informants in numerous other cases as well, according to the *Tribune's* investigation, but backed off after defense attorneys challenged their truthfulness and threatened to expose their backgrounds.

Snitch testimony helped convict or condemn 4 of the 12 Illinois Death Row inmates who were later exonerated. In two other cases, prosecutors had jailhouse informant testimony ready but did not use it.

While prosecutors say jailhouse snitches can provide important—and truthful—testimony, informants have little to lose by lying on the witness stand. Rarely are they charged with perjury. Instead, they often have something very real to gain: time shaved off their sentence, creature comforts in jail, or some other favor from prosecutors.

Informants who fabricate stories can glean details of a crime from newspapers or another inmate's legal papers and stitch them together into a compelling confession. In the most notorious cases, prosecutors and police have been accused of providing them with false stories to tell.[23]

The risks of executing the innocent based on the testimony of a single jailhouse snitch should be obvious. Yet, even when the snitches are doubled up, the risks created by payoffs for testimony override the benefit of two witnesses. In a case out of Idaho, which received national notoriety in 2001, Mr. Charles Fain was proven definitively not guilty by DNA testing. Simply put, scientific proof showed that Mr. Fain could not have been the man who committed the murder. Two jailhouse snitches had cut deals with the prosecutor to put Mr. Fain on death row.

Some of the most damning evidence against Mr. Fain was the testimony of two jailhouse informers. The men gave lurid details of what they said Mr. Fain had told them about what he had done to [the victim].

It is not clear why the two men gave what now appears to be false testimony. One of Mr. Fain's appellate lawyers, Spencer McIntyre, said it showed how jailhouse informers manipulate the system, knowing that if they cooperate, the authorities will go easier on them—even without an explicit promise or deal.[24]* (bracketed language mine)

What if there are three jailhouse snitches? One is tempted to think that surely with three snitches giving uniform testimony, the credibility must be high. Unfortunately not. This was the case in the prosecution of Joseph Amrine who was prosecuted in Missouri for a stabbing in the recreation room at Jefferson City Correctional Center.[25] The state's case against Amrine consisted of testimony by three inmates who claimed Armine stabbed the victim. Six inmates and a corrections officer testified that the deceased was involved in chasing a different person than Amrine just before the stabbing and that Amrine was playing cards in a different part of the recreation room. No physical evidence existed to connect Amrine to the murder. Nonetheless, the jury convicted Amrine on the testimony of the three snitches and sentenced him to death.

Over the next several years, two of the inmates who had testified against Amrine came forward under oath and recanted their testimony. The appeals courts allowed the conviction and death sentence to stand because there was still the unrecanted testimony of one inmate against Amrine in the trial record. Finally, Amrine's lawyers found the third jailhouse snitch. Now, he too recanted his testimony.

Did the appellate courts proclaim that the state was morally or ethically derelict for continuing to prosecute a man whose only three accusers had all confessed to lying for favorable treatment in their own situations?

No. Instead, the courts held that the recantation by the first jailhouse snitch was "unworthy of belief" because he claimed he had lied under the pressure of threats by authorities. The court refused to believe that such threats really occur.[26] The same court found that the recantation by the second jailhouse snitch was also not believable. In a separate proceeding, the trial court decided that the third jailhouse snitch "was not a credible witness and that his recantation could not be relied upon."[27]

Amrine found himself facing the death penalty based upon the testimony of three jailhouse snitches, all of whom had recanted under oath and had been found by the courts to be lacking in credibility. Yet, the state of Missouri continued to push for Amrine's execution. (Please see chapter 14 for further developments in the case of Joseph Amrine.)

We have our answer. The biblical truth of Torah/Pentateuch and the provisions of Talmud necessary to fulfill those scriptures reveal that the American death penalty is woefully derelict biblically when it comes to the qualifications that must be met by witnesses or with respect to prohibiting testimony from persons who have something to gain by lying. Deals by prosecutors with criminals and reprobates in exchange for testimony, which are pervasive under the American death penalty, are an abomination to biblical truth.

The American ideal for testimony in capital cases is that only *reliable* snitch testimony with independent corroboration would be allowed after full disclosure to the judge and jury of the witness's possible conflict of interest or duress. The actual practice in America is that even inherently unreliable snitch testimony is freely allowed and is earnestly sought by the prosecution. Both the ideal and the practice fall far short of the biblical standard, which would strictly prohibit any testimony by persons of impugned moral character in a capital case.

THE USE OF CONFESSIONS IN CAPITAL CASES

How does the American death penalty stack up against biblical truth with respect to the prohibition against using confessions in capital cases? The constitutional requirements that must be met in order to use a confession in an American death penalty case appear to be met if the police testify that the confession was freely and voluntarily given. I have not been able to find any case where the detective that took a confession stepped forward and said, "Sorry, your honor. I coerced this confession from the defendant."

Under the biblical death penalty, it is irrelevant whether a confession is given freely or voluntarily. That is a standard of man's law under the U.S. Constitution. Under the biblical truth of Torah/Pentateuch and the provisions of Talmud necessary to fulfill those scriptures, confessions are not allowed as evidence. Period.

Those who are familiar with the inner workings of America's death penalty machinery know that confessions play a significant role. Yet actual studies or reports on how confessions impact the system are hard to find. In a rare study of the use of confessions,[28] the *Chicago Tribune* "examined thousands of murder cases filed in Cook County since 1991 and found at least 247 where police obtained incriminating statements that were thrown out by the courts as tainted or failed to secure a conviction."[29]

Although not all of the cases in the study were capital cases, the tactics revealed in these cases allow a window into the hidden world of coerced confessions in American homicide investigations.[30] The innocent are imprisoned. The guilty remain free. What kind of confessions were discovered by the investigation? Preposterous confessions: from defendants "who, according to records, were in jail when the crime occurred"; that "contradicted the facts of the crime"; that were "refuted by DNA evidence"; that were given by children under ten years of age or by "mentally retarded men with IQs in the 40s, 50s and 60s."[31]

False confessions are especially a problem regarding juveniles and the mentally retarded. "At least two dozen of the 247 defendants" involved in the cases reviewed by the study "were mentally retarded, or had significant learning disabilities."[32] In another notorious case, two juveniles under nine years old confessed to the murder of an eleven-year-old boy. DNA evidence (semen) from the crime scene later proved the juveniles were innocent and a man in his thirties was charged with the crime.[33]

A recent case from Alabama underscores the problem of confessions and the mentally retarded. In this bizarre case, three mentally retarded individuals confessed to participation in the murder of a baby that never existed.

A capital murder charge against a mentally retarded man was dropped Friday as he pleaded guilty to a misdemeanor in the 1999 death of a newborn who may never have existed.

Medell Banks, Jr., 31, was freed after . . . a prominent gynecologist determined the purported infant's mother could not have been pregnant due to prior surgery. . . .

Choctaw County Sheriff Donald Lolley, who had insisted Banks took part in a newborn's killing, declined comment. . . .

Banks, his estranged wife, Victoria Banks, and her sister, Dianne Tucker, all pleaded guilty to manslaughter and got 15-year sentences after being charged with capital murder in 1999 in the death of the newborn. But after the pleas, defense lawyers argued that all three are mentally retarded and were intimidated—then introduced the gynecologist's finding Victoria Banks was actually sterile [from a successful tubal ligation]. . . .

Prosecutors denied any wrongdoing in taking the confession. . . . [N]o evidence of the baby or the burial site were found. . . .

. . . [T]he sheriff had said early in the case that Victoria Banks, who had been in jail, was clearly pregnant. "I can usually tell by looking at a lady if she appears to be pregnant or not," he said.[34] (bracketed language mine)

Should such people be allowed to play with the power of life and death over American citizens? That question and the issue of whether a confession turns out to be coerced or false are really American legal questions. As people of biblical faith, we ask whether we should be using confessions at all. Biblical truth says no. Maybe biblical truth is smarter than we are.

A recent investigative report by the *Miami Herald*[35] supports that conclusion by offering the first comprehensive review of murder confessions in south Florida.[36] Since 1990 almost forty murder confessions had been thrown out, rejected, or abandoned in Broward County, where Fort Lauderdale, Florida, is located. The reasons included "illegal interrogation, coercive questioning and flawed fact-checking." Some defendants confessed to murder but gave the wrong year or location of the crime or failed to properly identify their alleged weapon or victim; others who confessed were homeless persons, juveniles, and mentally retarded, one with a mental age of seven. Several of the "confessed killers" have since been established to be "unquestionably innocent."[37]

Our human nature doesn't want to believe that American law enforcement would coerce or fraudulently obtain murder confessions. That certainly was how the judge felt in the case of Jerry Frank Townsend.

> [Townsend] served 22 years in prison in the most notorious case of false-confession in recent South Florida history. At Townsend's 1980 trial, when [his defense attorney] suggested that the confessions might be false, Broward Circuit Judge Arthur Franza ridiculed him.
>
> "I would have to indict three major police departments of the state of Florida (to acquit Townsend), and I'm not about to do that," Franza replied, alluding to the Miami, Fort Lauderdale, and Broward departments.
>
> Transcripts reveal that detectives led the malleable Townsend, fed him facts, corrected his fictions and ignored obvious inaccuracies in building a case that led to six murder convictions. Townsend has the mental age of a 7- or 8-year-old.
>
> Townsend's confession to one Miami murder gave the victim the wrong name. His confession to a Broward murder gave the wrong year.
>
> Snippets of tape reveal detectives steering the suspect toward the facts they wanted rather than recording the facts he knew. When Townsend strayed too far from the truth, the tape would go off.[38]

Such cases are by no means limited to the mentally retarded. The same investigative report details the use of similar techniques by detectives in obtaining false confessions from a man named Wood who had suffered an alcoholic blackout: "Wood gave two detailed confessions to the murder. . . . A review of the transcripts shows that Wood's knowledge of the crime increased over time. Wood said detectives rehearsed the facts with him between sessions. Detectives deny any impropriety."[39]

Wood was released after a different man was identified as the triggerman.

False confessions can also be easily obtained from the mentally ill. The same investigation revealed the following:

John Gordon Purvis, a schizophrenic, spent nine years in prison for the murder of a neighbor before new evidence led to the victim's estranged husband.

[The victim, a thirty-eight-year-old woman, was found brutally murdered in her home, dead for about a week. Her eighteen-month-old daughter was found in the house, dead from neglect.]

Police set their sights on Purvis, a 43-year-old man with mental illness who lived three doors away.

Detectives and prosecutors paid little attention to the numerous inconsistencies in Purvis' statement. . . .

"John's a very suggestible guy," [his longtime psychiatrist] told the jury [at Purvis' murder trial]. "I think John, under these circumstances, would say whatever was wanted of him, and I think that's what took place."[40] (bracketed language mine)

False confessions can also be obtained from healthy people through threats. In a civil lawsuit against the sheriff's office of Broward County, Florida (Fort Lauderdale and Deerfield Beach), a witness recently testified that he spent sixteen months in jail after confessing to a murder that he did not really commit, claiming the detectives threatened him with the electric chair if he didn't confess and also implicate two other innocent men. Furthermore, he claims to have cracked after only three hours of pressure from detectives who convinced him that confessing was his only way out of the death penalty.[41]

Experts are scurrying to establish procedures that will make murder confessions trustworthy. In truth, however, under the standards of biblical truth in Torah/Pentateuch and the provisions of Talmud necessary to fulfill those scriptures, all confessions— true, false, coerced, or voluntary—are prohibited from being used as evidence in a capital case. We can see the wisdom in this, especially when we experience the power of false confessions to overcome all other evidence to the contrary.

Experts in interrogation techniques know how easy it is to obtain a false confession. Regular citizens who have never experienced being deprived of sleep for over thirty hours or sitting on the floor of a small room chained to a radiator for thirty or forty hours, without food and without any ability to relieve themselves except inside their own clothes, cannot imagine anyone confessing to something they did not do. This gives tremendous evidentiary power to any confession, even a false one.

In one case reviewed by the *Chicago Tribune* study,[42] the defendant had given a false confession. He did so hoping to bring his abusive treatment by police to an end, and expecting to straighten the matter out later. Afterward he protested to detectives that he could not have committed the crime because he was locked in the county jail when the crime occurred. The police checked their records and found out he was telling the truth. He could not have been at the park (scene of the crime) because he was in jail.

The case was prosecuted anyway and local street toughs were solicited by the state to testify. The jury chose to ignore the police records from the jail and accept the confession. The defendant was convicted of a crime committed at a park while he was locked in the county jail. This case, which involved a life sentence, not a death sentence, reveals the tremendous power of a coerced confession. "The witness who put [the defendant] in the park now says he lied at the request of detectives, and later was rewarded with leniency on a narcotics charge."[43]

We must marvel at the wisdom revealed by biblical truth in the strict prohibition against confessions. Although the American ideal for testimony in capital cases is that only *reliable* confessions would be allowed as evidence, the actual practice in America is that even inherently unreliable confessions are freely allowed as evidence and are used by the prosecution because they are extremely persuasive with juries. Both the ideal and the practice fall far short of the biblical standard, which would strictly prohibit any confessions in a capital case, regardless of the circumstances.

TESTIMONY BY A CHILD AGAINST HIS FATHER

In a current Florida case, from the same county that was investigated in the reports by the *Miami Herald*, confessions of both a father and his son were used.[44] The police arrested both the defendant and his then fifteen-year-old son. The father attests that he was concerned about his son's condition, especially after the police fired off a gun right near the teenager's head to scare him into talking. The father agreed to say anything the police wanted if they would release his son. He gave a taped statement that he had shot the victim, and the police then released his son. The defendant wrongly assumed that once he and his son were out of police custody, they could get everything worked out.

He also claims that originally his son told police he was never anywhere near the crime scene, but then police coerced his son into giving a contradictory statement that accused the father of the crime. The father claims that there is no physical evidence or forensic evidence connecting him to the crime scene. The use of the father's own confession, given under duress for the sake of his child, and his son's revised testimony were pivotal to the state's case. The Florida Supreme Court denied the defendant any relief, even though his attorney was discovered to have been addicted to and using drugs and severely abusing alcohol during the time of preparation for his trial.[45] The father has been on Florida's death row for over seventeen years.

Such testimony by a child against his father and a confession given by the father under duress for the sake of his son would never be allowed under the biblical truth of Torah/Pentateuch and the provisions of Talmud that fulfill those scriptural limitations.

The answer for us is clear. Biblical truth reveals that the American death penalty fails miserably when it comes to the prohibition against using confessions in capital cases.

THE USE OF A SOLITARY WITNESS IN CAPITAL CASES

Multiple witnesses whose testimony agrees as to all material facts are critical under the standards of the biblical death penalty. Our modern experience verifies the wisdom of this biblical requirement. The American ideal for testimony in capital cases is that only the *reliable* eyewitness testimony of a *perfect witness* would be allowed as evidence. That is a far cry from the actual practice in America where prosecutors frequently use solitary eyewitnesses who are corroborated with circumstantial evidence; moreover, when there are multiple witnesses, discrepancies in their testimony do not prevent the use of their statements in evidence.

Both the ideal and the practice fall far short of the biblical standard, which would strictly prohibit any solitary witnesses, and requires two or more witnesses whose testimony is in total agreement on all material facts.

Eyewitness testimony can be tricky. The mind has the power in recollection to subtly fill in details as though they were perceived in the event. How does America measure up under this standard revealed by biblical truth? The *Chicago Tribune* squarely faced this question in a 2003 Pulitzer Prize–winning editorial, "When Believing Isn't Seeing."

Thanks to a generation's worth of research, we know an awful lot about the fickleness of memory. We know eyewitness accounts of crimes are fragmented and suggestible. We know they're apt to go from shaky to confident between the time a cop confirms a witness' lineup choice ("You picked the right guy") and the start of trial. . . .

Gary Wells, a professor of psychology at Iowa State University, has spent more than 20 years studying police "sixpack" lineups and photo spreads, as well as the memory of eyewitnesses to a crime. Through repeated experiments with staged crimes in front of college students, he has found that the practice of lining a bunch of suspects up at once has a higher error rate than if suspects are shown to witnesses individually, in sequence. The same is true with photo spreads.

Why? Because when all suspects are viewed at once, the eyewitness is tempted to make a relative judgment (Who most resembles the suspect among those present?) rather than an absolute one (Is this the person who committed the crime?).

When the real perpetrator is not in the sequential lineup, witnesses tend not to pick anyone. In group lineups, witnesses are more likely to pick somebody in the interest of being helpful.[46]

An illustration of the risks of eyewitness testimony is the case of Chicagoan James Newsome.

His was not a capital case, but the lessons apply to all felony prosecutions. Newsome was driving with a friend on Halloween in 1979 when police stopped them, guns drawn, as possible suspects in the robbery of a prostitute.

One of the officers thought Newsome resembled a composite sketch of a suspect in a murder that occurred a day earlier. Next thing he knew, Newsome was being marched into a live lineup at the police station, where three eyewitnesses fingered him as the man who gunned down South Side convenience store owner Mickey Cohen.

Newsome, who had never before been arrested, spent 15 years in a rat-infested prison serving a life sentence. That's how long it took for fingerprint technology to develop that would prove the prints left at the scene by the killer weren't Newsome's. For five years police knew, but didn't divulge, that the prints belonged to Dennis Emerson, a career criminal.

Newsome and Emerson didn't even look alike.

Newsome was nearly three inches taller.

Newsome had a mole on his nose. Emerson didn't.

Newsome had short-cropped hair. Emerson had more of an Afro.[47]

Perhaps the most compelling answer to this question arises in the context of every prosecutor's dream—the perfect witness. Surely, biblical truth must allow for that rarest of circumstances when one eyewitness is all that is needed because he or she is the perfect witness. That appeared to have been the case in a North Carolina rape. Although the crime did not carry the death penalty, it is profoundly illustrative of the biblical concern about reliable evidence, even when it is the eyewitness testimony of a "perfect witness."

Jennifer Thompson was the perfect student, perfect daughter, perfect homecoming queen. And when her perfect world was ripped apart, the petite blonde with the dark, expressive eyes became something she could never have imagined.

The perfect witness.

Police had never seen a victim so composed, so determined, so sure.

Just hours after her ordeal, after a jaded doctor swabbed her for semen samples in a hospital, she sat in a police station with Detective Mike Gauldin, combing through photos, working up a composite. She picked out his eyebrows, his nose, his pencil-thin mustache. She picked out his photo.

A week later, she sat across a table from six men holding numbered cards. There was no one-way mirror to shield her. Each walked up and repeated the words, "Shut up or I'll cut you." Thompson picked number five. "That's my rapist," she told Gauldin.

In court, she put her right hand on the Bible and swore to tell the truth. Then she looked directly into the expressionless face of the suspect. "He is the man who raped me," she said.

She had never been so sure of anything.

His name was Ronald Cotton and he was the same age as she. . . .

When Thompson picked him out of the lineup, everyone was sure they had the right man. . . .

On Jan. 17, 1985, the day Cotton was sentenced to life in prison, Thompson toasted her victory with champagne. "It was the happiest day of my life," she said. . . .

One day, about a year after Cotton was convicted, another man joined him working in the prison kitchen. His name was Bobby Poole. He was serving consecutive life sentences for a series of brutal rapes. And he was bragging to other inmates that Cotton was doing some of his time. . . .

Cotton . . . put his faith in God. And when he learned he had won a second trial, his heart filled with hope.

Another woman had been raped just an hour after Thompson: same Burlington neighborhood, same kind of attack. Police were sure it was the same man. An appeals court had ruled that evidence relating to the second victim should have been allowed in the first trial.

At the new trial, the witnesses would get a look at Poole, who was subpoenaed by Cotton's lawyer. Finally, Cotton thought, he would be set free.

He had forgotten the power of Jennifer Thompson. Back on the stand, she was as confident as ever. She looked directly at

Poole and she looked directly at Cotton. Fifteen feet away he could feel the hatred in her heart. Cotton is the man who raped me, she told the jury. Are you sure? Yes, I'm sure.

The second victim was less convincing, but she pointed to him, too. Cotton hung his head. He had no words left inside him. . . .

The knock on the door of [Jennifer's] Winston-Salem home came out of the blue. The detective hadn't just dropped by casually to say hello. It had been 11 years. Standing in Thompson's kitchen, Gauldin struggled to break the news. "Jennifer," he said, "you were wrong. Ronald Cotton didn't rape you. It was Bobby Poole."

For a moment nothing registered in her mind, nothing but the deep blue walls of her kitchen and the yellow chicken pictures that her children had painted. They were hanging right behind Gauldin's head. Then everything started spinning— blues and yellows, the fuzzy glint of his police badge. And those words, thundering round and round in her head:

"You were WRONG . . ."

There was new evidence, Gauldin was saying. DNA tests. New scientific proof that hadn't been available before.

Eleven years of nightmares, of Cotton's face taunting her in the dark. Eleven years of struggling to move on, of building a life with her husband and children. Eleven years of being wrong.[48]

CLOSING THOUGHTS

The biblical truth of Torah/Pentateuch and the provisions of Talmud that satisfy those scriptural requirements demand at least two eyewitnesses whose testimony agrees in every material respect. Furthermore, the exchanges of words between the perpetrator and the witness that are required in the giving of the warning, discussed in chapter 13, establish a premise of interaction between the two that adds credibility to the memory.

Our American system of using single eyewitness testimony in death penalty cases falls far short of this biblical standard of reliability. As for confessions and jailhouse snitches, both the American ideal and the practice fall far short of the biblical standard, which would strictly prohibit any confessions and any testimony by persons of impugned moral character in a capital case.

Perhaps we will fare better in looking at the actual evidence allowed in a capital case.

Chapter Thirteen

AN INNOCENT PERSON YOU SHALL NOT SLAY

EVIDENCE PERMITTED

As we approach the question of evidence to be permitted in a capital case, it is helpful to remember that the primary concern of the biblical death penalty is the fear of executing the innocent. This is rooted in the Bible itself (Exod. 23:7). The nature of permissible evidence under the biblical death penalty and the statements and questions that judges are required to make and to ask flow from the scriptural mandate to avoid the execution of an innocent man. Above and beyond that, there is further biblical basis for these requirements.

> A single witness may not validate against a person any guilt or blame for any offense that may be committed; a case can be valid only on the testimony of two witnesses or more. Deut. 19:15 TNK

> [A]t the mouth of two witnesses, or at the mouth of three witnesses, shall the matter be established. Deut. 19:15 AV

> A matter must be established by the testimony of two or three witnesses. Deut. 19:15 NIV

If anyone kills a person, the manslayer may be executed only on the evidence of witnesses; the testimony of a single witness against a person shall not suffice for a sentence of death. Num. 35:30 TNK

Whoso killeth any person, the murderer shall be put to death by the mouth of witnesses. Num. 35:30 AV

But no one is to be put to death on the testimony of only one witness. Num. 35:30 NIV

The Bible mandates that the guilt of a person subject to capital punishment must be established by the testimony of at least two witnesses. A witness can only testify to what he has seen or heard. Consequently, the elements of premeditated murder must be established by explicit testimony of at least two witnesses. This results in the following rules for permitted evidence in capital cases under the standards of the biblical death penalty.

First, all material facts must be established by testimony of firsthand witnesses. Circumstantial evidence is prohibited.

According to the Torah, evidence is valid only if substantiated by two witnesses. These men must be men who have attained their majority, have never been accused of criminal offenses of any kind, and are not related to the litigants, the judges, or one another.[1]

Circumstantial evidence, however convincing, was not accepted. A witness was only allowed to testify who saw the crime actually committed.[2]

Circumstantial evidence is essentially any evidence other than eyewitness testimony of the ultimate fact in issue. With respect to murder, any evidence other than the testimony, "I saw him do it. It was at such and such a time, in such and such a place, and he used such and such a means" would be circumstantial evidence.

Many of us who have grown up on a diet of murder mysteries and cop shows have learned to take circumstantial evidence for granted. Reasonable deductions and logical conclusions are assumed to be part of the process of coming to a decision of "beyond a reasonable doubt." That is modern. That is American. None of that has anything to do with the biblical death penalty.

Reasonable deductions and logical conclusions are prohibited under the standards of the biblical death penalty. The standard of guilt under the biblical death penalty is "absolute certainty." The actual act of killing must itself be witnessed. For example:

> So that [the witnesses] should not say, "We saw [*the accused*] running after [*the victim*], with a sword in his hand. [The victim] ran in front of him into a shop, and then the other went after him into the store. We went in after them and found the victim slain on the floor, with a knife in the hand of the murderer, dripping blood."
>
> Now lest you say [*to the accused*], "If not you, then who killed him" – you must be admonished that this is not valid evidence.[3] (brackets without italics in original; brackets with italics mine)

In the facts just stated, even the small inference necessary to connect the accused to the murder of the victim is not allowed under the standards of biblical truth. In America we have become accustomed to the logic of the proverbial "smoking gun." That means that when a person is found standing over a dead body with a smoking gun in his hand, he is assumed to be guilty. The smoking gun is not even allowed to be mentioned in testimony under the biblical death penalty. The judges of biblical times were required to drive this point home by addressing the witnesses before they gave testimony. A form of the specific words of the admonition required have been recorded as follows:

> Perhaps the evidence you are about to give is based on conjecture or hearsay, or something said by another witness, or the statement made by a person in whom you have confidence. Perhaps, also, you are unaware that we shall subject you to a searching cross-examination. Take note that criminal cases are not like civil cases. In the latter a man forfeits his money and makes atonement; but in criminal cases the responsibility of his blood and the blood of his seed rests upon him until the end of the world. Thus do we find it in connection with Cain who killed his brother, of whom it is said, "The voice of thy broth-

er's bloods crieth unto Me from the ground" (Genesis 4:10). The text does not read "thy brother's blood" but "thy brother's bloods," meaning his blood and that of his seed. For that reason was man first created a single individual, to teach the lesson that whoever destroys one life, Scripture ascribes it to him as though he had destroyed a whole world; and whoever saves one life, Scripture ascribes it to him as though he had saved a whole world.[4]

This admonition is not for purposes of emphasizing the guilt of the accused. It is to emphasize the guilt of the witnesses if they are involved in the conviction and execution of an innocent man. Some courts felt this admonition did not go far enough. Such courts believed that the deliberations should be opened by the judge saying to the witnesses, "Who is to say that it happened just as you say it did?"[5]

This would place the witnesses on the defensive because the court would open discussion of the testimony by suggesting that the witnesses are lying and are involved in a plot against the accused. Others feared that such a frontal assault on the credibility of the witnesses would have the effect of "muzzling" them, intimidating them into retracting their testimony even if it had been truthful. However, less brazen, indirect techniques to unsettle witnesses and shake liars into retracting false testimony were considered normative under the biblical death penalty:

We move the witnesses from place to place, in order that their minds become unsettled, so that they will retract their testimony if it is untrue.[6]

The judges bring the witnesses into a room to examine them and then abruptly shift them to another room before examining them. After moving to the second room they again postpone hearing the testimony and shift to yet a third room.[7] This is done to wear down the witnesses and induce them to back out of testifying [on the assumption that witnesses will be less likely to persevere if they are not telling the truth].[8] (bracketed language in original)

Again we see that the overriding concern of the biblical death penalty is to avoid execution of the innocent.

Second, even the interior disposition of the accused as to intent to commit murder must be established by objective testimony. Malicious intent, premeditation, cannot be inferred from other actions.

An essential element that must be proved in any American crime is mens rea, the criminal intent to commit the act without any legally recognized excuse or justification. With respect to crimes against one's physical person, we frequently call this *malice aforethought* or *premeditation*. Under the American system, this criminal intent with respect to murder can be inferred from circumstantial evidence.

Unlike the implied intent of malice aforethought for first-degree murder in the United States, the standards of the biblical death penalty require that requisite premeditation, malice aforethought, be established by eyewitness testimony. First of all, the biblical death penalty does not allow for transferred intent or for felony murder.

> If one intended to kill an animal but killed a man instead . . . he is not liable to execution. If one intended to strike [someone] on his loins and the [blow] was not sufficient to kill him on his loins, but it landed on his chest and it was sufficient to kill him on his chest and he died, [the assailant] is not liable to execution. If he intended to strike him on his chest, and [the blow] was sufficient to kill him had it landed on his chest, but it landed on his loins instead, and it was not sufficient to kill him on his loins, but he died anyway, [the killer] is not liable to execution.
>
> . . . If one intended to strike an adult, and [the blow] was not sufficient to kill the adult, but it landed on a child instead, and it was sufficient to kill the child, and [the child] died, [the killer] is not liable to execution. If he intended to strike a child, and [the blow] was sufficient to kill the child, but he struck an adult instead, and the [blow] was not sufficient to kill the adult, but [the adult] died anyway, [the killer] is not liable for execution.[9] (bracketed language in original)

Even in cases where the killer succeeds in killing the person who is the intended victim, the biblical death penalty requires that malice aforethought, premeditation, must be established by objective witness testimony.

> According to the Torah, a man cannot be sentenced to punishment (flogging or execution) unless he committed the deed with malice aforethought. [*Jewish law does not allow for assuming premeditation on the basis of the actions and preparations for the crime. There must be specific and objective proof of the intent.*] This is the purpose of the warning . . . witnesses attest not only to the deed but also to the fact that he was cautioned, that is, told just before committing the crime that the act he was about to commit was forbidden by law and that the punishment for violation was death. Furthermore, it was not sufficient to utter the warning; it was necessary to verify that the defendant had taken note of it and accepted it by saying: "I know and I take it upon myself." Without these elements there is no possibility of proving malicious intent.[10] (bracketed language mine)

The warning (*hatra'ab*) required to be given and attested to in testimony by at least two agreeing eyewitnesses is explicitly set forth under the biblical death penalty, as follows:

> [T]hey convict then only on the testimony of witnesses, after warning, and after they inform him that [what he is going to do] subjects him to liability to the death penalty in court. . . .
> Whether all those who testify against him have given him warning, or only some of those who testify against him have given him warning, he is liable. . . .
> [If] they warn him and he was silent, or if they warn him and he nods his head, even though he says, "I know" – he is exempt – unless he will say, "I know it, and it is with that very stipulation that I am doing what I am doing!" . . .
> [If] they saw him profaning the Sabbath, [and] said to him, "You should know that it is the Sabbath today, and Scripture says, *Those who profane it will certainly die* (Exod. 31:14)"—even though he said, "I know"—he is exempt unless he says, "I know, and it is with that very stipulation that I am doing what I am doing!" . . .
> [If] they saw him killing somebody, and said to him, "You

should know that that man is subject to the [divine] covenant, and it is said, *Whoever sheds the blood of man by man shall his blood be shed* (Gen. 9:6)"—even though he said, "I know it"—he is exempt unless he says, "I know, and it is with that very stipulation that I am doing what I am doing!"[11] (bracketed language and italics in original)

Some courts placed even more stringent requirements upon the warning, insisting that the accused must have been warned specifically of the sort of death penalty to which he would be subjected.[12] Another held that the accused could not warn himself through a spontaneous declaration: "Lo, if he should warn himself, he is exempt, since it is said, *If an unrighteous man rise up to testify against him of wrongdoing* (Deut. 19:16)—that he should warn others, and not that he should warn himself."[13] (italics in original)

Regardless of one's opinion about the more restrictive view, it is absolutely clear that the biblical death penalty precludes execution unless the offender was given the warning and responded in a fashion that indicated he intended to incur the ultimate penalty for his act. Presumably this is based upon the scriptural truth that only God can judge the human heart; malice aforethought resides in the human heart. No human being is capable of judging its presence unless the accused himself has stated in the moment that it exists inside.

The third principle of the biblical death penalty with respect to permitted evidence is that if the testimony of the witnesses on any material fact is in disagreement, the witnesses and their testimony are excluded.

After the court has admonished the witnesses with the statement concerning their responsibility for the blood of an innocent man, the court is required to ask the seven standard questions: "They would examine [the witnesses] with seven questions: In which seven-year period did you see the crime? In which year? In which month? On which day of the month? On which day of the week? In which hour? In which place?"[14] (bracketed language in original)

The primary purpose of the seven standard questions is to pinpoint the time and place of the alleged event so as to allow for the possibility of the witnesses being refuted, having their testimony contradicted and excluded.[15] The biblical death penalty also requires supplementary questions to be asked in murder cases: "Did you recognize [the victim]? Did you warn [the accused]?"[16] (bracketed language in original) Judges are free to add additional supplementary questions. In fact, under the biblical death penalty, the more supplementary questions a court asks, the more esteemed is the court.[17]

Finally, the biblical death penalty makes a distinction between the standard questions and the supplementary questions as follows: "In the case of the standard questions, if one says, 'I don't know,' their testimony is null. In the case of the supplementary questions, however, if one says, 'I don't know,'—or even if two say, 'We do not know,' their testimony is upheld. Concerning both the seven standard questions and the supplementary questions, whenever [the witnesses] contradict one another, their testimony is null."[18] (bracketed language in original)

As we shall see later in this book, there is also a distinction made between the two sets of questions for purposes of subjecting false witnesses to the death penalty. In the meantime, however, our search requires us to measure the American death penalty against these three very fundamental principles of the biblical death penalty.

CIRCUMSTANTIAL EVIDENCE IN CAPITAL CASES

How does the permitted evidence under the American death penalty stack up against the evidence allowed under the standards of biblical truth from Torah/Pentateuch and the provisions of Talmud necessary to fulfill those scriptures?

The overwhelming majority of evidence presented in court in American death penalty cases would be excluded under the biblical death penalty as circumstantial evidence. Tire tracks, footprints, fingerprints, hair comparison analysis, blood splatter testimony, records of phone calls, purchase receipts, paint analysis, clothes and carpet fiber analysis, and similar forensic testimony all fall far short of the biblical standard of being accused in the matter by eyewitnesses to the murder.

Although the American ideal for use by the prosecution of circumstantial evidence in capital cases is that it could be used only if proven *reliable* and the expert witness has impeccable credentials and reputation, the actual practice in America is that the circumstantial evidence is allowed to be used even if it is inherently unreliable (e.g., hair analysis) and even if the expert witness has been rebuked by the U.S. Justice Department. Both the ideal and the practice fall far short of the biblical standard, which would absolutely prohibit any circumstantial evidence in a capital case.

It is interesting to speculate about the fate of DNA evidence under the biblical death penalty. We believe that the outcome of DNA testing is even more reliable than eyewitness testimony. Yet, the factors in the chain of analysis (e.g., was the right blood tested against the right sample, was the test performed under the right calibrations, etc.) introduce the kind of vagaries that worried the biblical death penalty, small gaps that result in a conclusion just short of actual certainty. Consequently, I believe that under the biblical death penalty, DNA evidence would be allowed to show evidence of innocence (establish doubt as to guilt), but would not be allowed for proving guilt. This would be consistent with the biblical truth, which always allies against the death penalty.

Are such concerns about forensic test results merely theoretical, or is there a reality here that biblical truth requires us to scrutinize? The following recent events indicate that the latter is true.

WEST VIRGINIA AND TEXAS

The credibility of the criminal justice system in West Virginia has been lambasted by the discovery that a state serology expert has been falsifying results for sixteen years.

Mr. Zain sat in the defendant's spot, accused by special state prosecutors of systematically faking scores of test findings in a 16-year career of cases in which the innocent were said to have been victimized and the state defrauded of justice. . . .

The criminal action against Mr. Zain comes after seven convictions relying on his testimony have been overturned upon challenge in [West Virginia and Texas] with millions of dollars in settlements paid to those who complained of deliberate injustice.

Other convictions are under challenge, impelled by a finding by the West Virginia Supreme Court that discredited Mr. Zain's work in 1993, years after the state first received complaints about his methods from colleagues and others. After a review of 189 of his cases, the court warned that "any testimony or documentary evidence offered by Mr. Zain at any time should be deemed invalid, unreliable and inadmissible." . . .

. . . George Castelle, the chief public defender in Charleston, said the case against Mr. Zain was well justified in exposing his methodology as "a blueprint on how to convict an innocent person." . . .

. . . Castelle said he was shocked to have found Mr. Zain regularly praised and promoted for his trial work . . . even though . . . two laboratory colleagues had been complaining about his bias against defendants and even presented evidence to state officials showing some of his laboratory tests contradicted his trial testimony.[19]*

We have not yet heard of any inmates actually executed based on Zain's erroneous scientific evidence or misleading scientific testimony. That is not the case with respect to the mistakes in Oklahoma.

OKLAHOMA

Joyce Gilchrist was the forensic scientist for the Oklahoma City Police Department. That means she performed basic scientific analysis of blood and hair samples, fibers, and similar circumstantial evidence. She then would testify as to her scientific conclusions at criminal trials. Gilchrist is reported to have made horrendous mistakes with thousands of cases tainted by her faulty scientific testimony, including twelve cases of men on death row

*Copyright © 2001 by The New York Times Co. Reprinted with permission.

and another eleven cases where the men had already been executed.*

A preliminary FBI study of eight cases found that in at least five, she had made outright errors or overstepped "the acceptable limits of forensic science." Gilchrist got convictions by matching hair samples with a certainty other forensic scientists found impossible to achieve. She also appears to have withheld evidence from the defense and failed to perform tests that could have cleared defendants. . . .

. . . [T]he allegations also underscore a national problem: the sometimes dangerously persuasive power of courtroom science. Juries tend to regard forensic evidence more highly than they regard witnesses because it is purportedly more objective. But forensic scientists work so closely with the police and district attorneys that their objectivity cannot be taken for granted.

[As far back as 1987, colleagues, including John Wilson, had filed complaints.]

. . . "We've been screaming in the wind, and nobody has been listening." . . .

How did her career last so long? "She couldn't have got away with this if she weren't supported by prosecutors, ignored by judges and police who did nothing," says Wilson. . . . "The police department was asleep at the switch."[20] (bracketed language mine)

Could innocent people have been executed because of such mistakes? Malcolm Rent Johnson was executed in January 2000 for a rape murder. A memorandum issued within the Oklahoma City Police Department in July 2001 is reported to have said that some of the scientific evidence that Gilchrist relied upon to place Johnson at the scene of the crime, "evidence she swore to does not exist."[21]

Such harrowing tales accentuate the biblical concern over possibilities of error in death penalty cases. No wonder biblical truth requires a rock-bottom standard of absolute certainty of guilt for the death penalty.

*© 2001 TIME Inc. Reprinted by permission.

Perhaps something inside us wants to believe that the horrendous experiences of local crime labs in West Virginia, Texas, and Oklahoma are only a scattered phenomenon, an exception to the rule. Unfortunately, that is not what the experts in the field are telling us.

An editorial by Dr. Cyril H. Wecht, past president of the American Academy of Forensic Sciences, notes that crime labs are overwhelmingly backlogged with work and that deficiencies of personnel, space, and equipment in forensic science labs often lead to shoddy practices and erroneous test results. Dr. Wecht notes:

> There can be little doubt in the minds of trained, experienced forensic scientists that testing defects, backlog pressures, inadequately qualified personnel, and prosecutorial bias exist in many other DNA labs even though they have not yet been uncovered and publicly reported. . . . Until these glaring deficiencies are identified, objectively reviewed, and carefully corrected, society cannot expect that justice will be served.
>
> . . . State lawmakers should carefully scrutinize DNA labs that use inferior testing methods that lead to inaccurate results. *An immediate freeze on executions is essential* until scrupulous federal and state reviews of all DNA labs have been accomplished. This is the only just way to proceed. Close attention to this critical problem will not only lower the risk of executing innocent people, it will also facilitate the capture and conviction of the guilty.[22] (emphasis mine)

The problem appears pervasive. Yet, surely we must have a level of complete certainty when the forensic testing is performed by a national organization of outstanding reputation and credentials instead of a local police laboratory.

THE FEDERAL BUREAU OF INVESTIGATION (FBI)

Unfortunately, the opposite is true. Larger operations with national scope just seem to spread the errors more effectively to more cases across more of the country. At least that is the lesson of the now infamous Malone fiasco at America's FBI. In "Good Cop, Bad Cop: Special Report: Fallout from an FBI Scandal," the Pulitzer Prize–winning reporter, Sydney P. Freedberg, published a comprehensive investigative report of the Malone story in the *St. Petersburg Times.* The following account is based upon that report.[23]

Michael P. Malone, a famous and popular crime analyst in the FBI crime laboratory, specialized in hair and fiber analysis. In case after case where the state had only circumstantial evidence, Malone would bulwark the prosecution with scientific certainty. He was often the difference between death row or prison on the one hand and no case at all on the other. The trouble started in 1997 when a U.S. Justice Department report slammed Malone and other crime lab specialists for faulty technique and the propensity for giving as sworn testimony scientific conclusions that could not be supported by science. Because of Malone's involvement, 263 cases in Florida and 3,000 cases nationwide had to be reevaluated.

The overwhelming majority of the cases where Malone's testimony could have falsely accused innocent defendants involved hair evidence. Malone believed that studying hair could reveal "a person's race, the area of the body the hair came from and whether it fell out or was pulled." In reality, until DNA testing became available, there were no scientific standards for hair analysis. The lab scientist relied on his or her ability to eyeball the specimen and on "educated guesswork."

When defense attorneys began looking behind Malone's conclusions, cases started to fall apart. In Florida, the state supreme court overturned convictions that were obtained on the basis of Malone's testimony. Finally,

> [i]n 1989, William Tobin, the FBI's chief metals expert, accused Malone of intentionally giving false testimony in a case. . . .
>
> . . . [I]n a six-page memo, he detailed 26 other instances where Malone made "false . . . contrived/fabricated . . . deceptive" statements under oath.
>
> Things looked bad for Malone. "Sad to say, you are right on every point," Tobin's supervisor wrote on a Post-it note.
>
> But when the memo reached a higher up, nothing happened. Instead, the quiet, easygoing Malone kept moving up

the FBI's career ladder—nominated twice for the bureau's top award.[24]

Just as occurred in West Virginia when two laboratory colleagues complained about improprieties in Mr. Zain's work and testimony, just as occurred in Oklahoma when John Wilson filed complaints about the methods and testimony of Joyce Gilchrist, so too in the FBI, Tobin's allegations against Malone were simply ignored.

The standards of biblical truth absolutely prohibit educated guesswork as evidence in a capital case. Under the best of circumstances, the forensic work generated by Malone at the FBI lab was anathema to biblical truth. Eventually, however, the standards of his work deteriorated to far worse than the best. Yet, Malone remained popular with Florida prosecutors because he could deliver on the witness stand.

The inertia in Oklahoma, West Virginia, Washington, D.C., and Florida seems to be the same: if the forensic evidence and testimony is successful at obtaining convictions, prosecutors and police better not raise questions about whether or not it is convicting the innocent. Despite that inertia, Malone's star began to fall.

In 1996 and again in 1997, Justice Department investigators grilled him. . . . Malone acknowledged that at times, he testified as a "layman," not an expert, but he insisted the prosecutor knew that. He said he made minor misstatements but denied deliberately lying under oath. . . .

When then-Inspector General Michael Bromwich released his 517-page report in April 1997, he hammered Malone for "testifying falsely."

The report stopped short of accusing anyone of fabrication of evidence. . . .

Still, [Malone's] work in up to 5,000 cases—including 500 trials (more in Florida than anywhere)—became suspect. . . .

In Lake County, Malone fended off a charge he embellished evidence against James Duckett, a former police officer on Florida's death row for raping and killing an 11-year-old girl.[25]

And he shrugged off a new nickname: Jay C. Smith, a former

Pennsylvania school principal freed from death row, dubbed Malone "Agent Death" because, Smith says, Malone could find hair and fiber evidence where none existed.

By the fall of 1999, new reports trickled in from the Justice Department, showing Malone had made forensic errors in at least four Tampa Bay area homicide cases. But like past obstacles, the new ones didn't prove to be a problem. In December 1999, Malone quietly retired, leaving the FBI on good terms, with a full pension.[26] (bracketed language and note mine)

Why did Mike Malone function as he did? Was it purely personal proclivities? Or is there an atmosphere in the police lab culture that rewards those who reach beyond science for conclusions that will support convictions? Were Malone's critical faculties swamped by a prosecutorial environment in which scientists were too closely allied with the state? Does Malone express regret or remorse? "'Nobody's convinced anybody in a black robe that I've done anything wrong,' Malone says. 'I did the best I could. Crime labs aren't perfect. People aren't perfect.'"[27]

Do the key players in the criminal justice system, police and prosecutors, hide their heads in shame at the prospect of having destroyed the lives of innocent citizens, having put innocent people on death row, even having possibly executed innocent Americans, all based on Malone's predictably pro-prosecution "scientific" testimony? "To police and prosecutors, Malone remains a hero. [In December of 2000], in fact, he was in Tampa having a quiet dinner with two buddies from the Hillsborough County Sheriff's Office. Two mornings later, he was in the spotlight again, testifying for the Hillsborough state attorney in a death penalty case."[28]

For people of strict biblical faith, the foregoing true accounts are a death knell for the American death penalty. The scriptures of Torah/Pentateuch and Talmud may not have reckoned with the specifics of forensic testimony, but they knew enough to prohibit any evidence that could be skewed or perverted to the point of rendering a guilty verdict against an innocent person in a capital case.

The fact that such nonsense occurs in *any* American death penalty cases should be enough to make every person of biblical faith stand up and demand an end to the practice. Yet, the truth is that such nonsense is hardly unusual in American capital cases. A *Chicago Tribune* investigation found that the use of inherently unreliable hair comparison analysis is remarkably frequent in death penalty cases.[29] According to their report, the technique was used by Illinois prosecutors in obtaining death sentences against at least 20 defendants out of 285. In some of those cases, the state's case consisted of only hair comparison evidence corroborated by testimony from a snitch or an accomplice. In other words, highly unreliable circumstantial evidence corroborated by highly unreliable testimony, the latter usually given in exchange for a deal.

CIRCUMSTANTIAL EYEWITNESS TESTIMONY

Unless we think biblically we don't realize that most eyewitness testimony in an American death penalty case is circumstantial, not direct. Witnesses are frequently testifying that they saw the defendant in the vicinity of the crime or saw his car or heard her voice. This is all circumstantial evidence. It is extremely rare to have an eyewitness who knew the defendant and the attacker and witnessed the murder itself. This is not to say that such forensic evidence is false. That is not the purpose of our inquiry. Our inquiry is to understand what the biblical truth of Torah/Pentateuch and the provisions of Talmud that fulfill those scriptural limitations reveal about the American death penalty.

On the basis of the forensic and other circumstantial evidence typically presented in court in an American capital case, we must conclude that our American death penalty is not biblical and cannot be supported biblically.

MALICE AFORETHOUGHT AND INCONSISTENT WITNESSES

We must come to the same conclusion with respect to the required warning that objectively proves malice aforethought. There is no required warning of any kind under the American death penalty. Not only that, but the requisite malice aforethought, premeditation, is inferred from the outside circumstances.

In most states, including Florida, the requisite premeditation for first-degree murder is met by any space of time, no matter how brief, in which reflection could have taken place. It can be a split second.[30]

Under the American common-law doctrine of felony murder, one does not have to intend to kill anyone. The accused does not even have to be the one who pulled the trigger. If he is part of a group that is engaged in a felony, such as a bank robbery or a convenience store holdup, and one of his confederates kills a person, he can be liable for the death penalty in several American jurisdictions.

Rather than the net of capital crimes in America growing more limited, it is being widened to catch more and more defendants of varying and lesser degrees of culpability. Jurisdictions are able to "conflate degrees of criminality, permitting, for example, the punishment of manslaughterers as if they were murderers."[31] Even fundamental legal protections are being eroded through procedural devices, e.g., shifting the burden of proof "with respect to defenses that define culpability, such as requiring defendants accused of murder to prove self-defense."[32]

Also, the American death penalty does not require the exclusion of testimony from witnesses that are inconsistent on essential, material facts of the crime. Those matters are simply submitted to the jury for their consideration.

CERTAINTY OF GUILT

There is no mechanism in the American death penalty that even allows us to argue with a straight face that absolute certainty of guilt is required as a condition to execution. It just is not there. The standard is simply guilty "beyond a reasonable doubt."

Although the American ideal for testimony in capital cases might be *moral certainty of guilt*, as proposed by Governor Keating, or *clear and overwhelming evidence of guilt*, as proposed by the Southern Baptist Convention in Resolution No. 5, the actual practice in America is simply guilty beyond a reasonable doubt. Both the ideal and the practice fall far short of the biblical standard, which requires absolute certainty of guilt and does not allow for even the slightest unreasonable doubt. The American death penalty is far, far below the threshold of absolute certainty of guilt required by biblical truth.

There was a moment, historically, when it might have been possible to raise the American standard closer to the biblical one. After the U.S. Supreme Court overturned all the existing death penalty statutes in 1972,[33] many states wrote statutes that closely paralleled the recommendations of the American Law Institute's (ALI) Model Penal Code.[34] Indeed, in *Gregg v. Georgia*, which gave approval to some states' new statutes, the Supreme Court specifically referred to the Model Penal Code as a source for constructing an acceptable new statute.[35]

In the Model Penal Code, there was an attempt to minimize mistaken executions by allowing the trial court to withhold a death sentence if the evidence left some doubt about the defendant's guilt, presumably any doubt that was less than a reasonable doubt. The drafters of the code realized the lingering possibility of innocence despite a conviction "beyond a reasonable doubt." Unfortunately, neither Florida nor any other state that employs the American death penalty has adopted this protection against the execution of the innocent. There is no place in the United States where the standard for the death penalty is absolute certainty of guilt.

> Gov. Frank Keating [a prominent faith-based conservative] recently suggested that a "moral certainty" standard replace the "beyond a reasonable doubt" standard now needed for a capital conviction. "[I]f you intend to take another person's life [through capital punishment] the only way we who believe in it can ensure that it will survive is that no innocent person be mistakenly put to death," Keating said. "And for us, to raise that bar and require that a capital crime, when you are taking a person's life, be a moral certainty standard, I think is not only appropriate, I think it is essential."[36]

CLOSING THOUGHTS

Governor Keating said he would seek to have the higher standard of moral certainty written into Oklahoma law. So far, neither

Oklahoma nor any other American state has incorporated the "moral certainty" of guilt standard for capital punishment. None have adopted the much higher biblical standard of absolute certainty of guilt into their death penalty laws.

We have our answer. The biblical truth of Torah/Pentateuch and the provisions of Talmud that fulfill those scriptural demands reveal that the American death penalty does not meet biblical standards when it comes to certainty of guilt and the kinds of evidence and testimony required to establish the guilt of the accused.

The next stop in our search is the issue of evidence of innocence. Perhaps the American death penalty will fare better under biblical truth on that score.

Chapter Fourteen

AN INNOCENT PERSON YOU SHALL NOT SLAY

INNOCENCE VERSUS CLOSURE

One of the hottest political issues concerning the American death penalty has been the struggle between closure of cases and allowing posttrial evidence of innocence. On the one hand, it seems reasonable to some Americans that executions should occur within five years of a death sentence. Efforts to make this happen have focused upon curtailing appeals and barring new evidence. But what about late-discovered evidence of innocence?

The biblical death penalty also had to deal with this issue. The primary concern of the biblical death penalty is the fear of executing the innocent. The biblical basis for this concern (Exod. 23:7) is the driving force behind the procedures for posttrial evidence under the biblical death penalty. The biblical death penalty is intensely concerned that no one be executed if he is innocent or has evidence of mitigating factors. Mitigating factors are facts in the case establishing that even if the accused committed the killing, he should not receive the death penalty.

Under the biblical death penalty, such evidence of innocence and mitigation is to be sought by the court and to be heard by the court right up to the very moment of execution.

Once a verdict has been reached and the defendant is pronounced guilty, they take him out to stone him. The stoning place was located outside the courthouse. . . . While the condemned is being escorted to the execution grounds, one man stands at the courthouse door with flags in his hand, and another sits astride a horse at a distance from him, but still within his sight. If someone says: I have grounds to argue for his acquittal, [the flagman] waves the flag as a signal, and the horse with its rider races to the execution party and halts them. And even if [the condemned] himself says, "I have grounds to argue for my own acquittal," they return him to the courthouse to consider his arguments. He is returned again and again, even four or five times, as long as there is substance to his words.[1] (bracketed language in original)

Although this passage from the Mishnah specifically discusses a verdict of stoning, the same pre-execution procedure applies for all the methods of execution: stoning, burning, beheading, and strangulation.[2] The purpose of this elaborate procedure is to preserve the ability to stop a wrongful execution right up to the last possible moment.

A man sits astride a horse as far as possible from the one with the flags so that if the flags are waved to signal that the case has been reopened, he will have the best possible chance to reach the prisoner in time to prevent his execution. Obviously, he must remain within sight of the flagman so that he will see him if he signals.[3]

The flagman signals the horseman, who races to the execution party to stop the proceedings until it can be determined if this new evidence is sufficient to reverse the court decision.[4]

Because the concern is to avoid the execution of an innocent person, the standards of the biblical death penalty place no limit on the number of times that the defendant may be returned to the court to hear new evidence:

Even if the condemned states this four or five times, he is returned each time. These numbers are used arbitrarily; there is

actually no limit to the number of times he may be brought
back for reconsideration of his case so long as the situation
meets the [following requirement]:[5]

If he presents an argument that seems to have some validity,
he is returned to the court for consideration of his argument.[6]
(bracketed language mine)

The place of execution is required to be both outside the city
and at a significant distance from the courthouse. This means that
if the courthouse is already outside the city, the place of execution must still be at least six thousand paces farther away from
the courthouse.[7] Why such a far distance? "Placing the execution
grounds at a distance from the court means the condemned man
must travel some time to get there. This allows extra time for
someone to approach the court with new evidence or arguments
that could lead the court to reverse its decision."[8]

Under the biblical death penalty, what does it mean that the
condemned man is returned if there is "substance to his words"?
For the first and second time, the condemned is given a presumption of the benefit of the doubt. He is returned to the courthouse
the first two times whether or not it appears there is substance in
his words. "The first two times he is returned even if his argument
appears baseless, for it is possible that he indeed has a valid argument but is unable to express it due to his fright. When he returns
to the courthouse, his mind will become more settled and he will
be able to present his case more coherently."[9]

Once the man is returned to the courthouse, the evidence is
heard and a new decision entered. In addition to the flagman
and the horseman, whose presence ensure the ability to halt the
execution, the biblical death penalty also requires an affirmative
effort to seek out evidence of innocence or mitigation right up to
the moment of execution. "If they found a reason to acquit him,
they would acquit him; but if not, he goes out to be stoned. A
proclamation would be called out before him, worded in the following way: 'So-and-so the son of So-and-so is being taken out
to be stoned, for he has transgressed such-and-such a prohibition,
and So-and-so and So-and-so are his witnesses. Whoever knows
any grounds for his acquittal, let him come forward and present
them.'"[10]

Under the standards of the biblical death penalty, nothing takes priority over making sure that an innocent man is never executed. The requirement for a crier seeking out evidence to exonerate the condemned applies to every death sentence, even the first.

> Whenever someone is being taken out to be executed, whether following the original verdict or after subsequent reconsideration, an official crier would travel in advance of the procession. He would announce who was being executed and for what transgression, as well as the names of the witnesses whose testimony led to his conviction.[11]

> The crier makes the declaration so as to alert anyone who knows something that could overturn the verdict. If someone does, in fact, come forward to present new facts or arguments, the case is reconsidered as described above.[12]

There were some opinions that the biblical death penalty even required an affirmative effort to find evidence that would impeach the witnesses against the accused. In certain cases, this evidence could result in the death penalty being imposed on the false witnesses: "And it is also necessary to say: 'The transgression was committed on such-and-such a day at such-and-such a time, and in such-and-such a place.' This is necessary because there might be people who know that these witnesses could not possibly have witnessed the alleged crime, and they will come and discredit [the witnesses]."[13] (bracketed language in original)

These additional statements would add to the power of the standard questions for purposes of subjecting false witnesses to the death penalty. We will address that process in the next chapter. For the time being, however, our search focuses on the standards set by biblical truth with respect to posttrial evidence of innocence or mitigation. "Jewish law is deeply concerned with factual guilt, so much so that it is absolutely clear that only the guilty can be convicted."[14]

How does the admission into court of posttrial evidence under the American death penalty stack up against the standards of biblical truth with respect to late-discovered evidence of innocence under the scriptures of Torah/Pentateuch and the provisions of Talmud necessary to meet those requirements?

POSTTRIAL EVIDENCE OF INNOCENCE OR MITIGATION

Unfortunately, under the American death penalty, in some cases it appears that we are less concerned about executing the innocent than about making sure we execute somebody.

> There is considerable evidence that the crisis of wrongful death penalty convictions has worsened: the annual average of people released from death row because of their innocence has increased . . . while the opportunity to appeal and to raise newly discovered evidence of one's innocence has recently shrunk dramatically. . . . Some courts have now taken the position that it is permissible for executions to go forward even in the face of considerable doubt about the defendant's guilt.[15]

Many, perhaps even most, of the people being released from America's death rows after exoneration are being freed because of the efforts of those outside the system: journalism students, volunteers, pro bono experts. Instead of these releases standing as evidence that the system is working, they stand as a poignant indictment of the inaccuracies and errors in America's death penalty system.

Those who have been through the system know this best of all. In Alabama, Randall Padgett spent seven years on death row before he was released in 1997, exonerated from guilt for the murder of his wife. Ronald Thompson, prosecutor in the case of Padgett, said the case reflects imperfections in the judicial system: "'The jury system isn't perfect,' Thompson said. 'It doesn't acquit everyone who is innocent and it doesn't find guilty everyone who is guilty.'"[16]

Perhaps Randall Padgett would be inclined to agree.

> Padgett said he used to think that the police always got the right man. Now he knows differently:
>
> When I heard something on the news, that we arrested someone at such and such time, I would say, "Well, good. They finally got the criminal." I thought in the good ol' U.S. of A., that when you went to court and you went to trial, the truth was supposed to be foremost and the court endeavors to

seek out the truth, you know, but I know firsthand that's not how it is.[17]

The system itself has "circled the wagons," responding to the constant flow of newly discovered wrongful death penalty convictions by making it more difficult for people to establish their innocence. Some of those efforts aim at prohibiting evidence of innocence from being heard in a court. In Florida,[18] a condemned man can only introduce evidence of innocence within one to two years after the Florida Supreme Court affirms his death sentence.[19] In Texas, one can only do so within eighteen months after being sentenced to death.[20] In Virginia the deadline is twenty-one days, but it has been temporarily extended to ninety days.*

Virginia's deadline for allowing new evidence of innocence— the toughest in the nation—has come under increasing scrutiny in recent years as stories of wrongly convicted inmates in Virginia and across the country make headlines.

The state had long barred the introduction of any new evidence more than three weeks after sentencing. But a 2001 law gave inmates the right to ask for DNA tests anytime and Virginia voters last fall approved a constitutional amendment that allows felons to present that scientific evidence to the Virginia Supreme Court to seek a "writ of actual innocence.". . .

[Senator Kenneth W. Stolle (R-Virginia Beach) said on January 8, 2002] that he believes Virginia's current system works well, but that he was moved to take action because there is public sentiment that three weeks is not enough time. His bill would extend the deadline from 21 days to 90 days.

"I think 21 days is sufficient," Stolle said. "The only reason I'm doing this is the perception of the public. There is a general recognition that we have to have the confidence of the public for the criminal justice system to work."

Stolle predicted that his 90-day deadline would become law this year.[21]

The public sentiment he refers to is the Virginia state constitutional amendment approved by voters in the fall of 2002 "that

*© 2003, The Washington Post. Reprinted with permission.

allows felons to present scientific evidence to the Virginia Supreme Court and to seek a writ of actual innocence."[22] Not everyone is as comfortable as Senator Stolle that twenty-one days or even ninety days is enough when the question involves execution of the innocent: "'What's fundamentally unfair about the 21-day rule will not change by doubling or tripling the time period,' said Peter Neufeld, co-director of the Innocence Project. 'If a man can demonstrate to the court that new evidence discovered five years after conviction proves his innocence, to keep him behind bars for any reason is irrational and unjust.'"[23]

Other efforts around the country have attempted to clear the way for executions to proceed despite evidence of innocence. For example, in Texas the court is prohibited from considering evidence of innocence after the 180-day period unless the condemned shows either that the evidence didn't exist during the 180-day period or that a violation of the U.S. Constitution caused him to be wrongly convicted or wrongly sentenced to death. The fact that the evidence shows him to be innocent is virtually irrelevant.[24]

In Florida, a law was passed making it a second-degree felony for someone to recant prior sworn testimony in a capital case even though the prior testimony was untrue.[25] Yes, in Florida, it can now be a felony to tell the truth under oath in a death penalty case. The statute adds that it is not necessary to prove which, if any, of the contradictory statements are not true.[26] Unlike the previous law, the prosecution need only prove that a witness has changed his testimony about a material element, not that he is in fact lying in his testimony. This allows prosecutors who bargained for false testimony to threaten prosecution of witnesses who now want to tell the truth in order to prevent the execution of an innocent man. Even if the new testimony is the truth, the fact that it contradicts prior testimony is sufficient to jail the witness.

Lest anyone be lulled into thinking that the law is for show, merely to discourage witnesses from changing what has been said under oath, rest assured, the law has teeth. And Florida prosecutors who have had their cases overturned are not hesitant to use them. In November 2003, the two witnesses who recanted their testimony in the case of Rudolph Holton were each sentenced on a "single charge of perjury by conflicting statements in a capital case."[27] One was sentenced to thirteen years, the other to fourteen years, in state prison.

There has not, however, been any word of any investigation into the prosecutors who cut the deals for those witnesses to testify for the state against Mr. Holton in exchange for favorable treatment from the state. Nor has there been any clamoring in the state capitol in Tallahassee for legislative reforms that would stop the practice.

Perhaps the most dramatic example of how Florida's felony "by conflicting statements in a capital case" plays out in favor of the state against innocent citizens is the case of James Duckett, a former policeman in rural Florida. Mr. Duckett claims he was framed by small-town politics and has been on Florida's death row for over fifteen years.[28] The state's star witness has recanted her testimony "in at least six separate interviews to different people."[29] But if she does so under oath in court, the prosecutor can escort her from the witness stand to the jail. The defendant's attorneys have asserted that

[t]his statute [the felony by conflicting statements in capital cases law] was proposed and passed as a response to witnesses in capital cases admitting that they had previously lied to assist the state in gaining a capital conviction. Presumably, the legislature felt that these capital defendants should not have a second bite at the apple (despite the fact that the first bite was poisoned by false testimony).[30] (parenthetical in original; bracketed language mine)

If that is in fact the purpose of the statute, then it seems to be working. Duckett's situation has been reported by the *Orlando Sentinel*:

It took a little more than a year for the state's case to start disintegrating.

In an Aug. 3, 1989, deposition with a defense lawyer, Gurley, the one witness who said she saw Duckett drive off with "a small person" in his patrol car, said she made her testimony up.

Gurley said she went along with whatever detectives and

prosecutors told her to say—an allegation they deny—because she was pregnant, in jail and facing a long prison sentence.

During one of Duckett's appeals in the fall of 1997, defense attorneys expected Gurley to say she never saw Duckett drive off with anyone that night. Instead, she refused to answer any questions about what she did or didn't see.

Florida law says if you lie during a capital-murder case, you can be sent to prison for seven years. Gurley said in a recent interview that she was aware of the law when called to testify during the 1997 appeal, and that's why she wouldn't say anything.[31]

James Duckett is still sitting on Florida's death row, and the state is still pressing toward his execution.

Historically, the federal courts were a place to seek redress from such evidentiary disasters. Not anymore. The Anti-Terrorism and Effective Death Penalty Act of 1996 severely limits the ability of federal courts to hear posttrial evidence of innocence that state courts have refused to consider: "The law . . . will have a devastating impact on poor people convicted of crimes. While the poor are entitled to legal representation for trials and one appeal, lawyers are not provided for post-conviction review. Thus, many people will be unable to comply with the time limit as they will not have lawyers to prepare and file the necessary legal documents."[32]

Most important, for purposes of our discussion, the law impedes federal review of late-found evidence of innocence: "Additionally, it places barriers to the filing of a second petition for review. Even if new evidence that was not known to the convicted person when the first petition was filed is found, the courts are barred from hearing the case."[33]

The shortened time limits created by the Anti-Terrorism and Effective Death Penalty Act pose an especially egregious risk of executing poor defendants with late-discovered evidence of innocence. Because they lack the resources to hire an attorney, they may be unable to meet the shorter time limits allowed for federal courts to review new evidence. "[The shortened time periods] came less than one year after Congress eliminated federal funding for capital resource centers which provided representation to condemned people during post-conviction review. . . .

"[We have lost] a fundamental safeguard that protected poor people facing the death penalty from unconstitutional executions."[34]

Instead of imitating the biblical death penalty by preserving the ability to introduce all credible evidence up to the last minute, the American death penalty is moving away from the biblical standard. Before 1996, America allowed some late-discovered evidence of innocence, even though the procedural hurdles were formidable. Now, very little of such late-discovered evidence is allowed and the procedural impediments have been drastically increased. Both the pre-1996 situation and the current one are completely inconsistent with the biblical standard that required freely admitting any evidence of innocence at any time, without procedural hurdles of any kind, right up to the moment that an execution was beginning.

Despite the increasing legal impediments against allowing a court to hear posttrial evidence of innocence, more and more wrongfully convicted people are walking off America's death rows. Who can guess how many would be able to show their innocence if the barriers to court review of their evidence were dropped?

What kinds of posttrial evidence cannot be heard after the short time periods have expired? The following is a sampling of actual cases from around America.[35]

FLORIDA

In Florida, at least twenty-three inmates, including Frank Lee Smith who died of cancer on death row, have been exonerated. Twenty-two Florida inmates have walked off death row—in three cases within sixteen hours of execution—after evidence emerged that they were wrongly convicted. Frank Lee Smith died before the DNA testing exonerated him. No state has found more wrongfully condemned prisoners on its death row than Florida.[36]

In at least 50 percent of these cases, it took longer than five years for the condemned men to establish their innocence.[37] Even so, Florida's death penalty system fought for years to prevent courts from hearing DNA test results: "In some states, new DNA technology has cleared inmates who had been convicted of murder or rape. In Florida, some prosecutors have resisted such DNA tests, citing a two-year limit on the introduction of new evidence."[38]

Florida still has people on death row who claim they are innocent and have always claimed they are innocent. In at least two cases, death row defendants pleaded for years for DNA testing of the evidence that was used to convict them.[39] One of those cases involves William "Tommy" Zeigler, a fifty-six-year-old man from Winter Garden, Florida, who has been on death row for over twenty-seven years, charged and convicted of the 1975 Christmas Eve slaughter of his wife and in-laws at the family furniture store.

The prosecuting attorney, a renowned DNA expert, fought for over three years to proceed with killing Zeigler without DNA testing. In August 2001 Zeigler asked again for DNA testing of the crime scene blood in order to prepare his clemency petition to the governor. An Orange County circuit judge ruled that the DNA tests could be performed because of the judicial need for "an abundance of caution" and "to instill confidence in the judicial system."[40]

The initial DNA test results supported the defendant's innocence and completely contradicted the blood splatter testimony that the state had used to win a conviction at trial.[41] The local press ran a story, with quotes from the state attorney's office, claiming that the DNA test results did not matter.[42] Almost unnoticed was the fact that a different judge was assigned to the case to replace the judge who allowed DNA testing in this high-profile matter.

The Florida case of Mr. Zeigler, which has gained international notoriety,[43] provides additional examples of facts that the courts are not allowed to review, including that the prosecution "buried" the original police report and used a "revised" police report at trial. (The original police report did not support the guilt of the accused; the revised police report did.) No jury has ever seen the original police report.

The state also "buried" a tape recording of the state's investigator suggesting to the only independent eyewitnesses that they might revise their memory to help the state's case if they wanted to be called as witnesses (and be given a free trip from Minnesota back to Florida). Those witnesses did not testify at the trial in

1976. The state did not call them and never told the defense of their existence or of their statements.

These facts and other "hidden" evidence came to light in 1987. The defendant, Zeigler, who has always maintained his innocence, has been trying for seventeen years to get the evidence heard by a court. No court has yet been able to hear the evidence because the time period had expired before the evidence came to light.[44]

Now, facing a DNA test report that is favorable to the defendant, the state has moved to limit any evidentiary hearing to only the DNA test results and to exclude all the other posttrial evidence of innocence.[45] This legal maneuver is to prevent the court from looking for the first time at the massive accumulation of other posttrial evidence of innocence in addition to the DNA test results. The state's motion was granted, so now the state will argue that the DNA test results *standing alone* do not prove the defendant is innocent and, therefore, the state should be allowed to execute him.

The state has consistently followed a two-pronged strategy in the Zeigler appeals: (1) arguing to the courts that the evidence of innocence is too old to be evaluated and (2) arguing to the public, in the media, that "Zeigler has appealed his conviction repeatedly and lost."[46] The public is thus lulled into thinking that the courts have reviewed Zeigler's evidence of innocence repeatedly and found it without merit.

The state never tells the public that they have spent untold hundreds of thousands—if not millions—of dollars in legal maneuvering to prevent the courts from considering Zeigler's evidence of innocence. Nor has the state ever disclosed to the public that the courts could immediately review Zeigler's guilt or innocence on the merits, once and for all, if the state simply agreed to allow the judge to consider all the new evidence and to make a decision.

Based upon the state's arguments in Zeigler's case, it is clear that actual guilt or innocence is irrelevant in Florida. The goal is execution notwithstanding the mountain of evidence of innocence discovered after the trial.

With respect to other inmates with DNA-testable evidence,

Florida has finally passed a statute allowing DNA testing but only for inmates who did not agree to a plea bargain.[47]

TEXAS

When Leonel Herrera's attorneys tried to introduce evidence that another man had confessed to the crime for which Leonel was facing execution, the federal courts concluded that such evidence was irrelevant to their deliberations. Leonel Herrera may have been innocent, but he was not innocent enough to satisfy the U.S. Supreme Court.[48]

A former Texas judge submitted an affidavit stating that another man had confessed to the crime for which Herrera was facing execution. Numerous other pieces of new evidence also threw doubt on his conviction. Still, the U.S. Supreme Court said that at the late stage of his appeal, he needed an extraordinary amount of proof to stop his execution. He was executed in Texas in 1993. One U.S. Supreme Court justice, who had been a long-time death penalty supporter, dissented from the court majority, writing: "Of one thing, however, I am certain. Just as an execution without adequate safeguards is unacceptable, so too is an execution when the condemned prisoner can prove he is innocent. *The execution of a person who can prove he is innocent comes perilously close to simple murder.*"[49] (italics mine)

VIRGINIA

Since the death penalty was reinstated in 1976, there have been inmates with reasonably credible claims of innocence who were nevertheless executed, some without a full review of those claims. One is Roger Keith Coleman.

Coleman was convicted of raping and murdering his sister-in-law in 1981, but both his trial and appeal were plagued by errors made by his attorneys. Coleman's representation at trial was shoddy. On appeal, his new attorneys misread the state statute governing the time for submitting an appeal and filed their brief one day too late. The Virginia state courts held that this late filing was the same as no filing and refused to review his issues. The federal courts then said that he could not raise a federal claim because he had waived his state review. The mistake by Coleman's attorneys in failing to file by the deadline was legally treated as a waiver of his rights to review.

The U.S. Supreme Court refused to consider the merits of his petition because his state appeal had been filed one day late. Finally, the Supreme Court said that he could not complain that it was his attorney who erred, since he was not entitled to an attorney in the first place.[50]

Considerable evidence was developed after the trial to refute the state's evidence, and that evidence might well have produced a different result at a retrial. Coleman was executed without a full review of his innocence claims.

It must be noted that Governor Wilder considered a commutation for Coleman, but allowed him to be executed when *Coleman failed a lie detector test on the day of his execution*. Unfortunately for Coleman, a lie detector test measures stress as a way of determining whether one is lying. Can anyone imagine a person not being stressed on the day of his execution?

THE WEST COAST

When Paris Carriger brought both his constitutional and innocence claims before the U.S. Court of Appeals for the Ninth Circuit, he was still denied relief. The chief witness against Carriger was a police informant, Robert Dunbar, who was given immunity for three felonies in exchange for his testimony. Later Dunbar admitted that it was he, not Carriger, who had committed the murder and that he had lied at the trial. He even admitted his guilt in court and again just before his death.[51]

When a three-judge panel of the court of appeals reviewed this new evidence, they concluded that the recantation did raise "serious doubts about Dunbar's credibility," a highly significant issue because the government relied heavily on Dunbar's testimony in prosecuting Carriger.[52]

Doubt about the government's chief witness led to doubt about Carriger's guilt. The court wrote, "Compared to many other capital cases we have seen, the evidence of guilt here is not overwhelming."[53] However, the court would still not grant Carriger any relief because the flimsiness of the state's case is not enough to stop an execution "under *Herrera* and its progeny, which put the burden on the petitioner to show he is unquestionably innocent. This Carriger has not done."[54]

The *Herrera* standard, which is now law in the American death penalty, imposes upon innocent defendants with significant evidence of innocence a daunting task. To avoid execution, they must meet the postconviction standard of establishing "unquestionable innocence." This is almost insurmountable.

In regard to posttrial evidence of innocence, biblical truth requires that the defendant be shown to be unquestionably guilty. The American death penalty requires that the defendant show he is unquestionably innocent. The two are at opposite ends of the spectrum.

MISSOURI

Some prosecuting attorneys have now gone so far as to argue that the courts do not even have the legal authority to stop the execution of an innocent man:

> Frank Jung, an assistant to Missouri Attorney General Jay Nixon, recently told the Missouri Supreme Court that it should not concern itself with mounting evidence that death row inmate Joseph Amrine might be innocent. Jung said the Court's sole consideration must be whether Amrine's constitutional rights had been violated, and he noted that even if DNA evidence conclusively exonerated an inmate, the court would need a constitutional violation to stop an execution.
>
> One judge asked Jung, "Is it not cruel and unusual punishment to execute an innocent person?"
>
> Jung responded, "If there is no underlying constitutional violation, there is not a right to relief."[55]

The Missouri Supreme Court rejected the state's argument in the Amrine case and overturned the conviction, but only by a four-to-three margin. Originally the state of Missouri filed new charges against Amrine for the same crime;[56] however, in July of 2003, the prosecution dropped the case and Amrine was released.[57]

The critical factor regarding evidence of innocence in a capital case under the American system is timing. If one is fortunate enough to have competent counsel and the resources to thoroughly investigate the case before trial, and if the necessary evidence of innocence is available then, and if the police and the prosecutors have not buried the evidence of innocence, there is a chance that a conviction and death sentence can be avoided by an innocent person.

On the other hand, if the competent counsel or the new evidence does not become available until after trial, the same evidence will often be rejected on technical procedural grounds. This is called "procedural default."

"Procedural default" and "procedural bar" work as follows: A man who claims innocence has been sentenced to death. Three or five or ten years or more after his trial, he or his lawyer discovers evidence that would have shown him innocent at trial. He asks the court to review his newfound evidence. "Procedural default" and "procedural bar" say, "Sorry, you are too late. The court could have heard your evidence of innocence last year, last month, last week, last decade, but the time for hearing evidence has expired. We have deadlines in order to expedite executions. It is a shame that you and your lawyer did not discover this evidence sooner, but maybe if you had tried harder, you would have found it in time."

The man is said to be "in procedural default" because the time limitations for his filing were not met. His evidence of innocence is said to be "procedurally barred" because no court can hear it. That is it. Period. The evidence of innocence will not be heard.

There is no such thing as "procedural default" or "procedural bar" under the standards of the biblical death penalty. Procedural default and procedural bar are both an abomination to the Bible and an abdication of the moral responsibility required of us by biblical faith.

"Closure," "expediency," and "cost cutting" may be politically valued, but they are not biblical values when it comes to the death penalty. Biblical truth reveals that nothing is allowed to interfere with the binding command that we shall not slay the innocent. Nothing.

The biblical truth of Torah/Pentateuch and the provisions of Talmud necessary to fulfill those scriptures mandate that we spend whatever money is necessary and take whatever time is necessary to assure absolute certainty of guilt before an execution. If we do not have the time or cannot afford the money, then biblical truth tells us that we cannot afford the death penalty.

POTENTIAL FOR WRONGFUL CONVICTIONS

Clearly, the American death penalty is not biblical when it comes to matters of posttrial evidence of innocence or mitigation, especially with respect to procedural default. Can we instead take solace in an assumption that our American system is safely reliable in convicting only the guilty?

Unfortunately, contrary to what we might assume, the potential for error and the risk of erroneous conviction is greater in death penalty cases than in ordinary American criminal cases.[58] Part of the reason for this is that the death penalty has become more and more political as legislators, prosecutors, and even judges promote the death penalty in their campaigns as an easy way to garner votes.[59]

Incumbents who will be running for reelection champion bills to expand the death penalty to cover more crimes. Prosecutors seeking political notoriety may pursue a death sentence even when the evidence is weak, and they may be reluctant to change course when contradictory evidence later arises.[60] Wrongful prosecution can be the unintended by-product of excessive zeal and political ambition. "A common route to the bench is through a prosecutor's office, where trying high-profile capital cases can result in publicity and name recognition for a prosecutor with judicial ambitions."[61]

When we add to this political momentum behind possibly erroneous death penalty cases the fact that recent changes in the appeals process, especially in federal courts as mentioned earlier, have made it more likely that executions will proceed even in the face of evidence raising doubts about a defendant's guilt,[62] it becomes all too clear that America's death penalty is falling below any standard of biblical accountability. Perhaps that explains why wrongful convictions in American death penalty cases are more likely than in other criminal cases.

Professor Samuel Gross, a noted author and researcher at the University of Michigan Law School, recently explored the reasons why this is true.[63] Among the reasons he gave are: the great pressure on police and prosecutors to "solve" the most notorious murders in a community; typical lack of eyewitness testimony and reliance upon unreliable witnesses; heightened publicity at trial; death-qualified juries (Juries in death penalty cases are always quizzed about their attitudes on capital punishment before the start of the trial. Those who could not impose a death verdict are eliminated from the jury pool.); and heinousness of the facts alone can make it more likely that the jury will ignore reasonable doubts and return a guilty verdict.

Another facet of the problem is the inaccuracy of our best efforts to investigate and solve crimes through circumstantial forensic evidence.[64] A view of the scope of the problem of error in the American criminal justice system is contained in a 1996 Department of Justice report on the use of DNA evidence. The report catalogs numerous cases, mostly from the late 1980s, in which previous convictions were overturned upon DNA testing. Some of these cases involved defendants on death row.[65] In commentary accompanying the report, Peter Neufeld and Barry Scheck note how often the police focus on the wrong suspect:

> Every year since 1989, in about 25 percent of the sexual assault cases referred to the FBI where results could be obtained . . . the primary suspect has been excluded by forensic DNA testing. . . . The fact that these percentages have remained constant for 7 years, and that the National Institute of Justice's informal survey of private laboratories reveals a strikingly similar 26-percent exclusion rate, strongly suggests . . . underlying

systemic problems that generate erroneous accusations and convictions.[66]

It is indeed disturbing that one out of four defendants accused of a serious crime and at least one[67]—maybe as many as four or five[68]—out of every one hundred persons condemned to the death penalty in America are in fact innocent. Such a record would be totally unacceptable for a car company whose cars were so defective that one out of every one hundred vehicles produced a fatal crash; or a hospital where service was so incompetent that one out of every one hundred patients died erroneously. Yet that is the case with the American death penalty system.

INNOCENCE VERSUS TECHNICAL FLAWS

We must be very careful to distinguish between factual innocence on the one hand and constitutional or technical legal violations on the other. Both can result in appellate courts granting new trials. The media and some politicians mix the two as though they were interchangeable. For example, a 2001 editorial in a major Florida newspaper stated that "Florida leads the nation in the number of people—21—who have been removed from death row in the past two decades because the defendants were later found innocent or because of serious flaws in the way cases were handled."[69] In reality over 70 percent of Florida's death sentences have been reversed for serious constitutional flaws. The number referenced in the editorial was for those that have come off Florida's death row because of significant evidence of innocence (that number now stands at 23). They are not the same.

Since 1973, 114 people in twenty-five states have been released from death row in America with evidence of their innocence.[70] The average number of years between being sentenced to death and exoneration has been more than 9.0 years.[71] DNA evidence played a substantial factor in establishing innocence in thirteen of those cases.[72]

Those numbers do not include reversals of convictions for constitutional and technical legal reasons. A study that reviewed 5,760 American death penalty cases between 1973 and 1995 found that in 68 percent, seven out of every ten, reviewing courts found serious reversible constitutional or other legal error: "only 313 (5.4%; one in 19) resulted in an execution during that period."[73]

A new follow-up study by the same researchers[74] finds that states and counties that make the most use of the death penalty— applying it to a wide range of crimes instead of reserving it for "the worst of the worst"—are also the most prone to flawed verdicts. This prompted one observer to note that when it comes to the American death penalty, practice does not make perfect.[75]

This high percentage of reversals, which is based on violations of complicated constitutional procedures, must be distinguished from the problem of the inability of death row inmates to introduce before a court posttrial evidence of innocence or mitigation. Both matters are serious concerns, yet each is a separate problem.

A FLOOD OF EVIDENCE-DRIVEN APPEALS

We've all heard the laments from politicians and prosecutors about the incredible number of death row appeals based on incompetence of the condemned man's trial lawyer. Only by investigating that situation did I find out what is really going on.

One of the few legal exceptions that will allow posttrial evidence of innocence to be heard by a court after the time period has expired is if the condemned man's trial attorney was incompetent. In case after case after case, appeals are clogging our court systems with claims of attorney incompetence. But that is not the real issue.

The real issue is that evidence of innocence or mitigation has come to light after trial—in many cases evidence that was hidden by the police or the prosecutors—and the defendant wants a court to hear the evidence. The prosecutors have responded that the time for new evidence has expired. So, the only way the condemned man can try to get his evidence heard in court is by claiming his trial lawyer was incompetent.

A secular observer who is not concerned about biblical standards might simply observe that this whole system is crazy, the worst of both worlds, and a gross waste of taxpayers' money without producing justice. That is not our concern.

We are searching for evidence as to whether America's death penalty meets the standards of the biblical death penalty with respect to concerns about executing the innocent. Consequently, the concerns of judges involved in the process are of interest to us. The following is a sampling from different levels of courts around the country.

ILLINOIS

Justice Harrison, recently retired from the Illinois Supreme Court, wrote:

Despite the courts' efforts to fashion a death penalty scheme that is just, fair, and reliable, the system is not working. Innocent people are being sentenced to death. . . . The prognosis for wrongly accused defendants facing capital charges is not improving. To the contrary, legislatures and the courts appear to have abandoned any genuine concern with insuring the fairness and reliability of the system.

Achieving "finality" in death cases, and doing so as expeditiously as possible, have become the dominant goals in death penalty jurisprudence. . . . It is no answer to say that we are doing the best we can. If this is the best our state can do, we have no business sending people to their deaths.[76]

FLORIDA

Retired Florida Supreme Court chief justice Gerald Kogan, a former homicide detective and prosecutor before eventually rising to chief justice of the Florida Supreme Court, has said he had "grave doubts" about the guilt of some of the people executed in Florida:

There are several cases where I had grave doubts as to the guilt of a particular person.[77]

I estimate that, in the last 40 years, I have participated either as a prosecutor, as a defense attorney or a trial judge or as an appellate judge on the Supreme Court in the disposition of more than 1,200 capital cases. I don't know of anyone else in the State of Florida who has that kind of experience or, for that matter, that kind of varying type of experience. So, when I speak to you, I speak to you based upon what, I hope, has been those things I have learned in the last 40 years. . . .

. . . [T]here is no question in my mind, and I can tell you this having seen the dynamics of our criminal justice system over the many years that I have been associated with it, prosecutor, defense attorney, trial judge and Supreme Court Justice, that convinces me that we certainly have, in the past, executed those people who either didn't fit the criteria for execution in the State of Florida or who, in fact, were, factually, not guilty of the crime for which they have been executed. . . .

. . . [Y]ou have to ask yourself, how many persons did we execute prior to the arrival of DNA evidence who would have been released, had we had that tool working for us 25, 30, 40, 50 years ago?[78]

TEXAS

Senior state district judge C. C. Cooke recently expressed his concerns about the fairness of the death penalty during a legal seminar. The Texas judge recalled how the eleven death penalty cases he presided over during his twenty-three years as a judge altered his feelings about capital punishment. Cooke helped craft the state's death penalty law when he served as a state representative: "I was looking at it as a young politician, with about 90 percent of my district supporting the death penalty. Now, from a judge's perspective and taking care of people's rights, I think it has a lot of flaws. . . . I think the mood is changing in this country and people are realizing there are deficiencies in the system. We always think we've got the right person, but the system is not infallible."[79]

ARIZONA

Former Arizona court of appeals judge Rudolph J. Gerber expressed his concerns about the death penalty in a recent article in the *Arizona Law Review*. Gerber, who spent over twenty-five years as a prosecutor and judge, wrote: "[T]here remain the disturbing facts . . . that our capital punishment falls disproportionately on minorities . . . and sweeps some innocent defendants . . . in its wide nets."[80]

FEDERAL DISTRICT COURT

Federal trial judge Michael Posner felt the need to set the record straight on the American death penalty system, even under the best of circumstances: "The experience left me with one unavoidable conclusion: that a legal regime relying on the death penalty will inevitably execute innocent people—not too often, one hopes, but undoubtedly sometimes. Mistakes will be made because it is simply not possible to do something this difficult perfectly, all the time. Any honest proponent of capital punishment must face this fact."[81] U.S. district judge Jed S. Rakoff held "that the federal death penalty is unconstitutional because it creates 'undue risk' of executing innocent defendants":

> In brief, the court found that the best available evidence indicates that, on the one hand, innocent people are sentenced to death with materially greater frequency than was once supposed and that, on the other hand, convincing proof of their innocence often does not emerge until long after their convictions. It is, therefore, fully foreseeable that in enforcing the death penalty, a meaningful number of innocent people will be executed who otherwise would eventually be able to prove their innocence. It follows that implementation of the Federal Death Penalty . . . creates an undue risk of executing innocent people."[82]

Judge Rakoff refused to accept the government's argument that "Congress, in the exercise of its legislative prerogatives, could constitutionally decide to knowingly execute a foreseeable class of mistakenly convicted but actually innocent persons in the belief that their deaths were outweighed by the potential deterring of the murders of other innocent people."[83] "[T]he unacceptably high rate at which innocent persons are convicted of capital crimes, when coupled with the frequently prolonged delays before such errors are detected . . . compels the conclusion that execution under the Federal Death Penalty Act, by cutting off the opportunity for exoneration, denies due process and, indeed, is tantamount to foreseeable, state-sponsored murder of innocent human beings."[84]

Pro–death penalty voices disagreed with Judge Rakoff, claiming that the U.S. Constitution does not require that people be guilty in order to be executed. A spokesperson for the Criminal Justice Legal Foundation, a California-domiciled organization that advocates for the death penalty, criticized the ruling because the judge implies that the U.S. Constitution requires certainty of guilt as a condition to legal executions, and, in their opinion, "that is not the law."[85]

U.S. SUPREME COURT

This disastrous state of affairs was acknowledged by pro–death penalty U.S. Supreme Court justice Sandra Day O'Connor. In a speech to a women's law group in Minneapolis on July 2, 2001, O'Connor said that "serious questions were being raised about whether the death penalty is being fairly administered." O'Connor attributed much of the problem to the disparity in legal representation between those who have money and those who do not. "If statistics are any indication, the system may well be allowing some innocent defendants to be executed," she said.[86]

More recently, at the Nebraska State Bar Association's annual meeting, Justice O'Connor again expressed her concern about the possibility of executing the innocent and the need for better representation of indigent defendants: "More often than we want to recognize, some innocent defendants have been convicted and sentenced to death."[87]

CLOSING THOUGHTS

A sea change has occurred in our concern about executing the innocent. We are 180 degrees away from where we started.

> It used to be unthinkable that we would execute an innocent person. But now many proponents of capital punishment say it is acceptable to execute an innocent person. Representative Bill McCollum from Florida said recently that he did not think there was any question that some day somebody who was innocent would be executed, but that is just a risk we have to accept. We have gone from the concept that it was better that the guilty go free than that an innocent person be convicted, to the notion that innocent people who may be executed are acceptable casualties in the war on crime.[88]

Given this deplorable inability of the American death penalty to consistently achieve the most basic justice, the identification of those who are guilty and those who are innocent, it is not surprising to hear the following from conservative columnist George F. Will:

> Horror, too, is a reasonable response to what Barry Scheck, Peter Neufeld and Jim Dwyer demonstrate in *Actual Innocence: Five Days to Execution and Other Dispatches from the Wrongly Convicted*. You will not soon read a more frightening book. It is a catalog of appalling miscarriages of justice, some of them nearly lethal. Their cumulative weight compels the conclusion that many innocent people are in prison, and some innocent people have been executed.[89]

We have our answer.

We cannot in any way, shape, or form support the American death penalty with biblical truth when it comes to courts seeking out and hearing posttrial evidence of innocence or mitigation. In fact, the American death penalty is 180 degrees opposite from the most minimum of standards set by biblical truth.

Now, let us turn our attention to how the Bible and the American death penalty deal with false witnesses. Hopefully, we will score better on that standard.

Chapter Fifteen

LET IT BE DONE TO THEM AS THEY SOUGHT TO DO TO HIM

FALSE TESTIMONY AND PROSECUTORIAL MISCONDUCT

The primary focus of the biblical death penalty is the fear of executing the innocent. The Bible is the basis for this concern (Exod. 23:7). The biblical death penalty is intensely concerned that no one be executed if he is innocent. All evidence except eyewitness testimony is excluded. That protects against the fallacies of circumstantial evidence. The biblical death penalty also has to deal with the problem of witnesses who lie. What was to be done about the problem of dishonest witnesses? The answer is in the Bible. *Those who provide false testimony in a capital case are subject to the death penalty themselves.*

And the magistrates shall make a thorough investigation. If the man who testified is a false witness, if he has testified falsely against his fellow, you shall do to him as he schemed to do to his fellow. Thus you will sweep out evil from your midst; others will hear and be afraid, and such evil things will not again be done in your midst. Nor must you show pity: life for life, eye for eye, tooth for tooth, hand for hand, foot for foot. Deut. 19:18–21 TNK

And the judges shall make diligent inquisition: and, behold, if the witness be a false witness, and hath testified falsely against his brother; then shall ye do unto him, as he had thought to have done unto his brother. . . . And thine eye shall not pity; but life shall go for life, eye for eye, tooth for tooth, hand for hand, foot for foot.   Deut. 19:18–21 AV

The judges must make a thorough investigation, and if the witness proves to be a liar, giving false testimony against his brother, then do to him as he intended to do to his brother. . . . Show no pity: life for life, eye for eye, tooth for tooth, hand for hand, foot for foot.   Deut. 19:18–21 NIV

The biblical death penalty follows this mandate to the letter, even to the point of requiring the same form of execution: "All perjurers and illicit lovers go and suffer the form of death which they had brought on their victim: if by stoning, they are stoned, if it was by burning, they are burned."[1]

Such a false witness was treated with the utmost severity. There was some disagreement as to the interpretation of the biblical law on the subject. The disagreement, however, was not about *whether* false witnesses should be executed but rather *when* they should be executed. The Pharisees said false witnesses were to be executed at end of the trial. The Sadducees held that false witnesses were to be executed only after the defendant had been executed.[2]

The biblical death penalty distinguished between those who gave inaccurate ancillary testimony and those who gave false material testimony. False testimony was determined through a process called *hazamah*. This category was intended to detect those who were attempting to frame an innocent man. The acid test was whether they were in fact at the scene of the crime, were in fact eyewitnesses. Irregularities in other testimony that was not material nullified the testimony but did not subject the witness to the scripturally mandated death sentence.

Hazamah was the biblical death penalty process for detecting and punishing those who knew or should have known that what was being presented to the court was material and false. As we saw in chapter 13, under the biblical death penalty the court was required to establish the basis for *hazamah* by asking the seven standard questions.[3]

There were some opinions that the biblical death penalty even required an affirmative effort to find evidence that would impeach the witnesses against the accused. Therefore, the crier that led the procession to execution was required to make the additional proclamation: "'The transgression was committed on such–and-such a day at such-and-such a time, and in such-and-such a place.' This is necessary because there might be people who know that these witnesses could not possibly have witnessed the alleged crime, and they will come and discredit [the witnesses]."[4] (bracketed language in original)

These additional statements would ferret out possible counter-witnesses for purposes of *hazamah*, subjecting false witnesses to the death penalty.

> *Hazamah* is a special process by which those testifying to a crime can be discredited by a second pair of witnesses who dispute their account. The second pair claims that the first ones could not possibly have witnessed the crime in question, for the first ones were with them in a different place at the very time that the crime supposedly occurred. When *hazamah* occurs, the testimony of the first witnesses is deemed false, and the court subjects them to the identical punishment they sought to inflict upon the accused. In our *Gemara*, Abaye points out that the official criers must pinpoint exactly when and where the alleged crime took place, so as to make possible a refutation through *hazamah*.[5]

As we have noted, this pressure on the courts to seek out false testimony required the judges "to walk a fine line between defending the accused and serving the needs of justice."[6] The biblical death penalty supports judges in finding innovative ways to discredit the prosecution without subjecting the witnesses to *hazamah* if they told the truth. For example, the judges are encouraged to ask the accused for help in discrediting the witnesses against him: "This is what we say to the accused, 'Do you have other witnesses to discredit [these witnesses] through *hazamah*?'"[7] (bracketed language in original)

This will work because the first witnesses are not in danger of the death penalty unless the accused is first condemned to death.

Therefore, they are free to retract their testimony before the death sentence has been imposed. The Gemara continues with another example of this technique: "Rather, Rabbah said: We say to [the accused], 'Do you have witnesses to contradict [the accusing witnesses]? This statement suggests an avenue for acquittal that at the same time avoids any suggestion of liability for the witnesses.'"[8] (bracketed language in original)

The duty on the court to discover false testimony is so important that the biblical death penalty requires the court to open its deliberations by suggesting the possibility of finding such witnesses.[9] And those who attempt to subvert justice by providing false material testimony in capital cases are to be executed in the same manner that they had sought to inflict on the defendant.

FALSE WITNESSES UNDER THE AMERICAN DEATH PENALTY

How does the American death penalty measure up to this standard of the biblical death penalty? Before answering that question, we must address a difference in the roles of certain participants in the biblical system and the American system. Under the biblical death penalty, "the case for the prosecution was conducted by the witness to the crime."[10] "The trial was not adversarial. Rather, the judges were actually required to act in defense of the accused."[11]

In the American system, the decision whether or not to prosecute someone in a capital case is made by the prosecutor—local, state, or federal. These are the people charged by oath to review the evidence and seek justice by pursuing only those likely to be guilty. That same oath demands prosecutors suspend pursuing conviction of a suspect when evidence comes to light making it apparent that they have focused on the wrong person.

The American death penalty relies on prosecutors to protect American citizens from wrongful indictment, conviction, and condemnation. Is it working? Apparently not, according to Harvard University law professor Alan Dershowitz: "Winning has become more important than doing justice. Nobody runs for the Senate saying I did justice."[12]

Even a significant law enforcement figure from a major city has felt the need to speak out on this issue:

Houston Police Chief C. O. Bradford said that criminal defendants in Texas are at the mercy of prosecutors in an unfair system that emphasizes winning rather than justice. Bradford voiced support for changes that would help to balance the Texas justice system, which he believes currently works in favor of prosecutors. . . .

. . . He described the attitude in the district attorney's office as, "What can I do to win? Win, win, win."[13]

What in heaven's name is going on for that to be the perception of the chief of police in a major American city?

PROSECUTORIAL MISCONDUCT

The rigors of a free and open democracy dictate the need for top-notch, diligent defenders of the common good. None of us want to live under a criminal-dominated society. We need excellent prosecutors on the federal and state levels. Having said that, one must also acknowledge that checks and balances on power—even prosecutorial power—should be endemic to the American spirit. In fact, however, the trend has been in exactly the opposite direction with respect to the powers of prosecutors: "The power and prestige of the American prosecutor have changed dramatically over the past twenty years. Three generalizations appropriately describe this change. First, prosecutors wield vastly more power than ever before. Second, prosecutors are more insulated from judicial control over their conduct. Third, prosecutors are increasingly immune to ethical restraints."[14]

The Center for Public Integrity, a nonprofit, nonpartisan, tax-exempt organization in Washington, D.C., has the mission of using public service journalism to "provide the American people with the findings of investigations and analyses of public service, government accountability and ethics related issues."[15] The center has published a new in-depth report: *Harmful Error: Investigating*

America's Local Prosecutors, which reports a distressing level of prosecutorial misconduct.

> Local prosecutors in many of the 2,341 jurisdictions across the nation have stretched, bent or broken rules while convicting defendants. . . . Since 1970, individual judges and appellate court panels cited prosecutorial misconduct as a factor when dismissing charges at trial, reversing convictions or reducing sentences in at least 2,012 cases. . . .
>
> . . . In thousands more cases, judges labeled prosecutorial behavior inappropriate, but allowed the trial to continue or upheld convictions using a doctrine called "harmless error."[16]

Despite the large number of cases, the study found that since 1970, only two prosecutors have been disbarred for such misconduct. It would seem that prosecutors know they are virtually bulletproof against charges of hiding evidence that a defendant is innocent or introducing false testimony in court. As bad as this state of affairs is with respect to any criminal charges, even minor ones, it is beyond comprehension when capital charges or homicide are involved.

In capital cases, the risk of harm from unbridled abuses of prosecutorial power is the greatest. A first-of-its-kind *Chicago Tribune* analysis of "thousands of court records, appellate rulings and lawyer disciplinary records from across the United States" finds the American justice system is not working very well when it comes to homicide cases:

> With impunity, prosecutors across the country have violated their oaths and the law, committing the worst kinds of deception in the most serious of cases.
>
> They have prosecuted black men, hiding evidence the real killers were white. They have prosecuted a wife, hiding evidence her husband committed suicide. They have prosecuted parents, hiding evidence their daughter was killed by wild dogs.
>
> They do it to win.
>
> They do it because they won't get punished.

They have done it to defendants who came within hours of being executed, only to be exonerated.[17]

The study found that since 1963, at least 381 defendants nationally have had a homicide conviction thrown out because prosecutors concealed evidence suggesting innocence or presented evidence they knew to be false. What are the consequences for this violation of oath and duty? "The U.S. Supreme Court has declared such misconduct by prosecutors to be so reprehensible that it warrants criminal charges and disbarment. But not one of those prosecutors was convicted of a crime. Not one was barred from practicing law. Instead, many saw their careers advance, becoming judges or district attorneys. One became a congressman."[18]

And although we are often told that such individual cases are unusual, the *Chicago Tribune* study shows that such deceit happens frequently and in nearly limitless ways.

Prosecutors have concealed evidence that discredited their star witnesses, pointed to other suspects or supported a defendant's claim of self-defense. They have suppressed evidence that a murder occurred when the defendants had alibis, or that it occurred not in a defendant's home, as alleged, but in someone else's cornfield far away. In one case prosecutors depicted red paint as blood. In another they portrayed hog blood as human.[19]

Given this disastrous state of "prosecutorial misconduct," which is the polite term used when prosecutors lie, cheat, and deceive the courts and juries, how does the American death penalty measure up to the biblical mandate: *Let it be done to them as they sought to do to him?* Prosecutors are almost never punished, even if their conduct is outrageous.

A dramatic example is provided by the 381 homicide defendants who received new trials because prosecutors hid evidence or allowed witnesses to lie. The appellate courts denounced the prosecutors' actions with words like "unforgivable," "intolerable," "beyond reprehension," and "illegal, improper and dishonest." At least a dozen of the prosecutors were investigated by state agencies charged with policing lawyers for misconduct.

But so far, here is what has happened to the prosecutors in those hundreds of cases: One was fired, but appealed and was reinstated with back pay. Another received an in-house suspension of 30 days. A third prosecutor's law license was suspended for 59 days, but because of other misconduct in the case.

Not one received any kind of public sanction from a state lawyer disciplinary agency or was convicted of any crime for hiding evidence or presenting false evidence, the *Tribune* found. Two were indicted, but the charges were dismissed before trial. . . .

However, a *Tribune* search failed to turn up a single prosecutor who was disbarred for securing a conviction while engaging in such misconduct in any kind of criminal case. And it found only two cases where prosecutors were convicted of criminal charges for such misconduct. Both of those convictions, one in an Ohio rape case and the other in a New York robbery case, were misdemeanors that resulted in $500 fines.

Instead, the prosecutor's career advances.[20]

Bennett Gershman, a law professor at Pace University in White Plains, New York, has written extensively about misconduct by prosecutors and calls it a "serious cancer in our system of justice." "There is no check on prosecutorial misconduct except for the prosecutor's own attitudes and beliefs and inner morality."[21]

I have practiced law as a corporate lawyer for over twenty years with both private and public sector clients. If a corporate lawyer ever suggested to his clients that they should trust his inner morality, attitudes, and beliefs and just pay his bill for professional services without any itemization or receipts, not only would they fire him, but investigations and audits by their professional staff and probably by the government would be certain.

How can we leave matters of life and death to the whims of human beings' attitudes and beliefs and inner morality? It is probably un-American. It is definitely anti-biblical.

Although the American ideal for imposing consequences for prosecutorial misconduct would at least involve loss of pay, loss

of job, or even disbarment, in actual practice there are virtually
no negative consequences for it. Even if the misconduct is discovered and established, the likelihood is that the guilty verdict will
be upheld and the prosecutor's prestige and career will be enhanced.

Without advocating for imposition of the death penalty
against prosecutors, which I do not advocate, we can still see that
the severity of the consequences for prosecutorial misconduct in
America are miniscule in the ideal and laughable in practice compared with the biblical standard that applied the death penalty
for false evidence or testimony in a capital case.

For those who are working on the state side, convictions, especially death penalty convictions, can be very helpful to promo-
tion, raises, and political ascendancy. Wrongful convictions have
no negative impact on any of those payoffs and offer very little
risk of negative consequences.

> Virtually every aspect of the prosecutor's function . . . reflects
> excess and abuse. Serious prosecutorial misconduct that under-
> mines a fair trial is increasingly insulated from judicial review
> by the aggressive application of the harmless error rule. By the
> same token, the need to prove substantial prejudice has ren-
> dered grand jury and other investigative abuses virtually unas-
> sailable. A prosecutor's violation of the obligation to disclose
> favorable evidence accounts for more miscarriages of justice
> than any other type of malpractice, but is rarely sanctioned by
> courts, and almost never by disciplinary bodies. . . . Due proc-
> ess of law, at one time a significant protection against egregious
> prosecutorial misconduct, has also been given an increasingly
> limited application, and in some instances deemed entirely ir-
> relevant.[22]

Some who are involved day in and day out in the legal practice
areas that are most affected by prosecutorial misconduct attest to
the drastic alteration that has occurred, changing from a focus on
integrity to an emphasis on convictions at any cost:

> [T]he leadership needed to help bring about justice is missing.
> There was a time when the Attorney General of the United

States and the attorneys general in many of the states were concerned not just with getting convictions, but also with fairness, integrity, and the proper functioning of the adversary system. . . .

. . . But those days are gone.[23] (citations omitted)

. . . In response to findings by federal courts of constitutional violations in state capital cases, prosecutors have urged stricter enforcement of procedural default rules to avoid dealing with the violations, not better counsel to avoid those unconstitutional trials in the first place.[24] (citations omitted)

The following is a sampling of this problem in cases from around America.

PENNSYLVANIA

Dennis Counterman was released because of prosecutorial misconduct in his case. The freed man has an IQ in the mid-seventies, and his wife is mentally retarded.

Eleven years after he was sentenced to death, Dennis Counterman was granted a new trial. [In July of 2001] Pennsylvania state court judge Lawrence Brenner threw out Counterman's 1990 conviction for setting a fire that killed three children, holding that prosecutors withheld critical evidence and repeatedly violated a duty to turn over exculpatory information. Among the information kept from defense lawyers were statements from neighbors that Mr. Counterman's oldest son had a history of setting fires and liked to play with lighters. In addition, before handing over police interviews to the defense, prosecutors whited out Mrs. Counterman's statement to the police that her husband had been asleep when the fire started. Brenner ruled that these statements would have cast "substantial doubt" on Mrs. Counterman's testimony against her husband.

In his opinion, Judge Brenner concluded that the trial was "fundamentally unfair" and the verdict was unreliable. He added that, had the prosecution not withheld the exculpatory evidence, "there is a reasonable probability that the outcome of the trial could have been different."[25]

In the case of Anthony Porter, the man released for innocence after seventeen years on Illinois' death row, the line between malicious misconduct and outright arrogance blurs.

[Alstory] Simon and Inez Jackson [the two people who came forward and gave the sworn videotaped testimony that resulted in Porter's release] offered identical accounts of their dealings with police. They said detectives came to their home the morning after the murders to talk to them and show them photographs of suspects.

But, they said, police were not interested in what they knew, and they did not suspect them. Instead, they said, the police simply were after Porter.[26] (bracketed language mine)

Texas has had numerous cases of prosecutorial misconduct. At least one such case, that of Randall Dale Adams, is infamous.

Adams was convicted in Texas in 1977 of murdering a policeman. He was sentenced to die largely on the testimony of a juvenile with a lengthy criminal record who made a secret deal with the prosecutor to implicate Adams,[27] and the testimony of two purported eyewitnesses to the killing. The juvenile actually murdered the policeman, as he later admitted. At Adams' trial, however, the prosecutor suppressed information about the secret deal, and successfully kept from the jury the juvenile's lengthy criminal record. The prosecutor also withheld from Adams' attorney proof that the two eyewitnesses had failed to identify Adams in a lineup, and even solicited from these witnesses testimony that they had made a positive identification of Adams. A Texas court . . . freed Adams [finding] that the prosecutor "knowingly used perjured testimony and knowingly suppressed evidence."[28] (bracketed footnote in original; citations omitted)

OKLAHOMA

The sentence of Alfred Brian Mitchell, an Oklahoma death row inmate, was overturned by federal court because of the false and misleading testimony at trial by Joyce Gilchrist, an Oklahoma City police chemist. The judges also denounced prosecutors for withholding exculpatory evidence from the defense and for deliberately misleading jurors, stating that such conduct "strikes a heavy blow to the public's trust" of prosecutors. The prosecutor's duty is not to win cases, said the court, it is to see "that justice is done."[29]

ALABAMA

Walter "Johnnie D." McMillian said love letters to a white woman sent him to death row.[30]

"That's the only thing I can think of," said McMillian, 59. "They wanted to get rid of me because they caught me with a white lady." . . .

District Attorney Tommy Chapman, elected to office during McMillian's stay on death row, doesn't think McMillian was even at the scene of the crime.

A second investigation conducted by the Alabama Bureau of Investigation convinced Chapman that someone else committed the murder. . . .

Walter McMillian of Monroeville sat on death row for years until his murder charge was overturned. "From Day One, I was framed up," McMillian said.

Before becoming a victim of prosecutorial misconduct, McMillian was sure only the right guy went to death row: "'I had always believed in the police. I always thought the police were right,'

McMillian said. 'I tell people if I hadn't been caught in this trap I would still be blind.'" A "do-gooder" intervened on McMillian's behalf:

> Lawyer Bryan Stevenson, who heads the Montgomery-based Equal Justice Initiative, appealed McMillian's case.
>
> Investigators targeted McMillian, Stevenson said, because he was black and poor.
>
> "He's no more guilty than you or I," Stevenson said. "The community owes Mr. McMillian an apology."
>
> Stevenson doesn't find it hard to believe McMillian's theory that being a black man and dating a white woman contributed to his conviction.
>
> "Race still matters in the administration of criminal justice," he said.

The prosecutor in the original case failed to provide a safeguard against false testimony.

> Both Chapman and Stevenson said the investigation was handled poorly.
>
> "It was just a comedy of errors," Chapman said.
>
> One of those errors involved the testimony of Ralph Myers, who McMillian described as "low-down." . . .
>
> Stevenson began to take a look at Myers' testimony.

Ultimately, the state court of appeals took a fresh look at the case:

> "Unquestionably Myers was the key witness for the prosecution," the state court of appeals later wrote. "Without his testimony, the state could not have obtained a conviction."
>
> And, the court said, it appeared as though lawmen coerced the evidence against McMillian.
>
> In 1992 at an appeals court hearing, Myers admitted that he had never seen McMillian on the day Morrison was killed.
>
> "This way we can all get out of this courtroom and we can let an innocent man go on home, if that's what the law will let happen," Myers said. "Me, I can simply look in your face or

anybody else's face dead eye to eyeball and tell you that anything that was told about McMillian was a lie."

Myers told his doctors who examined him that he felt pressure to implicate McMillian.

The appeals court also said investigators withheld evidence from the defense, including testimony that cast doubts on the time frame presented by prosecutors.

The court also found a tape recording not entered into evidence in which Myers denied being a part of the Morrison murder and denied McMillian had him kill Morrison.

"We conclude that there is a reasonable probability that had Myers' prior inconsistent statement been disclosed to the defense prior to trial, the results of the proceedings would have been different," wrote Judge John Patterson.

The case was overturned. Chapman decided not to retry McMillian and "Johnny D." became the first man to be freed from death row directly into society in Alabama.

Stevenson said others could be railroaded in Alabama.

"White or black, they can put him on death row," he said. "If he's not strong and fighting to get someone trying to help him, he'll get electrocuted."

Because our inquiry is focused upon the biblical standard, *Let it be done to them as they sought to do to him*, we must also note that the Alabama "courts ruled that the officials couldn't be held liable for withholding evidence" in McMillian's case.

FLORIDA

Florida was cited as well in the *Chicago Tribune* investigation mentioned earlier in this chapter. One of the examples given was the case of James Richardson:

> In the case of James Richardson, a Florida man wrongly convicted in the poisoning deaths of his seven children, certain evidence undermining the state's case surfaced only after being stolen from a prosecutor's office by a man dating the prosecutor's secretary.[31]

Richardson was condemned to die . . . in 1967. The prosecutor argued that Richardson, a penniless farm worker, killed his
children to collect insurance. A state judge . . . overturned the
murder conviction, finding that the prosecutor had suppressed
evidence that would have shown Richardson's innocence. The
undisclosed evidence included a sworn statement from the
children's babysitter that she had killed the youngsters, a sworn
statement from a cellmate of Richardson's that he had been
beaten by a sheriff's deputy into fabricating a story implicating
Richardson, statements from other inmates contradicting their
claims that Richardson had confessed to them, and proof that
Richardson had never purchased any insurance.[32] (citations
omitted)

Richardson was set free in 1989 after serving twenty-one years on
Florida's death row.[33]
Even more infamous than the case of James Richardson is the
Florida case of James "Shabaka" Brown:

Brown's murder conviction . . . was reversed by the Court of
Appeals for the Eleventh Circuit [U.S. appeals court in Atlanta,
Georgia]. Brown was hours away from being executed; he was
measured for his burial suit and asked to order his last meal.
The federal court found that the prosecutor "knowingly allowed material false testimony to be introduced at trial, failed
to step forward and make the falsity known, and knowingly
exploited the false testimony in its closing argument to the
jury." The subornation of perjury[34] related to the testimony of
a key prosecution witness who falsely denied that a deal had
been made with the prosecutor, and the prosecutor's misrepre-
sentations of that fact to the trial court. In addition the prosecutor misrepresented to the jury that ballistics evidence proved
the defendant's guilt, when in fact the prosecutor knew that
the ballistics report showed that the bullet that killed the deceased could not have been fired from the defendant's
weapon.[35] (bracketed note mine; citations omitted)

According to the Florida Supreme Court, speaking in the recent death row appeal decision in the case of Walter Ruiz, "it

is finding prosecutorial misconduct in death penalty cases with 'unacceptable frequency.'" (One of the prosecutors in that case has advanced her career to the U.S. state attorney's office.)[36] The case involved the kind of misconduct that is easy to detect: inflammatory statements to the jury on the record.[37]

Prosecutorial misconduct, however, can occur in many different ways, e.g., hidden evidence, destroyed evidence, fabricated evidence, or concealment of exculpatory witnesses. One example is the case of Frank Lee Smith from Fort Lauderdale, Florida. When Smith died of cancer, he had been on death row for over fourteen years. Postmortem DNA testing in late 2001 definitely established his innocence of the rape-murder.

> No physical evidence linked him to the crime, but a jury convicted him in 1986 based largely on an eyewitness. A judge sent him to death row.
>
> Gov. Bob Martinez signed a death warrant on Oct. 16, 1989, but less than a month before Smith's execution, the eyewitness, Chiquita Lowe, recanted. She testified she wrongly identified Smith after police pressured her, telling her Smith was dangerous.
>
> A week before he was to die, the Florida Supreme Court stayed the execution.
>
> But then a judge in Broward turned down his request for a new trial after prosecutors depicted Lowe as a liar.
>
> In fact, Lowe never wavered from her testimony that she saw someone else lurking outside the victim's house that night: Eddie Lee Mosely, an insane killer who was the prime suspect in a number of other rapes and killings in the same neighborhood.[38]

No one has explained why the police focused on Smith, even pressured Lowe into fingering Smith, when her original reports identified a man who was suspected of similar crimes in the same neighborhood. Did the prosecutors provide a check on this possible police misconduct at the investigation stage? Not a chance. They fought against the truth right to the end.

> In 1998, Smith's attorneys began pressuring for DNA testing. But the Broward State Attorney's Office said that under long-

standing court rules it was too late for Smith to get his conviction overturned—even if the semen found in the victim belonged to someone else.

At one hearing, prosecutor McCann accused Smith's lawyers of "playing games" to delay justice.[39]

What does the prosecutor, who objected to DNA testing as a waste of time and fought against it for years, say to the fact that the DNA tests proved Smith was innocent? "No prosecutor wants this to happen," McCann said. "Unfortunately, we're in an imperfect system where the guilty go free, and sometimes innocent people are convicted."[40]

People of biblical faith might well ask, should such an imperfect system be taking human life?

Everyone might ask, how did the police allow this to happen? How did the investigators who put Frank Lee Smith on death row fare under the American death penalty system? They were cleared of lying and manufacturing evidence in this case. Why? Failure to document their work resulted in a lack of any evidence for investigation and, consequently, no charges.[41]

Part of the problem is that the laws have been skewed to protect the state's side. Record-keeping requirements for police and law enforcement are a case in point.[42] Personnel records must be retained until fifty years after an officer leaves the force. But records of investigations into misconduct can be destroyed five years after the investigation.

Joseph Nahume Green was convicted in 1992 and the charges dismissed in 2000. Green was released after spending seven years on Florida's death row. Green always maintained his innocence. He was convicted on the testimony of the state's only eyewitness, Lonnie Thompson. The Florida Supreme Court overturned Green's conviction, holding that Thompson, whose testimony was "often inconsistent and contradictory," had not been competent to testify.

Thompson is mildly retarded and suffered head traumas that have caused memory problems, the ruling said. Thompson also admitted to drinking eight cans of beer and using cocaine and marijuana before [the shooting].

He also told police at first that a white man [was the shooter]. Green is black. . . .

There was no physical evidence . . . linking Green to the crime.[43]

The court dismissed the charges, saying:

"The state can produce no witness who is able to place [Green] at the scene of the crime at the time the crime occurred."

The physical evidence "does not tie [him] to the crime in any way," the judge wrote. . . .

With that, Green became the 21st person[44] condemned to die in Florida since 1972 who was ultimately released from death row. . . . Florida leads the nation in wrongful death [penalty] cases. . . .

For months, prosecutors tried to orchestrate a face-saving way to close the case without admitting a mistake. . . .

[They] said a jury could "infer" Green is guilty because he matched a description given by [the victim] to a paramedic as she lay dying. . . .

She told the medic a skinny black man tried to rob her, then shot her and fled.[45] (bracketed language and note mine)

In other words, the prosecution's position would support the conviction and execution of anybody who is a "skinny black man." As tenuous as that position is, the facts revealed after Green was freed raise even worse concerns:

The witness, Lonnie Thompson, told a Bradford County Jury that Green shot [the victim] outside a convenience store. . . .

Now, however, Thompson says he doesn't know who committed the murder. In an affidavit obtained [in November 2001] by one of Green's former lawyers, the 40-year-old handyman says he was just trying to stay out of trouble when he identified Green. . . .

Green's civil lawyer, George Nachwalter of Miami, said the affidavit shows that police and prosecutors coached Thompson, a man with memory problems who had been drinking and taking drugs that night, into giving false testimony.

"The whole case against Joseph was an out-and-out lie,"
Nachwalter said.[46] (bracketed language mine)

The affidavit signed by Thompson explains how he was subtly
pressured into lying: "'At first I told the truth . . . that I couldn't
tell who the man was that shot [the victim],' the affidavit says.
'[The police] kept on asking me if the man was Joseph Green no
matter what I said. So finally I said, yes, it was Joseph Green so
he would leave me alone.'"[47] (bracketed language mine)

In another Florida case, William Kelley was sent to death row
twenty-three years ago for a murder that had occurred fifteen
years earlier.

Kelley's first trial was declared a mistrial because the jury found
[the testimony of John Sweet, the state's star witness]—the
only solid evidence connecting Kelley to the murder—to be
suspect because Sweet got an immunity deal for testifying.

But at Kelley's second trial in 1984, the immunity deal was
withheld from the jury, and Kelley was convicted of first-
degree murder. When the jury sent the note asking if Sweet
had "anything to gain from his testimony," [the prosecutor]
responded that "Sweet had nothing to gain by his testimony."
. . .

Sweet did, indeed, get immunity for a string of crimes in
exchange for his testimony against Kelley.

[Judge] Roettger wrote: "Disclosure of [Sweet's] immunity
. . . would have resulted in a markedly weaker case for the
prosecution and a markedly stronger one for the defense."

Because [the prosecutor] also withheld documents and transcripts from the defense that would have disclosed the immunity deal, Roettger goes further: "[The prosecutor in this case]
has a habit of failing to turn over exculpatory and impeach-
ment evidence."[48]

In response to questioning from the federal judge, the former
prosecutor said: "It was never my intention to lie. But maybe the
way the words came out is not how they should have come out."[49]
The federal district judge in Miami ordered a new trial for Kelley
"on the grounds of prosecutorial misconduct."[50]

The day before Kelley was to be freed, the state appealed the ruling to the U.S. Court of Appeals for the Eleventh Circuit. Even if the state's appeal is denied and Kelley retains his right to a new trial, the typical appellate timetables will result in Kelley living on Florida's death row for at least a year or more after he was to have been released. If the appellate court overturns Kelley's right to a new trial, the state could execute him.[51]

Is this appeal by the state of Florida based upon a substantiated conviction that the right man has been found guilty and worthy of death? No, not even remotely. A state attorney involved has already acknowledged to the press that there will be no retrial, because the state could not possibly win a retrial. The assistant state attorney who heads the homicide division has agreed, acknowledging that the state has no evidence against William Kelley.[52] Kelley's case serves as a stark reminder that the death penalty has less to do with justice and more to do with winning.

What about the morality and ethics of keeping Kelley on death row and seeking the death penalty against him when there is not even a shred of evidence tying him to the crime? Should not that, in and of itself, be called prosecutorial misconduct?

At least in the case of Rudolph Holton the state prosecutors had the decency to call it quits. Florida death row inmate Rudolph Holton received a new trial, ordered by a Hillsborough County circuit judge. Since Holton's first trial, witnesses have admitted lying about seeing him with the victim the night she was murdered. A key state witness, a jailhouse snitch who testified that Holton confessed to him, has also recanted. (As noted in chapter 14, both witnesses have been sentenced to prison for recanting their false testimony and telling the truth under oath.)[53] In addition, a hair found on the victim, which was used at trial to link Holton to the victim, has undergone new DNA testing. The tests show that the hair does not belong to Holton.[54]

Holton was released on January 24, 2003, becoming the twenty-third person to be exonerated on Florida's death row.[55] The prosecutor refused to admit Holton's innocence saying, "The [state] does not have a reasonable likelihood of obtaining a conviction. Therefore, I am ethically precluded from going forward. It does not mean he is innocent."[56]

What? If the state doesn't have enough evidence to go to court, then he is legally innocent. Only God knows the human heart. The law does not read the human heart. The *law* says that one is innocent unless proven guilty in a court of law beyond a reasonable doubt. In Holton's case, the state has so little to go on that it would be unethical for the prosecuting attorney to even accuse Holton of the crime, unethical to put the evidence before a jury and ask them to decide "guilty" or "not guilty." The state's case is so nonexistent that Rudolph Holton cannot even be charged let alone tried. He is no guiltier than any other person plucked at random from off the street. One cannot help but wonder if that is how Holton was picked for prosecution in the first place.

NEW YORK

The Northeast also has its share of shameful stories of prosecutorial misconduct. A compelling example is the case of Eric Jackson:

> Jackson's murder conviction was . . . vacated by a New York state court. Jackson was convicted of starting a fire in a Brooklyn supermarket that resulted in the death of six firefighters. If New York had a death penalty at the time,[57] Jackson might have been sentenced to death. The court found that the prosecutor concealed evidence that would have shown that the fire was not arson-related, but was caused by an electrical malfunction. During a . . . court hearing, the prosecutor consistently maintained that nothing had been suppressed. When the judge ordered the prosecutor's file to be submitted to him for his inspection, he found two internal memoranda from the trial prosecutor to an executive attorney in the prosecutor's office. The memoranda stated that an expert witness who had examined the evidence concluded that the fire had not been deliberately set, and that the expert's conclusion presented a major problem for the prosecution. None of this information was ever revealed to Jackson's lawyer.[58] (bracketed note mine; citations omitted)

PROSECUTORIAL MISCONDUCT IN THE FLORIDA
PORTION OF THE FEDERAL SYSTEM

As with the case of Eric Jackson, prosecutorial misconduct is not
limited to capital cases. In Tampa, Florida, four cases of prosecutorial misconduct have surfaced in the U.S. attorney's office. At
least these four cases show that sanctions for prosecutorial misconduct are possible. One involves a prosecutor lying to a grand
jury; another, the destruction of records in a criminal case; and
yet another, the concealment of a witness's identity.[59] In the latter
case, an assistant U.S. attorney resigned her position after receiving a one-year suspension from the state supreme court.[60]

And then there is also the infamous *Aisenberg* case in which a
Tampa area couple was being charged with the death of their
child. A federal prosecutor and his assistant told the judge that
the couple could be heard making "incriminating statements" on
official surveillance tapes.[61] When the judge finally listened to the
tapes, the voices were "inaudible," leading the judge to conclude
that the government's case had been built on "lies and half-
truths."[62] The lead prosecutor, who had been involved in prosecutorial misconduct before, was demoted and both were being investigated by the Justice Department.[63]

A special prosecutor appointed by governor Jeb Bush probed
the way the *Aisenberg* case was handled. The Florida bar also
opened its own investigation,[64] and recently, the assistant prosecuting attorney on the case was quietly shunted to the civil division.[65]

What happens to the police and investigators who are involved
in such misconduct? As reported in the *St. Petersburg Times*,[66] judge
Mark Pizzo issued a blistering report that ran for over sixty pages,
saying that the sheriff's detectives "made up facts" to obtain permission to bug the Aisenbergs' home and evidenced a "reckless
disregard" for the truth. The report of Norman Wolfinger, the
appointed special prosecutor, labeled certain of their actions "cur-
sory," "irresponsible," and "reckless." So what happened to the
offending officials? Virtually nothing. "The two lead detectives
. . . received written reprimands for failing to follow Sheriff's Office procedure and inattention to duty. [The major] who oversaw
the investigation, also received a written reprimand for failing to

follow procedure. None of them were demoted or docked pay, and no one else at the Sheriff's Office faces any formal discipline in connection with the case."[67]

This case shows the extent to which an investigation can be distorted and perverted, even result in the destruction of the personal lives of innocent citizens, without any negative consequences for the government officers and staff who skewed the investigation. The standards of biblical truth reveal that this state of affairs is abhorrent.

JUMPING ON THE BUS

It would be a mistake to create the impression that prosecutorial misconduct is just a Florida problem. Florida is not alone. The problem of prosecutorial misconduct is a severe problem on both state and federal levels and pervades our criminal justice system nationwide. A multiyear investigative report by the *Pittsburgh Post-Gazette* exposed a culture of prosecutorial misconduct on the federal level:

Hundreds of times during the past 10 years, federal agents and prosecutors have pursued justice by breaking the law.

They lied, hid evidence, distorted facts, engaged in cover-ups, paid for perjury and set up innocent people in a relentless effort to win indictments, guilty pleas and convictions, a two-year *Post-Gazette* investigation found.

Rarely were these federal officials punished for their misconduct. Rarely did they admit their conduct was wrong.[68]

There should not be any surprise that such a federal problem has manifestations in the Florida part of the federal system:

In Florida, prisoners call the scam "jumping on the bus," and it is as tantalizing as it is perverse. Inmates in federal prisons barter or buy information that only an insider to a crime could know—often from informants with access to confidential federal crime files.

The prisoners memorize it and get others to do the same.

Then, to win sentence reductions, they testify about crimes that might have been committed while they were in prison, by people they've never met, in places they've never been. The scam succeeds only because of the tacit approval of federal law enforcement officers. Those who practice this misconduct are almost never penalized or disciplined. . . .

[The *Post-Gazette*] found that powerful new federal laws designed to snare terrorists, drug smugglers and pornographers are being aimed at business owners, engineers and petty criminals.

Whether suspects are guilty has come to matter less than making sure they are indicted or convicted or, more likely, coerced into pleading guilty.

Promises of lenient sentences and huge government checks encourage criminals to lie on the witness stand. Prosecutors routinely withhold evidence that might help prove a defendant innocent. Some federal agents work so closely with their undercover informants that they become lawbreakers themselves.[69]

Lest one hope that the examples of prosecutorial misconduct related in this chapter are anomalies, Professor Gershman is the bearer of much sadder news:

These cases are indeed shocking, but they are neither unique nor aberrational. They represent a recurring and largely unsolved problem in American criminal litigation. An exhaustive article in the *Stanford Law Review* in 1987 concluded that an innocent person was convicted in 350 capital cases, and that 23 of those condemned were executed, with 21 narrowly winning reprieves. A significant number of those cases involved claims of prosecutorial suppression of evidence. Neither the judiciary nor disciplinary bodies have been able to prevent the recurrence of this conduct.[70]

Those who practice this misconduct are almost never penalized or disciplined. A former U.S. attorney known for his faith-based conservative principles offered his assessment of the current state of affairs in America with respect to prosecutorial misconduct. " 'It's a result-oriented process today, fairness be damned,' said Robert Merkle, whom President Ronald Reagan appointed U.S. Attorney for the Middle District of Florida, serving from 1982 to 1988. 'The philosophy of the past 10 to 15 years [is] that whatever works is what's right.' "[71]

CLOSING THOUGHTS

The biblical death penalty requires that those who attempted to subvert justice by providing false material testimony in capital cases are to suffer the same fate that they had sought to inflict on the defendant. How does the American death penalty measure up to this standard? The pervasive presence of prosecutorial misconduct throughout the criminal justice system, especially in capital cases, without any negative consequences to those responsible flies in the face of biblical principles. "Indeed, the increasing incidence of prosecutorial misconduct suggests that it has become 'normative to the system.' Sanctions for misconduct are so infrequent as to appear almost non-existent. The courts focus on the impact of the misconduct upon the verdict, and professional disciplinary bodies appear unable or unwilling to grapple with ethical violations by prosecutors."[72] (citations omitted)

We do not need to go so far as to propose the execution of prosecutors, police, and government investigators who provide false material evidence of guilt or hide exculpatory evidence of innocence. We can simply observe that the American death penalty provides virtually no punishment, monetary or criminal, for such conduct. In fact, the rules of the American death penalty encourage such conduct. As we have seen in chapter 14, if suppressed evidence of innocence can be kept hidden long enough, the wrongfully condemned man may not even be able to get a new trial when the evidence does come to light. The atmosphere of gaming and calculation that results from this state of affairs has nothing to do with justice and nothing to do with biblical truth.

Clearly, biblical truth reveals that the American death penalty completely fails to meet any semblance of the biblical principles concerning prosecutorial misconduct and other forms of false testimony.

Chapter Sixteen

LEVELS OF CULPABILITY AND DIMINISHED CAPACITY

AGE, MENTAL ILLNESS, AND MENTAL RETARDATION

As we have already seen, the primary focus of the biblical death penalty is the fear of executing the innocent. The Bible is the basis for this concern (Exod. 23:7). A corollary to this concern is the fear of executing those who are "morally innocent" through lack of culpability. That category would include children and those under the effect of impairment in their mental ability. This means that under the biblical standards of Torah/Pentateuch and the provisions of Talmud necessary to fulfill those scriptures, minors, the mentally retarded and the mentally ill were forbidden to be executed. The following rules apply with respect to diminished capacity under the standards of the biblical death penalty.

First, minors are not subject to capital punishment: "[A minor is] 'someone who has not yet reached maturity. A minor is not considered legally competent. He bears no responsibility for his acts.'"[1]

The calculations of minority and time periods under the biblical death penalty are admittedly complex. Although for certain purposes one becomes an adult in the eyes of the community at his bar mitzvah (age thirteen), the age of majority for death penalty purposes is much older. Mendelsohn, the twentieth-century scholar of the jurisprudence of the ancient Hebrews, summarizes the provisions as follows: "[S]ince with reference to crime, the Talmud does not divide the different stages of minority, but considers the end of the period the same as the beginning thereof, we may reasonably conclude that, according to Talmudic law, liability to capital punishment begins with the beginning of the person's majority—*at the age of twenty."*[2] (italics in original)

Second, the biblical death penalty exempts from execution any person with a diminished mental capacity, whether it affects reasoning or emotional ability to harbor malice. The exemption applies whether the disability is permanent or intermittent, so long as it was in effect at the time of the crime.

The biblical death penalty recognizes a condition called *idiocy,* in which

> a person is not presumed to be possessed of the capability of premeditation or willing in general, and of malice in particular. Accordingly, Talmudic jurisprudence declares . . . when they inflict injury, they cannot be held responsible.[3] (citations omitted)

> By *Idiot* the Talmud understands not only the confirmed lunatic, but also the monomaniac: as the one who habitually and unnecessarily exposes himself to danger; or who betrays general destructive proclivities, as by willfully tearing his clothes; or who manifests other reprehensible idiosyncrasy.[4] (citations omitted)

Another English translation of the term is *imbecile:* "A person so intellectually and emotionally unstable that he is not responsible for his actions."[5]

The biblical death penalty provides that a person who phases in and out of diminished mental capacity is only responsible for his actions during periods of normalcy: a mentally unstable person who has periods of sanity and insanity is responsible for his actions during periods of lucidity. However, during his periods of insanity, he is not considered responsible for his behavior.[6] This is the basis for an insanity exclusion from the biblical death penalty.

Another description of the classification of those with mental impairments appears in Maimonides' Mishneh Torah with respect to those who are excluded as witnesses because their condition excludes them from breaking the laws:

> The mentally deficient is incompetent by biblical law, because he is not subject to the commandments. By "mentally deficient" is to be understood not only one who walks around naked, breaks things, and throws stones, but anyone who is confused in mind, invariably mixed up with respect to some matters, although with respect to other matters he speaks to the point and asks pertinent questions; nevertheless his evidence is inadmissible and he is included among the mentally deficient.
>
> In case of an epileptic, during a fit he is ineligible; in the interval (between fits), he is eligible, whether the paroxysm occurs periodically or at irregular intervals, provided that he is not mentally disordered all the time, for there are epileptics who are always confused in mind. The question of the admissibility of the evidence of epileptics requires careful consideration.
>
> The inordinately foolish, who are unable to discriminate between contradictory matters and do not comprehend things as normal people do, also those who are impulsive and hasty in judgment and act like madmen, are classed with the mentally deficient.[7]

Minors, the mentally retarded, and the mentally ill were exempt from the biblical death penalty. How does the American death penalty measure up to this standard of the biblical death penalty? Not well. Juveniles (under the age of twenty) and the mentally ill can and are executed. Execution of the mentally retarded is supposed to be prohibited; however, as discussed later, forces are at work to define that prohibition into meaninglessness.

THE EXECUTION OF MINORS UNDER THE AMERICAN DEATH PENALTY

Since 1990, juvenile offenders are known to have been executed in only six countries in the world: Iran, Pakistan, Yemen, Nigeria, Saudi Arabia, and the United States.[8] Of all the countries in the world that either claim to be Christian or Jewish or claim to have

a Christian or Jewish religious majority, the only one that executes minors is the United States: "The United States is clearly
one of, if not the leader of, the execution of persons who committed crimes as juveniles. These executions are not a new phenomenon."[9]

A total of 225 juvenile death sentences have been imposed in
the United States since the *Furman* decision in 1973. Of the 225
post-1973 death sentences, only 75 remain active (as of October
6, 2003). The other 150 sentences resulted as follows: 22 (15
percent) were executed and 128 (85 percent) were reversed or
commuted.[10]

Currently, thirty-eight states and the federal government have
statutes authorizing the death penalty for certain forms of murder.[11] Of those jurisdictions, nineteen states and the federal government have expressly chosen age eighteen at the time of the
crime as the minimum age for eligibility for the death penalty:[12]
California, Colorado, Connecticut, Illinois, Indiana, Kansas,
Maryland, Missouri,[13] Montana, Nebraska, New Jersey, New
Mexico, New York, Ohio, Oregon, South Dakota, Tennessee,
Washington,[14] Wyoming, and the federal government. Five have
chosen age seventeen as the minimum: Florida,[15] Georgia, New
Hampshire, North Carolina, and Texas. The other fourteen of the
death penalty jurisdictions use age sixteen as the minimum age,
either through an express age in the statute (four states) or by
court ruling (ten states):[16] Alabama, Arizona,* Arkansas,* Delaware,* Idaho,* Kentucky, Louisiana,* Mississippi,* Nevada, Oklahoma,* Pennsylvania,* South Carolina,* Utah,* Virginia.

The execution of juveniles has been a part of the American
death penalty from the beginning. In 1642 Thomas Grauger of
the Plymouth Colony, Massachusetts, was the first recorded juvenile execution.[17] In the 358 years since that time, a total of approximately 366 persons have been executed for juvenile crimes,
constituting less than 2.0 percent of roughly 20,000 confirmed
American executions since 1608.

There are currently 75 death row inmates (all male) sentenced
for crimes committed as juveniles, about 2.0 percent of the total
death row population.[18] Twenty-eight (36 percent) of these juveniles are in Texas.[19] Sixty-six (88 percent) are in the Bible Belt.[20]

Twenty-two men have been executed in the United States for

crimes committed as juveniles since the reinstatement of the death penalty in 1976. Thirteen of the 22 executions have taken place in Texas. All 22 executions for crimes committed as minors have occurred in the Bible Belt.

These 22 recent executions of juvenile offenders make up 2.5 percent of the total of about 876 executions since capital punishment resumed in the United States in the 1970s. A sampling of recent juvenile capital cases is enlightening.[21]

MISSOURI

Chris Simmons, who was scheduled to be executed in Missouri on June 5, 2002, received a stay of execution from the U.S. Supreme Court. Simmons, a seventeen-year-old high school student at the time of the crime, was under the influence of drugs and alcohol and was also found to be suffering from schizotypal disorder, a mental illness. At trial, Simmons's attorney failed to present evidence of this mental disorder or evidence of Simmons's childhood abuse by his father.

In August 2003, by a four-to-three decision, the Missouri Supreme Court vacated the death sentence, stating that the juvenile death penalty violates the nation's evolving standards of decency and is therefore unconstitutional. Noting "a national consensus has developed against the execution of juvenile offenders," the court's opinion cited evidence such as the growing number of states that have banned the practice. The court resentenced Simmons to life in prison without parole.[22]

The U.S. Supreme Court will revisit the legality of the juvenile death penalty under the U.S. Constitution in fall of 2004.

OKLAHOMA

On February 4, 1999, Sean Sellers was executed. This was the first time in forty years that an offender was executed in the United States for a crime committed as a sixteen-year-old. Sellers had been diagnosed with multiple personality disorder, though that wasn't explained to the jury at his trial. The U.S. court of appeals noted that Sellers may be "factually innocent" of the murders because of his mental illness, but then went on to say that innocence alone is not sufficient to grant federal relief.[23]

TEXAS

Napoleon Beazley, originally granted a stay of execution by the Texas Court of Criminal Appeals just hours before his scheduled execution,[24] was seventeen at the time of the crime. The National Mental Health Association and others wrote letters to Texas governor Perry asking that he commute Beazley's sentence. At Beazley's trial, his codefendants testified against him, but have since signed affidavits admitting that much of their critical trial testimony was untrue. They also admit that they testified for the state against Beazley on the basis of an undisclosed deal that secured them life sentences. He was executed by the state of Texas on May 28, 2002.

GEORGIA

Alexander Williams was granted clemency by the Georgia Board of Pardons and Paroles on February 25, 2002. A spokeswoman for the board stated that Williams's mental illness, his status as a juvenile offender, and his history of abuse as a child were factors leading to the board's decision to commute his death sentence to life without parole. The board received many pleas for clemency.[25]

While Texas and Oklahoma remain far from the standards of the biblical death penalty in their handling of juveniles, Missouri and Georgia seem to be making steps in a biblical direction. Florida, however, may be running the other way.

FLORIDA

In Florida, capital punishment is permitted for those who were age seventeen or older at the time of commission of their crime. Originally, the Florida Supreme Court ruled that, regardless of any federal constitutional mandate, the Florida Constitution's prohibition against cruel or unusual punishment forbid the execution of fifteen-year-old offenders.[26] Some Florida leaders assumed that this ruling adopted the U.S. constitutional minimum of sixteen years old for execution of minors in Florida. It did not. The court simply held that fifteen-year-olds were too young under Florida's Constitution.

Then, on July 8, 1999, in the *Brennan* case, the Florida Supreme Court held that the execution of those who were sixteen years old at the time of their crime violated the Florida Constitution.[27] The minimum age for the death penalty under the Florida Constitution was seventeen based on the Florida Supreme Court's interpretation of cruel or unusual punishment.[28]

The Florida legislature was outraged by the court's prohibition against executing sixteen-year-olds in Florida. At tremendous cost to the taxpayers, the Florida legislature initiated a statewide constitutional referendum to overrule the Florida Supreme Court. The obliquely worded constitutional amendment was placed on the ballot for referendum in November 2002. The ballot referendum on the death penalty passed with over 70 percent of the votes. The lawyerly drafted ballot did not mention execution of juveniles; clearly, however, as passed, it appears to overrule *Brennan*, allowing execution of those who commit crimes as sixteen-year-olds and making Florida the first state in America to have the death penalty in its state constitution. In the 2003 legislative session, the Florida senate passed a bill banning juvenile executions. The law failed to pass in the Florida house. A similar bill again passed in the Florida senate in the 2004 legislative session but it's companion bill died in committee on the house side.[29]

The American death penalty is not in accordance with biblical principles when it comes to the execution of persons for crimes committed as juveniles. There are some indications of small steps in the right direction. Half of the death penalty states, however, allow execution of those under the age of eighteen (when the crime occurred). Most significantly, all the death penalty jurisdictions in America, including the federal government, allow execution of eighteen-year olds. Even if the U.S. Supreme Court bans juvenile executions, the benchmark in issue is age eighteen. This will continue to allow the execution of those under the age of twenty at the time of the offense throughout the United States. If we were applying the standards of the biblical truth of Torah/ Pentateuch and the provisions of Talmud that fulfill those scriptural limitations, there would be no one on America's death rows for crimes committed under the age of twenty.

THE EXECUTION OF MENTALLY ILL UNDER THE AMERICAN DEATH PENALTY

How does the American death penalty stack up against the biblical death penalty on the issue of exempting the mentally ill? We must start our answer by addressing the problem of criminalization of the mentally ill in America.

NAMI [formerly known as the National Alliance for the Mentally Ill] believes that, in the overwhelming majority of cases, dangerous or violent acts committed by persons with brain disorders are the result of neglect or inappropriate or inadequate treatment of their illness. State and local mental health authorities must develop policies and programs to provide care and appropriate treatment for persons who suffer from brain disorders that produce behaviors assessed and labeled by society as "criminal" or "violent." Where a mental illness and substance abuse co-occur they should be treated with integrated treatment.[30] (bracketed language mine)

NAMI points to recent research indicating that instead of treatment, many of America's mentally ill are falling into criminal incarceration:

A report issued by the United States Department of Justice in 1999 revealed that 16 percent of all inmates in state and federal jails and prisons have schizophrenia, manic-depressive illness (bipolar disorder), major depression, or another severe mental illness. This means that on any given day, there are roughly 283,000 persons with severe mental illnesses incarcerated in federal and state jails and prisons. . . .

Conditions in jails and prisons are often terrifying for people with severe mental illnesses. These settings are not conducive to effectively treating people with these brain disorders. Many correctional facilities do not have qualified mental health professionals on staff to recognize and respond to the needs of inmates experiencing severe psychiatric symptoms. Correctional facilities frequently respond to psychotic inmates by punishing them or placing them in physical restraints or administrative segregation (isolation), responses that may exacerbate rather than alleviate their symptoms.[31]

There is no secret as to how things became this way. In the 1960s and early 1970s, this country was swept by an enlightened and benign view that the best treatment of the mentally ill is deinstitutionalization. The mentally ill should be dispatched from mental hospitals and sent home to their communities where they would be supported by community mental health centers. The community mental health centers, funded by the money saved from downsizing mental hospitals, would enable America's mentally ill to live a quality life outside institutions.

To make a long story short, the easiest part of the plan was completed: hospital beds for the mentally ill were drastically reduced to a mere fraction of their former numbers, and the mentally ill were dumped back into their home communities. That is about as far as America progressed on the plan. "Fifty years ago . . . half a million mentally ill Americans lived in public mental health hospitals. . . . Today fewer than eighty thousand people live in mental hospitals and that number is likely to fall still further." (citations omitted)[32]

By the time we should have been funding the community mental health centers, the Arab oil embargo and its legacy had pushed the prime rate into the stratosphere. The economy was on life support; Iran had seized our embassy; the USSR was invading Afghanistan; and the cold war was perilously close to becoming hot. Money was tight, and whatever funds were available were needed for defense and economic stimulation. The deinstitutionalized mentally ill poured into our city centers, surviving day-to-day on the streets and in the alleys of the most violent neighborhoods in the country: "The federal government did not provide ongoing funding for community services and while states cut their budgets for mental hospitals, they did not make commensurate increases in their budgets for community-based mental health services."[33]

During the late 1980s and early 1990s, I was a volunteer handling trust funds for the mentally ill on the streets in Tallahassee, Florida's state capital. Aside from being robbed, raped, and constantly in fear for their lives, a primary concern of the mentally ill that I served was their frequent visits to the county jail. Not by design, but by pure default, the criminal justice system has become the treatment plan for our severely mentally ill. That means they end up behind bars because there is nowhere else for them to go. We are told it is a good thing because it saves taxpayers money. Punishment is cheaper than treatment. The numbers of incarcerated mentally ill are astounding: "According to the American Psychiatric Association, over 700,000 mentally ill Americans are processed through either jail or prison each year. In 1999, NAMI . . . reported that the number of Americans with serious mental illnesses in prison was three times greater than the number hospitalized with such illnesses."[34] (citations omitted)

Florida is no better or worse than the rest of the country. We are also imprisoning our severely mentally ill, turning them over to a massive state agency whose mission is punishment—not treatment. "At least one in nine state prisoners in Florida suffers from *severe* mental illness."[35]

That translates to about eight thousand severely mentally ill persons in Florida state prisons. And when the severely mentally ill cannot make it in prison, when they decompensate and act out, they are moved to solitary confinement, now called close management: locked for years at a time in a six-by-ten-foot steel and concrete cage behind a steel door without air-conditioning. They are fed through a hole in the door. This is one of the areas in which I minister as a chaplain. One prison alone has over a thousand such cells. A neighboring prison has several hundred more such cells now under construction.

Such is the fate of the mentally ill in America today. This fate falls disproportionately upon the poor and upon minorities. According to a U.S. surgeon general's report issued by Dr. David Satcher, these groups "suffer a disproportionate burden of mental illness." Services are less available and quality of care is lower for those at the lowest end of the socioeconomic ladder. Consequently, higher proportions of those groups find themselves with unmet needs for mental health services, including those who are incarcerated.[36]

Within the broad confines of those vulnerable and needy populations are the "survivors of traumatic experiences." This includes our military veterans who are a persistent presence among the mentally ill in our streets and those in our prisons.

With such huge problems surrounding the care and treatment for the mentally ill, it is inevitable that this issue would present itself in the area of America's death penalty. My personal experiences on death row indicate that the incidence of mental illness on death row is at least as high, if not higher, than those quoted for the prison population at large. The tragedy of this situation for a person of biblical faith is best described by the following true story from Florida's death row.

This is the story of Thomas Provenzano. Thomas lived on the streets of Orlando. He had been severely mentally ill for many years. Long before he was arrested, he believed he was Jesus Christ. This was a very ill man struggling to exist in the rough "survival of the fittest" streets of a large Florida city. "Fifteen years ago, Provenzano walked into the Orange County Courthouse muttering threats against two police officers who had charged him with disorderly conduct. Beneath his jacket, he had concealed a shotgun, an assault rifle and a revolver. The knapsack he carried held ammunition. When three bailiffs decided to search him, Provenzano opened fire. He killed one of the bailiffs and paralyzed two others."[37]

One can feel only gut-wrenching compassion for the paralyzed victims and the survivors of the deceased victim of this horrible crime. Many avenues of critical analysis might have followed this tragedy. An obvious line of thought would have started with the question: "Why was such a sick man, who suffered from psychotic delusions and paranoid schizophrenia, able to acquire a shotgun, an assault rifle, and a revolver and ammunition in downtown Orlando, Florida?" Such questions and lines of inquiry were not to be part of the public discourse.

The issue that monopolized the day was whether it is legal in Florida to execute a man who is so mentally ill that he believes he is Jesus Christ. The legal standard in the United States for executing a mentally ill person is simple: the condemned man must know he is about to be killed and he must know why. There is no requirement that the mentally ill man knows who he himself is or that he not be psychotic.

This level of discussion reached all the way to the state capitol building in Tallahassee. There were those who were appalled at the imminent execution of a man who was certifiably mentally ill before he even committed his crime, was denied treatment for mental illness by the state before he ever became violent,[38] and was now to be killed by the same government that had refused to treat him.

Others railed against making excuses for the mentally ill, claiming that it amounted to pampering and coddling criminals:

> A fed up House lawmaker suggested Wednesday that the state crucify Thomas Provenzano, a condemned killer whose delusions of being Jesus Christ have helped keep him out of the electric chair.
>
> Rep. Howard Futch, R-Indialantic, made the suggestion to fellow lawmakers at a House Criminal Justice and Corrections Council meeting.
>
> "I told them that if he thinks he is Jesus Christ, why don't we just crucify him," Futch said. "I'd make him a cross, and we could take it out there to Starke and nail him up."[39]

The tenor of Representative Futch's comments are even more baffling in light of the fact that Provenzano's family tried for years to obtain treatment for him. None was available. Florida ranks in the cellar of the fifty states in caring for its mentally ill. Yet, even as discussions were taking place in Tallahassee about crucifying Thomas Provenzano, the Florida governor's office had plans under way to close one of the state's few remaining mental hospitals, eliminating another 350 beds for mental health patients in Florida.[40]

Thomas Provenzano was executed. The mental hospital was closed in February 2002, with more than two hundred of the last three hundred patients being discharged to their home communities.[41] Where there are no community services being funded, that means "discharged to the streets."

This story is not unique. Take the case of Larry Robison from Texas. He was a young adult, twenty-one years of age, when he was honorably discharged from the air force after only one year of service. No explanation was given. He returned to his home state of Texas. It turned out he was manifesting the symptoms of paranoid schizophrenia.

The state of Texas refused to provide his treatment, saying that because of limited resources the state could not treat him for mental illness unless he had become violent. His mother ended up suing the state of Texas to try and obtain treatment for her severely mentally ill son's paranoid schizophrenia. In her civil lawsuit she was unsuccessful.[42]

On August 10, 1982, Robison experienced a complete psychotic break. It was the first time he had ever become violent. Under the delusion of instructions from God to liberate souls, he killed five people. Now his mother found herself trying to stop the state of Texas from executing him.[43]

The state of Texas, which had refused to spend any money to treat his mental illness, now expended an estimated $2.3 million to execute him.[44] "[E]xecuting a criminal who suffered from mental illness before he murdered and who lacked the resources for psychiatric care serves no public purpose. . . . [T]he nation's 2nd largest state ranks 48th for mental health investments overall."[45]

The state of Texas, which ranks forty-eighth of the fifty states in mental health services, executed Larry Robison on January 21, 2000.

The standards of biblical truth reveal that the American death penalty fails miserably when it comes to addressing the mentally ill.

THE EXECUTION OF THE MENTALLY RETARDED
UNDER THE AMERICAN DEATH PENALTY

Based upon a landmark decision rendered by the U.S. Supreme Court in June 2002, *Atkins v. Virginia*, it is unconstitutional in America to execute the mentally retarded.[46] In its opinion, the court noted:

Given the well-known fact that anticrime legislation is far more popular than legislation providing protections for persons guilty of violent crime, the large number of States prohibiting the execution of mentally retarded persons (and the complete absence of States passing legislation reinstating the power to conduct such executions) provides powerful evidence that today our society views mentally retarded offenders as categorically less culpable than the average criminal. The evidence carries even greater force when it is noted that the legislatures that have addressed the issue have voted overwhelmingly in favor of the prohibition. Moreover, even in those States that allow the execution of mentally retarded offenders, the practice is uncommon.[47] (citations omitted)

The Court also identified specific concerns about the mentally retarded as capital punishment defendants:

The risk "that the death penalty will be imposed in spite of factors which call for a less severe penalty," is enhanced, not only by the possibility of false confessions, but also by the lesser ability of mentally retarded defendants to make a persuasive showing of mitigation in the face of prosecutorial evidence of one or more aggravating factors. Mentally retarded defendants may be less able to give meaningful assistance to their counsel and are typically poor witnesses, and their demeanor may create an unwarranted impression of lack of remorse for their crimes.[48] (citations omitted)

The Court noted the clinical definition of mental retardation:

[C]linical definitions of mental retardation require not only subaverage intellectual functioning, but also significant limitations in adaptive skills such as communication, self-care, and self-direction that become manifest before age 18. Mentally retarded persons frequently know the difference between right and wrong and are competent to stand trial. Because of their impairments, however, by definition they have diminished capacities to understand and process information, to communicate, to abstract from mistakes and learn from experience, to

engage in logical reasoning, to control impulses, and to understand the reactions of others. There is no evidence that they
are more likely to engage in criminal conduct than others. . . .
Their deficiencies do not warrant an exemption from criminal
sanctions, but diminish their personal culpability.[49]

What the U.S. Supreme Court left open in its decision is the
basis for determining the existence of mental retardation. This
has been left up to each of the states to determine for itself. On a
sophisticated level, that issue centers around a debate over
whether mental retardation should be determined solely on the
basis of IQ or should be a composite standard melding IQ and
other developmental and adaptive factors. That level of discussion is too complicated for sound-bite politics.

The new battle line on this issue for political purposes is being
drawn as follows: what is the IQ level appropriate to establish
mental retardation for exclusion from the death penalty?

Part of the answer to that oversimplified question can be
gleaned from the facts in cases of the kind that *Atkins* hopes to
ameliorate. For example, there's the case of Jerry Frank Townsend,
forty-nine, a retarded man from Miami who spent twenty-two
years behind bars for six murders. He had pled guilty to four
murders and a rape and was convicted of two other murders.
DNA testing proved that he was not guilty of two of the crimes
for which he was serving seven life terms in prison. At the request
of the prosecuting attorneys, the other convictions were struck as
well.[50]

As mentioned by the U.S. Supreme Court in *Atkins*, the risk
of false confessions given to please police is exactly the kind of
vulnerability that makes it unconstitutional to execute the mentally retarded. Townsend has an IQ of about 60.[51] Can there be
any doubt that a man with that level of IQ should be exempted?

The actual condemned man in the U.S. Supreme Court case,
Daryl Atkins, has an IQ of 59. Clearly that is covered. There is
also a footnote concerning the case of Jerome Bowden, a man
executed by the state of Georgia in June 1986. In the footnote
the Court notes that Bowden "had an IQ of 65, which is consistent with mental retardation."[52] This will suggest to many observ-

ers that the Court is of the opinion that an IQ of 65 is definitely within the range they intend.

What about an IQ of 69? "In 1983, police convinced Earl Washington (with an IQ of 69) to make a statement concerning the rape and murder of a woman in Culpeper, VA, in 1982. The statements were used against him and in 1984 he was convicted and sentenced to death. Sixteen years later, DNA tests confirmed that Washington was innocent and he received an absolute pardon."[53] One would certainly think that an IQ of 69 precludes the death penalty based on the clear logic of the *Atkins* decision and the actual case of Earl Washington. Yet, when large numbers are at stake, things that should be clear seem to blur. The impact of this Supreme Court decision is not small. The numbers of mentally retarded involved in death row is more than one would guess. Although the mentally retarded make up only about 3 percent of the population at large, it is estimated that they account for about 10 percent of the men and women on death row.[54]

For at least the next few years, we can expect the media to report news about the battles over standards for mental retardation and the death penalty. Florida provides a good example of what the states will be experiencing as they each navigate this new standard.

THE FLORIDA EXPERIENCE WITH MENTAL RETARDATION

Since 1976, thirty-four offenders with mental retardation have been executed in the United States, four of them in Florida.[55] Then, on June 12, 2001, Florida became one of the eighteen death penalty states that prohibited execution of the mentally retarded before the *Atkins* decision. Governor Jeb Bush signed a bill prohibiting the execution of the mentally retarded.[56] The statute, however, did not set an IQ standard for mental retardation. "Instead, it allows two court-appointed experts to evaluate a defendant's mental capacity."[57] That is when Florida politicians started arguing about IQ levels. Under *Atkins* the arguments will now continue nationwide.

The IQ level of 69 is the standard that the state of Florida uses for providing social services to the adult mentally retarded.[58] Of the 365 inmates currently residing on Florida's death row, an estimated 10 to 15 percent have IQs under 70. If an IQ of 69 is the cutoff for exemption from the Florida death penalty, it is estimated that between twenty and forty people on Florida's death row would be affected.[59]

Pro–death penalty politicians, however, are arguing for some of the prior proposals suggested in Florida, such as setting the standard for mental retardation at an IQ of 50 to 55 or lower. If that standard is used, not one mentally retarded person on Florida's death row will be exempted from the death penalty. One Florida defense lawyer noted that for a person with an IQ of 50 to 55 to kill someone, he would have to fall out of a window onto the victim.

In August 2003, the Florida Supreme Court held oral arguments on its proposed rule to implement the ban on executions of the mentally retarded. Numerous parties argued for making the determination of mental retardation prior to the trial and setting a proof standard of "preponderance of the evidence." Supporters of this approach included circuit judge O. H. Eaton, chairperson of the Florida Supreme Court's Criminal Court Steering Committee; Michael Messer, executive director of the South Florida Chapter of the Association for Retarded Citizens; and defense lawyers.[60]

The current draft of the rule provides for making the determination only after the defendant has been found guilty and places the burden of proof on the defendant by "clear and convincing evidence," a significantly higher burden than "preponderance of the evidence." This is the approach supported by the Florida Prosecuting Attorneys Association.[61]

CLOSING THOUGHTS

Clearly, the American death penalty is nowhere close to the standards of the biblical death penalty with respect to juveniles and the mentally ill. We may be closer to biblical standards with respect to the mentally retarded than we are with any other aspect we've addressed. Yet, even on this count, we are not at the place revealed by the biblical truth of Torah/Pentateuch and the provisions of Talmud that fulfill those scriptural limitations. We have only begun to take a few small, tentative steps in that direction. In Florida, at least, on the issues of both mental retardation and juveniles, it has been one step toward the standards of biblical truth, followed by three steps backward. On mental illness, we are still moving in the wrong direction.

Before completing our search, we have just a few more topics to address: the troublesome issues of economics, race, and politics under the standards of the biblical death penalty and the American death penalty.

Chapter Seventeen

GOD IS BLIND TO WEALTH

NO PRIVILEGE FOR RICH OVER POOR

As we have already seen, the primary focus of the death penalty when the scriptures of Torah/Pentateuch and the provisions of Talmud necessary to fulfill them were setting the standards to be observed was the fear of executing the innocent. Other critical restrictions, however, also applied to the death penalty. *One of these concerns was the biblical mandate that all murder defendants are to be treated the same regardless of wealth.*

> You may not accept a ransom for the life of a murderer who is guilty of a capital crime.   Num. 35:31 TNK
>
> Moreover ye shall take no satisfaction for the life of a murderer, which is guilty of death.   Num. 35:31 AV
>
> Do not accept a ransom for the life of a murderer who deserves to die.   Num. 35:31 NIV

The purpose of this scriptural prohibition is to prevent the death penalty from falling on the poor while sparing the rich. The scriptures of Torah/Pentateuch contemplated that if the murderer comes from a wealthy family, his kin might seek to buy his way out of a death sentence by paying off a ransom to the family of the victim. Under the biblical death penalty, this practice was prohibited even when the family of the victim was willing to accept the money in lieu of a death sentence. Mendelsohn summarizes the rule as follows: "[The biblical death penalty] forbids taking blood-money from the murderer . . . in strict accordance with the Mosaic prohibition . . . even when the avenger is willing to compromise by the acceptance of a ransom."[1] (citations omitted)

Under the biblical death penalty, "the avenger" has the duty of bringing a murderer to justice. This role, which in modern America is vested in the prosecutors and district attorneys, rests biblically upon the "avenger of the blood," the nearest relative or heir of the victim of the crime, or in the case of a slave, the master. The avenger of the blood under the biblical death penalty is a carryover from the age of clan vengeance. Pre–Mosaic law, the avenger of the blood had the duty to carry out human vengeance.

Whether rich, poor or in-between, the biblical death penalty requires that the ultimate sanction apply equally to all the people. This is consistent with the more general biblical admonition about administering justice without regard to economic status:

Do not favor the poor or show deference to the rich.
Lev. 19:15 TNK

Thou shalt not respect the person of the poor nor honor the person of the mighty.   Lev. 19:15 AV

Do not show partiality to the poor or favoritism to the great.
Lev. 19:15 NIV

In a nutshell, biblical truth demands that the rich enjoy no advantage and the poor suffer no detriment in regard to the death penalty. How does the death penalty in America today measure up to the biblical requirement that everyone be treated the same regardless of economic status? Very, very badly. The American experience with capital punishment is that both the rich and the poor obtain all the justice they can afford.

THE FATE OF THE POOR UNDER THE AMERICAN DEATH PENALTY

The problem of capital punishment being reserved for those who are without capital has plagued the American death penalty from the beginning. "The one characteristic of almost all people who receive the death penalty, however, is that they are poor."[2] Justice William O. Douglas summed it up well in his words in the *Furman v. Georgia* decision: "One searches our chronicles in vain for the execution of any member of the affluent strata in this society."[3]

In biblical times, economic inequalities were reflected by the ability of one's kin to pay a ransom. In modern America, the inequities of wealth are reflected by one's ability to retain competent legal counsel for defense at trial and for appeals. Attorney Stephen B. Bright is one of the most knowledgeable Americans about the problem of economic disparities and America's death rows. In addition to being the director of the Southern Center for Human Rights in Atlanta, Georgia, he is a visiting lecturer in law at Yale Law School and Harvard Law School. Bright, who has been involved in representation of those facing the death penalty at trials, on appeals, and in postconviction proceedings since 1979, observes: "Poor people accused of capital crimes are often defended by lawyers who lack the skills, resources, and commitment to handle such serious matters. This fact is confirmed in case after case. It is not the facts of the crime, but the quality of legal representation, that distinguishes [cases], where the death penalty was imposed, from many similar cases, where it was not."[4] (citations omitted)

The problem of disparate resources is exacerbated by America's completely adversarial legal system. Under this system, each side has a lawyer whose job it is to investigate the facts, research the law, and argue the case before a judge. The judge sits as a referee, and a jury decides guilt or innocence. In such a system, the resources available for investigation and research and the relative abilities of the parties' respective attorneys can make the difference as to which side wins. That can result in some very unjust verdicts in civil cases where small folk are pitted against huge corporate or government interests. Even worse, when access to a fair trial in the criminal justice system is governed by open market parameters, "best lawyers go to the highest bidder," the result is plea bargains and slipshod representation for many of the poor while silk-stocking representation is provided to the rich.

THE WORST LAWYERS FOR THE POOR FACING DEATH

Bright notes that this perversion of justice is not an occasional problem; rather, it is endemic to our American death penalty system: "Inadequate legal representation does not occur in just a few capital cases. It is pervasive in those jurisdictions which account for most of the death sentences. The American Bar Association concluded after an exhaustive study of the issues that 'the inadequacy and inadequate compensation of counsel at trial' was one of the 'principal failings of the capital punishment systems in the states today.'"[5] (citations omitted)

The disparity in representation based on wealth is a major issue that goes to the essence of whether the American death penalty is fair and just, not only in individual cases, but systemwide: "The process of sorting out who is most deserving of society's ultimate punishment does not work when the most fundamental component of the adversary system, competent representation by counsel, is missing."[6] (citations omitted)

From his review of hundreds of cases, Bright concludes that the American death penalty fails to provide justice:

> Imposition of the death penalty was not so much the result of the heinousness of the crime or the incorrigibility of the defendant, but rather of how bad the lawyers were. In consequence, a large part of the death row population is made up of people who are distinguished by neither their records nor the circumstances of their crimes, but by their abject poverty, debilitating mental impairments, minimal intelligence, and the poor legal representation they received.[7] (citations omitted)

The resulting injustices are so dramatic that the imposition of the American death penalty begins to resemble a lottery more than a justice system. "The *National Law Journal*, after an extensive study of capital cases in six Southern states, found that capital trials are 'more like a random flip of the coin than a delicate balancing of the scales' because the defense lawyer is too often 'ill trained, unprepared . . . [and] grossly underpaid.'"[8] (ellipsis and brackets in original; citations omitted)

The disparity in representation due to wealth reaches beyond the trial and into the appeals process as well: "The adversary system often breaks down at the appellate level as well. The poor defendant usually does not receive representation equal to that of the prosecution."[9] (citations omitted)

As noted earlier, the impact of these discrepancies is magnified under America's adversarial legal process. At least under the standards of the biblical death penalty, only the witnesses were adversarial. The judges were mandated to seek out the truth. Under the American death penalty system, the accused without wealth is stuck with whatever representation the state provides. Neither the state nor the judge is required to intervene. In fact, the worse the legal representation is for a poor defendant, the better it is for the state because it makes the prosecutor's job of obtaining a conviction easier—whether the accused is really guilty or not. Bright points out that

> [s]tate trial judges and prosecutors . . . have allowed capital trials to proceed and death sentences to be imposed even when defense counsel fought among themselves or . . . referred to their clients by a racial slur . . . slept through part of the trial, or [were] intoxicated during trial. Appellate courts often review and decide capital cases on the basis of appellate briefs that would be rejected in a first-year legal writing course in law school.[10] (citations omitted)

Bright pulls no punches in establishing the root cause: "There are several interrelated reasons for the poor quality of representation in these important cases. Most fundamental is the wholly inadequate funding for the defense of indigents."[11]

For the biblical death penalty, money is a danger. Biblical truth knows that if the death penalty is in force, money should not be allowed to buy ransom; otherwise, the poor are punished for their lack of wealth. The same rules must apply equally to rich and poor alike. Under the American death penalty, money is a problem. Money is a determining factor in who sits on death row and who goes free, in who is killed and who lives.

Although it is rare indeed for the courts under the American death penalty to recognize that the amount of funding for defense counsel can jeopardize the constitutional guarantee of a fair trial, anyone familiar with the system knows that it is true.

The United States Court of Appeals for the Fifth Circuit, finding that Federico Martinez-Macias "was denied his constitutional right to adequate counsel in a capital case in which [his] actual innocence was a close question," observed that, "The state [Texas] paid defense counsel $11.84 per hour. Unfortunately, the justice system got only what it paid for." What is unusual about the case is not the amount paid to counsel, but the court's acknowledgement of its impact on the quality of services rendered."[12] (citations omitted)

While $11.84 per hour would have been a high wage for many of the poor and destitute who now sit on America's death rows, high-profile, experienced criminal defense attorneys charge ten times that or more in Texas. The extent to which the problem of disparate legal representation based on wealth pervades the American death penalty is easily glimpsed by sampling results of newspaper investigations into the issue. While not many states have had the benefit of such investigations, those investigations that have been done show amazingly similar results.

TEXAS

In a special investigative series, "Death Penalty in America,"[13] the *Chicago Tribune* explored the underpinnings of the death penalty systems in several states, including Texas.[14] The *Chicago Tribune's* findings about the death penalty in Texas include the following.[15]

Of the 131 cases where a death row inmate has been executed in Texas (from the beginning of 1995 until the end of 1999), 29 included a psychiatrist who gave testimony that the American Psychiatric Association condemned as unethical and untrustworthy; 43 included defense attorneys publicly sanctioned for misconduct—either before or after their work on cases; and 40 involved trials where the defense attorney presented no evidence or only one witness during the sentencing phase.

Among the 131 cases, the following irregularities also appeared: 23 included jailhouse informants, considered among the least credible of witnesses, and 23 included visual hair analysis that has consistently proved unreliable. In 34 of the 43 cases mentioned earlier, the sanctioned attorney was disbarred, suspended, or given what is called a "probated suspension." A probated suspension allows the lawyer to continue practicing if certain requirements are met—for example, seeking drug treatment or paying restitution to victimized clients. In the other 9 cases, the attorney was reprimanded.

Lest there be any doubt that the appointment of inadequate counsel for poor defendants in capital cases is a part of the American death penalty system, the investigative report noted: "Most of the sanctioned attorneys in Texas were appointed by local judges to represent defendants too poor to hire their own lawyer."[16]

And, of course, there is the legendary sleeping defense lawyer. In Texas it has become an art form. "Joe F. Cannon, a Houston attorney . . . was infamous for sleeping during trials and speeding through cases to please judges with heavy backlogs." He never received any sanction, but his clients paid dearly for his bad habits. "Cannon was the court-appointed attorney for three men executed [during the five years of the study]."[17]

The study also found that the state spent large amounts of money to "purchase" expert testimony in its favor. According to the *Chicago Tribune* investigation, a Dallas psychiatrist who had been expelled from the American Psychiatric Association in 1995 "because it found his testimony unethical and untrustworthy" was known to predict a defendant's future dangerousness without even examining him. Public records showed that, even at rates of $150 per hour, prosecutors called on him so frequently that he "usually earned more than $150,000 a year."[18]

In the American legal system it is not unusual for decisions to hinge on "expert testimony," which is the testimony of someone with special knowledge and training in specialties such as doctors, psychologists, or psychiatrists. An expert, who usually gives opinion testimony on behalf of one side at a trial, is paid by that side. Many trials boil down to a battle of the experts, who have been hired by each side. For example, in a circumstantial evidence case, there may be tire marks, or blood splatter or cloth fibers that have been recovered from the crime scene. The state may hire experts, chemists, and scientists, who will testify for the state in favor of convicting the defendant.

In many cases, an indigent defendant lacks the resources to hire experts to combat such testimony. Their underpaid, and sometimes incompetent, lawyers lack the skills or the resources to discredit such testimony. Consequently, prosecutors in the state of Texas were virtually able to purchase death sentences through acquisition of such canned expert psychological testimony.

TENNESSEE

The magnitude of this problem is not limited to Texas. In an extensive investigative report by the *Tennessean*, the death penalty in Tennessee is put under the microscope. "Special Report: Tennessee Death Penalty," a five-part series consisting of twenty-five articles,[19] addresses various aspects of the death penalty system in that state, including the appointment of incompetent counsel to represent indigent defendants.

Dozens of lawyers who have defended clients facing the death penalty in Tennessee have been in trouble themselves—disciplined by the state for unethical, unprofessional or illegal activities, a *Tennessean* search of public records has found.

Eleven of them appear on a current list of lawyers who meet Tennessee Supreme Court standards for future appointment in death penalty cases.

This list of eligible defense attorneys, circulated to trial judges by the state Supreme Court as a guide, includes a lawyer convicted of bank fraud, a lawyer convicted of perjury, and a lawyer whose failure to order a blood test let an innocent man linger in jail for four years on a rape charge.

In the past quarter century, at least 39 Tennessee lawyers

who have been disciplined by the state have represented defendants in capital cases, which federal courts repeatedly have
said require the highest legal standards. Most of the lawyers'
misconduct did not result in a death sentence being overturned, even in cases where the misconduct was directly related.[20]

According to the *Tennessean's* investigative report, there is no
confusion about the fact that such lawyers should not be handling
capital cases: " 'There are a lot of lawyers on your list who should
not have been defending a capital case,' said Lance Bracy, chief
disciplinary counsel for the Board of Professional Responsibility,
which investigates complaints against lawyers. 'They were wrecks
waiting to happen.' "[21] Yet these sanctioned attorneys were foisted
upon defendants who were too poor to pay for their own counsel:
"Trial judges use the list to make appointments when defendants
cannot afford a lawyer and where a public defender cannot take
the case—usually because of a client conflict or because the demands of a capital case would overwhelm the defender's office."[22]
    This has taken place in spite of general knowledge that capital
cases demand more skills and more caution than any other criminal case. According to David Keefe of the state Public Defender
Conference's capital division, which trains defense lawyers:
"There are dozens of cases from the U.S. Supreme Court that talk
about the need for heightened reliability and the need for extreme
precision and care in death penalty cases. To appoint a lawyer,
when you know right from the starting blocks that you've got
some evidence this lawyer does not always perform up to par,
gives the lie to that standard."[23]
    Few laypeople would imagine that judges might assign lawyers
to cases against their will. The *Tennessean* documented that such
assignments do take place. Consider the case of "Harry Scruggs
Jr., a Memphis lawyer suspended after he was sentenced to a federal prison term of one year for theft and obstructing justice."

When Scruggs petitioned for reinstatement, colleagues testified to his good moral character and he testified he would con-
fine his practice to civil, not criminal, law. Even so, judges later
assigned Scruggs to capital cases.

He briefly represented convicted cop-killer Philip Workman on appeal and later defended at trial Timothy Harris, sentenced to death for a 1990 Memphis murder.

"Man, I was trying to sneak out the door when the judge appointed me to Harris," Scruggs recalled recently. "I really didn't want to do anything more complicated than DUI or divorce."[24]

NORTH CAROLINA

A recent report issued by the Common Sense Foundation[25] reveals a shocking situation in North Carolina with respect to many of those lawyers who have been appointed to handle the defense for death penalty cases. The following is from a summary of the report, which was prepared by the executive director, David Mills.

More than one in six current death row inmates was represented at trial by lawyers who have been disciplined by the North Carolina State Bar, according to a new report released today by the Common Sense Foundation, a statewide public policy organization based in Raleigh.

One of the attorneys cited . . . represented current death row inmate Kenny Neal at his capital trial in 1996. The state appointed [the attorney] to the case not long after he was released from serving time in federal prison for child pornography charges. Jurors said after the trial that they knew about [the attorney's] felony conviction and it affected their perception of his arguments. . . .

The report includes only attorneys who were formally disciplined, so the numbers do not reflect many cases in which court-appointed attorneys performed poorly. The lawyer for a man executed last year admitted to drinking 12 shots of rum every night during the capital trial. He was not formally disciplined by the Bar.

State officials recently overhauled the way lawyers are appointed to represent indigent clients, confirmation that they too recognize the flaws in the old system—the system under which the 208 current death row inmates were convicted and sentenced. . . .

Thirty-five of the inmates currently awaiting execution were represented by disciplined attorneys. Mills says there is only one way for the state to respond to the report: grant new trials for all 35 inmates.[26] (bracketed language mine)

WASHINGTON STATE

The problem of inadequate legal representation of the poor in capital cases is by no means confined to the Bible Belt. The northwest corner of the continental United States is about as far as one can get from the Bible Belt. When it comes to the death penalty, however, the appointment of counsel for the poor is no different from that in the Deep South.

In "Death Penalty: Uncertain Justice," a three-part series consisting of twelve articles,[27] the Seattle Post-Intelligencer delved into the realities of Washington's death penalty. The report concluded that, although the "state authorizes the death penalty," it does not take the steps necessary to make sure "that defendants are represented equally." Illustrating this conclusion was the fact that at least one out of every five persons on Washington State's death row was represented by attorneys who "had been, or were later, disbarred, suspended or arrested."[28]

The lead article of the series,[29] which focused upon the crisis in legal representation of the poor, documented pervasive problems with the funding of legal services and selection of defense attorneys for indigents in capital cases. In addition to broad discrepancies in the handling of such matters throughout the state, the report determined that judges appoint "inexperienced local lawyers" in such cases "instead of those recommended by the state"; and then, the woefully inadequate lawyers are paid woefully inadequate fees to handle the cases. The inevitable result is shoddy defense, "putting convictions and sentences on shaky legal ground."

The article went on to elaborate that in death penalty cases, the accused receives only the quality of lawyer for which the state is willing to pay by showing that although the rate of disbarment among Washington's lawyers at large is less than 1 percent, the rate of disbarment among lawyers handling death penalty cases is approximately 500 percent higher.[30]

In other words, just like in biblical times, the root of the issue is about money. However, the Bible prohibited the poor from being penalized for being poor, while in America, the justice system assures that the poor, including the innocent poor, are many times more likely to be convicted and sentenced to death than the wealthy.

ALABAMA

In the five-part investigative report "Execution of Justice," the *Birmingham Post-Herald* put the spotlight on the death penalty in the state of Alabama.[31] One of the major issues addressed was the lack of adequate provision, by funding or otherwise, of lawyers for capital murder trials and death row appeals.

Bo Cochran was on Alabama's death row for twenty years before he was released in 1997. Many believe that it was lack of resources that put him there. His new lawyer, Richard Jaffe, won his release: "'His lawyers, although good lawyers, had their hands tied behind their back,' Jaffe said. 'They had no funds. At the time they were given $1,000 (to represent Cochran). There is no way someone can get a fair shake with those kinds of limitations.'"[32]

As bad as that sounds, the stories get worse. Another article in the series, "Justice at 50 Cents an Hour: Defending Death Row Case Drove Lawyer into Bankruptcy," reveals the quandary of a death row lawyer who must either fail to adequately represent his client or go bankrupt doing it right.

The state paid Bob French about 50 cents an hour to try to save Judith Ann Neelley's life.

French said he worked thousands of hours preparing the defense for the 1983 capital murder trial. He argued that Neelley was a battered wife, that her husband had forced her to inject a 13-year-old girl with drain cleaner then shoot her in the back in DeKalb County. Neelley was indigent, so French was appointed to handle the case.

He doesn't remember exactly, but he said the state paid him between $500 and $1,000 for his work. By French's estimate, he and his Fort Payne office sank $340,000 into the case. It pushed him into bankruptcy.

"I don't want any more capital murder cases," he said.

The Neelley case is an extreme example of what death penalty lawyers faced for more than two decades in Alabama. The state wouldn't pay a lawyer more than $2,000, plus overhead expenses, for work on a capital case.[33]

The tale gets even worse than that, however, for the many inmates on Alabama's death row. As also reported in the *Birmingham Post-Herald*, the Alabama practice appears to be: No lawyer? No money for a lawyer? Too bad.

Everyone accused of a crime has a right to an attorney.

But in Alabama, that right disappears at some point during the appeals process, leaving about 40 of 185 death row inmates without representation.

Alabama is the only state that doesn't guarantee a lawyer or fund an office to help death row inmates find lawyers. And since the state pays so little to handle an appeal of a capital case, few attorneys vie for the privilege.[34]

As presented earlier, investigative journalists have, in many states, allowed us to peek behind the veil of the American death penalty to see if the same rules apply to rich and to poor. Not every state has had the benefit of a journalistic investigative report into the funding of trial defense and appellate counsel for death row inmates. That does not mean, however, that in other states the system is any better.

OHIO

Recently, Stephen Bright addressed a gathering of lawyers in Ohio concerning the inadequate system of indigent defense in capital cases in Ohio, stating the following:

Twenty-four counties here in Ohio pay less than $20,000 to the two lawyers appointed to defend a death penalty case. If the two together spend 1,000 hours defending that case it means that they are going to be paid less than $20 an hour; in some counties, they will be paid $5 per hour. Most of the business people and most of the lawyers in this room know what kind of legal representation you are going to get for $20 an hour. . . .

. . . I once defended a capital case and was paid so little that I could have gone to McDonald's and flipped hamburgers and made more than I made defending someone whose life was at stake. There are not many lawyers who are willing to do that. That is why this problem is not isolated to Houston, not isolated to Philadelphia, but is pervasive.[35]

MISSOURI

In her in-depth look at the process of clemency in death penalty cases—a nonfunctioning process that is defined less by what it accomplishes than by what it fails to do—Cathleen Burnett makes passing mention of legal disasters she stumbled upon in her research on Missouri's death row. "Robert Sidebottom was executed without having a lawyer to handle his appeals; Jessie Wise, in part, acted as his own lawyer; Bert Hunter pled guilty without a trial and without a lawyer to counsel him; and Gary Roll waived his right to a jury in both the trial and sentencing."[36]

She also mentions having been told that the state of Missouri offered to pay one attorney only three thousand dollars to take a case.[37] As we can see, the problems of paying for adequate defense for those facing execution covers the country, from coast to coast and all the way to the center.

FLORIDA

The disparities in treatment between capital defendants with money and those without it can be manifest even in states that provide state-funded counsel for defense at trial and for appeals. Florida is an excellent example of this fact.

Florida and California, which have two of the country's three largest death rows, have public defender programs, but many capital cases in those states are handled by assigned counsel outside of the public defender system. Florida has an elected public defender in each judicial circuit. . . . Even though these programs cannot handle the huge volume of capital cases in those states, they have annual training programs and provide materials which improve the quality of representation in those states. No similar programs exist in Texas or many other states with large death row populations.[38] (citations omitted)

Death penalty appeals for indigent death row inmates in Florida are handled by attorneys employed by the state agency known as the Capital Collateral Regional Counsels (CCRC). This is the three-pronged successor to the Capital Collateral Representative (CCR). CCR, which was never adequately funded, was finally dissolved by the Florida legislature and CCRC was created instead. "It is generally believed that CCRC serves the purpose of making it look like indigent death row inmates have counsel, but is intentionally hamstrung to prevent effective representation."[39] This perception is not helped by the fact that under the new CCRC, public defenders no longer submit suggestions to the governor for the heads of the offices. "Now the heads of all three offices are former prosecutors."[40]

Every attorney knows that former prosecutors frequently make the best defense lawyers—at least so long as their clear and sole responsibility is the defense of their client. Yet, in the structure of CCRC, the political control of the agency by the governor and legislature definitely poses the threat of a serious conflict of interest. Lawyers handling appeals of death penalty cases have to make decisions on which issues to raise and how aggressively to represent their clients. Are the lawyers at CCRC forced to make such decisions while looking over their shoulder at the people who cut their paycheck? After all, the governor is the same person who signs the death warrants.

The best way to avoid any appearance of impropriety would be to allow the lawyers to zealously represent their clients and to adequately fund the costs of vigorous defense. The state of Florida has done just the opposite. A lawsuit was filed challenging the underfunding of CCRC as creating a sham. The following quotes are taken from an affidavit of an outside expert filed with the Florida Supreme Court in those proceedings:

At the end of my first visit in late February 1998, based upon my extensive and detailed work in Florida since 1986 and over two decades of conducting studies both nationally and in many states around the country, it was my firm professional judgment that the current system is totally unable to safeguard the rights of indigent post conviction capital defendants whose cases are currently before the Florida and federal courts.[41] . . .

As of today [March 17, 1998] there are only 27 CCRC attorneys available to represent more than 230 defendants in state post conviction and federal habeas corpus cases. . . . This situation in my professional judgment is unconscionable.[42] (bracketed language mine)

The Florida Supreme Court ordered that this situation be remedied. In response, the Florida legislature passed the Death Penalty Reform Act of 2000. This law, enacted in a hasty January special session of the Florida legislature, attempted to take control of the death penalty process in Florida out of the hands of the Florida courts and put it under the control of the legislature by preempting the authority of the Florida Supreme Court to establish rules of procedure. The Florida Supreme Court held Florida's Death Penalty Reform Act of 2000 unconstitutional.

Many observers believe, however, that the Florida legislature's desired limitations on representation of the poor on death row by CCRC are being accomplished in practice by consistent underfunding of the agency. Underfunding results in too few lawyers for the agency's caseload, thus creating a state of constant triage. The prosecutorial side is adequately funded.

Florida has now taken the next step in dismantling legal representation for the poor. In January 2003, governor Jeb Bush proposed eliminating CCRC and replacing the state agency with a "privatized" system of private lawyers. The fees and costs would be limited enough to save $3.8 million per year. Experts in the field expressed concern about attempting to speed up executions without adequately addressing problems of legal representation.[43]

State of Florida attorney general Charlie Crist, known as "Chain Gang Charlie," also registered his support for the abolition of CCRC.[44]

Such a drastic step would be amazing, especially to save a paltry $3.8 million. In the first place, the agency was created in 1985 at the behest of Jim Smith, a Republican who was then Florida's attorney general, because not enough private lawyers were making themselves available to handle death penalty appeals.[45] Second, the meager savings are likely illusory. Experts testified in hearings that the average case being handled on appeal by CCRC has at least twenty-five boxes of documents. Some have as many as forty boxes. Assuming just twenty-five boxes per case for the 218 active cases, and seven hours per box for new attorneys to review and become familiar with each case, the required statutory fees for new private lawyers on the 218 cases would total $4.76 million—an immediate increase in cost of almost $1 million.[46] No one seemed interested in dealing with the fact that outright abolition of the Florida death penalty could save the state as much as $51 million per year.[47]

Some observers believe that the move to abolish CCRC is not about money. Rather, the CCRC lawyers have made powerful political enemies among pro–death penalty politicians.[48] The agency may have had too many successes in overturning death sentences and obtaining the release of innocent people from Florida's death row.[49] Even though death penalty experts, the official who oversees the Florida registry of private attorneys for death penalty appeals, the Florida legislature's Office of Program Policy and Government Accountability, and some of the attorneys on the registry all agree that the abolition of CCRC is a large mistake, the first step toward that end was approved in the 2003 Florida legislative session.[50] The Tallahassee office of CCRC, which covers the northern third of the state, was abolished.

CLOSING THOUGHTS

In our search for what biblical truth reveals about the American death penalty, we must ask whether our monetary and other limitations upon the representation of indigent defendants facing execution comply with the biblical mandate that the wealthy shall have no privilege over the poor when it comes to the death penalty.

Clearly, such limitations in Florida and elsewhere throughout American death penalty states, whether by statute or underfunding, fail any semblance of compliance with the biblical mandate. Biblical truth reveals that if we cannot afford to expend the same resources for defense that we expend on prosecution, we cannot afford the death penalty.

There may have been times when the legal profession attempted to police itself in regard to justice for the poor, when the search for justice was considered more important than winning. Our search shows that such lofty goals and high-minded moral injunctions have fallen prey to the glories of victory, individual political ambitions, the desire for vengeance, and the willingness to punish the poor for simply being poor. Stephen Bright gives voice to our collective lament that those days have slipped from our grasp:

> [T]he leadership needed to help bring about justice is missing. There was a time when the Attorney General of the United States and the attorneys general in many of the states were concerned not just with getting convictions, but also with fairness, integrity, and the proper functioning of the adversary system. . . .
>
> . . . But those days are gone.
>
> Today, the United States Department of Justice, state district attorneys, and state attorneys general use their power and influence to make this shameful situation even worse. They take every advantage of the ignorant, incompetent lawyers foisted upon the poor. They have defended in the courts even the most outrageous instances of incompetence on the part of defense counsel and used the ineptness of counsel as a barrier to prevent courts from addressing constitutional violations in capital cases.
>
> Despite abundant evidence of poor lawyering and egregious constitutional violations in capital cases, the Justice Department and many prosecutors have proposed shortcuts and procedural traps to paper over the problems and speed up the

process of sending those sentenced to death at unconstitutional trials to their executions. In response to findings by federal courts of constitutional violations in state capital cases,
prosecutors have urged stricter enforcement of procedural default rules to avoid dealing with the violations, not better counsel to avoid those unconstitutional trials in the first place."[51]
(citations omitted)

Is the goal of wealth-blind justice an impossible pie-in-the-sky
moral ideal? No. The Bible shows us that basic justice, regardless
of economic status, is a practical necessity. As people of biblical
faith we have a duty to make sure that justice is not a commodity,
available at a price, but is a fundamental right of all people regardless of their wealth.

The American death penalty is nowhere close to the standards
revealed by biblical truth with respect to equal treatment of rich
and poor. If anything, America is experiencing tremendous pressure in the opposite direction, pressure to save money—not by
abandoning the death penalty, but rather by abandoning even the
semblance of adequate representation for the poor who are facing
the death penalty. Any movement to economize by abandoning
adequate representation for the poor facing capital punishment is
an abomination to God's word.

We are nearing the conclusion of our search. Next we must
engage one of the most sensitive issues in America today: race.
What does biblical truth reveal to us about the racial disparities
in America's death penalty?

Chapter Eighteen

GOD IS BLIND TO COLOR

ALL VICTIMS ARE OF EQUAL VALUE;
ALL OFFENDERS ARE TO BE TREATED EQUALLY

There is an additional critical restriction that applied to the death penalty under biblical standards. This concern could easily slip by without notice because it is buried in the fundamental theology and understanding of the Hebrew people of biblical times. Consequently, we must look to the evidence of this principle in the biblical texts, which are based on this essential truth. *Under the biblical death penalty, all victims are of equal value and all offenders are to be treated equally.*

> He who fatally strikes a man shall be put to death. . . . When a man schemes against another and kills him treacherously, you shall take him from My very altar to be put to death. He who strikes his father or his mother shall be put to death. He who kidnaps a man—whether he has sold him or is still holding him—shall be put to death. He who insults his father or his mother shall be put to death.   Exod. 21:12, 14–17 TNK

> He that smiteth a man, so that he die, shall be surely put to death. . . . [I]f a man come presumptuously upon his neighbor,

to slay him with guile; thou shalt take him from mine altar, that he may die. And he that smiteth his father, or his mother, shall surely be put to death. And he that stealeth a man, and selleth him, or if he be found in his hand, he shall surely be put to death. And he that curseth his father, or his mother, shall surely be put to death.   Exod. 21:12, 14–17 AV

Anyone who strikes a man and kills him shall surely be put to death. . . . [I]f a man schemes and kills another man deliberately, take him away from my altar and put him to death. Anyone who attacks his father or his mother must be put to death. Anyone who kidnaps another and either sells him or still has him when he is caught must be put to death. Anyone who curses his father or mother must be put to death.   Exod. 21:12, 14–17 NIV

These scriptures state a profound truth by omission. There is no distinction between different classes of Hebrews for the category of murder. One could miss the tremendous significance of these scripture passages, and many others that parallel them, unless one is aware of the complex and detailed delineations made under Torah and Talmud for tracking Hebrew lineage.

During the times when the scriptures of Torah/Pentateuch and the provisions of Talmud necessary to fulfill them were the law of the land, there were ten categories of lineage within the Jewish people, as follows:

(1) Priests. (2) Levites. (3) Israelites. (4) Children of priests disqualified from the priesthood. (5) Converts. (6) Freed slaves. (7) Illegitimate offspring. (8) Gibeonites. (9) Children whose father's identity is unknown. (10) Foundlings.

The first three categories may marry freely among themselves. Levites, Israelites, converts and freed slaves may marry freely among themselves. Similarly, categories (5) to (8) may marry freely among themselves. Categories (9) and (10) cannot even marry people in their own category. They may marry people in categories (5), (6), and (8).[1]

The scripture verses cited earlier establish that when it comes to capital punishment for murder, the Bible mandates absolute equality of treatment among all Hebrews regardless of their class. Consequently, we are able to distill this set of rules into the following two maxims for capital cases under the standards of the biblical death penalty:

All victims are of equal value. There can be no variations in application of the death penalty based upon the nature of the victim.
All offenders are to be treated equally. There can be no variations in application of the death penalty based upon the nature of the offender.

Biblical truth reveals that even in the ancient Hebrew society that had so many different social classes for other purposes, absolute equality for purposes of justice and capital punishment were required.[2] How does the death penalty in America today measure up to the biblical requirements that every victim be treated with equal value and every offender be treated equally?

The most significant factor in determining whether a murderer receives the death penalty is the race of the victim.[3] Even though, on a nationwide basis, only 50 percent of murder victims are white, the race of the victim in completed capital cases is overwhelmingly white.[4] (See table 18.1.)

Table 18.1
Race of Victim in Completed Capital Cases

Race	Percentage
White	81%
Black	14%
Hispanic	4%
Asian	2%

The statistics are abundantly clear with respect to interracial murders as well.[5] (See table 18.2.)

The disparities in the American death penalty based on race also hold true with respect to the race of the defendant. Black Americans are heavily overrepresented (compared with percentage of overall population) on America's death rows and in terms of the number of inmates actually executed. (See table 18.3.)

Table 18.2

Persons Executed for Interracial Murder (U.S.) Since 1976

	Number	Percentage
White defendants executed for killing a black victim	12	6%
Black defendants executed for killing a white victim	188	94%
Total	200	

Table 18.3

Racial Disparity in Capital Cases

Race	Defendants on Death Row (%)[a]	Number Executed (%)[b]	Percentage of Population[c]
Black	1,473 (42.05%)	310 (34.1%)	12.2%
Hispanic	353 (10.08%)	57 (6.5%)	11.9%
White	1,596 (45.56%)	518 (57.2%)	71.3%
Other	81 (2.31%)	22 (2.4%)	4.6%

[a]DPIC *Race of the Executed.*
[b]DPIC *Race of the Executed.*
[c]U.S. Census Bureau, "Resident Population Estimates of the United States by Sex, Race, and Hispanic Origin: April 1, 1990, to July 1, 1999, with Short-Term Projection to November 1, 2000," http://www.census.gov/population/estimates/nation/intfile3-1.txt.

Numerous studies have reported this problem over the last two decades. Even Congress commissioned a study to determine if there was systemic racial prejudice in the application of the American death penalty.[6]

In the late 1980s, Congress asked the General Accounting Office ("GAO") to review the empirical studies on race and the death penalty that had been conducted up to that time. The agency reviewed 28 studies regarding both race of defendant and race of victim discrimination. Their review included studies utilizing various methodologies and degrees of statistical sophistication and examined such diverse states as California, Florida, Georgia, Illinois, Kentucky, Louisiana, Mississippi,

New Jersey, and Texas. Their conclusion in 1990, based on the vast amount of data collected, was unequivocal:

> In 82% of the studies, race of victim was found to influence the likelihood of being charged with capital murder or receiving a death sentence, i.e., those who murdered whites were found to be more likely to be sentenced to death than those who murdered blacks. This finding was remarkably consistent across data sets, states, data collection methods, and analytic techniques. The finding held for high, medium, and low quality studies.[7]

One of the most sophisticated of the studies reviewed by the GAO was the study of race and the death penalty in Georgia. This study looked at 2,400 cases processed in Georgia over a seven-year period and controlled for hundreds of variables, such as the level of violence in the crime and the prior criminal record of the defendant. It showed that even when controlling for the many variables that might make one case worse than another, defendants whose victims were white faced, on average, odds of receiving a death sentence that were 4.3 times higher than similarly situated defendants whose victims were black.[8]

In a recent report prepared for the American Bar Association,[9] David Baldus, professor of law at the University of Iowa College of Law, and George Woodworth, professor of statistics at the University of Iowa,[10] have expanded on the GAO's review of studies on race discrimination in capital cases. They found that there are some relevant data in three-quarters of the states with prisoners on death row.

> In 93% of those states, there is evidence of race-of-victim disparities, i.e., the white race of the person murdered correlated with whether a death sentence will be given in a particular case. In nearly half of those states, the race of the defendant also served as a predictor of who received a death sentence. . . .
>
> These disparities reveal a disturbing and consistent trend indicating race-of-victim discrimination.[11] (emphasis in original)

The significance of this racial disparity is highlighted by comparing it to a smoker's increased odds of dying from coronary artery disease. A pivotal study found smokers' odds of dying were approximately 1.7 times higher than for nonsmokers of similar ages,[12] a factor smaller than that linking race and the death penalty. Such statistical evidence about the dangers of smoking led the surgeon general to conclude that "cigarette smoking is a cause of coronary heart disease,"[13] which, in turn, helped trigger legislation and significant reform. Yet the correlation between race and the death penalty is much stronger and has been met with virtual silence.

We have already seen in chapter 6 that some of America's death penalty statutes were originally taken from the scriptures of Torah/Pentateuch. How did we veer so far from a biblically based death penalty to one that is racially biased?

THE TWO ROADS TO EXECUTION: NORTH VERSUS SOUTH

Under Torah only crimes against people and God were dealt with as criminal offenses, i.e., deserving of punishment. Matters involving money, even theft, were treated as civil matters to be settled through damages and restitution.[14] The New England colonies followed the general model of Torah, thus treating property crimes as noncapital offenses and treating sexual and religious crimes as death-eligible: "The early northern colonies were far more lenient than England for crimes against property. . . . For what today would be called consensual crimes or crimes against morality, by contrast, the early northern colonial penal codes were often harsher than English law, because of the religious origins of many of these colonies."[15]

The northerners' use of the scriptures from Torah/Pentateuch for authority was conscious and intentional. Their religious-based founding in the New World allowed them to appeal to scriptural authority for the colonial criminal laws. On occasion this was even done by counsel for the benefit of the accused: "The lawyers for a Connecticut slave named Cuff, condemned in 1749 for raping fourteen-year-old Diana Parrish, argued (apparently without success) that the colony's statute establishing rape as a capital offense ought to be interpreted in light of the Old Testament, which they asserted punished with death only the rape of a *betrothed* virgin, not that of an unbetrothed virgin like the victim."[16]

The southern colonies, on the other hand, followed the English common law model, which stressed crimes against property:

> Except for a very brief period in early seventeenth-century Virginia, the early southern colonies did not enact criminal codes as the northern colonies did, but simply used English law. In the seventeenth century the law in the southern colonies thus included capital punishment for more property offenses and fewer morality offenses than in the northern colonies. As the northern colonies gradually decapitalized blasphemy and the like, the southern colonies were left with the greater number of capital crimes, particularly where property was concerned.[17]

Not only were more offenses treated as capital crimes in the South, but there was also a much greater resort to the use of the death penalty, especially with respect to slaves. Between 1706 and 1784, 555 slaves received death sentences in Virginia alone. No northern state came close to such numbers.[18] The South followed a pattern of ever-broadening death penalty statutes, which in many cases grew to include all blacks, whether slave or free. "Criminal law in the southern states tended to lump together all blacks, slave or free. The North Carolina Code of 1855 is full of instances: thus 'Any slave, or free Negro, or person of color, convicted of . . . an assault with intent to commit rape, upon the body of a white female, shall suffer death.'"[19] (citations omitted) And in another example, "The Virginia law that made it a crime to use 'provoking language or menacing gestures' to a white person, applied to any 'negro,' not just a slave."[20] (citations omitted)

The laws in the South also provided for different punishment depending upon whether the victim was black or white. In Mississippi, as late as 1860, it was still not a crime to rape a black woman *over* twelve years old.[21] As for North Carolina:

> Thus, as one court put it, "in the nature of things," the "homicide of a slave may be extenuated by acts, which would not produce a legal provocation if done by a white person." The

year was 1820, the place North Carolina. Tackett, a journey-
man carpenter, shot and killed Daniel, a slave; and a jury convicted him of murder. The appeals court reversed, because the
jury had not been properly instructed. If the slave had been
"turbulent and disorderly," if he offered "provocations," the
crime might be "extenuated," even though, if the victim had
been white, these would be no excuse or defense. Slavery altered the rules.[22] (citations omitted)

Virginia drew a distinction based on slavery, which was racial in
effect: "Virginia provided the death penalty for slaves who committed any crime for which free people would serve a prison sentence of three years or more."[23] (citations omitted) Georgia placed
the racial differences right in the statutes: "Georgia law provided
that the rape of a white female by a black man 'shall be' punishable by death, while the rape of a white female by anyone else
was punishable by a prison term of not less than two nor more
than twenty years. The rape of a black woman was punishable 'by
fine and imprisonment, at the discretion of the court.'"[24] (citations
omitted) In the South, race of the perpetrator and the victim both
mattered: "Throughout the South attempted rape was a capital
crime, but only if the defendant was black and the victim white."[25]
(citations omitted) In some cases, the laws specifically targeted
any threat to the "peculiar institution" known as slavery: "In Louisiana, meanwhile, it was a capital crime to print or distribute material, or to make a speech or display a sign, or even to have a
private conversation, that might spread discontent among the free
black population or insubordination among slaves."[26]

During the period leading up to the mid–eighteen hundreds,
the religiously based death penalty in the North was the subject
of serious and widespread reevaluation. Movements for repeal of
capital punishment in the North were gaining momentum and
many northern states limited their capital crimes extensively, in
some cases to only murder and treason.

This was not the case in the South. "The debate over capital
punishment that engulfed the northern states in the first half of
the nineteenth century was virtually absent from the South. The
difference was a product of slavery."[27]

The South's retention of capital punishment for blacks was
surely a direct result of slavery. In the middle of the nineteenth

century whites formed a minority of the population in South
Carolina, Mississippi, and Louisiana. Blacks made up more than
a third of the residents of Virginia, North Carolina, Georgia,
Florida, and Alabama. From the perspective of slaveowners,
harsh punishments were necessary to manage such large cap-
tive populations. The institution of slavery prevented southern
states from developing alternatives to the death penalty for
blacks. Incarceration or forced labor would not have been
much worse than slavery itself. . . . With two million captives
on their hands, southern state governments saw no solution
other than capital punishment.[28]

Despite the role of capital punishment as a linchpin holding
together the societal social structure of slavery, there were signs
that aspects of the practice were becoming unpalatable. For example:

The South Carolina lawyer William Grayson recalled that in
the early nineteenth century, when the ringleaders of an incipi-
ent slave conspiracy were convicted and decapitated and their
heads placed on poles along the highway, the "sight was so
disgusting that some of the younger people refused to bear it.
They so far disregarded the majesty of the law as to take down
the hideous butcher's work and bury it where it stood." An
aggravated punishment for slaves that had been routine in the
eighteenth century was becoming unbearable in the nineteenth
century.[29]

By the Civil War there was a wide gulf between the northern
and southern states in their use of capital punishment.[30]

The Civil War ended the relationship of slavery and capital
punishment. In the waning days of Reconstruction, the next phase
of the road to race-biased legal executions began to unfold.

CHAIN GANGS AND LYNCHING AS PROLOGUE TO LEGAL EXECUTIONS

An adage claims that the more things change, the more things
stay the same. This is a fairly accurate description of the last forty

years of the nineteenth century for many American blacks in the South.

> With the end of slavery, southern whites feared what a young Charleston woman called "the foulest demoniac passions of the Negro, hitherto so peaceful and happy, roused into being and fierce activity by the devilish Yankees." . . .
>
> . . . White southerners perceived themselves to be in a constant state of crisis with respect to their former slaves. . . .
>
> As a result, most of the southern states' capital crimes on the eve of the Civil War were still capital nearly a century later.[31]

How could an economy formerly based on slavery and a white populace terrified of retribution for slavery reshape the social and legal structure in a manner that would keep things, as much as possible, the way they had been before?

> [T]he state courts in the South provided the freed slaves no protection at all. Instead, they played a major role in continuing their oppression. Perhaps the worst example of this defiance was the involvement of the courts in many states, including Alabama, Arkansas, Florida, Georgia, Mississippi, North Carolina, South Carolina, Tennessee, and Texas, in maintaining a system of convicting and leasing people that was the virtual perpetuation of slavery. Convict leasing "was designed for black, not white, convicts." When a work force was needed, men would be arrested for vagrancy and other minor crimes, convicted and then leased to plantations, railroads, turpentine camps, or others who needed cheap labor. One participant in the practice admitted, "[I]t was possible to send a negro to prison on almost any pretext but difficult to get a white there, unless he committed a very heinous crime." Many convicts were literally worked to death. One historian has observed that "[t]he South's economic development can be traced by the blood of its prisoners."[32] (citations omitted)

The "ultimate sanction," the really heavy structure that propped up the labor system of the South, was the penal system. Typically, southern convicts (overwhelmingly black) were leased out for work on chain gangs or labor gangs. The lessees were worse than Simon Legree; they worked black bodies as hard as they could; they made use of "shackles, dogs, whips, and guns," and "created a living hell for the prisoners." The mortality rates on these chain gangs were staggering. Two hundred eighty-five convicts were sent to build the Greenwood and Augusta railroad between 1877 and 1880. Almost 45 percent of them died—and these were young black men in the prime of their lives. You can imagine what it would take, what cruelty, what conditions of work, to kill almost half of these men.[33] (citations omitted)

Condemnation to the chain gang was a likely death sentence. Even worse was the unofficial justice of the mob, manifested through lynching.

The practice of lynching, which reached its peak in the South in the late nineteenth and early twentieth centuries, provided an additional barrier to change. Lynching was a form of unofficial capital punishment, adjudication of guilt and execution by groups lacking the formal authority for either. . . . At its peak, lynching was much more common than official capital punishment. In Kentucky, for instance, between 1865 and 1940 there were 229 executions and 353 lynchings. Lynchings outnumbered executions 82 to 6 in the 1870s and 92 to 40 in the 1890s. A culture that carried out so much unofficial capital punishment could hardly be squeamish about the official variety.[34] (citations omitted)

Through the institution of lynching, the double standards of punishment based upon the race of the victim and the race of the accused were continued into the twentieth century.

Disparate punishments—exacted by the courts and by the mob—based upon the race of the victim and the race of the defendant continued in practice after the abolition of slavery. At least 4,743 people were killed by lynch mobs. More than ninety percent of the lynchings took place in the South, and three-fourths of the victims were African-Americans. The threat that Congress might pass an anti-lynching statute in the early 1920s led Southern states to "replace lynchings with a more '[humane] . . . method of racial control'—the judgment and imposition of capital sentences by all-white juries."[35] (ellipsis and brackets in original; citations omitted)

[T]he racial pattern of capital punishment in the South closely resembled that of lynching. Of the 771 people of identified race known to have been executed for rape between 1870 and 1950, 701 were black. For robbery, 31 of 35 were black; for burglary, 18 of 21. . . . Throughout the South, for all crimes, black defendants were executed in numbers far out of proportion to their population. The death penalty was a means of racial control.[36]

"In places where executions are prevalent today, extrajudicial lynchings used to be quite common as well. Lynchings, of course, were often racially motivated."[37] The racially biased process of lynching laid the foundation for a racially biased death penalty. "The death penalty is a direct descendant of lynching and other forms of racial violence and racial oppression in America."[38]

FROM LYNCHING TO LEGAL EXECUTIONS

Sometimes we crave the false comfort of disconnecting our present from our past. Unfortunately, with respect to the racial bias in America's death penalty, the thread to racial bias under slavery and lynching is a time-woven steel cable that defies denial. These disparities reached a climax of sorts in the 1950s when the whole world was astounded at the racially biased injustice of the American death penalty in the South. "In 1958, when Jimmy Wilson was sentenced to death in Alabama for robbing a white woman of $1.95, the case was known around the world. . . . Alabama Governor James Folsom called a press conference to announce that he was 'snowed under' by more than three thousand letters he received in a single box from Toronto. . . . Folsom commuted Wilson's sentence."[39] (citations omitted)

Yet, the inequities of the American death penalty based on race continue to the current day. The following true account, which is taken from "Can Judicial Independence Be Attained in the South? Overcoming History, Elections, and Misperceptions about the Role of the Judiciary," occurred in the late eighties to late nineties of the twentieth century:[40]

> The relationship of this history to what happens in criminal courts today is illustrated by the Texas case of Clarence Lee Brandley. A police officer charged Brandley, a janitor, with the rape and murder of a white high school student instead of white suspects because "the nigger," as the officer referred to Brandley, "was big enough to have committed the crime; therefore, 'the nigger [is] elected.'" Brandley was tried twice. On both occasions, the prosecutors used all their peremptory strikes against blacks to get all-white juries, as was the normal practice of the Montgomery County prosecutor's office. Although "a powerful feeling of prejudice and racial tension pervaded the courtroom" at the first trial, the jury was unable to agree on a verdict. At a second trial, where a reviewing judge found that a "'project like' mentality" on the part of the judge, prosecutor and court clerk "overbore any sense of justice and decency," the all-white jury sentenced Brandley to death.
>
> Brandley was freed after the CBS News program 60 Minutes publicized his innocence, and the Texas Court of Criminal Appeals was forced to acknowledge the unfairness of his trial. The treatment of Brandley was consistent with the treatment that black people had long received in Montgomery County:

> > The story of Clarence Brandley rang with echoes from [the lynching of a black man a few days before Christmas in 1885]: the rules of law that had been abandoned; the judge who had fallen in with the mob; the press that had relished his fate; the "leading citizens of the county" who had committed the crime; the bodyguard of new civil rights that had turned and deserted him; the whole town that had stood by and let it happen. And that was the loudest echo of all. . . .

> > It was part of the corruption that had become a way of life. . . . Not only had the whites always got away with it, but they had also always been able to justify it. Killing one

black man was a means of disciplining the whole of his community. Just as a secret police force tries to quell the courage
of a whole people by arresting its figureheads, just as terrorists try to frighten a whole society by throwing fear into
the lives of each of its members, so the white people of
Montgomery County had for years ruled black people with
fear by picking off their young men. Murder was disguised
as a necessary social task. . . .

The ordeal Clarence Brandley suffered was an attempt at
a legal lynching. It was the law, not an old rope, that was
twisted into a deadly weapon, but the intention of those
who attacked him was just as surely to kill him, as their
predecessors had killed young black men in the past.[41] (citations omitted)

The history of the death penalty in the South, through slavery
and lynching, has created other imbalances that help to perpetu-
ate the anti-biblical condition of disparate treatment for victims
and offenders. For example:

Other vestiges of discrimination that occurred years ago still
infect the courts and affect their decisions. One of the most
significant is that African-Americans and other minorities remain largely excluded from the justice system. The history of
legalized oppression has resulted in very few people of color
sitting as judges. [As of 1995] [o]f Alabama's 381 district, circuit, probate and appellate judges only eighteen are black. Of
Florida's 456 circuit judges, only sixteen are black and eighteen
are Hispanic. Of Georgia's 152 Superior Court judges, only
nineteen are black. Of South Carolina's forty-three circuit
judges, only four are black. Of Texas' 396 district court judges,
only twelve are black and forty-two are Hispanic. There is
little likelihood that the bench will become more representative in the next several decades since states are allowed to elect
judges from districts in which the voting power of black citizens is diluted. Members of racial minorities continue to be
underrepresented in jury pools and excluded in the jury selection process.[42] (citations omitted; bracketed language mine)

RACIAL BIAS IN THE AMERICAN DEATH PENALTY TODAY

As was noted earlier in this chapter, the GAO Report and major studies conducted by other institutions have determined that there is a profound racial bias in the American death penalty at large. The Racial Justice Act, a proposed model law that would create a legal right to challenge a racially motivated death sentence, has been passed in only one American jurisdiction, the Commonwealth of Kentucky.[43] Except for that, no definitive legislative action has been taken to remedy this problem. The refusal by legislative bodies to enact legislation to deal with the problem of racial disparities in the American death penalty is in spite of an abundance of statistical evidence that has named and quantified the problem.

> Although African-Americans make up only twelve percent of the total population of the United States, they have been the victims in about half of the total homicides in this country in the last twenty-five years. In some states in the South, where capital punishment is often imposed, African-Americans are the victims of over sixty percent of the murders. Yet eighty-five percent of the cases in which the death penalty has been carried out have involved white victims.[44] (citations omitted)

> A congressional study found stark disparities in the use of the federal death penalty. Racial disparities have been documented by other observers.[45] (citations omitted)

> Despite pronounced racial disparities in the infliction of the death penalty in both state and federal capital cases, Congress and state legislatures have failed to limit application of the death penalty or provide remedies for racial discrimination, such as the Racial Justice Act.[46] (citations omitted)

We will now look at the actual facts from a sampling of states and the federal government.

TEXAS

Recently, Texas executed a white person for killing a black person. It was the first time in several decades that such an execution had occurred in that state.[47] Racial bias in the Texas death penalty is a problem that exists in other ways as well. "A study in 1994 of death sentences in Harris County, Texas, a single county which has carried out more executions and sentenced more people to death than most states, found that 'Harris County has sent blacks to death row nearly twice as often as whites during the last ten years, a growing imbalance that eclipses the pre–civil rights days of 'Old Sparky' the notorious Texas electric chair.'"[48] (citations omitted)

FLORIDA

In Florida, which has the nation's third largest death row, the Racial and Ethnic Bias Commission of the Florida Supreme Court found that "the application of the death penalty in Florida is not colorblind."[49]

However, in the year 2001, a special task force established by Florida's Governor to study the death penalty concluded that there is no racial bias in Florida's death penalty. This conclusion is nothing short of phenomenal in light of the following facts: (1) Since capital punishment began in Florida in 1769, the state has never executed a white person for killing an African-American.[50] (2) Of Florida's (then) 366 inmates on death row, only five whites await execution for killing a black. (3) Depending on the study cited, in Florida a defendant's odds of receiving a death sentence range from 4.8 times higher[51] to 3.4 times higher[52] if the victim is white than if the victim is black in similarly egregious cases. (4) In Florida, whites are the majority on death row. But blacks make up a disproportionate percentage. Only 12 percent of Florida's population is black, but 34.5 percent of the men on Florida's death row are black.[53]

ALABAMA

The recently published investigative report by the *Birmingham Post-Herald* on the Alabama death penalty offers additional insights as to how the workings of the death penalty of the eighteen hundreds continue to cast a shadow into the twenty-first century. Talladega County is a lesson in itself. The following is excerpted from "Talladega: Death Row Country: Is Fairness Missing from the State's Use of Capital Punishment?"[54]

There is perhaps no better place in the nation to understand the workings of the death penalty than Talladega County, located about an hour's drive east of Birmingham.

Talladega, with a population of 80,000, has sent more people per capita to death row than any county in the state. And Alabama, which trails only Nevada in the percentage of residents on death row, leads the nation in residents per capita sentenced to death since 1994.

Fourteen men convicted in Talladega County await execution, more than the individual totals of New York and 10 other states that use the death penalty. . . .

No place seems to have a greater bond with the death penalty than Talladega County, best known for its speedway that stages NASCAR races. . . .

Why the county should send so many people to death row is a bit of a mystery. . . . [S]ome people point to race as an explanation.

Talladega County is 31.5 percent black, and half of the 14 men Talladega has sent to death row are black. But the county district attorney and all of its judges are white.

In "Does Race Decide Who Dies? Some Say Color of Defendant, Victim Plays Significant Role," the *Birmingham Post-Herald* tackles the issue of race and the death penalty in Alabama head-on:[55]

Pretend a white man is accused of the robbery and murder of a young black woman in a mostly black Alabama town.

Pretend further that the judge is black. So are the prosecutor and all of the jurors except one.

And all of the witnesses are black.

"Do you think the white defendant in this hypothetical would receive a fair trial?" asked Bryan Fair, a law professor at the University of Alabama, in a paper about the death penalty.

Fair said his hypothetical case was based on a real capital murder trial in Alabama, except with the races reversed of everyone involved. No imagination needed in that scenario. . . .

Of all the homicides committed by black Alabamians in the past five years, 11 percent were committed against whites. But 57 percent of blacks on death row are there for killing whites. Only 43 percent are on death row for killing other blacks, even though 89 percent of homicides committed by blacks are against other blacks.

"I would be dishonest if I said it doesn't matter if you are African-American," said Barrown D. Lankster, who was Alabama's only black elected district attorney in the 1990s. "It matters in this state, and it matters in this country. It matters because you have individuals who are making the decision to pursue the death penalty, and they bring their own biases to that."

While people can speculate about reasons, the actual statistics in Alabama are clear, unequivocal, and undisputed. The following information is provided by the Equal Justice Initiative of Alabama:[56]

1. Black people in Alabama constitute 2 percent of the prosecutors, 4 percent of the criminal court judges, 26 percent of the total population, and 63 percent of those in prison.
2. Although only 6 percent of all murders in Alabama involve black defendants and white victims, over 60 percent of black death row prisoners have been sentenced for killing someone white.
3. Nearly 70 percent of those executed in Alabama in the past twenty years have been black.

Each year in Alabama, nearly 65 percent of all murders involve black victims. However, 80 percent of the prisoners currently awaiting execution in the state were convicted of crimes in which the victims were white.

GEORGIA

As with Alabama, the modern death penalty in Georgia is visibly anchored in the practices of the nineteenth century:

Georgia became the nation's primary executioner, carrying out the most executions in the twentieth century before the death penalty was declared unconstitutional in 1972. Between 1924 and 1972, Georgia executed 337 black people and 75 white people.[57] (citations omitted)

[A]lthough African-Americans were the victims of sixty-five percent of the homicides in the Chattahoochee Judicial District [Georgia], eighty-five percent of the capital cases in that circuit were white victim cases.[58] (citations omitted; bracketed language mine)

It can be difficult to conceptualize how this racially biased outcome occurs in the criminal justice system of an American state. A window into the mechanics of this bias is provided by the following data.[59]

Prosecutorial Discretion in Seeking the Death Penalty[60]

Georgia prosecutors have complete discretion in deciding whether to seek the death penalty in any eligible case.

Percentage of cases involving African-Americans charged with crimes against white persons in which Georgia prosecutors seek death   70%

Percentage of the cases involving white persons charged with the murder of another white in which Georgia prosecutors seek death   32%

Percentage of cases involving African-Americans charged with the murder of another African-American in which Georgia prosecutors seek death   15%

Percentage of cases involving white persons charged   19%

with murders of African-Americans in which Georgia
prosecutors seek death

Sentencing Disparities in Capital Cases[61]

Percentage of cases involving white victims in which death is imposed	11%
Percentage of cases involving African-American victims in which death is imposed	1%
Percentage of cases involving an African-American accused of a crime against a white in which the death penalty is imposed	22%
Percentage of cases involving a white person accused of a crime against a white in which the death penalty is imposed	8%
Percentage of cases involving an African-American accused of a crime against an African-American in which the death penalty is imposed	1%
Percentage of cases involving a white person accused of a crime against an African-American in which the death penalty is imposed	3%

Executions and Lynchings in Georgia[62]

Number of executions by the state of Georgia, 1608–present	1,154
Number of lynchings documented in Georgia, 1608–present	460
Number of executions by the state of Georgia since 1900	673
Number of death sentences imposed under current law adopted in 1973	324
Number of African-Americans executed between 1930 and 1972	337

Number of whites executed between 1930 and 1972	75
Number of African-Americans executed under current death penalty statue (upheld in 1976 by U.S. Supreme Court)	12
Number of white persons executed under current statute	8
Number of African-Americans executed under current capital statute who were sentenced to death by all-white juries	6
Percentage of homicides in Georgia in which the victim of the crime is African-American	65%
Percentage of cases in which executions have been carried out in which the victim of the crime was white	90%

> Although over 60 percent of the victims of murders in Georgia each year are African American, 18 of the 20 cases in which executions have been carried out under the current law involved white victims. Over 80 percent of those on Georgia's death row are there for the murders of white victims."[63]

MARYLAND

In May 2002, governor Parris N. Glendening placed a moratorium on executions in Maryland pending the completion of a comprehensive study of the death penalty in that state. Criminal justice professor Raymond Paternoster headed the University of Maryland study of almost six thousand Maryland homicide cases over twenty years:

> Maryland prosecutors are far more likely to seek the death penalty for black suspects charged with killing white victims, a racial disparity that mirrors national trends and raises questions about whether capital punishment is being administered fairly. . . .
> "The kind of disparities we're finding are systemic," Paternoster said. . . .

"Offenders who kill white victims, especially if the offender is black, are significantly and substantially more likely to be charged with a capital crime," the report states. The probability is "twice as high as when a black slays another black." . . .

Paternoster said the explanation for the disparities lies with the state's attorneys, not juries, although he was careful not to impugn the prosecutors' motives.*

"Let me be clear," he told a news conference. "It doesn't mean there is racial animus involved."[64] Rather, he said, it illustrates how "the product of their action does result in racial disparity."[65] (bracketed note mine)

What is happening to the death penalty in Maryland as a result of the study? The death penalty is on the verge of resuming without any changes to Maryland's system.[66]

WASHINGTON

The death penalty in Washington State appears heavily determined by racial factors.

Research compiled by the Washington Death Penalty Assistance Center, revealed that death notices have *never* been filed in a case with a white defendant and a black victim, while such notices have been filed in 42% of murder cases with a black defendant and a white victim. Of the 10 individuals currently on death row in Washington, nine cases involved a white victim and *none* involved a black victim. In addition, *every* juror that convicted and sentenced the black defendants was white.[67]

THE FEDERAL SYSTEM

Attorney general John Ashcroft continues to aggressively seek capital convictions, despite the racially biased outcomes of the federal death penalty:

Since taking office [in early 2001], Ashcroft has reversed the recommendations of federal prosecutors 12 times, ordering

*© 2003, The Washington Post. Reprinted with permission.

them to seek the death penalty in cases where they had recommended against doing so. . . . These include at least one case in which a tentative plea agreement had already been reached. . . .

The data also indicate that racial disparities in the application of the death penalty . . . have lingered during Ashcroft's tenure.

Since Ashcroft became attorney general, the Justice Department has been three times more likely to seek death for black defendants accused of killing whites than for blacks alleged to have killed nonwhites, according to the Federal Death Penalty Resource Counsel Project, which was established by the courts to monitor capital cases.[68]*

RACIALLY BASED MISTREATMENT

It is clear that the standards of the biblical death penalty cannot abide disparate application based on the "value" of the victim. White victims must not be treated as more valuable than black victims. It also does not allow for disparate treatment of the accused based on one being more valuable than another. White murderers are not to be treated differently from black murderers. The American death penalty falls far short of this biblical standard on both counts.

Moreover, equal treatment of all offenders would—at the very least—imply not using racial slurs and epithets in the judicial process. Again, the American death penalty, with its strong bias from history, fails to comply:

[R]acial discrimination not acceptable in any other area of American life today is tolerated in criminal courts. The use of a racial slur may cost a sports announcer his job, but there have been capital cases in which judges, jurors and defense counsel have called an African-American defendant a "nigger" with no repercussions for anyone except the accused. For example, parents of an African-American defendant were referred to as the "nigger mom and dad" by the judge in a Florida case. The judge

*© 2003, The Washington Post. Reprinted with permission.

did not lose his job; the Florida Supreme Court merely suggested that judges should avoid the "appearance" of impropriety in the future. [This event took place in the mid-1980s.]

Similarly, a death sentence was upheld in a Georgia case where jurors used racial slurs during their deliberations. . . . No state or federal court so much as held a hearing on the racial prejudice which infected the sentencing of Henry Hance before he was executed by Georgia in 1994, even though jurors signed affidavits swearing racial slurs had been used during deliberations. In at least five capital cases in Georgia, the accused were referred to with racial slurs by their own lawyers at some time during the court proceedings.[69] (citations omitted; bracketed language mine)

In February 2000, Scott D. Makar, a highly respected lawyer with an extensive background in statistics, was serving, at governor Jeb Bush's request, on the Governor's Capital Cases Task Force. One of the issues to be addressed was the racial disparity in Florida's death penalty. Mr. Makar published a letter in the *Florida Times-Union* in response to misstatements of the facts by the editorial staff of the paper:

The Jan. 31 editorial discussing criminal justice statistics seriously misstates that "courts have not discriminated against murder defendants, based on race, since the death penalty was reinstated nearly a quarter of a century ago."

I wish that were true. Ironically, as I read the editorial, I had a 1986 Florida Supreme Court case in front of me where the trial judge called the defendant's family a bunch of "n——ers."

The murder defendant's conviction and death sentence were thrown out on other grounds, and he was acquitted on retrial.

In other words, a black defendant who was not guilty of the crime charged was close to being wrongfully executed by a judicial process that was tainted with the N-word.

My point is that race can play a role in individual murder cases, whether statistics bear it out or not.[70]

Mr. Makar makes an excellent point about the individual risks of racial prejudice in every capital case, whether the statistical studies catch it or not. Yet, what happens when the statistics show that racism permeates the entire American death penalty machine and skews the system into racially disparate outcomes? According to the U.S. Supreme Court, a body that hardly functions within the penumbras of biblical truth, when it comes to the death penalty, systemic racism doesn't really matter.

RACIAL BIAS AND THE COURTS

In the late 1980s, the U.S. Supreme Court was asked to review the racial disparity in Georgia's death penalty system. The nature of the review required that the court employ one of two tests to guide its reasoning. The two tests can be called the "objective test" and the "subjective test."

Under the objective test, one compiles accumulated statistical data over time and many samples, which shows that the outcome is racially biased. This outcome-focused test has been used in legal battles for virtually all areas of discrimination.

The other option available to the court was to require that the accused must prove that specific individuals intentionally and knowingly discriminated against him because of his race. This is the subjective test and it is an impossible hurdle unless the prejudiced actor as much as admits he is prejudiced and intentionally discriminated against the accused.

In the Georgia case, the statistics and the studies mentioned earlier were presented to the Court. Based on the legal approach utilized by the Court in areas of housing, education, employment, etc., the Court could have consistently applied the objective test. To a startled world, the sharply divided U.S. Supreme Court issued a five-to-four ruling holding that the subjective test applied to the American death penalty, and the objective test could not be used.

> In *McCleskey v. Kemp*, the [U.S. Supreme] Court accepted the racial disparities in the imposition of the death penalty as "an inevitable part of our criminal justice system." . . .
>
> In rejecting McCleskey's claim under the Eighth Amendment, the Court . . . held that evidence that blacks who kill

whites are sentenced to death at nearly twenty-two times the rate of blacks who kill blacks did not "demonstrate a constitutionally significant risk of racial bias affecting the Georgia capital sentencing process."[71] (citations omitted)

[The] Court ruled . . . that to prevail under the Equal Protection Clause the defendant must present "exceptionally clear proof" that "the decision makers in his case acted with discriminatory purpose."[72] (citations omitted)

In other words, the U.S. Supreme Court held that the defendant had to show that he was personally and intentionally discriminated against in the course of the prosecution. "Merely" showing a disturbing pattern of racial disparities in Georgia over a long period of time was not sufficient to prove bias in his case.[73]

The *McCleskey* ruling has virtually halted and thwarted any possible progress, through the courts, in bringing the American death penalty into alignment with the racially unbiased requirements of biblical truth. This obstruction has been felt at all levels of government, federal and state.[74]

In another example, a prior U.S. attorney general issued a report on the federal death penalty. While the report did not render a conclusion as to racial basis, it did publish the actual statistics, which showed that the federal death penalty is not race neutral. Americans were confused when Mr. John Ashcroft, the current attorney general, issued a new report concluding that the federal death penalty is not discriminatory. The explanation of the difference in the showings of the first report and the conclusions of the second report is that the initial report looked at the racially biased outcomes of the federal death penalty. Mr. Ashcroft primarily used the subjective approach.

The *McCleskey* ruling by the U.S. Supreme Court has also obstructed progress by the states.

Other courts have followed the Supreme Court's head-in-the-sand approach. [In 1993 the] Florida Supreme Court, by a 4–3 vote, refused to require a hearing on the racial disparities in the infliction of the death penalty. [In 1994 the] Georgia Supreme Court upheld the denial of a hearing on racial discrimination in a capital prosecution against an African-American accused of the murder of a white person in Cobb County, a county which has a long history of racial discrimination.[75] (bracketed language mine; citations omitted)

CLOSING THOUGHTS

In a word, when it comes to racial bias and the death penalty, America is stuck. Attorney Stephen Bright has summarized our plight succinctly:

> The legal system is the institution in our society that has been least affected by the civil rights movement. . . . The judges are white, the prosecutors are white, the lawyers are white and, even in communities with substantial African-American populations, the jury may be all white. In many cases, the only person of color who sits in front of the bar in the courtroom is the person on trial. . . .
>
> . . . [T]he death penalty remains, as it always has throughout our history, a matter of race.[76] (citations omitted)

We could continue discussion at length on social questions, political issues, and even ethical points about the racial disparity in America's death penalty. That is not our purpose. Our question is very focused.

Does the American death penalty meet the standards revealed by biblical truth with respect to showing no preferential treatment for any offender over any other offender and that all victims be treated as equal in value?

Our answer is quite clear. The biblical truth of Torah/Pentateuch and the provisions of Talmud necessary to fulfill those scriptures reveal that the American death penalty fails miserably in meeting this standard. Worse than that, under the current state of the law, no progress in this regard can be expected through the workings of the court system unless the U.S. Supreme Court overturns its decision in *McCleskey*.

We have exhausted our search into the procedural standards demanded by biblical truth. Now it is time to look at who should decide who dies.

Chapter Nineteen

IMPARTIALITY IN THE DECISION MAKERS

THE POLITICS OF DEATH

As we have already seen, the primary focus of the biblical death penalty is the fear of executing the innocent. The Bible is the source for this concern (Exod. 23:7). A fair and impartial judiciary is the most effective means of avoiding such a terrible result. Thus, it should be no surprise that the Bible also provides the basis for a fair and impartial court and judicial structure.

In what is considered one of the seven commands binding on all humankind under the Noahide law, God mandated the creation of a system of judicial courts:[1]

You shall appoint magistrates and officials for your tribes, in all the settlements that the LORD your God is giving you, and they shall govern the people with due justice. Deut. 16:18 TNK

Judges and officers shalt thou make thee in all thy gates, which the LORD thy God giveth thee, throughout thy tribes: and they shall judge the people with just judgment. Deut. 16:18 AV

Appoint judges and officials for each of your tribes in every town the LORD your God is giving you, and they shall judge the people fairly.   Deut. 16:18 NIV

This biblical source actually incorporates two explicit commands: the establishment of courts, and the obligation to administer the courts with justice, in a fair and impartial manner. The biblical death penalty was to be administered under a court system fashioned upon this scriptural foundation: "It is a positive biblical command to appoint judges and executive officials in every city and every district, as it is said: *Judges and officers shalt thou make thee in all thy gates* (Deut. 16:18). Judges refers to the magistrates assigned to the court, before whom litigants appear."[2] (italics in original)

During the times that the scriptures of Torah/Pentateuch and the provisions of Talmud necessary to meet the requirements of those scriptures were the law of the land, the critical components of this judicial system were the Supreme Court, called the Great Sanhedrin, and the local courts, each called a Small Sanhedrin. "The Great Sanhedrin was composed of seventy-one judges, and a lesser one was composed of twenty-three judges."[3] "Capital cases are judged by a court of twenty-three judges."[4]

In chapter 8 we addressed the scriptural basis for the numbers of judges in each court and for the requirement of judicial ordination. For purposes of this chapter, however, our focus is the characteristics and qualifications required under the biblical death penalty for judges who sit in a capital case. What are the essential requirements for judicial qualifications under the biblical death penalty? They are extensive. *Judges are to be moderate, neither too harsh nor too forgiving.*[5] "Neither a very aged man nor a eunuch is appointed to any Sanhedrin, since these are apt to be wanting in tenderness; nor is one who is childless appointed, because a member of the Sanhedrin must be a person who is sympathetic."[6] *Judges must be reluctant to impose a sentence of death and be absolutely impartial toward each accused.* "Since there were standing instructions to courts to refrain, insofar as possible, from passing the death sentence, it was customary to remove from the bench any man who was believed incapable of maintaining an impartial attitude toward the defendant."[7]

Judges are not to glide along with the flow of community sentiment. The biblical death penalty forbids judges from simply following the direction of the prevailing political winds. "The strong emphasis on the importance of witnesses in the [Torah/Pentateuch] implies that judgment is to be made on the facts of the case at hand, not on a general feeling about the defendant or the politics of the situation."[8] The basis for this judicial mandate is scriptural:

> You shall neither side with the mighty [multitude] to do wrong. Exod. 23:2 TNK

> Neither shalt thou speak in a cause to decline after many to wrest judgment. Exod. 23:2 AV

> Do not pervert justice by siding with the crowd. Exod. 23:2 NIV

This scriptural command results in a judicial duty of independent thinking under the biblical death penalty:

> Any judge in a capital case, whose vote—either for acquittal or for conviction—voices not his own carefully considered opinion but that of a colleague, transgresses a negative command. Concerning him Scripture says: *Neither shalt thou bear witness in a cause to turn aside* (Exod. 23:2). It has been learned by tradition that this injunction means, "Do not say when the poll is taken, it is good enough if I follow So-and-so; but give expression to your own opinion."[9] (italics in original)

Every judge must "possess the following seven qualifications: wisdom, humility, fear of God, disdain of gain, love of truth, love of his fellow men, and a good reputation."[10]

All of these requisites are explicitly set forth in Torah. Scripture says *wise men and understanding* (Deut. 1:13), thus stating (that those chosen) must be men of wisdom; *and beloved of your tribes* (ibid.), that is, men with whom the spirit of their fellow creatures is pleased. What will earn for them the love of others? A good eye, a lowly spirit, friendly intercourse, and gentleness in speech and dealing with others.

Elsewhere it is said *men of valor* (Exod. 18:21), that is, men strong in the performance of the commandments, and strict with themselves, men who control their passions, whose character is above reproach, aye, whose youth is of unblemished repute. The phrase *men of valor* implies also stoutheartedness to rescue the oppressed from the hand of the oppressor, as it is said: *But Moses stood up and helped them* (Exod. 2:17). And just as Moses, our teacher, was humble, so every judge should be humble. *Such as fear God* (Exod. 18:21)—this is to be understood literally; *hating gain* (*ibid.*), that is, they are not anxious about their own money and do not strive to accumulate wealth, for he that hastens after riches, want shall come upon him; *men of truth* (*ibid.*), that is, they pursue righteousness spontaneously and of their own accord; they love the truth, hate violence, and flee anything that savors of unrighteousness.[11] (italics and bracketed language in original)

Judges must not be appointed based upon their appeal to the masses.

Say not, "So-and-so is a handsome man, I will make him a judge; So-and-so is a man of valor, I will make him judge; So-and-so is related to me, I will make him a judge. So-and-so is a linguist, I will make him a judge." If you do it, he will acquit the guilty and condemn the innocent, not because he is wicked, but because he is lacking in knowledge.[12]

Judges shall not be appointed based upon their financial means. In biblical times, those wrapped in judicial robes were sometimes referred to as "gods" (with a small *g*). Hence, the literal understanding from scripture: "Moreover, the injunction *Thou shalt not make with Me gods of silver or gods of gold* (Exod. 20:20) has been interpreted by the Sages to mean: gods who come into being through the influence of silver or gold, that is a judge who owes his appointment to his wealth only."[13] (italics in original)

Anyone who seeks judicial office is automatically disqualified from it.

It was the habit of the early Sages to shun appointment to the position of judge. They exerted their utmost endeavors to avoid sitting in judgment unless they were convinced that there were no others so fit for the office as they, and that were they to persist in their refusal, the cause of justice would suffer. Even then they would not act in the capacity of judges until the people and the elders brought pressure upon them to do so.[14]

Finally, the biblical death penalty is absolutely unforgiving of anyone who has obtained his judicial office through financial means: "It is forbidden to rise before a judge who procured the office he holds by paying for it. The Rabbis bid us slight and despise him, regard the judicial robe in which he is enwrapped as the packsaddle of an ass."[15]

Mendelsohn summarizes these requirements for judicial qualification under the biblical truth of Torah/Pentateuch and the provisions of Talmud necessary to fulfill them as follows:

Numerous and varied are the qualifications required to render one eligible to judicial honors. Besides being a worthy man, possessed of true piety and an untarnished character . . . [h]e is required to be affable, of good appearance, and not haughty. He is to be advanced in years, i.e., a man of experience, but not too old, for high age is frequently accompanied by high temper; and must be the father of a family, that he may always be animated by paternal feelings. . . . Nor do we meet in the Talmud with examples of modern electioneering. Office-hunting is thoroughly repugnant to the spirit of Talmudic law.[16]

We must confront the unhappy issue of how judicial qualifications and independence under the modern American death penalty stack up against the rigorous list revealed by biblical truth. Also, because in most states the last resort for death row inmates is a clemency appeal before the governors, we must include them in our assessment.

JUDGES AND POLITICS UNDER THE AMERICAN DEATH PENALTY

In his address to the American Bar Association Annual Meeting in the summer of 1996, U.S. Supreme Court justice John Paul Stevens made the following disturbing statement:

Persons who undertake the task of administering justice impartially should not be required—indeed, they should not be permitted—to finance campaigns or to curry the favor of voters by making predictions or promises about how they will decide cases before they have heard any evidence or argument. A campaign promise to "be tough on crime," or to "enforce the death penalty," is evidence of bias that should disqualify a candidate from sitting in criminal cases.[17]

This warning about the impact of modern-day electioneering on our American death penalty system is actually the tip of the iceberg. Others are sounding the alarm that a new wave of campaign finance–driven vested interest is cornering the market on American justice.

Everyone who cares about judicial independence and the rule of law should be alarmed when the president of a large state's bar comments, "[t]he people with money to spend who are affected by Court decisions have reached the conclusion that it's a lot cheaper to buy a judge than a governor or an entire legislature and [the judge] can probably do a lot more for you." The comment was made after a candidate spent $1 million to defeat the incumbent Chief Justice of Ohio who spent $1.7 million. The newly-elected chief justice then voted to rehear thirty cases that had been decided in the final weeks of the incumbent's term.[18] (citations omitted)

Our focus is the effect of this development upon the judicial administration of America's death penalty. One would imagine that even most laypeople, with no legal expertise whatsoever, could appreciate the disastrous results to be expected from courts vetted by public opinion. Yet, that is not the case.

Notwithstanding the fact that many polls show voters concerned about the influence of campaign contributions on judicial decision making, many ballot initiatives to set up appointed judgeships do not succeed. For example, a November 2001 Florida referendum to replace elected county judges with appointed judges failed.[19] Now, the Florida press is again raising concerns about the implications of the swelling reelection coffers of county trial judges that are being filled by vested interests. The average amount of political contributions per county trial judge in Florida has increased 9 percent in two years.[20] The ramifications of a reelection-driven judiciary are clear. U.S. Supreme Court justice Byron White summed it up for all of us: "If a judge's ruling for the defendant . . . may determine his fate at the next election, even though his ruling was affirmed and is unquestionably right, constitutional protections would be subject to serious erosion."[21] Such a state of affairs would not seem to be in anyone's best interest.

> The very purpose of a Bill of Rights was to withdraw certain subjects from the vicissitudes of political controversy, to place them beyond the reach of majorities and officials and to establish them as legal principles to be applied by the courts. One's right to life, liberty, and property, to free speech, a free press, freedom of worship and assembly, and other fundamental rights may not be submitted to vote; they depend on the outcome of no elections.[22]

Why would any American want to see judges subjected to political pressure to compromise the law? Biblical truth knew to avoid this pitfall at all costs. Yet in America we have seen a political cycle of judicial pledges to "get tough on crime" and "increase executions."

> The greater use of the death penalty today is very much a product of the competition among politicians to show who can be the toughest on crime. Politicians compete to show who can be most for the use of the death penalty, who can be most in favor of cutting back on review of death sentences, who can be for speeding up the process so we have faster executions, and who can be for longer prison sentences.[23]

> Judicial candidates who promise to base their rulings on "common sense," unencumbered by technicalities, essentially promise to ignore constitutional limits on the process by which society may extinguish the life of one of its members.[24] (citations omitted)

Meanwhile, judicial attempts to honor the requirements of the federal and state constitutions and the Bill of Rights court disaster and are derided as mere technicalities.

For a judge to follow the law and the constitution can have perilous consequences.[25]

The Bill of Rights guarantees an accused certain procedural safeguards, regardless of whether those safeguards are supported by popular sentiment at the time of the trial, in order to protect the accused from the passions of the moment. But nothing protects an elected judge who enforces the Constitution from an angry constituency that is concerned only about the end result of a ruling and may have little understanding of what the law requires. Judges who must keep one eye on the next election often cannot resist the temptation to wink at the Constitution.[26]

This political pressure to find defendants guilty, to sentence them to death, to sustain death sentences, and to deny clemency, despite facts or requirements of law, exists at the trial level and the appellate level, both state and federal. It is manifested in prosecutorial decisions to seek the death penalty. It lurks behind both judicial elections and judicial appointments.

In 32 of the 38 states with the death penalty, judges are subject to election. Some of those elected judges have abandoned the independence of their office by such actions as throwing a noose over a tree outside the courthouse, coming into court displaying brass knuckles and a gun, revealing their death verdicts before the defendant even comes to trial, boasting about being a "hanging judge," and issuing election press releases prejudicing a capital defendant during trial. . . .

Ultimately, the integrity of the justice system suffers. . . . The outcomes of individual cases can be affected as judges feel the pressure to uphold death sentences, and even innocent defendants can find themselves facing an execution if the judge might lose his or her job in the next election for faithfully interpreting the law.[27]

The "higher authority" to whom present-day capital judges may be "too responsive" is a political climate in which judges who covet higher office—or who merely wish to remain judges—must constantly profess their fealty to the death penalty. . . .

Not surprisingly, given the political pressures they face, judges are far more likely than juries to impose the death penalty.[28]

The recent decision of the U.S. Supreme Court in *Ring v. Arizona*[29] held it unconstitutional to have a trial judge decide on death sentences without any jury involvement. This may mitigate the direct effect of political pressure on judges in capital sentencing cases in most states. The decision did not address the hybrid situation in four states—Alabama, Florida, Delaware, and Indiana—which allows judges to make the sentencing decision after advisory input from a jury.[30] The hybrid sentencing schemes in those states are working their way toward a U.S. Supreme Court decision at this time.

The U.S. Supreme Court has not yet ruled as to whether the *Ring* decision is retroactive.[31] Also, the *Ring* decision does not address the numerous indirect ways a trial judge can impact the outcome in a death penalty case, e.g., through rulings on motions, decisions on recusal, attitude toward the accused, etc. Consequently, it is worthwhile to touch on some actual cases from around the country that show the wisdom of the standards of the biblical death penalty, which separate politics from capital punishment. The following excerpts are from *Killing for Votes: The Dangers of Politicizing the Death Penalty Process* and other sources.[32]

ALABAMA

The case of Walter McMillian, a black man who was in a romantic relationship with a white woman, was mentioned in chapter 15. This account concerning his case addresses the circumstances of his trial:

Sometimes innocent defendants are caught up in the zealousness of the judge to impose a death sentence. Walter McMillian had been placed on death row in Alabama even before his trial. He was a black man accused of murdering a well-liked young white woman. McMillian was already unpopular because he was dating a different white woman. After the murder had gone unsolved for months, the police convinced some witnesses to testify against McMillian. . . . Through his arrest and trial, McMillian maintained his innocence. The evidence against him was weak. The jury convicted him of murder, but given the lack of physical evidence, they recommended a life sentence. But the judge, Robert E. Lee Key, had the ultimate decision on sentencing. . . .

. . . When McMillian's life was placed in Key's hands, he rejected the jury's caution in this racially charged case and declared, "The only appropriate sentence is death by electrocution." Six years later the key witnesses from the trial admitted that they had lied. In their zeal to solve this troubling murder, the prosecution had focused on the wrong man and the judge overruled the jury and sentenced him to die. But for the extraordinary intervention of the Alabama Resource Center in showing his innocence, he would have been executed.

It is impossible to know why Judge Key acted as he did, since the law does not require any explanation in overriding the jury. But when a black man is convicted of killing a young white woman in a small, outraged southern town, and the judge, who is subject to election, is given the power to make a strong political statement through his sentencing, there is great danger of improper influence.[33]

MISSOURI

In Missouri, judge Earl Blackwell issued a signed press release related to his judicial election announcing his new affiliation with the Republican Party while presiding over a death penalty case against an unemployed African-American defendant. The press release stated, in part:

> [T]he Democrat party places far too much emphasis on repre-
> senting minorities . . . people who dont' [sic] want to work,
> and people with a skin that's any color but white. . . . I believe
> the time has come for us to place more emphasis and concern
> on the hard-working taxpayers in this country . . . [the] major-
> ity group of our citizens seems to have been virtually forgotten
> by the Democrat party.

The judge denied a motion to recuse himself from the trial.
The defendant, Brian Kinder, was convicted and sentenced to
death.[34]

AMERICAN DEATH PENALTY POLITICS AND PROSECUTION

Not infrequently, the local prosecutor's office is both a pressure
point for political influence on application of the death penalty
and a source of politicizing of the local judiciary. "Some prosecutors brag about their death penalty convictions as if they were
notches on their guns. They campaign for office, knowing that it
is almost impossible to appear 'too tough' on crime. For example,
Bob Macy, the District Attorney of Oklahoma City, proudly
listed as the first item in his campaign literature that he had sent
44 murderers to death row."[35]
The unreviewable decision of the prosecutor to seek the death
penalty can be heavily influenced by political support in his current job and aspirations for judicial office:

> A capital case provides a prosecutor with a particularly rich
> opportunity for media exposure and name recognition that can
> later be helpful in a judicial campaign. Calling a press confer-
> ence to announce that the police have captured a suspect and
> the prosecutor will seek the death penalty provides an oppor-
> tunity for a prosecutor to obtain news coverage and ride popu-
> lar sentiments that almost any politician would welcome. . . .
> A capital trial provides one of the greatest opportunities for
> sustained coverage on the nightly newscasts and in the news-
> papers. A noncapital trial or resolution with a guilty plea does
> not produce such coverage.[36] (citations omitted)

A judge who has used capital cases to advance to the bench

finds that presiding over capital cases results in continued public attention.[37]

TEXAS

According to the Death Penalty Information Center in Washington, D.C., Johnny Holmes, the district attorney of Harris
County, Texas, made a career out of the death penalty.[38] He sent
more people to the execution chamber between 1976 and 1996
than any *state*, except Texas itself. In the DA's office was a chart
entitled the "Silver Needle Society," which listed all those from
Harris County who had been executed by lethal injection.[39]

However, a . . . decision in federal court sharply criticized the
reckless attitude of some of the prosecutors in Holmes's office.
In overturning the capital conviction of Ricardo Guerra of
Houston, Judge Kenneth Hoyt castigated the police and prosecutors: "The police officers' and the prosecutors' actions described in these findings were intentional, were done in bad
faith, and are outrageous."[40] He particularly pointed to the political side of this prosecutorial misconduct, which he said "was
designed and calculated to obtain a conviction and another
'notch in their guns' "[41]

AMERICAN DEATH PENALTY POLITICS AND STATE APPELLATE COURTS

The intrusion of politics into the independent thinking and integrity of justices is not confined to the prosecutorial or trial levels.
The judges who are charged with the constitutional duty to review death penalty cases are not immune from the pressure to
affirm death sentences without regard to law or facts. It starts at
the lowest appeals court level and continues through to the highest. "A judge's votes in capital cases can threaten his or her eleva-
tion to a higher court. No matter how well qualified a judge may
be, perceived 'softness' on crime or on the death penalty may
have consequences not only for the judge, but also for those who
would nominate or vote to confirm the judge for another court."[42]

Let us take a brief look at how this outcome-oriented death penalty political pressure forces appellate judges to look over their shoulder when making decisions.

TEXAS

Stephen Bright relates the following factual account:

After a decision by the Texas Court of Criminal Appeals, reversing the conviction in a particularly notorious capital case, a former chairman of the state Republican Party called for Republicans to take over the court in the 1994 election. The voters responded to the call. Republicans won every position they sought on the court that year. One candidate for the court, Stephen W. Mansfield, campaigned on promises of greater use of the death penalty, greater use of the harmless-error doctrine, and sanctions for attorneys who file "frivolous appeals especially in death penalty cases." Before the election, it came to light that Mansfield had misrepresented his prior background, experience, and record; that he had been fined for practicing law without a license in Florida; and that—contrary to his assertions that he had experience in criminal cases and had "written extensively on criminal and civil justice issues"—he had virtually no experience in criminal law. Nevertheless, Mansfield received fifty-four percent of the votes in the general election, defeating the incumbent judge, a conservative former prosecutor who had served twelve years on the court and had been supported by both sides of the criminal bar. After his election, *Texas Lawyer*[43] declared Mansfield an "unqualified success."[44] (citations omitted)

ALABAMA

One finds that some appellate judges do not feel free to describe the corruption of the judicial review process through political pressure until they are off the bench.

William Bowen Jr., the former presiding judge of the Alabama Court of Criminal Appeals, spoke out against the state's jury override provision which allows a judge to impose a death sentence even after the jury has recommended life in prison. Bowen said most judges would prefer not to have this power because it increases political pressure on judges to impose the death penalty. In Alabama, nearly a quarter of the death row inmates were sentenced to death by an elected judge exercising the jury override power. "Judicial politics has gotten so dirty in this state that your opponent in an election simply has to say that you're soft on crime because you haven't imposed the death penalty enough," said Bowen. "People run for re-election on that basis, because the popular opinion in the state is, Let's hang 'em."[45]

AMERICAN DEATH PENALTY POLITICS AND STATE SUPREME COURTS

Such a state of affairs would be bad enough if it was limited to the intermediate level of state appeals courts. The sad truth, however, is that even attaining the rare status of a state supreme court justice offers no protection against the outcome-oriented political heat to affirm death sentences without reference to law or facts.

MISSISSIPPI

In "Political Attacks on the Judiciary: Can Justice Be Done Amid Efforts to Intimidate and Remove Judges from Office for Unpopular Decisions?"[46] Stephen Bright documents the incredible story of a justice on the Mississippi Supreme Court:

Justice James Robertson was voted off the Mississippi Supreme Court in 1992. His opponent in the Democratic primary ran as a "law and order" candidate with the support of the Mississippi Prosecutor Association. Robertson was attacked for a concurring opinion he had written expressing the view that the Constitution did not permit the death penalty for rape where there was no loss of life. However, Robertson and his fellow justices who had taken an oath to uphold the Constitution of the United States had no choice. The United States Supreme Court had held ten years earlier that the Eighth Amendment did not permit the death penalty in such cases.[47] (citations omitted)

Robertson had also filed a dissent in another case, stating that because the trial judge failed to give the jury proper instructions at the sentencing hearing, the case should be returned to the trial court for a new sentencing hearing properly conducted. Eventually, four years later, the U.S. Supreme Court took the same position as Robertson and ordered a new sentencing hearing.[48] "Thus, had Justice Robertson's view prevailed on the initial appeal, it would have saved four years and considerable costs before the resentencing. If anything, Justice Robertson's dissent is an indication of his abilities as a judge, not a basis for removing him from the court."[49] The law and order campaign painted him as a criminal-coddling judge, and he was removed for making correct statements of constitutional law.

CALIFORNIA

Use of the governor's bully pulpit to "beat up" on state supreme court justices has become an art form in California, the state with America's largest death row population:

In 1986, the Governor of California, George Deukmejian, publicly warned two justices of the state's supreme court that he would oppose them in their retention elections unless they voted to uphold more death sentences. Obviously, he did not know the legal issues presented by those cases; all he was interested in was results. Deukmejian had already announced his opposition to Chief Justice Rose Bird because of her votes in capital cases. Apparently unsatisfied with the subsequent votes of the other two justices, the governor carried out his threat. He opposed the retention of all three justices, and all lost their seats after a campaign dominated by the death penalty. Deukmejian appointed their replacements in 1987.[50] (citations omitted)

Once a governor has been successful in politicizing the state's supreme court, it is almost inevitable that his successors will feel compelled to do the same: "California Governor Gray Davis said that his judicial appointments should follow his political lead on such issues as the death penalty or resign. Erwin Chemerinsky, a law professor at the University of Southern California calls Davis' comments 'outrageous.' 'A judge is not a Cabinet member who is there to carry out a governor's or a president's policies,' said Chemerinsky."[51]

TENNESSEE

The story of Tennessee Supreme Court justice Penny White serves to remind us that the political pressure to force state supreme court judges to affirm death sentences, regardless of the law or the facts, is not limited to the west side of the Mississippi.

Justice White is [a] recent example of a state court judge removed from office after campaigns that promised results—more death sentences, not justice—and that relied on distortions of a judge's record to make the judge appear "soft on crime."[52] (citations omitted)

Justice Penny White was the only woman on Tennessee's Supreme Court. . . . She had served admirably . . . on the lower appellate court and, in fact, confirmed the overwhelming number of criminal convictions which she reviewed.[53]

In the first death penalty case before her on the Supreme Court, she joined the unanimous vote of the other justices in affirming the conviction of Richard Odom, but overturning his death sentence. She also joined, but did not write, a three-judge majority opinion in the same case which found insufficient evidence to uphold Odom's death sentence for the rape and murder under Tennessee's capital punishment law.[54]

Justice White's opponents . . . blamed her for the fact that Tennessee has not carried out any executions in the last thirty-six years. But the Odom case was the only capital case that came before the court during White's nineteen months on the court.[55] (citations omitted)

Justice Penny White was voted off the Tennessee Supreme Court.[56] (citations omitted)

Yet immediately after Penny White was voted off the Tennessee Supreme Court in a retention election that was nothing but a referendum on the death penalty, Governor Don Sundquist said, "should a judge look over his shoulder [when making decisions] about whether they're going to be thrown out of office? I certainly hope so." And just in case the message was lost, he pointed out that the other four members of the court would be on the ballot in two years.[57] (bracketed language in original)

FLORIDA

In general, the judiciary, especially the Florida Supreme Court, has been under vicious attack by outcome-oriented death penalty politicians:

"What I hope is that we become like Texas: bring in the witnesses, put them on a gurney and let's rock and roll." Said Brad Thomas, Governor [Jeb] Bush's top advisor on the death penalty. . . .

[Former] House Speaker John Thrasher, [speaking on the Florida Supreme Court's reversal of death penalty cases,] wrote, "[It] raises serious questions about whether the death penalty is being enforced by the courts."[58] (bracketed language mine)

Even when reversal of a death penalty case is obviously required because of violation of the most fundamental constitutional rights, the court is castigated for doing its job. For example, in July 2003, the Florida Supreme Court overturned the death penalty conviction of Harold Lee Harvey based on ineffective assistance of counsel. The decision, reported in the online edition of the *Vero Beach Press Journal*,[59] is based upon the fact that Harvey's attorney conceded guilt to first-degree murder in his opening statement. That is incredible. Once his lawyer had made such a statement, what was the purpose of a hearing? The whole proceeding was rendered a sham.

Did the prosecutor acknowledge this factual reality? Did he affirm the state supreme court's duty to uphold the constitutional right to an attorney who doesn't advise the jury that you are guilty before they have even heard the facts of the case? No. He bashed the court in the media. "This court will look for any reason to overturn a death-penalty case."[60]

Another example is Florida's battle over the new DNA testing statute. The language desired by the pro–death penalty leadership of the state legislature limited testing to those "tried and found guilty." This eliminated all inmates who had entered a plea bargain.

The Florida Bar Association requested Florida Supreme Court rules allowing testing for any inmate, including those who had entered guilty pleas. This was based on the reality that most defendants are poor and unable to afford counsel. They are represented by overworked public defenders and are the most likely defendants to enter pleas, even in cases where they are innocent.

Tom Feeney, then Florida House Speaker, was infuriated, claiming such a step would exceed the court's authority. The legal reality is that the Florida Supreme Court has the inherent authority to let innocent people out of prison. The court was already considering DNA testing rules before the legislature even passed their own bill.[61]

Yet, in an effort to avoid further political acrimony over the death penalty, the Florida Supreme Court yielded to the Speaker's pressure. When the Florida legislature passed a statute that limits postconviction DNA testing to inmates who have not entered guilty pleas,[62] the Florida Supreme Court kept the peace by adopting a postconviction DNA testing rule that mirrored the statute.[63]

The DNA law was just another battle in the series of skirmishes between Florida's Supreme Court and the outcome-oriented death penalty politics of Florida's legislature. The legislative backers of Florida's Death Penalty Reform Act of 2000 were irate when the Florida Supreme Court heard arguments on its constitutionality. The goal of the act was to execute everyone within five years of their trial. The Florida Supreme Court, during oral arguments, expressed concern that the changes drastically increased the risk of executing an innocent person because they prohibited the hearing of new evidence of innocence (unless procedural violations could be proven).[64] The Florida Supreme Court held that the Death Penalty Reform Act of 2000 was unconstitutional.[65]

The political attack on the judiciary was immediate.[66] One proposal sought to stack the Florida Supreme Court with additional justices who would be committed to doing whatever the legislature wanted.[67] Other outcome-oriented death penalty politicians prepared a new law to strip the court of certain powers and to put the legislature in control of court procedures.[68] This attempt was reinitiated and expanded in the Florida House of Representatives.[69]

The key proponent of a legislative takeover on the Florida judiciary roiled about a criminal procedure rule, adopted by the Florida Supreme Court, which allows defense lawyers to take depositions during discovery before a criminal trial. The purpose of the rule is to minimize hidden or fabricated evidence or lying witnesses. In other words, the rule is to reduce the risk of prosecutorial misconduct and wrongful conviction of the innocent. The rule has the additional benefit of confronting such problems up front instead of dealing with them in endless appeals. The outcome-oriented death penalty politician castigated the court for the rule because, in his words, it is "a waste of money."[70]

The latest attack on the Florida Supreme Court has been the legislatively initiated state constitutional amendment, which attempts to force the court to treat all U.S. Supreme Court decisions as binding on interpretations of Florida's Constitution. The language is long and convoluted, but the primary purpose is generally believed to be the overturning of the *Brennan* decision (discussed in chapter 16) with respect to execution of juveniles. (In *Brennan*, the Florida Supreme Court interpreted the Florida Constitution as prohibiting execution of minors for crimes committed under the age of seventeen.) Now that the constitutional amendment passed in November 2002, Florida can execute minors whose crimes were committed at the age of sixteen, the minimum age allowed by the U.S. Constitution.

The serpentine wording of the amendment, which never mentions execution of juveniles, opens a Pandora's box of problems in areas other than the death penalty. Many commentators are sure that the amendment is an unconstitutional encroachment upon the separation of powers, which mandates that judicial, executive, and legislative functions remain independent.

STATE JUDICIARIES POLITICIZED BY CAMPAIGN FUND-RAISING

The news gets worse. Many state high court judges also need to raise money for expensive statewide campaigns or retention elections. The very same process that has been identified as having mortgaged our legislative bodies to vested interests are now also extending to our states' top judges. A recent editorial raised the alarm that in "39 states, at least some judges face elections to get or keep their offices." Campaigns for two Ohio Supreme Court positions spent "an estimated $9 million," while—not to be outdone by its neighbor—the "race for three [Michigan] Supreme Court seats cost at least $16 million." Elizabeth A. Weaver, a Michigan Supreme Court justice, warned that there is "danger ahead" because of "aggressive campaigning that has become part of judicial politics."[71]

Given the political realities of outcome-oriented death penalty politics for state supreme court judges, it should not be surprising that some state supreme courts might choose to overlook erroneous death sentences, hoping the mistakes will be mopped-up by review in the federal courts. "A Georgia Supreme Court justice acknowledged that the elected justices of that court may have overlooked errors, leaving federal courts to remedy them via habeas corpus, because '[federal judges] have lifetime appointments. Let them make the hard decisions.'"[72]

Before 1996, that may have been a viable strategy for deflecting political heat in tough death penalty cases. But under the federal legislation that was passed in the early and mid-nineteen nineties, the ability of federal courts to review and correct legal errors, even review claims of innocence, in death penalty cases has been severely curtailed. The intrusion of America's death penalty politics into the judicial integrity of federal judges in capital cases has taken other forms as well.

AMERICAN DEATH PENALTY POLITICS AND FEDERAL COURTS

The broad swath of outcome-oriented death penalty politics, the pressure to increase executions without reference to law or facts, includes the process of federal judicial appointments. In the mid-nineties, the Senate Republicans gave notice that they would challenge any judicial nominee whom they considered to be insufficiently committed to the death penalty.[73] In effect, this has resulted in the judicial selection processes around the nation screening out any judge who shows concerns about capital punishment—even if it is just a concern about executing the innocent. An example is the case of justice Rosemary Barkett.

> Considerable opposition . . . was mounted against the Chief Justice of the Florida Supreme Court when she was nominated for the U.S. Court of Appeals. Despite the fact that Justice Rosemary Barkett had upheld the death sentence in more than 200 cases, Senator Orrin Hatch wanted to see if she was "serious enough about the death penalty."[74] (citations omitted)

> Rosemary Barkett participated in more than 12,000 decisions during her eight years on the Florida Supreme Court and wrote more than 3,000 opinions. Yet, she was condemned for a dissenting opinion that another member of the court wrote.[75] (citations omitted)

The assaults never mentioned that

> Barkett voted to uphold the death sentence in 275 cases, even on occasion when the court reversed, and that she was endorsed for retention in 1992 by the Fraternal Order of Police, the Police Officers Benevolent Association, and the Peace Officers Association.[76] (citations omitted)

> None of the materials used to attack Barkett mentioned the

legal analysis behind her decision or that she had voted to uphold more death sentences than she voted to reverse.[77]

The fallout from outcome-oriented death penalty politics has a wide dispersal pattern at the federal level. In political fights in other states, senators who had voted to confirm former Florida Supreme Court justice Rosemary Barkett for a seat on the U.S. Court of Appeals for the Eleventh Circuit were attacked based on the claim that she was soft on crime and weak on the death penalty. Supporters of her appointment were assaulted in their own reelection campaigns with claims that Barkett voted to let a child murderer "off the hook."[78]

In fact she had joined in a dissenting opinion with the then most conservative justice on the Florida Supreme Court. The majority of the court had voted to affirm the death sentence. No one had been let off the hook. The attack also misrepresented two other cases in which Judge Barkett had written opinions concerning very specific legal issues, one concerning jury instructions on mitigating factors, the other concerning the execution of a mentally retarded and mentally ill man with psychotic delusions and an IQ of 60. Both decisions were characterized as coddling criminals with willful disregard for the victims.[79]

The clear message is that any judicial vote for resentencing or retrial in a death penalty case, even if legally correct, even if actual innocence is involved, will be punished politically. In addition to the screening of appointments based upon outcome-oriented death penalty politics, a flanking operation is now under way to impeach federal judges who grant relief in death penalty cases. "A judge spoke recently . . . at Emory and said we all know when we make these controversial decisions what the impact is going to be when we run for office. And now members of Congress are even suggesting that we should impeach federal judges for unpopular decisions."[80]

All this political bickering and rivalry over the decisions of judges has taken a tremendous toll on our judicial system.

The price paid for an elected judiciary in Alabama, California, Georgia, Texas, and other states has been the corruption of the judges and the courts of those states. Once a judge makes a decision influenced by political considerations, in violation of the oath he or she has taken to uphold the law, both the judge and the judicial system are diminished, not only in that case, but in all cases. . . . Once the public understands that courts are basing their rulings on political considerations—even when the courts are giving the voters the results they want, as the California Supreme Court is now doing—it undermines the legitimacy and the moral authority of courts as enforcers of the Constitution and law.[81]

AMERICAN DEATH PENALTY POLITICS AND CLEMENCY

Clemency is the last resort for intervention before execution. It is only available after all the state and federal court reviews have been exhausted. Among the states that have the death penalty, clemency is usually reserved to the governor (fourteen states).[82] Nine states provide that the governor must have a recommendation of clemency from a board or advisory group,[83] and nine other states provide for a nonbinding recommendation from such a board or advisory group.[84] In three states a separate advisory group makes the decision,[85] while in three others the governor sits on the board that makes the decision.[86] In the federal system, clemency is vested in the president of the United States.[87] "Since 1976, 225 death row inmates have been granted clemency for humanitarian reasons. Humanitarian reasons include doubts about the defendant's guilt, questions about the defendant's mental capacity, rehabilitation of the defendant, or the personal convictions of the governor."[88] Of the 225 cases, 171 were involved in the clemency and blanket commutations granted by Governor Ryan of Illinois in January 2003. That means only 54 clemencies for humanitarian reasons, a very small number of cases, have been granted outside that unique situation. After surveying the extent of outcome-oriented death penalty political pressure on our judges, who are supposed to be somewhat insulated from such influence, one can imagine the political pressure on governors to avoid clemency. In *Killing for Votes*, a former chair of Louisiana's pardon board gives an account of what transpired in an actual case. The chairperson was serving on the pardon board after appointment by the governor.

> When we left the [pardon board] hearing and went behind
> closed doors to decide [the inmate's] fate, I just couldn't convince myself that the man was really guilty and deserved to
> die, and right there from the room where we were meeting I
> called the Governor's office. His chief legal counsel . . . came
> to the phone, and when I told him about the case—I was upset,
> I was crying—I said that if our job was to dispense mercy, that
> this seemed as clear a case for mercy that I had yet seen, but
> [the Governor's lawyer] told me that I knew the governor did
> not like to be confronted with these cases and wanted us to
> handle it.[89]

After the telephone conversation, the Board rendered its
unanimous decision upholding [the] death sentence. [The
chairman] later commented, "I lacked the courage to vote on
the basis of how I felt and what I believed. I gave in to the
prestige and power, the things that went with my job. I knew
what the Governor, the man who had appointed me, wanted:
no recommendation for clemency in any death case."[90] (bracketed language mine)

In my home state of Florida, the role of public pressure in
wiping out clemency review is legendary. No Florida governor
has granted clemency in any death case since governor Bob Graham in the early 1980s.[91]

As stunning evidence that this state of affairs continues in present-day Florida, one need only address the recent example of
Amos Lee King Jr., convicted of killing a Florida widow in 1977.
Governor Jeb Bush delayed for thirty days the scheduled execution of King in order to allow DNA testing of the blood found
on King's shirt at the time of the crime. The *Miami Herald* came to
the governor's defense in an op-ed piece when he was "skewered"[92] by death penalty advocates for allowing this brief delay.

What is the hurry? Should we not use every available means to
determine whether or not a person is guilty before killing him?
What does biblical truth reveal about our blood lust?

The dimensions of a clemency process that exists only on

paper are especially frightening when we read the infamous *Herrera* case. In effect, the U.S. Supreme Court handed the hot potato to the governors of the states. The court distinguished its role of reviewing compliance with constitutionally required procedures from the job of clemency, which belongs to the governors, thereby leaving it to the clemency process to catch the cases of innocence and mitigation. In the political reality of America's nonexistent clemency process, that is tantamount to saying that no one is willing to take the political heat for preventing the execution of a person who might be innocent. Not the governors and not even the U.S. Supreme Court.

As this sobering and startling reality sets in, we can only marvel at the wisdom of biblical truth in mandating a separation of the judicial from the political. We also can better understand some of the confusing responses to the American death penalty from around the world.

For example, on June 6, 1995, the Constitutional Court of the Republic of South Africa, the nation reconstituted from the one that our society condemned and boycotted in moral outrage because its policy of apartheid fell so far below our standards of moral decency, handed down its decision on the constitutionality of the death penalty under the republic's new constitution.[93] The court focused on a contrast between the U.S Constitution and the new constitution of South Africa. Their distinction, simply put, was the fact that the U.S. Constitution guarantees fundamental fairness of procedures but does not guarantee any right to life. The court then distinguished the constitution of the Republic of South Africa, which, it held, guarantees the "right to life": "The unqualified right to life vested in every person by section 9 of our Constitution is another factor crucially relevant to the question whether the death sentence is cruel, inhuman or degrading punishment within the meaning of section 11(2) of our Constitution. In this respect our Constitution differs materially from the Constitutions of the United States and India."[94]

BLANKET CLEMENCY: THE ILLINOIS CLEMENCY AS A CASE STUDY

In the wake of the national publicity concerning the erroneous capital conviction of Anthony Porter, Illinois' Republican governor George Ryan, a longtime death penalty supporter, imposed a moratorium on the Illinois death penalty on January 31, 2000.[95] Porter had come within forty-eight hours of execution and "was released from death row following an investigation by journalism students who obtained a confession from the real murderer in the case."[96] During the period of the moratorium, Governor Ryan appointed a special commission to study the death penalty in Illinois. The fourteen members of the commission represented diverse viewpoints, including eleven members with prosecutorial experience and a former general counsel to the Chicago Police Department.[97]

The commission was appointed by the governor "to study and review the administration of the capital punishment" in Illinois, "to determine why that process has failed," and "to examine ways of providing safeguards and making improvements."[98] The work of the commission could not have been conducted more diligently or thoroughly. Subcommittees gave detailed study to specific issues, the whole commission held monthly daylong meetings, subcommittees met monthly, public hearings were held three times in both Chicago and Springfield to accept public input, and private meetings were held with both survivors of murder victims and with some of the thirteen men who had been exonerated and released from Illinois' death row. "Commission members reviewed the recommendations contained in written reports from other groups that had already studied the system . . . and conducted its own research to develop suggestions for improvements."[99] They examined the cases of the thirteen men released from Illinois' death row, reviewed more than 250 Illinois cases in which the death penalty was levied, studied victim issues and the impact of various factors on the death sentencing process, reviewed death penalty laws in the thirty-seven other jurisdictions with the death penalty, took expert input in areas such as police practices and eyewitness testimony, and analyzed existing efforts throughout the country to address the systemic problems of capital punishment prosecutions.

These are some of the very issues of greatest concern under the light of biblical truth. Such an effort is exactly the utilization of resources and talent to study the death penalty that a person of biblical faith would hope for during a moratorium. The depth and breadth of the review is calculated to truly redefine the role and scope of capital punishment in a way that will alleviate the errors and injustice that have plagued the American death penalty. The commission's official report recommends eighty-five changes that must be made to the system of capital punishment in Illinois in order to eradicate injustice and minimize the potential of wrongful executions. In an attempt to save capital punishment in Illinois, Governor Ryan introduced legislation that would make the recommended changes.[100] The Illinois legislative bodies refused to pass any of the changes.[101] The inaction of the Illinois legislators set the stage for a weekend of the most dramatic action taken by any governor in the American death penalty arena in recent history.[102] The first step took place on Friday, January 10, 2003.

> Governor Ryan . . . pardoned four condemned prisoners who long maintained Chicago police tortured them to confess to murders they did not commit.
>
> "What I can't understand is why the courts can't find a way to implement justice," Ryan told a classroom of law students. "So here we have four men, who were wrongfully convicted and sentenced to die by the state for crimes the courts should have seen they did not commit.
>
> "They are perfect examples of what is so terribly broken about our system. They have repeatedly cried out for justice, and their cries have fallen on deaf ears."[103]
>
> "The only evidence that there were against these four people were obtained through brutal beatings, electrocutions and suffocations," Ryan said.[104]

In granting the four pardons, Governor Ryan said: "Today, I am pardoning them of crimes for which they were wrongfully prosecuted and sentenced to die. The system has failed for all four men, and it has failed the people of this state."[105]

On Saturday, January 11, 2003, the second act of this historic weekend was unveiled. Ryan stated bluntly that Illinois' capital punishment system was "haunted by the demon of error" and "commuted the sentences of every inmate on Illinois' Death Row . . . 164 inmates, including four women."[106]

In his speech at Northwestern University Law School, Governor Ryan spoke at length, explaining how he had reached the decision that only blanket clemency could be appropriate:

I never intended to be an activist on this issue. I watched in surprise as freed death row inmate Anthony Porter was released from jail. A free man, he ran into the arms of Northwestern University professor Dave Protess who poured his heart and soul into proving Porter's innocence with his journalism students.

He was forty-eight hours away from being wheeled into the execution chamber where the state would kill him.

It would all be so antiseptic and most of us would not have even paused, except that Anthony Porter was innocent of the double murder for which he had been condemned to die.

After Mr. Porter's case there was the report by *Chicago Tribune* reporters Steve Mills and Ken Armstrong documenting the systemic failures of our capital punishment system. Half of the nearly 300 capital cases in Illinois had been reversed for a new trial or resentencing.

Nearly half!

Thirty-three of the death row inmates were represented at trial by an attorney who had later been disbarred or at some point suspended from practicing law.

Of the more than 160 death row inmates, 35 were African-American defendants who had been convicted or condemned to die by all-white juries.

More than two-thirds of the inmates on death row were African-American.

Forty-six inmates were convicted on the basis of testimony from jailhouse informants.

I can recall looking at these cases and the information from the Mills/Armstrong series and asking my staff: How does that happen? How in God's name does that happen? I'm not a lawyer, so somebody explain it to me.

But no one could. Not to this day.

Then over the next few months, there were three more exonerated men, freed because their sentence hinged on a jailhouse informant or new DNA technology proved beyond a shadow of doubt their innocence. . . .

How many more cases of wrongful conviction have to occur before we can all agree that the system is broken? . . .

I have had to consider not only the horrible nature of the crimes that put men on death row in the first place, the terrible suffering of the surviving family members of the victims, the despair of the family members of the inmates, but I have also had to watch in frustration as members of the Illinois General Assembly failed to pass even one substantive death penalty reform. Not one. They couldn't even agree on *one*. How much more evidence is needed before the General Assembly will take its responsibility in this area seriously?

The fact is that the failure of the General Assembly to act is merely a symptom of the larger problem. Many people express the desire to have capital punishment. Few, however, seem prepared to address the tough questions that arise when the system fails. It is easier and more comfortable for politicians to be tough on crime and support the death penalty. It wins votes. But when it comes to admitting that we have a problem, most run for cover. Prosecutors across our state continue to deny that our death penalty system is broken, or they say if there is a problem, it is really a small one and we can fix it somehow. It is difficult to see how the system can be fixed when not a single one of the reforms proposed by my Capital Punishment Commission has been adopted. Even the reforms the prosecutors agree with haven't been adopted.

So when will the system be fixed? How much more risk can we afford? Will we actually have to execute an innocent person before the tragedy that is our capital punishment system in Illinois is really understood? . . .

The legislature couldn't reform it.

Lawmakers won't repeal it.

But I will not stand for it.

I must act.

Our capital system is haunted by the demon of error, error in determining guilt, and error in determining who among the guilty deserves to die. Because of all of these reasons today I am commuting the sentences of all death row inmates.[107]

How have leaders responded to this courageous act of clemency in the face of a broken death penalty system that courts could not fix and legislators would not fix? Some hope that sweeping reform will occur in Illinois and throughout America. "'It is inevitable that momentum will follow this announcement,' said David Elliot, spokesman for the National Coalition to Abolish the Death Penalty. 'It's going to reinforce the emerging impression that in the minds of the American public that the death penalty system is fundamentally flawed.'"[108] Others believe that a backlash against Ryan's acts will stymie reform: "Sen. Peter Roskam, a Republican who proposed more modest death penalty changes than Ryan pushed, said the backlash from victims' families and prosecutors could hold back reform efforts. 'I don't think the public will understand why people who have committed vile, brutal crimes on children and women and men in Illinois will not get the ultimate punishment.'"[109]

In the state of Florida, where twenty-three people have been exonerated from its death rows, both those in favor of the death penalty and those against it agreed that Florida would not review its system of capital punishment.

The independent review that led the outgoing Illinois governor to empty his state's death row last week would be virtually impossible in Florida where politicians strongly support capital punishment and show little interest in examining its fairness.

. . . Republican Gov. Jeb Bush . . . has said no moratorium or wide-ranging study is needed.

Attorney General Charlie Crist, a Republican whose office represents the state in appeals from death row, said Florida doesn't have "this wholesale problem . . . that I heard might be in Illinois." . . .

Several Republicans and Democrats in the Legislature said . . . they see no need for study, either. State Sen. Rod Smith, a Gainesville Democrat and former prosecutor, noted several Illinois cases involved police officers who had coerced confessions or tampered with evidence.

"I know nothing like that's been suggested in this state," Smith said. "I believe our capital penalty in Florida has proven itself time and again to give ultimate protection against error."[110]

Such assertions about the well-being of Florida's death penalty are so inconsistent with the actual facts, which we have reviewed in the prior chapters, that one can only attribute them to wishful thinking at best. The reality of the death penalty in Florida comports more closely with the conclusions of a *Miami Herald* editorial in the wake of Ryan's commutations, wherein the editors acknowledged that the "factual basis" for Governor's Ryan's decision also exists in Florida, and, although Florida's governor would be under political pressure to ignore the problems in Florida's death penalty, he should at least investigate them and possibly declare a moratorium.[111]

CLOSING THOUGHTS

There is plenty of room for philosophical debate about the facts presented in our brief walk through the political realities of the American death penalty, both as to judges and as to clemency. We could discuss the pros and cons of a judiciary that is responsive to its citizens, especially on such crucial issues as abortion and euthanasia. We could debate the plusses and minuses of governors who act for the mood of the people versus governors who act for the sake of justice.

Our core question, however, is very focused. What does biblical truth reveal about the American death penalty with respect to judges and clemency? Let us assume that every judge in America possesses the qualifications of wisdom, humility, fear of God, disdain of gain, love of truth, love of fellow men and women, and a good reputation. What about the rest of the standards revealed by biblical truth?

Does a judge who is elected or appointed promising to "get tough on crime" and "speed up executions" meet the standard of the biblical death penalty that judges are to be moderate, reluctant to impose a sentence of death, and absolutely impartial toward each accused?

Does a judge who must appease execution-oriented electors and must look over his or her shoulder at outcome-oriented death penalty politicians meet the standard of the biblical death penalty that judges must not be appointed based upon their appeal to the masses and are forbidden to glide along with the community in the direction of the prevailing political winds?

Does a judge who must run for election or retention or seek judicial appointment meet the standard of the biblical death penalty that anyone who seeks judicial office is automatically disqualified from it?

Does a judge who must raise funds to finance an election, reelection, or retention campaign meet the standard of the biblical death penalty that no judge shall be appointed based upon his or her financial means, and that anyone who has been so appointed is to be treated with the dignity of the packsaddle of an ass?

Does a governor who is terrified to grant clemency, even in appropriate cases, because of media lynching and the consequent political fallout meet the standards of biblical truth?

Our answer is quite clear. The American death penalty fails hopelessly in meeting the standards revealed by biblical truth with respect to clemency and with respect to judges who preside in capital cases.

There's little left to scrutinize. Let us now turn to the issue of balancing the respective interests of the accused and of the families of the victims.

Chapter Twenty

FOR WHOM IS IT A DETRIMENT?

THE AMERICAN DEATH PENALTY AND FAMILIES OF THE VICTIMS

In October 1999, I was in southeastern Michigan for the final days of my sister's valiant struggle with cancer. Thumbing through a copy of the *Detroit Free Press*, I stumbled across an incredible article, "Now, the Healing Can Begin: Man Is Found Guilty of 4 Claw-Hammer Murders after Home Break-In."¹ The article quietly attests to a truth that is barely mentioned or breathed in the Bible Belt: the fact that the death penalty brutalizes the family and loved ones of the murder victim, again and again and again.

> Now, perhaps, the healing and living can begin for relatives of the four people Michael Barnhart killed in the Nov. 1 bloodbath that rocked Oakland County, after a jury on Monday found the unemployed construction worker guilty of one second-degree and three first-degree murder charges. . . .²

Prosecutors and the victims' families requested that Barnhart be sentenced to life in prison without possibility of parole. As noted at the end of chapter 10, the former Governor of Michigan is proud that his state abolished the death penalty 150 years ago because its absence keeps Michigan's murder rate lower. The absence of capital punishment also is a tremendous blessing to the families and loved ones of the victims. When a sentence of life imprisonment is pronounced at the end of the trial, the formal part of the ordeal is over. The healing can begin. In a death penalty state, the healing would not begin for the victim's family and loved ones for at least another ten or fifteen years after the trial.

Some respond flippantly to such facts, asserting that speeding up executions will cure the problem. In the prior nineteen chapters, we've combed through reams of evidence showing that the risk of erroneous prosecution is much higher in death penalty cases than in life imprisonment cases and that the average time needed to show actual innocence after wrongful conviction in a capital case is at least nine years. We do not need to rehash all that here in order to know that speedier executions promise little except for more wrongful executions.

Yet, there is the nagging question of the plight of the loved ones of the victim. Their need must be addressed. Does the biblical truth of Torah/Pentateuch and the provisions of Talmud that fulfill those scriptural limitations offer any guidance in this regard? In fact, it does: "[F]or whom is the defendant's acquittal detrimental in a capital case? The Gemara answers: This is not difficult, because the acquittal of a person accused of murder would be to the detriment of the avenging relative of the victim."[3] The Hebrew word translated as *avenging relative* actually means *redeemer of the blood* and "refers to a close relative of a murder victim."[4] "Under certain circumstances, this relative has the right to avenge his relative's murder by pursuing and killing the murderer (see, Num. 35:19). Since the avenger will suffer emotionally if the murder conviction is reversed (thereby leaving the victim's death unavenged), the reversal is deemed to the detriment of the avenger."[5]

The Talmud struggles, however, because the issue is whether or not the court should reverse a death sentence. The judges believe that there are proper grounds for relieving the defendant from execution. The judges are also concerned about the plight of the survivors of the murder victim. Whose interest should hold sway? "Because of the detriment of the avenging relative, shall we refrain from reversing the guilty verdict and kill this person?"[6]

We all recognize this question. It is an ancient formulation of the current dilemma under the American death penalty. Our way of expressing this question is a little different: If we reverse a death sentence because of innocence or constitutional error or legal error, will not our act reopen the wounds of the family and loved ones of the victim? The answer is, "Yes, probably it will." That was true three thousand years ago, and it is true now. The biblical truth of Torah/Pentateuch and the provisions of Talmud necessary to fulfill those scriptures then proceeds to answer the underlying issue. "If the judges have found legal grounds to reverse the guilty verdict, it seems highly improper to proceed with the defendant's execution simply because it seemed detrimental to the avenger!"[7] And of course, given the difficult situation that one is already stuck in the machinery of the death penalty, that is the answer. Some are waking up, however, and realizing that the death penalty is not necessarily good for the family and loved ones of the victim. A healing process that can begin after the verdict and sentencing in the trial may be worth a lot more than a "life for a life." At least one prosecutor in Nebraska has become aware of this truth.

> Lancaster County Attorney Gary Lacey announced that he would not seek the death penalty against Randolph Reeves at an upcoming resentencing hearing. Reeves, a Native American, was convicted and sentenced to death in Nebraska in 1981 for killing two women. The case drew national attention when some of the family members of the victims began actively opposing his execution, which was scheduled for January 12, 1999. The execution was stayed by the state Supreme Court, which ordered a new sentencing hearing for Reeves.
>
> In announcing that he will not pursue the death penalty again, Lacey stated, "I had the power to put an end to all the suffering in this case. . . . I have the power to do that, and over the weekend I decided that's what I'm going to do."
>
> Since the state is not going to seek the death penalty, Reeves will likely be resentenced to life in prison.[8]

Two other aspects of the plight of the victim's loved ones are almost never mentioned. I am aware of the first one because my wife and I make ourselves available to minister to families and loved ones of murder victims. It is a sobering and gut-wrenching undertaking. One cannot overestimate the horror and agony that has been thrust into the lives of these innocent people. Their suffering is real and will continue long after the newspapers have tired of the details. The death penalty will inflict another blow on most of them before their healing can start. It happens this way.

The reality is that our American Constitution will not allow the execution of every person that commits a murder. No matter what the law does in terms of procedures, capital punishment is only fitting under our laws for a small fraction of the thousands of murders committed every year in America. That means for each of the families of victims whose murder will be avenged by seeking the death penalty, hundreds, maybe thousands, of other families will be told that the death penalty is not appropriate in the case of their loved one's murder.

No matter that the conclusion by the prosecutor is the legally correct one. No matter the legal explanation that is given for the decision. None of that matters. Regardless, most of those people will hear the message, "Your loss is not as bad as someone else's." The mere fact that the death penalty is available on a limited basis turns it into a second bludgeoning of all the surviving loved ones of persons whose murder is not death penalty qualified. That encompasses the overwhelming majority of survivors of murder victims.

PREJUDICE AGAINST VICTIMS' FAMILIES THAT OPPOSE CAPITAL PUNISHMENT

What about the families and loved ones of murder victims who oppose capital punishment? How are their needs being addressed? In fact, almost no one even mentions them. A January 2003 letter to the editor in the *Florida Times-Union* expressed the plight of such victims extremely well:

I read with dismay George Will's Jan. 19 column titled "Ryan left a dubious legacy," regarding the commutation of the death sentences of 167 inmates in Illinois.

Will stated that it is disrespectful of victims' survivors not to take a life for a murder. He further suggested that grieving survivors need capital punishment to feel a sense of "equilibrium being restored to the world."

Despite having lost two loved ones to murder, I beg to differ with Will. My father was a New York state trooper who was shot and killed in the line of duty in 1974. Ten years later, my boyfriend of four years was also murdered. Yet, I still oppose the death penalty. A life does not replace a life; and two wrongs don't make a right.

As a survivor, I am not alone in my opposition to capital punishment. Murder Victims' Families for Reconciliation is a group comprised of family members of both homicide and state killings who oppose the death penalty in all cases.

Established in 1976, all of us refuse to respond to our loss with a pursuit for more killing, a state-sanctioned killing. Our loved ones who were murdered deserve more honorable memorials.

Executions are not what will help us heal. For those of us seeking a more peaceful world, capital punishment only undermines our efforts.[9]

Syndicated columnists are not the only ones who pretend that murder victims' family members who oppose the death penalty don't exist. The criminal justice system has all but perfected this denial. In *Dignity Denied: The Experience of Murder Victims' Family Members Who Oppose the Death Penalty*,[10] Murder Victims' Families for Reconciliation (MVFR) addresses an undiscussed yet incomprehensible reality: throughout America, prosecutors, judges, police officers, policymakers, and the victim services community treat victims' family members who oppose the death penalty as though they are not really victims.

In "Ain't *I* a Victim," the introduction to this astounding report, Renny Cushing, whose father was killed in the hallway of his own home, spells out a form of discrimination that most of us could never have imagined:

As Executive Director of MVFR, I regularly hear stories that reflect this widespread assumption that victims' families want the death penalty. . . .

. . . Today, as MVFR publishes this account of silencing and discrimination against anti–death penalty victims, *we are not aware of a single protocol in the office of any prosecutor in the United States* that alerts victim assistants to the possibility that some family members of victims may oppose the death penalty and that they are entitled to the same assistance as those who support it. Though we are a national clearinghouse for information on these issues, we are not aware of any laws or policies prohibiting discrimination against victims who oppose the death penalty, or mandating that services intended for survivors of homicide victims be provided equally to those who support the death penalty and those who oppose it.[11] (italics in original)

Cushing does not attribute this discrimination to bad faith; rather, it seems to be driven by erroneous presumptions. "An assumption exists in the United States that people who have had a family member taken from them by murder believe that justice is achieved only if the perpetrator is killed. This unquestioned assumption is so widespread that prosecutors and policymakers assume they are advocating for victims when they advocate for the death penalty. Yet some victims' family members feel differently."[12]

Anti-victim discrimination against family survivors who fail to support the death penalty is not ethereal. It is real and concrete. For example, nothing is so basic to survivors' rights as the right to speak and be heard in the formal legal process. The constitution of the state of Nebraska guarantees this right. A Nebraska court, however, held that murder victims' families who do not support the death penalty are not victims for purposes of the constitutional protection.

In early 1999 the Nebraska Board of Pardons met to consider holding a hearing about the possibility of granting a commutation of death sentence to [a murderer]. Three family members of the [deceased] asked to present testimony to the Board of Pardons, but only one was allowed to do so. [The deceased's husband and daughter who oppose capital punishment] were denied the right to speak or to present written testimony, but [the deceased's] sister, who supports the death penalty was allowed to have her views read into the record of the meeting.[13] (bracketed language mine)

The husband and daughter of the deceased went to court against the Nebraska Board of Pardons, claiming that the board had violated their rights under the Nebraska Constitution, including the rights of victims to "be informed of, present at, and make an oral or written statement at sentencing, parole, pardon, commutation, and conditional release proceedings."[14] The district court ruled that they are not victims. "It appeared that, because [they] wanted to speak at the clemency hearing in support of the defendant, they could not be considered victims. Victims, the judge's ruling effectively said, are those who oppose the defendant and support the state's efforts to impose the death penalty."[15] (bracketed language mine)

The attorneys for the members of the murder victim's family who are opposed to execution summarized the state of the law in Nebraska:

> The district court's callous declaration that [the members of the murder victim's family who are opposed to execution] are not victims does not obviate the loss they have endured. Rather, the ruling . . . adds insult to injury when their public plea not to desecrate the memory of their loved one by the taking of another life is met with a legal pronouncement that they are *persona non grata* under the Nebraska law. . . . If the district court is correct in its findings and conclusions, then the Victim's Bill of Rights in Nebraska means that the state helps victims only when the victims are willing to help the state. . . . To shut out of the process people who are not willing to do the state's bidding as victims further victimizes people who have suffered a terrible loss.[16] (bracketed language mine)

As bad as that account seems, the reality can be much worse. In other cases, survivors who are opposed to executions have been silenced even though they have assisted in the prosecution of the offender by testifying in the guilt phase of the trial. In a Florida case, a twenty-four-year-old woman watched her father die. She survived by holding her breath so that the murderer would believe she was already dead. When she was called as a witness during the penalty phase of the trial, she tried to honor her father by stating his opposition to the death penalty.

> It is difficult to imagine anyone failing to recognize [the victim's] right to speak, since she herself was repeatedly stabbed in the head during the attack that killed her father and came very close to losing her own life. Yet because of her opposition to the death penalty, she too was silenced during the criminal proceeding against the attacker. . . .
>
> . . . The judge interrupted her, saying, "There will be no discussion about the death penalty, period, and I'm advising you right now that if you violate my order, you will be in direct criminal contempt, and you face six months in county jail and a $500 fine."
>
> A videotape of this scene in the courtroom shows [the victim] on the witness stand, crying as she replies, "I don't know what to say. I feel like if I say one word I'm going to jail. I don't want to go to jail. That's not my purpose here." Years later, speaking at an MVFR conference, [she] commented about this moment: "I was wondering who was a criminal in that courtroom. They were treating me like I was the bad one."[17] (citations omitted; bracketed language mine)

In addition to being silenced, survivors of murder victims who oppose the death penalty also can find themselves shut out of any information about the progress of the case. For one such survivor, whose daughter was raped and murdered, "[o]nce she made her opposition to the death penalty known, it seemed to her that the district attorney's office cut off communication with her and did not inform her of [an] upcoming court hearing involving her daughter's murderer."[18]

Prosecuting attorneys have been known to "warn families that if they advocate against the death penalty the office will no longer communicate with them" or, in other cases, "the office may communicate with the family, but do so in a way that is incomplete, inaccurate, or misleading."[19]

In states where families of murder victims are entitled to assistance and advocacy, a "victim's opposition to the death penalty can mean that assistance and advocacy are *withdrawn*. . . . [S]ome advocates see victims who oppose the death penalty as more closely identified with the defendant than with their own status as victims, thus rendering them ineligible for (or undeserving of) advocates' help."[20]

A recent case in Delaware involved a man who was sentenced to death for the murder of his wife. No advocate from the state system was present to assist the couple's fourteen-year-old son through the process or comfort him after the execution was carried out.

It was members of MVFR who stepped in unofficially to support and assist this boy. Likewise, it was members of MVFR who accompanied the victims' family throughout the court proceedings when Texas was seeking the death penalty for Andrea Yates. . . . The family members . . . did not want the death penalty imposed. At one point during the trial, no seats were reserved for the Yates family, and they did not receive any acknowledgement or help from the victim assistant's office about this or any other aspect of the proceedings.[21]

This state of affairs would be bad enough if it simply reflected the attitudes of prosecutors and judges whose political ambitions are so paramount that they outweigh the First Amendment rights of survivors who wish to speak against the death penalty in the cases of the murder of their own loved ones. Unfortunately, that is only the tip of the iceberg. The problem permeates America's entire death penalty system.

It must also be acknowledged that silencing and discrimination exist on the broader levels of institutional policies and funding priorities. . . .

When the Victim Witness Coordinator for Cook County, Illinois organized a group of victims' families to testify before a legislative task force in support of the death penalty, public funds were being used to address the needs and represent the voices of that particular subgroup of victims. No publicly funded advocate helped or represented the victims' families in Illinois who wanted to speak out *against* the death penalty that day. Likewise, when the National Organization for Victim Assistance produced the video "Finding Resolution: Crime Victims as Witnesses to Executions," which featured only victims' families who support the death penalty and did not address the needs of those who oppose it, public funds were again being used to serve only one subset of the victims' population. Without an equal commitment of public resources, victims' families who oppose the death penalty experience clear economic discrimination [by the state].[22] (bracketed language mine)

Governor George Ryan perceptively hit upon this issue in his January 11, 2003, speech at Northwestern University Law School: "What kind of victims' services are we providing? Are all of our resources geared toward providing this notion of closure by execution instead of tending to the physical and social service needs of victim families? And what kind of values are we instilling in these wounded families and in the young people?"[23]

My personal experience is that the system is deaf to the needs of victims' families—other than the need for executions. In March 2002 I attended a debate on the death penalty hosted at a church in downtown Jacksonville, Florida.

The pro–death penalty speaker was a capital crimes lawyer from the local state attorney's office. A prominent lawyer from Tallahassee, the state capital, presented the failures and problems with the death penalty and proposed alternatives. I arrived early enough to grab a third-row seat. The rows in front of me were filled with members of a local crime victims' advocacy group.

A gray-haired woman seated with the advocates looked a bit overwhelmed by the size of the crowd and the pre-debate ruckus. I struck up a conversation with her. She described the murder of her loved one and her own emotional and psychological pain. I realized that it might be wounding to her if, after having confided in me, she heard me ask a question that indicated my lack of support for the death penalty. So, I gently broached the subject:

"I've come to the conclusion that I cannot support the American death penalty but it is not because I do not think your pain and your suffering are real and horrendous. It is because of my religious and biblical beliefs. Please understand that my heart goes out to you."

She looked at me a bit puzzled and replied, "I don't support the death penalty either."

I was amazed. "Do they know that?" I asked, pointing to the victims' advocates who had arranged for her presence in the group as a show of support for capital punishment.

"Oh, no," she shook her head. "They've never asked me what I think about it."

THE AMERICAN DEATH PENALTY AS AN OBSTACLE TO HEALING

There is a final way that the American death penalty continues to harm both the survivors of the victim and the community. The article from Detroit about a quadruple homicide, mentioned earlier in this chapter, reveals it almost accidentally:

> Last week, Barnhart's family released a statement expressing remorse and asking for forgiveness for him, saying he wasn't the man they remember before he became addicted to drugs.
>
> On Friday, the Barnharts met privately with victims' relatives.
>
> "They wanted to apologize," [a loved one of the victims] said Monday. "They can't help what their son did. We feel terribly for them, too. This was all his sole responsibility."[24]

This is the kind of reconciliation that begins deep healing for the victims' loved ones, the family of the perpetrator, and the community. The community has been shocked and torn asunder by such a horrible crime. Everyone needs healing.

Unlike the experience of the families and community described in the Michigan article, it is almost impossible for healing to begin in a case where the death penalty is being sought. This is true for several reasons.

First, any attempt by the family of the perpetrator to reach out to survivors of the victim is suspect as a ploy to try and save the neck of their own loved one. Also, because the value of the deceased and the magnitude of his or her suffering is riding on whether or not the death penalty is granted, the surviving family feels duty bound in loyalty to avoid "softening up" to the family of the perpetrator. "I was struck by the anger of the families of murder victims. To a family they talked about closure. They pleaded with me to allow the state to kill an inmate in its name to provide the families with closure. But is that the purpose of capital punishment? Is it to soothe the families? And is that truly what the families experience?"[25]

Second, the state and defense attorneys will try to keep the families apart so as to avoid statements that may become evidence in death sentence hearings later in the case. A battle will be under way for years to try and achieve or prevent execution of the perpetrator. The victim's family is now in the role of the avenger, seeking to kill the loved one of the perpetrator's family. The victim's family has become the avenger of the blood. The wounds and wounding continue without healing for anyone as the family of the perpetrator suffers the prolonged agony of preparing for their loved one's murder.

Many of these families live with the twin pain of knowing not only that, in some cases, their family member may have been responsible for inflicting a terrible trauma on another family, but also the pain of knowing that society has called for another killing.

These parents, siblings and children are not to blame for the crime committed, yet these innocent stand to have their loved ones killed by the state. . . . [T]hey are also branded and scarred for life because of the awful crime committed by their family member.

Others were even more tormented by the fact that their loved one was another victim, that they were truly innocent of the crime for which they were sentenced to die.[26]

Also, by the time either an execution is carried out or the perpetrator's sentence is commuted, the animosity between the families and the polarization of the community (where most of the members have taken up with one side or the other) are almost beyond recovery.

Contrast that situation with an incredible yet true account of healing that was recently reported in the *Florida Times-Union* in Jacksonville. The story began five years ago with a November 1998 crime that was ultimately revealed to be horrific. The entire northeast Florida community had been galvanized by the one-week search for the missing girl that preceded the grisly discovery of her body under the waterbed of her killer. The victim was just eight years old. The murderer was a fourteen-year-old boy. The families were neighbors, living across the street from each other. Both children had mothers. Almost two years after the crime, the boy's father, Steve, died.

The two mothers held each other and wept.

"Baby steps. Just take baby steps," Sheila Clifton whispered in Missy Phillips' ear.

Neighbors separated by a thin city street and a chasm of grief, they'd avoided each other for more than a year—since Phillips' 14-year-old son, Josh, murdered Clifton's 8-year-old daughter, Maddie, in one of Jacksonville's most infamous crimes.

"It was a year's worth of grief that poured out of us," Missy Phillips recalled last month. . . .

It was a far cry from that frenzied week in 1998. . . .

Five years later, both moms continue on the road to healing. Both have found it in some measure in their faith, in their relationships, in using their experiences to help others.

And both point to a reconciling moment in July 2000—when Sheila Clifton crossed the chasm to comfort Phillips after her husband's death.

"It felt good to let her know that I didn't hate her," said Clifton, now Sheila Delongis. "I don't hate her, and I never will. I don't hate Josh. I hate what he did." . . .

The two hadn't spoken since Maddie's death. Phillips said if she saw her neighbor in the yard, she would wait until she went inside before leaving her house.

"My instinct was to go out and hug her, but I didn't because I was afraid," Phillips said. "We both needed to do that, and we didn't know how."

Delongis, who said she felt a need to comfort Phillips on the death of her husband, walked into the living room and embraced her neighbor just a few feet from where Maddie died. She told her healing would come slowly.

"I just felt her loss was great, too," Delongis said. "I felt the hurt she was going through."

Together, the two women wept tears of pain and loss and grief.

"It wasn't just for Steve," Phillips said. "We cried for Maddie. We cried for everything that had happened."

But there were tears of healing, too, the same kind of healing Delongis tells other grieving families about, the kind that requires going through the hurt.[27]

As miraculous as such a healing between families is under any circumstance, it would have been beyond reach if the death penalty had been involved. Because the perpetrator was only fourteen years old, he could not face capital punishment. Instead, he was tried as an adult and sentenced to life imprisonment without possibility of parole. We can see, however, that if the death penalty had been involved and the two families had been polarized into the long-term death penalty fight, such healing could not have taken place. If one family was fighting to prevent their child from being executed and the other family was fighting to obtain that execution, no one could have crossed the line and offered the embrace that would unleash the tears of agony of both families.

The death penalty is not about healing. With respect to families of murder victims, there are two ways. One is the way of healing evidenced by the articles from Detroit and Jacksonville. The other is the way of vengeance and death, played out over and over again in the death penalty states in the cases where capital punishment is being sought.

For people of biblical faith, can there be any doubt as to which of these two approaches is most consistent with the restorative justice of the Bible?

For Christians of biblical faith, can there be any doubt as to which of these two approaches is most consistent with the spirit and the mind of Jesus Christ?

In light of the standards for substantive and procedural details under the biblical death penalty of Torah/Pentateuch and the provisions of Talmud necessary to fulfill those scriptures, can there be any doubt as to which of these two approaches is consistent with the revelations of biblical truth?

Then again, what are we to make of the appeals for closure? Is closure the same as healing? Does an execution really bring closure?

A former chief justice of the Florida Supreme Court, Gerald Kogan, has been involved in over twelve hundred capital cases in his professional career. He comforted and encouraged the survivors of the victim when he was a prosecuting attorney in death penalty cases. He represented death penalty defendants as a lawyer in private practice. He sat on the bench as a reviewing judge. And as chief justice of the state supreme court, he attended to the open phone line with the governor's office, first confirming that no stays were in effect and then listening as the electrocution commenced and the death was confirmed with the words: "The sentence of the Court has been carried out." We would be hard-pressed indeed to find anyone who has experienced as many cases and as many facets of the actual death penalty in America.

What does Justice Kogan have to say about executions bringing closure? "It's not real. An execution does not bring closure—it does not bring back the deceased loved one. The pain of that loss will continue for as long as the survivor lives. And as far as finality, there is no finality when an innocent man is executed. Nothing has been brought to finality or closure when the State has killed an innocent man."[28]

Justice Kogan's experience is confirmed by Mark Parker, a survivor of the Orlando courthouse shooting by Thomas Provenzano (discussed in chapter 16). Parker's work partner was killed. Parker was rendered a paraplegic for the rest of his life. In an interview with the *Tampa Tribune*, he avoided the word "closure" when describing the experience of witnessing Provenzano's execution: "I knew the minute he died I was not going to jump up out of my wheelchair."[29]

Yet some survivors of murder victims testify that healing is possible. When Aba Gayle's nineteen-year-old daughter was murdered in 1980, she found herself seeking revenge and consumed by bitterness. Although the district attorney assured her that she would feel better when the murderer was convicted and, in turn, executed, Gayle was not convinced that the death penalty would quell her anger and lead to the healing she desired. Today, Gayle shares her story with the public and speaks out against the death penalty:

"I knew that I didn't need the State of California to murder another human being so I could be healed," she notes. "It's time to stop teaching people to hate and start teaching people to love. The whole execution as closure idea is not realistic."

A member of Murder Victims' Families for Reconciliation, Gayle states, "Anger is just a horrible thing to do to your body. Not to mention what it does to your soul and spirit. Forgiveness is not saying what he did was right—it's taking back your power."[30]

Other brave survivors of murder victims tell similar stories revealing that they found their healing not in revenge but in forgiveness. In "Forgiving the Unforgivable," a true story by Johnnie Cabrera of Oklahoma City, she shares how she achieved healing from the brutal murder of her seven-year-old granddaughter. The beautiful little girl had gone outside to ride her bike near her house for a few minutes until the family dinner was ready. Her body was found in a dumpster "behind a WalMart. She had been sodomized, stabbed and drowned."

I asked the minister if I could speak to him. In the following months we talked. . . . Somewhere along the way, I forgave Kathy's killer.

After that, it was much easier to go on. When you forgive, you get that hatred out of your system—the hatred that consumes you. . . .

. . . [Her killer] wanted to die.

But I didn't want to see him die. I believe that God gave us life and only He can take it away. . . . Did you know that when a person is executed the death certificate reads HOMICIDE?[31]

Johnnie Cabrera ended up attending the execution of her granddaughter's killer by lethal injection—not because she wanted to, but because the killer asked her to: "There's no dignity to it. It's cold. It's impersonal. It's a barbaric ritual, sanctioned by the state. I saw Floyd Medlock die, and I can tell you this: Nobody gets closure by witnessing somebody else murdered. Forgiveness is the only thing that allows you to go on."[32]

Johnnie Cabrera has moved on. Her healing has taken deep

root. Her example challenges all of us. And the depth of her understanding that the nature of executions is homicide, no different from any other killing, is consistent with the understanding of the biblical death penalty:

> This respect for the individual is reinforced through the Biblical language on killing. In the Bible there are no words that distinguish between, of kill [sic], criminal homicide, justifiable homicide, and execution. They are all described through the same word; Kill (razach). This usage is also reflected in the language of the Rabbinate. . . . Thus, the language of ancient Israel made no distinction between types of killing. No matter their posture, justified or criminal, they are all described by the same word with the equal moral imprint, kill.[33]

What exactly are we called to offer to the victim's survivors: vengeance or healing? Governor Ryan, after commuting the death sentences of Illinois death row inmates to life imprisonment without possibility of parole, addressed this issue, saying that he hoped that "the family members of victims would ultimately turn away from 'the hope of revenge.'"[34]

Living for the hope of revenge is the way of vengeance. Johnnie Cabrera, Aba Gayle, Sheila (Clifton) Delongis, and Missy Phillips have shown us the path of healing. The two roads are very different. The road we choose will determine the outcome.

The choice we make cannot be made in a moral vacuum. As people of biblical faith, morality guides our choices. Surrender to mere vengeance would be to abscond from our duty to live out the fullest of our biblically moral potential. To those of us who see biblical truth as a guide, a tool to better living as well as a basis of faith, the choice is absolutely clear. Some judges have started to recognize this fact.

Baltimore County Judge Dana M. Levitz recently sentenced a man convicted of murder to two life terms without parole, in part because of its possible effects on the victims' families. Levitz said, "The devastating effect that this unending litigation has on the innocent families of the victims is incalculable. By imposing a death sentence, I ensure that the victim's families will be subjected to many more years of appeals."

Family members also noted that the decision gave them the peace of mind they have been searching for. A sister of the victim noted, "I'm pleased with the sentence because I think I might get some closure from this. I didn't want him out on the street anymore, but killing him wasn't the answer either."[35]

CLOSING THOUGHTS

So long as the American death penalty exists, it is a bludgeoning tool of further injury to the overwhelming majority of survivors of murder victims, those whose loved one's murder does not qualify for the death penalty. In those few cases where it can be applied, capital punishment effectively prevents healing of the survivors and the community for years and, if carried out, creates a new set of suffering victim survivors. For those survivors who oppose capital punishment, the existence of the death penalty can result in the state treating them like second-class citizens or worse, heaping further injury upon their trauma. When it comes to the concerns about families of the victims, the American death penalty does not meet the standards of biblical truth.

Our search is completed. It is now time to tally our results and calculate the answer to our question: *What do the biblical truths of Torah/Pentateuch and the provisions of Talmud necessary to fulfill those scriptures reveal about the American death penalty?*

Chapter Twenty-one

Summary of Part Two

In part 1 of this work, the standards of the biblical truth of Torah/ Pentateuch and the provisions of Talmud necessary to fulfill those scriptures reveal that the American death penalty is fatally deficient in terms of the substantive law and the authority to kill, as we summarized in chapter 11. Now we must summarize the results of viewing the procedures of the American death penalty in light of such biblical truth. The failings are overwhelming. Let us recap these differences by subject matter in scorecard fashion.

In terms of the standards of biblical truth for people permitted to be witnesses, does the American death penalty comply with the following requirements?

The witnesses must be of impeccable character with nothing to gain from their testimony.
No.

Anyone with something to gain from his or her testimony is disallowed as a witness.
No.

Anyone with a special relationship to the accused is disallowed as a witness.
No.

In terms of the evidence permitted under the standards of biblical truth, does the American death penalty comply with the following requirements?

All material facts must be established by testimony of firsthand witnesses who witnessed the actual killing.
No.

Circumstantial evidence is prohibited.
No.

There must be multiple witnesses who agree in every material respect on all essential facts.
No.

If the testimony of the witnesses on any material fact is in disagreement, the witnesses and all of their testimony are excluded.
No.

Confessions are prohibited as evidence.
No.

In terms of the culpability of the accused under the standards of biblical truth, does the American death penalty comply with the following requirements?

The criminal intent of the accused as to intent to commit murder must be established by objective testimony.
No.

Malicious intent, premeditation, cannot be inferred from other actions.
No.

There must be absolute certainty of guilt and premeditation through the giving of the warning to the murderer before the murder occurs.
No.

In terms of the admission into court of posttrial evidence of innocence or mitigation under the standards of biblical truth, does the American death penalty comply with the following requirements?

Any reasonable evidence of innocence or mitigation must be heard by the court right up to the moment of execution.
No.

The defendant must be shown to be unquestionably guilty.
No.

There is no such thing as "procedural default."
No.

Given the disastrous state of "prosecutorial misconduct," the polite term used when prosecutors lie, cheat, and deceive the courts and juries, does the American death penalty measure up to the following mandate of biblical truth?

Let it be done to them as they sought to do to him.
No.

In terms of those defendants of diminished mental and emotional capacity, does the American death penalty meet the following standards of biblical truth?

Minors (those under twenty years old) are not subject to capital punishment.
No.

Any person with a diminished mental capacity, whether it affects reasoning or emotional ability to harbor malice, must not be subject to capital punishment.
No.

Such persons are to be exempt from capital punishment whether the disability is permanent or intermittent, so long as it was in effect at the time of the crime.
No.

With respect to differences in social and economic conditions, does the American death penalty satisfy the following standards of biblical truth?

Whether rich, poor or in between, the ultimate sanction must apply equally to all the people.
No.

Justice must be administered without regard to economic status.
No.

With respect to differences in race, does the American death penalty satisfy the following standards of biblical truth?

All victims are of equal value.
No.

There can be no variations in application of the death penalty based upon the nature of the victim.
No.

All offenders are to be treated equally.
No.

There can be no variations in application of the death penalty based upon the nature of the offender.
No.

With respect to the characteristics of judges and of the manner of their selection, does the American death penalty satisfy the following standards of biblical truth?

Judges must be moderate, neither too harsh nor too forgiving.
No.

Judges must be reluctant to impose a sentence of death and be absolutely impartial toward each accused.
No.

Judges must not glide along with the flow of community sentiment.
No.

Judges are prohibited from simply following the direction of the prevailing political winds.
No.

Every judge must "possess the following seven qualifications: wisdom, humility, fear of God, disdain of gain, love of truth, love of fellow men and women, and a good reputation."

We hope it is true, but it is not required for the job.

Judges must not be appointed based upon their appeal to the masses.
No.

Judges shall not be appointed based upon their financial means.
No.

Anyone who seeks judicial office is automatically disqualified from it.
No.

Finally, does the American death penalty at least meet the concern of biblical truth for the suffering of the survivors of the victims?
No.

With respect to the basis for court authority to impose death, does the American death penalty meet the following requirements of biblical truth?

All judges must be ordained by the laying on of hands.
No.

The court system must be structured based upon the biblical court system.
No.

A majority of two is required to convict and only a majority of one is required to acquit.
No.

A unanimous first vote to convict requires acquittal.
No.

The Great Sanhedrin must be housed in the temple.
No.

The judges must be committed to Torah.
No.

The judges must acknowledge the dominion of the God of the Bible over the court proceedings.
No.

With respect to deterrence, does the American death penalty meet the following standards of biblical truth?

A moratorium must be placed upon executions when the death penalty is not a deterrent to capital crimes.
No.

Since it is obvious that the American death penalty does not meet any of the standards required by biblical truth, does the American death penalty qualify for biblical support as an extra-biblical death penalty on another basis, such as the following?

The inherent right of kings in the Davidic lineage.
No.

An exigency court for the protection of Torah or of God's reputation.
No.

As a mandate by God under Romans 13:4.
No.

Our conclusions are not ambiguous. The American death penalty fails miserably under the revelations of biblical truth. It cannot be conducted under biblical judicial authority. There is no scriptural foundation for the American death penalty as an extra-biblical death penalty, from either the Hebrew scriptures or the Christian scriptures. Finally, the American death penalty fails to satisfy even the deterrence requirement.

When it comes to balancing the concerns of justice and the plight of the survivors of murder victims, the American death penalty does not meet the standards of biblical truth. The American death penalty is a bludgeoning tool of further injury to the overwhelming majority of survivors of murder victims. In those relatively few cases where it can be applied, it effectively prevents healing of the survivors and the community for years and, if carried out, creates a new set of suffering victim survivors. For those survivors who oppose capital punishment, the existence of the death penalty can result in the state treating them like second-class citizens, heaping further injury upon their trauma.

As persons of biblical faith we may still want to maintain the American death penalty; however, we have no choice but to admit that doing so is a function of our will, not God's, and a matter of our desire for revenge. We cannot support the American death penalty based upon biblical truth or upon a proper under-standing of the biblical basis for an extra-biblical death penalty. Our comparison of the facts allows for no other conclusion.

Only one additional question remains in our search: How should people of biblical faith respond to this reality?

Chapter Twenty-two

A FAITH ALTERNATIVE

ABOLITION OR MORATORIUM OF THE AMERICAN DEATH PENALTY BY PEOPLE OF BIBLICAL FAITH

Our conclusion is inescapable. The American death penalty cannot be supported by biblical truth.

Now, our dilemma is to frame a response to this truth. What do we do?

When confronted with new facts, it is reasonable for thinking people to reassess their opinions and conclusions. The facts discovered by us in the process of our search have had just such an effect on others.

For example, the story of Jerry Townsend, the retarded man from Miami who was serving multiple life terms in prison until DNA testing proved he was wrongfully convicted, had a profound affect on one Florida assistant attorney general. Mark Schlein had been a detective who helped to nail down the convictions in that case. Then, he was a proponent of capital punishment, but "he changed his mind after recent DNA tests pointed to another suspect" and Jerry Townsend was set free from prison and exonerated. "[T]he criminal justice system in America is not perfect," said Schlein, who now works for the attorney general's office.

"Florida ought not be in the business of killing people. I'm deeply grateful he's alive today so he can walk free from jail."[1]

The facts have also had a deep impact on one Arizona Supreme Court justice who is painfully aware that he lacks God's unique ability to know the human heart:

> Arizona Supreme Court Justice Stanley Feldman recently stated that the fundamental issue of whether the death penalty should be retained in Arizona cannot be ignored. As the state Supreme Court's longest-serving justice, Feldman criticized efforts in Arizona to "perfect what I consider to be imperfectible" and noted:
>
> "There is no way to really do it right. The final decision has always come down to the members of our (Supreme Court) as to whether someone should live or someone should die. . . . I am not smart enough to make that decision on any fair and consistent basis given the tremendous range of facts and circumstances that affect every victim and every defendant and every set of facts that make up a case."[2]

A Texas judge has also gone on record as changing his mind about the American death penalty:

> Senior State District Judge C. C. Cooke recently expressed his concerns about the fairness of the death penalty during a legal seminar. The Texas judge recalled how the 11 death penalty cases he presided over during his 23 years as a judge altered his feelings about capital punishment. Cooke helped craft the state's death penalty law when he served as a state representative.
>
> "I was looking at it as a young politician, with about 90 percent of my district supporting the death penalty. Now, from a judge's perspective and taking care of people's rights, I think it has a lot of flaws."
>
> Among the flaws cited by Cooke were inadequate legal representation, access to DNA testing and the racial disparity of those executed. "I think the mood is changing in this country and people are realizing there are deficiencies in the system,"

said Cooke. "We always think we've got the right person, but the system is not infallible."[3]

Most significant of all, Governor Ryan of Illinois, a longtime death penalty supporter, has made history by his dramatic step in response to the facts of the American death penalty:

Four years ago I was sworn in as the thirty-ninth governor of Illinois. That was just four short years ago; that's when I was a firm believer in the American system of justice and the death penalty. I believed that the ultimate penalty for the taking of a life was administrated in a just and fair manner.

Today, three days before I end my term as governor, I stand before you to explain my frustrations and deep concerns about both the administration and the penalty of death.[4]

"I'd rather have somebody angry than have an innocent person killed," Ryan said. "If government can't get this right, it ought not be in the business of passing such final, irreversible judgment."[5]

We should not be surprised to find prominent Bible-believing Christians also announcing a change of their position on the American death penalty. Christian Josi, executive director of the American Conservative Union and a consultant to the campaign of former vice president Dan Quayle, wrote:

My fundamental problems with the death penalty began as a result of my personal concern, echoed by many on all sides of the political spectrum, that it was inconsistent for one to be "pro-life" on the one hand and condone government execution on the other. Pope John Paul II weighed in and cleared up the issue for me a bit, but dare I say, I still had my doubts.

Then came the talk of margin of error; the fact that in the course of business, the government had sentenced innocent people to death based on either just plain poor legal represen-tation or discoveries obtained through advanced DNA technology. . . .

The time has come for us to get beyond government executions.[6]

Josi's words seem directed toward abolition, the repeal of the American death penalty. As noted in chapter 11, abolition is the conclusion that I have reached as my faith response to America's death penalty.

Other people of biblical faith have weighed in strongly for a moratorium. Perhaps no one has summed it up better for Bible-believing Christians of the latter opinion than the Reverend Pat Robertson. In an assessment of the Christian response to the current state of the American death penalty, he said, "I think a [death penalty] moratorium would indeed be very appropriate."[7]

ACTION BY PEOPLE OF BIBLICAL FAITH

Abolition and moratorium are not common words in the vocabulary of most evangelical Christians. For one thing, the words sound political. For another, they smack of social action. Yet, either abolition or moratorium is exactly the right response for a biblical Christian and other people of biblical faith when confronted with the patently unbiblical American death penalty.

A statement of abolition by people of biblical faith says: "*Our faith position is that the American death penalty should be abolished.*" Abolition means it is to be ended.

How does a person, or a group of persons, make a clear and concise statement that as people of biblical faith they support abolition of the American death penalty? The easiest and most careful way is to sign or pass an abolition resolution for people of biblical faith. A short form of resolution for this purpose is reproduced in appendix A.

As noted earlier in the quote from Reverend Pat Robertson, some Christians and other people of biblical faith may feel that their most sincere response when confronted with the patently unbiblical American death penalty is to stand for a moratorium. A moratorium is a step short of abolition. Under a moratorium, the practice of the American death penalty is suspended, stopped, while the deficiencies are addressed and people of biblical faith are educated as to what biblical truth reveals about the American death penalty.

A statement of moratorium by people of biblical faith says: *"Our faith position is that the American death penalty must be stopped, subjected to a moratorium, while others of biblical faith learn what biblical truth reveals about the American death penalty."*

How does a person, or a group of persons, make a clear and concise statement that as people of biblical faith they support a moratorium on the American death penalty? The easiest and most careful way is to sign or pass a moratorium resolution for people of biblical faith. A short form of resolution for this purpose is reproduced in appendix B.

IF NOT DEATH, THEN WHAT?

Having determined that people of biblical faith cannot support the American death penalty, which fails to comply with the standards revealed by biblical truth and is unable to be rehabilitated to biblical standards, what are we to do with those who have committed murder? Are we left with no guidance from biblical truth? In fact, because of the strict requirements under Torah/Pentateuch and the provisions of Talmud necessary to satisfy those restrictions, the biblical death penalty had to deal with this issue just like we do. The guidance is there for our understanding. Biblical truth contemplated "[a] narrow, vaulted chamber in which certain serious criminals were imprisoned for life."[8]

The punishment being described here is life imprisonment for murderers, employed in order to fulfill the dictates of scripture. "The punishment is not mentioned in Torah, but was instituted by the Sages in fulfillment of the biblical expression: 'And you shall put the evil away from your midst.' (See, Deut.13:6, 17:7, 19:19, etc.) This punishment was reserved for known murderers who could not be executed because of legal technicalities."[9]

Imprisonment similar to what is available today in America is explicitly provided for under the biblical truth of Torah/Pentateuch and the provisions of Talmud necessary to satisfy those scriptures: "Regarding one who kills another soul not in the presence of witnesses, they place him in a cell and feed him 'sparing [portions of] bread and scant amounts of water.'"[10] (brackets in original) One would be hard-pressed to better describe the conditions of confinement in the modern American penal system—right down to the food. Our search has come full circle. We began with Cain whom God banished into a biblical exile remarkably similar in nature to our modern system of incarceration. The difference is that Cain was put outside the walls. Our offenders are placed inside the walls.

Having started at that point, we now return to the revelations of biblical truth for dealing with murderers that cannot be executed because of the inability to comply with the standards required by the scriptures in Torah/Pentateuch and the provisions of Talmud necessary to satisfy those rules. The answer is imprisonment.

We have available to us in America the option of life imprisonment as a punishment for murder. In many states, this life imprisonment can be without the possibility of parole. Thirty-five of the thirty-eight American states that provide for the death penalty also provide the option of life imprisonment without parole; the three exceptions are Kansas, Texas, and New Mexico.[11] Eleven of the twelve remaining states (all but Alaska) and the District of Columbia also provide for life imprisonment without possibility of parole.[12]

Biblical truth reveals that imprisonment is part of the solution to our problem. The Bible, however, has more to say on this issue than just imprisonment.

BIBLICAL RESTORATIVE JUSTICE

For people of biblical faith, the restorative justice principles of the Bible are sharply in evidence throughout the covenant relationship between God and his people. God is faithful, yet he calls his people to accountability, allowing them to face the consequences of their breaches (idolatry) while always, himself, remaining in the saving action of the dynamic initiated by God with Abraham.[13] We could learn a great deal from this biblical model.

My experience in over a dozen years of prison ministry is that our criminal justice system is almost devoid of accountability. First, there is a tremendous breach in the accountability of the offenders. This is a result of the plea bargain system. For years offenders have told me, "I'm not guilty of what I'm in here for." Initially, I disregarded such statements as "cons on the street guy."

Over time I realized, however, that the statements were literally true in many cases, not because of moral innocence, but rather because of the deals that were cut between lawyers for the defendants (mostly overworked public defenders who had to "plead clients out" in order to manage their case load) and lawyers for the state. The deals, called plea bargains, require the defendant to plead guilty to certain charges (which he may or may not have actually committed) and accept certain punishments as a way of clearing the court dockets and keeping the criminal justice system from collapsing under the weight of criminal trials. An unintended consequence of the fact that the overwhelming majority of criminal charges are dispensed with through plea bargains is that our prisons are full of men doing time for crimes that, literally, they did not commit or for which they have never been found guilty based on any evidence.

The inevitable conclusion of many offenders in such a "market-based" system of justice is that anyone who can afford a better lawyer is not guilty of anything. Thus, their real crime is being poor. Human denial can take an inch and turn it into a life script. The result is a tremendous lack of accountability by offenders for their wrongs to society.

The covenant relationship behind restorative justice requires mutual accountability.[14] That means we, as a society, must also face our failings to the offender. I cannot count the number of inmates who have half-laughed, half-cried as they told me about the "stupid rich man's society" that could have made them into a taxpayer by putting them through college for a few thousand dollars but instead would rather pay to keep them in prison where they can contribute very little to society.

"Tell me how that makes sense!" man after man challenges me. I've yet to come up with any answer that makes any sense of that situation, mathematically or economically, let alone morally or biblically.

Biblical restorative justice seeks to deliver us from merely punitive nonsolutions that make no sense. Punishment can be part of justice, but restorative justice goes beyond punishment by also seeking to restore the community, the victims, and the offender. Restitution is a concept of restorative justice for crimes against property that is evidenced in Talmud: "Although theft is prohibited from the religious viewpoint, it is considered by Jewish law to be a civil offense rather than a criminal act calling for physical punishment. The thief is obliged to restore the stolen object and in certain cases to pay a monetary fine to the owner (twice or more the value of the object), but he suffers no other punishment."[15]

Restorative justice becomes more difficult with crimes against persons, when a loved one has been maimed, raped, or murdered. How are the community, the victim—or in the case of murder, survivors of the victim—and the offender restored from such horrible crimes? As we have seen in the numerous true stories in chapter 20, forgiveness seems to play a very important role. The Bible is filled with examples of God's forgiveness. Unmerited mercy, forgiveness, is called grace.

For Christians of biblical faith, grace is a foundational concept. There should be no shortage of grace to deal with restorative justice, especially when Jesus admonished us that as we forgive, so shall we be forgiven. The impediments to accessing this grace for restorative justice seem to come from an exclusively "me and God" misunderstanding of the Bible (which speaks extensively about "we and God")[16] and dualistic theological formulations that distinguish between individual forgiveness as good and corporate forgiveness as bad, based upon our freedom in God to forgive individual infractions, but our supposed duty in God—as good citizens—to extract punishment for wrongs to our society.[17]

My personal experience is that restorative justice is something that God is doing whether we like it or not, whether we participate in it or not. I have met men in prison, even on death row, whose spirituality and faith shame my meager faith and spiritual shallowness. Such men have truly been restored. They have a great deal to offer to us. This should not surprise any person of biblical faith. God took the murderer Moses and used him to lead his people to freedom. God protected the reign of King David, even though he was a murderer by arrangement.[18] For Christians of biblical faith, God took the killer of Christians, Saul, and used him as the greatest evangelist of all time.[19] Our refusal to accept God's restoration of broken human flesh does not keep it from happening; we only prevent ourselves from sharing in the benefits of God's saving actions.

Ultimately, we all hope for restorative justice. Through years of ministry to dying people, people who were professionals, politicians, street people, even inmates, I have never, not once, had anyone pray on their deathbed to receive what they deserve. Every one of them has hoped for restorative justice from God.

Finding the ways and means to implement biblical restorative justice in our society will not be easy. The punitive justice we have pursued, however, has not been easy either. We have spent untold billions of dollars and millions of personnel hours conceiving and designing the ways and means of punitive justice that exist now. Similar allocations of effort and resources would undoubtedly be extremely effective in conceiving and designing the ways and means of biblical restorative justice.

WHY NOT A BIBLICAL DEATH PENALTY?

After the exhaustive search we have performed in the course of this book, a person of biblical faith might ask: Why not have America enact a biblical death penalty? We must examine that possibility based upon what we have learned.

First, a biblical death penalty is not limited to murder. Do we really desire execution for our teenage daughters who have engaged in premarital sex and for Sunday/Sabbath shoppers and the store personnel who wait on them? Are we prepared to begin execution of those who worship gods different from our own? Are we ready to levy the ultimate penalty for committing adultery; for being greedy or inciting greed in others; for playing with tarot cards or engaging in palm reading; for writing, printing, or reading horoscopes; for bad predictions by psychics; for cursing one's parents; or for being a rebellious son? Are we ready to slaughter most of our people? Of course not.

And what are we to do with the requirements for court structure, judicial ordination, vote-counting procedures, physical connection to the temple, and unqualified allegiance to Torah and the God of the Bible, all revealed by biblical truth as essential to biblical authority to exercise capital punishment? Are we ready to abandon America's secular governance, Constitution, and democracy in exchange for a king and decapitations? Are we ready to bring back monarchies and the guillotine? Of course not.

Are we prepared to expend the massive amounts of money and resources necessary to meet the procedural and judicial requirements of a biblical death penalty, all as detailed in the second part of this book? The cost of just a fair and equitable death penalty is astronomical. Can we really afford it? Yet, that standard is nowhere near the standards required for the minimums of a biblical death penalty. We would still be working with the relatively minimal standard: *guilt beyond a reasonable doubt*. That is far inferior to the biblical standard: *absolute certainty of guilt*. Who in America is willing to foot the bill for a system that guarantees absolute certainty of guilt before a death sentence can be levied? Who is kidding whom?

The answer is clear. A biblical death penalty in America two thousand years after the destruction of the second temple is a fantasy. We cannot afford it. We cannot make it work. We would end up in the same position as those who actually administered the biblical death penalty more than two millennia ago—it would be on the books but we could not use it.

Yet that is not the worst of matters. Most profoundly troubling of all for Christians of biblical faith is the truth that the biblical death penalty defies the atonement completed by Jesus Christ. The purpose of capital punishment under Torah/Pentateuch was redemptive. The sacrificial offering of the offender through biblical capital punishment brought atonement, redemption, to the offender and to the community, thus achieving reconciliation for both. Are those of us who are Christians of biblical faith prepared to take the position that the atonement by Jesus Christ was not enough? What Bible-believing Christian wants to participate in this?

The answer is evident. For people of biblical faith, especially Christians, in twenty-first-century America, there simply is no such thing as a biblical death penalty.

CONCLUSION: THE UNSETTLING HISTORY OF PARALLELS BETWEEN
AMERICAN SLAVERY AND CAPITAL PUNISHMENT

In the course of researching this book, I discovered unsettling parallels in American history between the biblical arguments supporting slavery in the eighteen hundreds and the biblical arguments supporting the death penalty in twenty-first-century America. As stunning as that realization has been, there are even more startling lessons from history for modern Americans of biblical faith.

Richard Furman was a devout and intelligent minister in the Carolinas of the pre–Civil War South. As noted earlier, he is recorded in history as *the man* who synthesized the biblical arguments that defended and supported the institution of slavery in the southern states. A ghastly lesson of history emerges into relief when we realize that Furman's critical biblical masterpiece was ultimately being used by his son, Reverend James Furman, not as a treatise defense of slavery, but rather as a means to excoriate the southern slave owners for mistreatment of slaves and call them to accountability under the biblical standards for treatment of slaves. "'We who own slaves,' wrote James Furman [the son], 'honour God's law in the exercise of our authority.' These words were not a defiant response to abolitionist rhetoric or a statement about the divine origins of black slavery. They were words of admonition to a fellow slaveholder . . . suspected of perverseness in his treatment of a male servant."[20] Furman attempted to elevate the treatment of slaves in the South by appealing to a scriptural basis of God-given authority for every slave owner's authority, thereby calling slave owners to live up to the biblical standards of their so-called God-given authority. In doing so, his writing became "a brief exposition of the Evangelical slaveholding ethic."[21] Poor Reverend Furman.

There were plenty of people of biblical faith back in Furman's time who were appalled, not with slavery itself, but with how the institution existed in practice. "Prominent Catholics and Jews joined Protestants in upholding the biblical sanction for slavery while they complained that Southern slavery fell short of biblical norms."[22] This position seems preposterous to modern Americans of biblical faith.

The lesson is that any call merely to biblical accountability for the standards of carrying out the death penalty will look very different in the eyes of history. We are in great danger if we appeal to a scriptural basis of God-given authority for government to kill its citizens in an effort to thereby call upon government to live up to the biblical standards of its so-called God-given authority. Do any of us, including myself, want to be remembered one hundred years hence as the people who synthesized a biblical defense, an evangelical ethic, for governmental killing of its own citizens through capital punishment?

There were enlightened southern theologians of the mid–eighteen hundreds who acknowledged that slavery was not consistent with the proper understanding of the unfolding of revelation in the Bible. Richard Fuller, also a minister in the South, "lamented the very existence of the slavery he was defending" and acknowledged that "slavery should not continue indefinitely."[23] He refrained from calling slavery a sin, yet considered the institution to be inconsistent with the Bible's revelation that, among men, "irresponsible power is a trust too easily and too frequently abused."[24]

There is no stretch of imagination in applying that statement equally to the actual facts of the American death penalty, facts through which we have labored in the last hundreds of pages of this book. Which of us wants to be remembered by history as a person who acknowledged that capital punishment is inconsistent with the unfolding revelation of the Bible about man and man's nature, yet in cowardice postponed the burden of the inevitable decision for abolition to a later time, to someone else, to anybody but ourselves?

Perhaps most enlightened among people of biblical faith struggling with arguments based on biblical standards for slavery were those who grasped that the biblical standards themselves would require a complete restructuring of southern society. "Two questions haunted the sincere Christians among white Southerners: First, did not the actual conditions of slave life in the South significantly lapse from biblical standards? And second, would not the changes necessary to bring Southern slavery up to biblical standards in fact replace slavery with a markedly different form of personal servitude?"[25]

We moderns in America should be dumbfounded at the pre-science of such questions, which fall squarely upon our own predicament in the twenty-first century with capital punishment. As we have already established, the American death penalty fails miserably in every possible respect to meet any of even the most minimal biblical standards. And deep in our hearts and in our bones, we know that making the changes necessary to replace American capital punishment with the standards of biblical criminal justice reviewed in this book would require a markedly different form of criminal justice in America—not just with capital punishment, but also with the system at large. What person of biblical faith dares to pretend it would not?

The last lesson of this history is perhaps the most disconcerting. The world is baffled at the mystery that America, long the bastion and the standard for democracy and principles of accountability by government to its people, is the only Western democracy that allows its government to lawfully kill its own citizens for crimes less than treason. How can this be?

A possible answer emerges from our history with slavery and the parallel use of scripture to defend capital punishment. Could it be that modern American capital punishment is the poisonous fruit of the poisonous tree of America's history with slavery? Could it be that the seeds of a defective scriptural interpretation and analysis, which rallied to defend God's word by defending American slavery, is yielding a harvest of defective scriptural interpretation and analysis, which is rallying to defend God's word by defending American capital punishment?

How much clearer must it be?

How much clearer could it be?

People of biblical faith must abolish the American death penalty, and we must do so in our time. Moratorium is a way of stopping the practice while others of biblical faith become educated to the biblical truth, a truth that demands nothing less than abolition.

APPENDIX A

Short Form of an Abolition Resolution
for People of Biblical Faith

Resolution of the [name of group] of [name of church, congregation, temple, or synagogue] [city], [state] USA

As people of biblical faith, we have determined that the American death penalty is not what we thought it was. We thought it was conceived in accordance with biblical truth. It is not.

As people of biblical faith we know that there is a death penalty in the Bible. What we are doing in America, however, has nothing to do with what is revealed by the biblical truth of Torah/Pentateuch and the provisions of Talmud that fulfill those scriptural limitations.

As people of biblical faith, we know that the biblical truth of the scriptures in Torah/Pentateuch and the provisions of Talmud that fulfill the limitations of those scriptures reveal that the American death penalty is completely at odds with its supposedly biblical support. Furthermore, with the constitutional requirements that apply to capital punishment in America, it is not clear that the differences could, or even should, be resolved.

As people of biblical faith, we do not want to engage the biblical list with respect to the issue of who is deserving of death. We have no desire to slaughter most of our people. We have no scriptural basis for picking only one offense off the biblical list and claiming that the other thirty-some capital offenses on the list were not to be taken seriously.

As people of biblical faith, we do not believe that God has mandated the literal understanding of *lex talionis*, the law of tit for tat. Therefore, we have no scriptural basis for insisting that God meant it literally only when he said, "life for life."

As people of biblical faith, we do not agree that Genesis 9:6 is God's mandate for capital punishment. Such an understanding would be inconsistent with God's own actions from the very beginning. Moreover, even such an interpretation of that scripture would not empower governments to kill, as there were no governments at that time.

As people of biblical faith, we know that biblical truth reveals requirements for courts and unqualified allegiance to Torah and the God of the Bible, all of which are insurmountable for America's secular governance.

As people of biblical faith, we conclude that there is no possible way to support the American death penalty based upon biblical truth. Consequently, since we cannot support the American death penalty based upon biblical truth, we cannot support the American death penalty at all. It must be abolished.

For Christians of biblical faith add:

As Christians of biblical faith, we know that it is not at all clear from a nonselective reading of scripture that God desires the death penalty, especially if one accepts the teachings of Jesus Christ. Furthermore, we know that proper understanding of Romans 13:4, based on the usage of the actual Greek words in the earliest scriptures and the specific problems addressed in that letter by Paul, makes it clear that the verse is not a mandate for capital punishment.

As Christians of biblical faith, we know that the biblical death penalty defies the atonement effected by Jesus Christ. The purpose of capital punishment under Torah/Pentateuch was redemptive. The sacrificial offering of the offender brought atonement, redemption, to the offender and to the community, thus achieving reconciliation for both.

As Christians of biblical faith, we cannot participate in this. The atonement effected by Jesus Christ was and is enough for all people, for all purposes, for all times, for all places. There is nothing that must be completed by the human sacrifice of biblical capital punishment.

ACCORDINGLY, OUR BIBLICAL FAITH POSITION IS THAT THE AMERICAN DEATH PENALTY MUST BE ABOLISHED.

NOW, THEREFORE, BE IT RESOLVED: That the undersigned people of biblical faith call for abolition of the death penalty in our state and in our nation.

BE IT FURTHER RESOLVED:

That the undersigned people of biblical faith call upon our governor, _____, and our state legislators, and U.S. president _____, and our U.S. representatives and senators in Congress, to enact and adopt legislation abolishing executions in this state and in our nation.

BE IT FURTHER RESOLVED:

That copies of this resolution shall be forwarded to our governor, _____, and our state legislators, and U.S. president _____, and our U.S. representatives and senators in Congress, and any religious or interreligious body that may assist in accomplishing the foregoing.

BE IT FURTHER RESOLVED:

That our fellow parishes, churches, temples, and synagogues of biblical faith are hereby implored to respond in solidarity to this moral crisis by passing resolutions similar to the foregoing.

[name of church, congregation, temple, or synagogue]

Date: _____

[names and signatures of members]

Resolution of the [name of group] of [name of church, congregation, temple, or synagogue] [city], [state] USA

As people of biblical faith, we have determined that the American death penalty is not what we thought it was. We thought it was being operated in accordance with biblical truth. It is not.

As people of biblical faith, we know that there is a death penalty in the Bible. What we are doing in America, however, has nothing to do with what is revealed by the biblical truth of Torah/Pentateuch and the provisions of Talmud that fulfill those scriptural limitations.

As people of biblical faith, we know that the biblical truth of the scriptures in Torah/Pentateuch and the provisions of Talmud that fulfill the limitations of those scriptures reveal that actual practices of the American death penalty are completely at odds with its supposedly biblical support. Furthermore, with the constitutional requirements that apply to capital punishment in America, it is not clear that the differences could, or even should, be resolved.

As people of biblical faith, we have become aware, through study and observation of the events currently taking place in our state and throughout our nation, that the American death penalty fails in any way, shape, or form to meet any of the standards revealed by biblical truth, e.g., we have a fallible judicial system that will likely kill the innocent; a standard of guilt far below the biblical standard of absolute certainty; a system rife with inequalities based on economic, racial, and other factors; execution of those with diminished capacity; time periods after which evidence of innocence cannot be heard by a court; and a host of other factors, every single one of which is in direct contravention of the truth revealed by God's word.

As people of biblical faith, we do not agree that Genesis 9:6 is God's mandate for capital punishment. Such an understanding would be inconsistent with God's own actions from the very beginning. Moreover, even such an interpretation of that scripture would not empower governments to kill, as there were no governments at that time.

As people of biblical faith, we have noted that the American death penalty fails to even meet the concerns of the biblical death penalty when it comes to balancing the concerns of justice and the plight of the survivors of murder victims.

As people of biblical faith, we conclude that there is no possible way to support the American death penalty based upon biblical truth. Consequently, since we cannot support the American death penalty based upon biblical truth, then we cannot support the American death penalty at all. There must be a moratorium upon the American death penalty so that all these issues can be addressed.

For Christians of biblical faith add:

As Christians of biblical faith, we know that it is not at all clear from a nonselective reading of scripture that God desires the death penalty, especially if one accepts the teachings of Jesus Christ. Furthermore, we know that proper understanding of Romans 13:4, based on the usage of the actual Greek words in the earliest scriptures and the specific problems addressed in that letter by Paul, makes it clear that the verse is not a mandate for capital punishment.

ACCORDINGLY OUR BIBLICAL FAITH POSITION IS THAT THE AMERICAN DEATH PENALTY MUST BE STOPPED, SUBJECTED TO A MORATORIUM, WHILE OTHERS OF BIBLICAL FAITH LEARN WHAT BIBLICAL TRUTH REVEALS ABOUT THE AMERICAN DEATH PENALTY.

NOW, THEREFORE, BE IT RESOLVED: That the undersigned people of biblical faith call for a complete and immediate moratorium on the death penalty in our state and in our nation.

BE IT FURTHER RESOLVED:

That the undersigned people of biblical faith call upon our governor, _____, and our state legislators, and U.S. president _____, and our U.S. representatives and senators in Congress, to enact and adopt legislation placing a moratorium upon all executions in this state and in our nation.

BE IT FURTHER RESOLVED:

That copies of this resolution shall be forwarded to our governor, _____, and our state legislators, and U.S. president _____, and our U.S. representatives and senators in Congress, and any religious or interreligious body that may assist in accomplishing the foregoing.

BE IT FURTHER RESOLVED:

That our fellow parishes, churches, temples, and synagogues of biblical faith are hereby implored to respond in solidarity to this moral crisis by passing resolutions similar to the foregoing.

[name of church, congregation, temple, or synagogue]

Date: _____

[names and signatures of members]

APPENDIX C

2000 Southern Baptist Convention Resolution on Capital Punishment
Passed in Orlando, Florida in June, 2000

WHEREAS, The Bible teaches that every human life has sacred value (Genesis 1:27) and forbids the taking of innocent human life (Exodus 20:13); and

WHEREAS, God has vested in the civil magistrate the responsibility of protecting the innocent and punishing the guilty (Romans 13:1–3); and

WHEREAS, We recognize that fallen human nature has made impossible a perfect judicial system; and

WHEREAS, God authorized capital punishment for murder after the Noahic Flood, validating its legitimacy in human society (Genesis 9:6); and

WHEREAS, God forbids personal revenge (Romans 12:19) and has established capital punishment as a just and appropriate means by which the civil magistrate may punish those guilty of capital crimes (Romans 13:4); and

WHEREAS, God requires proof of guilt before any punishment is administered (Deuteronomy 19:15–19); and

WHEREAS, God's instructions require a civil magistrate to judge all people equally under the law, regardless of class or status (Leviticus 19:15; Deuteronomy 1:17); and

WHEREAS, All people, including those guilty of capital crimes, are created in the image of God and should be treated with dignity (Genesis 1:27).

Therefore, be it RESOLVED, That the messengers to the Southern Baptist Convention, meeting in Orlando, Florida, June 13–14, 2000, support the fair and equitable use of capital punishment by civil magistrates as a legitimate form of punishment for those guilty of murder or treasonous acts that result in death; and

Be it further RESOLVED, That we urge that capital punishment be administered only when the pursuit of truth and justice result in clear and overwhelming evidence of guilt; and

Be it further RESOLVED, That because of our deep reverence for human life, our profound respect for the rights of individuals, and our respect for the law, we call for vigilance, justice, and equity in the criminal justice system; and

Be it further RESOLVED, That we urge that capital punishment be applied as justly and as fairly as possible without undue delay, without reference to the race, class, or status of the guilty; and

Be it further RESOLVED, That we call on civil magistrates to use humane means in administering capital punishment; and

Be it finally RESOLVED, That we commit ourselves to love, to pray for, and to minister the gospel to victims and perpetrators of crimes, realizing that only in Christ is there forgiveness of sin, reconciliation, emotional and spiritual healing, and the gift of eternal life.

ABBREVIATIONS AND NOTES
ON CITATIONS

URLs and Websites

Unless otherwise indicated in the note, the last date visited for all URLs is November 30, 2003.

Legal Citations

Unless otherwise indicated in the note, all cases cited are U.S. Supreme Court; all citations to cases and law journals are made in volume-title-page-date format.

Abbreviations

In citing certain works in the notes, short titles have been used. Works frequently cited have been identified by the following abbreviations.

Citations to Sources from the Death Penalty Information Center (DPIC)

The Death Penalty Information Center (DPIC) is a nonprofit organization serving the media and the public with analysis and information on issues concerning capital punishment. The DPIC was founded in 1990 and prepares in-depth reports, issues press releases, conducts briefings for journalists, and serves as a resource to those working on this issue. The DPIC is widely quoted and consulted by all those concerned with the death penalty. The executive director is Richard C. Dieter, an attorney who has written and spoken extensively on this subject. The DPIC is located at 1320 18th Street NW, Fifth Floor, Washington, D.C. 20036; phone: 202-293-6970; fax: 202-822-4787; website: http://www.deathpenaltyinfo.org.

All the DPIC reports with current updates are available online. A subject matter index is available. Richard C. Dieter has authored all of the reports and information pages referenced to the DPIC.

Citations to Printed Reports Issued by the DPIC

(All DPIC reports are available on-line, as well as in print, at http://www.deathpenaltyinfo.org. Therefore, citations to printed reports issued by the DPIC (other than the year end reports) are referenced to "text accompanying note," "text immediately following note" or "text immediately preceding note," thereby facilitating access for users of both print and electronic media.

DPIC 2003 Report	*The Death Penalty in 2003: Year End Report* (Washington, D.C.: DPIC, 2003)
DPIC 2002 Report	*The Death Penalty in 2002: Year End Report* (Washington, D.C.: DPIC, 2002).
DPIC 2001 Report	*The Death Penalty in 2001: Year End Report* (Washington, D.C.: DPIC, 2001).
DPIC 2000 Report	*The Death Penalty in 2000: Year End Report* (Washington, D.C.: DPIC, 2000).
DPIC Black and White	*The Death Penalty in Black and White: Who Lives—Who Dies—Who Decides: New Studies on Racism in Capital Punishment* (Washington, D.C.: DPIC, 1998).
DPIC Executing the Innocent: 1997	*Innocence and the Death Penalty: The Increasing Danger of Executing the Innocent* (Washington, D.C.: DPIC, 1997).
DPIC Killing for Votes	*Killing for Votes: The Dangers of Politicizing the Death Penalty Process* (Washington, D.C.: DPIC, 1996).
DPIC Law Enforcement	*On the Front Line: Law Enforcement Views on the Death Penalty* (Washington, D.C.: DPIC, 1995)

Citations to On-line Information Pages Maintained by the DPIC

All information pages are available at http://www.deathpenalty info.org/.

DPIC Cases of Innocence	*Cases of Innocence: 1973–Present*

(Washington, D.C.: DPIC, 2004,
continuously updated) (contains specific
information about the case of each
person released from death row for
innocence from 1973 to the present).

DPIC Clemency

Clemency: Clemency Process by State
(Washington, D.C.: DPIC, 2004,
continuously updated).

DPIC Deterrence

Facts about Deterrence and the Death Penalty
(Washington, D.C.: DPIC, 2004,
continuously updated).

DPIC Federal Death
Penalty

Federal Death Penalty of the U.S. Government
(Washington, D.C.: DPIC, 2004,
continuously updated).

DPIC Freed from Death
Row

Freed from Death Row (Washington, D.C.:
DPIC, 2004, continuously updated)
(contains a list of the people in the
United States released from death row
for innocence from 1973 to the present).

DPIC Innocence

Innocence and the Death Penalty
(Washington, D.C.: DPIC, 2004,
continuously updated).

DPIC Juvenile
Executions

Execution of Juvenile Offenders (Washington,
D.C.: DPIC, 2004, continuously
updated).

DPIC Juveniles

Juveniles and the Death Penalty
(Washington, D.C.: DPIC, 2004,
continuously updated), incorporating
Victor L. Streib, *The Juvenile Death Penalty
Today: Death Sentences and Executions for
Juvenile Crimes* (2003) (Ada, Ohio: Claude
W. Pettit College of Law, Ohio
Northern University, 2003); available at:
http://www.law.onu.edu/faculty/streib/
JuvDeathSept2003.htm (last updated
October 6, 2003).

DPIC LWOP	*Life without Parole* (Washington, D.C.: DPIC, 2004, continuously updated).
DPIC Mental Retardation	*Mental Retardation and the Death Penalty* (Washington, D.C.: DPIC, 2004, continuously updated).
DPIC Minimum Ages	*Minimum Death Penalty Ages by American Jurisdiction,* (Washington, D.C.: DPIC, 2004, continuously updated).
DPIC New Voices	*New Voices, Articles, and Statements on the Death Penalty* (Washington, D.C.: DPIC, 2004, continuously updated).
DPIC Polls	*Summaries of Recent Poll Findings* (Washington, D.C.: DPIC, 2004, continuously updated).
DPIC Race of the Executed	*Race of Defendants Executed Since 1976* (Washington, D.C.: DPIC, 2004, continuously updated; last updated with execution in Virginia on March 31, 2004).
DPIC What's New	*What's New* (Washington, D.C.: DPIC, 1998–2004, continuously updated).

Citations to Sources from the Southern Center for Human Rights (SCHR)

The Southern Center for Human Rights (SCHR) is a nonprofit, public interest legal project, founded in 1976, to enforce the constitutional protections against "cruel and unusual punishment" by challenging excessive and degrading forms of punishment and cruel and inhuman conditions of confinement. SCHR challenges discrimination against people of color, the poor, and the disadvantaged in the criminal justice and corrections systems of the South, raises public awareness of these issues, and works with community groups and individuals to improve the criminal justice and corrections systems and develop constructive, humane, and nonviolent solutions to crime.

SCHR receives no government funds. It is supported entirely by individuals, law firms, foundations, religious groups, and any attorney fees or honoraria collected in carrying out its work. Stephen B. Bright has been the director of the center since 1982. He has taught courses on criminal law, capital punishment, prisoners' rights, and international human rights at Yale, Harvard, Georgetown, Emory, Northeastern, Florida State, and St. Mary's law schools. Stephen B. Bright has authored, or is the lead author, of all the articles and reports referenced to the SCHR.

The SCHR is located at 83 Poplar Street, NW, Atlanta, Ga. 30303-2122; phone: 404-688-1202; fax: 404-688-9440; website: http://www.schr.org.

All the SCHR reports and current information about projects and programs are available on-line. A subject matter index is available at http://www.schr.org/center.

Citations to Reports and Articles by Stephen B. Bright and SCHR

An index of all the reports, articles, and lectures (with links to the on-line available versions of each of the following) is available at http://www.schr.org/reports. All the cited articles authored by Stephen B. Bright are available on-line, as well as in print. Therefore, citations to such articles are referenced to "text accompanying note," "text immediately following note," or "text immediately preceding note," thereby facilitating access for users of both print and electronic media.

SCHR Casualties and Costs	Stephen B. Bright, "The Death Penalty: Casualties and Costs of the War on Crime" (lecture, City Club of Cleveland, November 7, 1997).
SCHR Counsel for the Poor	Stephen B. Bright, "Counsel for the Poor: The Death Penalty: Not for the Worst Crime but for the Worst Lawyer," 103 *Yale Law Journal* 1835 (1994).
SCHR Fairness	Stephen B. Bright, "Is Fairness Irrelevant? The Evisceration of Federal Habeas

Corpus Review and Limits on the Ability
of State Courts to Protect Fundamental
Rights," 54 *Washington and Lee Law Review*
1 (winter 1997).

SCHR Judges and   Stephen B. Bright and Patrick J. Keenan,
Politics   "Judges and the Politics of Death:
                          Deciding between the Bill of Rights and
                          the Next Election in Capital Cases," 73
                          Boston University Law Review 759 (May
                          1995).

SCHR Judicial   Stephen B. Bright, "Can Judicial
Independence   Independence Be Attained in the South?
                          Overcoming History, Elections, and
                          Misperceptions about the Role of the
                          Judiciary," 14 *Georgia State University Law
                          Review* 817 (July 1998).

SCHR 1996 Act   Steven B. Bright, *Restrictions on Federal
                          Review of Death Sentences Passed by Congress
                          in 1996* (Atlanta: SCHR, 1997).

SCHR Political Attacks Stephen B. Bright, "Political Attacks on
                          the Judiciary: Can Justice Be Done Amid
                          Efforts to Intimidate and Remove Judges
                          from Office for Unpopular Decisions?"
                          72 *New York University Law Review* 308
                          (May 1997).

SCHR Racial   Stephen B. Bright, "Discrimination,
Discrimination   Death, and Denial: The Tolerance of
                          Racial Discrimination in the Infliction of
                          the Death Penalty," 35 *Santa Clara Law
                          Review* 433 (1995).

SCHR Twenty-first   Stephen B. Bright, "Will the Death
Century   Penalty Remain Alive in the Twenty-first
                          Century? International Norms,
                          Discrimination, Arbitrariness, and the
                          Risk of Executing the Innocent," 1
                          Wisconsin Law Review 1 (2001).

SCHR *Vengeance*   Stephen B. Bright, *A Preference for Vengeance: The Death Penalty and the Treatment of Prisoners in Georgia—A Report on Human Rights Violations in Georgia* (Atlanta: SCHR, 1996).

Citations to Sources from or about Talmud

Ancient Hebrews   S. Mendelsohn, LL.D., *The Criminal Jurisprudence of the Ancient Hebrews: Compiled from the Talmud and Other Rabbinical Writings, and Compared with Roman and English Penal Jurisprudence*, 2d ed. (New York: Hermon Press, 1968).

Dictionary of Jewish   R. J. Zwi Werblowsky and Geoffrey
Religion   Wigoder, eds., *The Oxford Dictionary of the Jewish Religion* (New York: Oxford University Press, 1997).

Essential Talmud   Rabbi Adin Steinsaltz, *The Essential Talmud*, trans. Chaya Galai (New York: Basic Books, 1965).

Everyman's Talmud   Rabbi Abraham Cohen, *Everyman's Talmud: The Major Teachings of the Rabbinical Sages* (New York: Schocken Books, 1949).

Ethics and Halakhah   Basil F. Herring, *Jewish Ethics and Halakhah for Our Time: Sources and Commentary*, (New York: KTAV Publishing and Yeshiva University Press, 1984).

Maimonides   *The Code of Maimonides (Book Fourteen): The Book of Judges*, trans. Rabbi Abraham M. Hershman, D.D., D.H.L., Yale Judaica Series (New Haven, Conn.: Yale University Press, 1949).

Talmud, *Kiddushin*   Rabbi Hersch Goldwurm, ed., *Talmud Bavli: Tractate Kiddushin*, ArtScroll Series,

Schottenstein Edition (Brooklyn:
Mesorah Publications, 1993).

Talmud, *Kethuboth*   Rabbi Dr I. Epstein, B.A., Ph.D., D.Lit.,
ed., *Hebrew–English Edition of the Babylonian
Talmud,* trans. Rabbi Dr. Samuel Daiches,
LL.B., and Rev. Dr. Israel W. Slotki,
M.A., Litt.D. (London: Soncino, 1971).

Talmud, *Makkoth*   Rabbi Hersch Goldwurm, ed., *Talmud
Bavli: Tractate Makkoth,* ArtScroll® Series
Schottenstein Edition (Brooklyn:
Mesorah Publications, 1993).

Talmud, *Sanhedrin*   Rabbi Hersch Goldwurm, ed., *Talmud
Bavli: Tractate Sanhedrin,* ArtScroll® Series,
Schottenstein Edition (Brooklyn:
Mesorah Publications, 1993).

Talmud Reference Guide   Rabbi Adin Steinsaltz, *The Talmud; The
Steinsaltz Edition: A Reference Guide* (New
York: Random House, 1989), © 1989 by
The Israel Institute for Talmudic
Publications and Milta Books.

Tosefta Sanhedrin   Jacob Neusner, *The Tosefta, Translated from
the Hebrew, Fourth Division NEZIQIN (the
Order of Damages)* (New York: KTAV
Publishing, 1981).

NOTES

PREFACE

1. In the 1972 case, *Furman v. Georgia*, 92 S.Ct. 2726, the U.S. Supreme Court held the death penalty statutes then existing in the United States unconstitutional as applied. Because the Court did *not* hold the death penalty itself unconstitutional, the states were free to enact new death penalty procedures that would conform to the constitutional requirements. Thirty-five states did so within four years.

2. *State v. Dixon*, 283 So.2d 1 (Florida Supreme Court, 1973); Standard Jury Instructions (approved by the Florida Supreme Court, 1990).

3. *Callins v. Collins*, 114 S.Ct. 1127 (1994), 1128, concurring in memorandum opinion and referring to the facts in *McCollum v. North Carolina*.

4. This is usually monitored by automatic appeal of every death sentence to the state supreme court. See, for example, U.S. Supreme Court approval of such arrangements in *Proffitt v. Florida*, 428 U.S. 242 (1976) and *Gregg v. Georgia*, 428 U.S. 153 (1976).

5. *Lockett v. Ohio*, 98 S.Ct. 2954 (1978).

6. *Callins v. Collins*, 1129, Justice Blackmun dissenting from memorandum opinion.

7. *Callins v. Collins*, 1129, Justice Blackmun dissenting from memorandum opinion.

8. *Callins v. Collins*, 1130, Justice Blackmun dissenting from memorandum opinion.

9. *Walton v. Arizona*, 110 S.Ct. 3047 (1990). This case was partially overruled in 2002 insofar as the U.S. Supreme Court found a constitutional requirement that juries must be involved in assessing the death penalty in each case.

10. *Callins v. Collins*, 1129, Justice Blackmun dissenting from memorandum opinion.

11. In one case, the Court even acknowledged that mental retardation and the murderer's abuse experienced as a child could influence a jury in *favor* of assessing the death penalty. *Penry v. Lynaugh*, 109 S.Ct. 2934 (1989), 2949. The issue of mental retardation was recently revisited (June 2002) in the case of *Atkins v. Virginia* (discussed in chapter 16). In that case the U.S. Supreme Court held that in America it is unconstitutional to execute the mentally retarded; however, they did not establish the standards for mental retardation.

12. *Stanford v. Kentucky*, 109 S.Ct. 2969 (1989), holding that the U.S. Constitution does not prohibit the execution of sixteen- and seventeen-year-old murderers. The issue of execution for crimes committed as a juvenile (discussed at length in chapter 16) is being revisited by the U.S. Supreme Court in the case of *Roper v. Simmons*, No. 03-633, which is expected to be argued in the fall of 2004.

13. In an effort to cut down the number of appeals that a convicted murderer can make to the U.S. Supreme Court, the Court has gradually identified a large number of issues that can only be asserted at early points in the case. The result is that even where a defendant has been able to develop highly credible evidence (postconviction) showing that he did not commit the murder, the U.S. Supreme Court will not stop his execution.

14. *SCHR Racial Discrimination*, text accompanying notes 230–38. See also David C. Baldus, Charles A. Pulaski Jr., and George Woodworth, "Arbitrariness and Discrimination in the Administration of the Death Penalty: A Challenge to State Supreme Courts," 15 *Stetson Law Review* 2 (1986), 133.

15. Michael L. Radelet and Glenn L. Pierce, "Choosing Who Will Die: Race and the Death Penalty in Florida," 43 *Florida Law Review* 1 (1991). Of the 191 executions occurring in Florida between 1769 and 1924, the race of the prisoner is known in 180 cases and 73.3 percent were black. This does not include the 178 lynchings that have been documented between 1889 and 1918, in which 90 percent of the victims were black. Between 1924 and 1964, Florida executed 196 prisoners, 67.5 percent of whom were black. At the time that the U.S. Supreme Court held death penalty statutes unconstitutional in 1972, 98 inmates were on death row in Florida and 66.3 percent were black. Three of those men have since been exonerated.

16. Radelet and Pierce, "Choosing Who Will Die," 7.

17. Radelet and Pierce, "Choosing Who Will Die," 2, note 3, citing the Espy Data archive in Headland, Alabama, as reputed to be the best and most comprehensive concerning executions in America. The Espy Data files are now available through the DPIC.

18. Radelet and Pierce, "Choosing Who Will Die," note 61, 7.

19. *Callins v. Collins*, 1135, Justice Blackmun dissenting from memorandum opinion and referring to *McCleskey v. Kemp*, 481 U.S. 279, 292 (1987) (discussed in chapter 18).

20. *McCleskey v. Kemp*.

21. Vittorio Zucconi, "O'Dell torna a sperare: La Corte Suprema ferma Il boia a poche ore dall'esecuzione," *La Repubblica* (Rome, Italy), December 18, 1996, 2.

22. Arturo Zampaglione, "Non è merito del Papa se O'Dell è ancora vivo," *La Repubblica* (Rome, Italy), December 19, 1996, 15.

CHAPTER ONE

1. *DPIC 2001 Report*, citing a May 2001 Gallup poll.

2. *DPIC 2001 Report*.

3. *DPIC Polls: National Polls*, quoting Gallup News Service, May 20, 2002.

4. *DPIC Polls: State Polls*, quoting "Press Release: Most New Jerseyans Support Moratorium on the Death Penalty New Eagleton Poll Reports," May 30, 2002. The study was conducted in New Jersey by the Eagleton Institute of Politics at Rutgers University.

5. *DPIC 2001 Report*.

6. *DPIC 2003 Report* and *DPIC 2002 Report*.

7. Alex Kotlowitz, "In the Face of Death," *New York Times Magazine*, July 6, 2003, 34.

8. *DPIC Federal Death Penalty: Recent Developments*, October 6, 2003, citing *New York Times*, June 15, 2003.

9. *DPIC Federal Death Penalty: Recent Developments*, October 6, 2003, citing the Federal Death Penalty Resource Counsel Project (2003).

10. The term "first-time" death sentence excludes persons resentenced to death following a new penalty-phase hearing ordered by an appeals court.

11. Source for information in this paragraph about Florida: Michael L. Radelet, "Recent Developments in the Death Penalty in Florida" (paper presented at Life over Death: Capital Litigators Training Conference, Florida Public Defender Association, Orlando, Fla., September 7, 2001; updated through December 21, 2001; available at http://www.fadp.org/pad/aresearch.html.

12. Source for information in this paragraph concerning years 1999 and 2000: *DPIC 2000 Report*.

13. *DPIC 2003 Report*.

14. Source: DPIC, citing Deborah Fins, Esq., *Death Row U.S.A.*, Winter 2004, *A Quarterly Report by the Criminal Justice Project of the NAACP Legal Defense and Education Fund, Inc.*

(New York: NAACP Legal Defense Fund, 2004); updated quarterly and available at http://www.deathpenaltyinfo.org/DEATHROWUSArecent.pdf.

15. Source for the information concerning use of scripture in courtroom death penalty arguments: John H. Blume and Sheri Lynn Johnson, "Limiting Religious Arguments in Capital Cases" (paper presented at A Call for Reckoning: A Conference Reader on Religion and the Death Penalty, sponsored by Pew Forum on Religious and Public Life, University of Chicago Divinity School, Chicago, Ill., January 25, 2002).

16. James J. Megivern, *The Death Penalty: An Historical and Theological Survey* (Mahwah, N.J.: Paulist Press, 1997), vii.

17. Brian C. Duffy, "Barring Foul Blows: An Argument for a Per Se Reversible-Error Rule for Prosecutors' Use of Religious Arguments in the Sentencing Phase of Capital Cases," 50 *Vanderbilt Law Review* 1335 (1997), 1357–59.

18. Daniel A. Rudolph, "The Misguided Reliance in American Jurisprudence on Jewish Law to Support the Moral Legitimacy of Capital Punishment," 33 *American Criminal Law Review* 437 (1996), 439.

19. Sydney E. Ahlstrom, *A Religious History of the American People* (New Haven, Conn.: Yale University Press, 1972), 715.

20. Ahlstrom, *A Religious History*, 667.

21. Henry Warner Bowden, *Dictionary of American Religious Biography* (Westport, Conn.: Greenwood Press, 1977), s.v. "Furman, Richard," 168–69.

22. Ahlstrom, *A Religious History*, 659.

23. Ahlstrom, *A Religious History*, 660.

24. Ahlstrom, *A Religious History*, 661.

25. Ahlstrom, *A Religious History*, 663–65.

26. Thomas C. Berg, "Religious Conservatives and the Death Penalty," 9 *William and Mary Bill of Rights Journal* 31 (December 2000).

27. Berg, "Religious Conservatives," 36–37.

28. Berg, "Religious Conservatives," 33, at note 11, referring to 2000 Southern Baptist Convention Resolution on Capital Punishment Passed in Orlando, Florida, in June, 2000 (reproduced in its entirety in appendix C to this book).

29. Bible Belt executions as of March 31, 2004: Tex. 8, Okla. 4, Va. 2, Ark. 1, Fla. 1, S.C. 1, N.C. 1.

30. "Juvenile execution" refers to those executed for a crime committed while a minor.

31. *DPIC Juvenile Executions.*

32. Associated Press, "Death Sentence Tossed over Reliance on Bible," *Florida Times-Union,* May 25, 2003.

33. Rudolph, "Misguided Reliance," 440–41.

34. T. Richard Snyder, *The Protestant Ethic and the Spirit of Punishment* (Grand Rapids, Mich.: Wm. B. Eerdmans, 2001), 19.

35. Lloyd Steffen, *Executing Justice: The Moral Meaning of the Death Penalty* (Cleveland, Ohio: Pilgrim Press, 1998), 7.

36. J. Denny Weaver, *The Nonviolent Atonement* (Grand Rapids, Mich.: Wm. B. Eerdmans, 2001), 78–79.

37. Dietrich Bonhoeffer, *The Cost of Discipleship*, rev. ed. (New York: Macmillan, 1959), 45–47.

38. Snyder, *Protestant Ethic and Punishment*, 33–37.

39. Snyder, *Protestant Ethic and Punishment*, 65–73.

40. David M. Goldenberg, *The Curse of Ham: Race and Slavery in Early Judaism, Christianity and Islam* (Princeton: Princeton University Press, 2003), 142.

41. Ken Camp, "Christian Life Commission Endorses Moratorium on Death Penalty," *Baptist Standard*, January 14, 2003.

CHAPTER TWO

1. For a description of these ancient Near East legal regimens, see John L. McKenzie, S.J., *Dictionary of the Bible* (New York: Collier Books/Macmillan, 1965), s.v. "Law," 495–96.

2. For an excellent discussion comparing the Torah with the other Near Eastern ancient laws, see Frank Crüsemann, *The Torah: Theology and Social History of Old Testament Law* (Minneapolis: Fortress Press, 1996).

3. Crüsemann, *Torah: Theology and Social History*, 14.

4. McKenzie, *Dictionary of Bible*, s.v. "Torah," 498.

5. Crüsemann, *Torah: Theology and Social History*, 1.

6. Irene Merker Rosenberg and Yale L. Rosenberg, "Lone Star Liberal Musings: 'Eye for Eye' and the Death Penalty," 1998 *Utah Law Review* 505, 510.

7. *Essential Talmud*, 11.

8. *Essential Talmud*, 12.

9. *Essential Talmud*, 13.

10. *Essential Talmud*, 13–14.

11. "Bible" in this quote refers to the scriptures that Christians call the Old Testament.

12. *Essential Talmud*, 14–15.

13. *Dictionary of Jewish Religion*, s.v. "Talmud," 668.

14. "The Jerusalem Talmud has always been regarded as inferior to the work produced in Babylonia. Fewer manuscripts of the former were produced, and it was disregarded by the great commentators." *Essential Talmud*, 80.

15. For more information on Maimonides and the Mishneh Torah, see *Dictionary of Jewish Religion*, s.v. "Maimonides, Moses," 436–37.

16. Crüsemann, *Torah: Theology and Social History*, 5.

17. Crüsemann, *Torah: Theology and Social History*, 5.

18. *Dictionary of Jewish Religion*, s.v. "Beit Din," 107.

19. *Essential Talmud*, 164–65.

20. *Essential Talmud*, 164.

21. *Essential Talmud*, 165.

22. The Great Sanhedrin is also referred to as the Great Beit Din; the Small Sanhedrin was called simply a Beit Din. Beit Din means a house of judgment. *Dictionary of Jewish Religion*, s.v. "Beit Din," 107.

23. For an excellent summary of the civil law under the Talmud, see *Essential Talmud*, 145–62.

24. Num. 35:30; Deut. 17:6; 19:15.

25. Talmud, *Sanhedrin* 80b¹ (Gemara), notes 6–7.

26. For an excellent summary of the procedural laws of capital punishment under the Talmud, see *Essential Talmud*, 167–72.

27. *Dictionary of Jewish Religion*, s.v. "Penal Law," 523.

28. Talmud, *Sanhedrin* 78b³–79a¹.

29. Talmud, *Sanhedrin* 76b²–77a².

30. Talmud, *Makkoth* 7b, 9a.

31. "There is no agency for transgression." *Talmud Reference Guide*, par. 2, 161. See also Talmud, *Kiddushin* 42b.

32. See *Dictionary of Jewish Religion*, s.v. "Penal Law," 524; and *Essential Talmud*, 169–70.

33. Megivern, *Death Penalty*, 13.

34. For an extensive discussion of the argument behind theonomy, see Greg L. Bahnsen, *Theonomy in Christian Ethics* (Nutley, N.J.: Craig Press, 1977).

35. Lewis B. Smedes, *Mere Morality: What God Expects from Ordinary People* (Grand Rapids, Mich.: Wm. B. Eerdmans, 1983), 120.

36. James F. Childress and John Macquarrie, eds., *The Westminster Dictionary of Christian Ethics* (Philadelphia: Westminster Press, 1986), s.v. "Bible in Christian Ethics," 57–61.

37. Christopher J. H. Wright, *Walking in the Ways of the Lord: The Ethical Authority of the Old Testament* (Downers Grove, Ill.: InterVarsity Press, 1995), 93.

38. Wright, *Walking: Ethical Authority*, 93.

CHAPTER THREE

1. Headline on op-ed page of *Florida Times-Union*, December 15, 1999, B6.

2. *Webster's Ninth New Collegiate Dictionary* (Springfield, Mass.: Merriam-Webster, 1990), s.v. "law," 678.

3. National Conference of Catholic Bishops/United States Catholic Conference, *To End the Death Penalty: A Report of the National Jewish/Catholic Consultation* (Washington, D.C.: NCCB/USCC, 1999), 1.

4. *To End the Death Penalty*, 2, citing "Statement to the Massachusetts Legislature by Jerome Somers, Chairman, Board of Trustees, Union of American Hebrew Congregations," March 22, 1999.

5. Malcolm Stewart, "Enactment of the Florida Death Penalty Statute, 1972: History and Analysis," 16 *Nova Law Review* 1299 (1992), 1300.

6. David Von Drehle, *Among the Lowest of the Dead: Inside Death Row* (New York: Fawcett Crest, 1995), 6.

7. Stewart, "Enactment of Florida Death Penalty," 1325.

CHAPTER FOUR

1. Please note that the scripture reference to Deuteronomy 19:21 deals with false witnesses and false testimony. The concept of retaliatory justice and proportionality to the harm intended carries through even in this instance. The issue of false testimony, false witnesses, and destruction or hiding of evidence (referred to as "prosecutorial misconduct" in modern American legal parlance) will be discussed in chapter 15.

2. Lawrence M. Friedman, *Crime and Punishment in American History* (New York: BasicBooks, 1993), 8.

3. Gardner C. Hanks, *Against the Death Penalty: Christian and Secular Arguments against Capital Punishment* (Scottdale, Pa.: Herald, 1997), 29–30.

CHAPTER FIVE

1. Hanks, *Christian Arguments*, 30.

2. For a description of Florida's leadership as a bellwether state for all major aspects of the death penalty in America, see Michael A. Mello, "Florida: The Buckle of the Death Belt," in *Dead Wrong: A Death Row Lawyer Speaks Out against Capital Punishment* (Madison, Wis.: University of Wisconsin Press, 1997), 30–33.

3. Megivern, *Death Penalty*, 15.

4. *Talmud Reference Guide*, par. 5, 261.

5. Megivern, *Death Penalty*, 15.

6. Aharon W. Zorea, *In the Image of God: A Christian Response to Capital Punishment* (Lanham, Md.: University Press of America, 2000), 65.

7. "The law does not prescribe the precise period of time which must elapse between the formation of and the execution of the intent to take human life in order to render the [killing] a premeditated one; it may exist only a few moments and yet be premeditated." *McCutchen v. State*, 96 So.2d 152, 153 (Florida Supreme Court, 1957).

8. Florida Statutes, sec. 921.141, Sentence of Death or Life Imprisonment for Capital Felonies, provides in relevant part:

(5) AGGRAVATING CIRCUMSTANCES . . .

(i) The capital felony was a homicide and was committed in a cold, calculated, and premeditated manner without any pretense of moral or legal justification. *West's Florida Statutes Annotated*, sec. 921.141(5)(2) (St. Paul: West, 2002).

9. Florida Statutes, sec. 921.141, Sentence of Death or Life Imprisonment for Capital Felonies, provides in relevant part:

(5) AGGRAVATING CIRCUMSTANCES . . .

(k) The victim of the capital felony was an elected or appointed public official engaged in the performance of his or her official duties if the motive for the capital felony was related, in whole or in part, to the victim's official capacity. *West's Florida Statutes*, sec. 921.141(5)(k).

10. Florida Statutes, sec. 921.141, Sentence of Death or Life Imprisonment for Capital Felonies, provides in relevant part:

(5) AGGRAVATING CIRCUMSTANCES . . .

(d) The capital felony was committed while the defendant was engaged . . . in the commission of . . . or flight after committing . . . any robbery . . . [Note: Stealing a slave from the possession of its master or supervisor is the robbery of property.] . . .

(g) The capital felony was committed to disrupt or hinder the lawful exercise of any governmental function or the enforcement of laws. (bracketed language mine) *West's Florida Statutes*, sec. 921.141(5)(d) and (g).

11. Florida Statutes, sec. 921.141, Sentence of Death or Life Imprisonment for Capital Felonies, provides in relevant part:

(5) AGGRAVATING CIRCUMSTANCES . . .

(e) The capital felony was committed for the purpose of avoiding or preventing a lawful arrest or effecting an escape from custody. *West's Florida Statutes*, sec. 921.141(5)(e).

CHAPTER SIX

1. Rudolph, "Misguided Reliance," 443–44.

2. *Ancient Hebrews*, sec. 26, note 91, 48.

3. *Ancient Hebrews*, sec. 26(18), 48.

4. *Ancient Hebrews*, note 100, 52–53.

5. *Furman v. Georgia*, note 47, 2775.

6. *Furman v. Georgia*, note 48, 2775.

7. Philip English Mackey, ed., *Voices against Death: American Opposition to Capital Punishment, 1787–1975* (New York: Burt Franklin, 1976), xi.

8. Friedman, *Crime and Punishment*, 32.

9. Friedman, *Crime and Punishment*, 34–35.

10. Friedman, *Crime and Punishment*, 35 (cf. Lev. 20:15–16).

11. *Wilkerson v. Utah*, 99 U.S. 130 (1879).

12. *In re Kemmler*, 136 U.S. 436 (1890).

13. *Ancient Hebrews*, sec. 25, note 85, 3–4.

14. "But a perverse tongue will be cut out" (Prov. 10:31 NIV).

15. For example, stoning is the punishment prescribed for a stubborn and rebellious son (Deut. 21:18–21).

16. For example, "If a priest's daughter defiles herself by becoming a prostitute, she disgraces her father; she must be burned in the fire" (Lev. 21:9 NIV).

17. "Blows and wounds cleanse away evil, and beatings purge the inmost being" (Prov. 20:30 NIV).

18. The foregoing punishments referred to in the Hebrew scriptures usually provided for public execution. Other lesser crimes in the same books of the Torah/Pentateuch provided for the offender to be "cut off from the people." For example, exile in the form of expatriation (Lev. 20:6). Expatriation as a punishment in America was held unconstitutional by the U.S. Supreme Court. *Trop v. Dulles*, 78 U.S. 590 (1958), 603.

19. *Essential Talmud*, 111.

CHAPTER SEVEN

1. Megivern, *Death Penalty*, 11–12.

2. *Ancient Hebrews*, note 100, 52–53.

3. *Ethics and Halakhah*, 156.

4. Friedman, *Crime and Punishment*, 41.

5. Friedman, *Crime and Punishment*, 41.

6. For example, see Maimonides, "Evidence," chap. 12, par. 1, 107–8, with respect to tying a knot on the Sabbath.

7. Talmud, *Sanhedrin* 15b[1] (Gemara).

8. *Ethics and Halakhah*, 161.

9. *Ethics and Halakhah*, 157, quoting Rabinowitz-Teomim.

10. Talmud, *Sanhedrin* 43b[1].

11. Maimonides, "Sanhedrin," chap. 13, par. 1, 37.

12. Talmud, *Sanhedrin* 43b[1], note 9.

13. Josh. 7:19–20.

14. Josh. 7:25.

15. Talmud, *Sanhedrin* 43b[1].

16. Talmud, *Sanhedrin* 43b[1], note 13.

17. Everett F. Harrison, Geoffrey W. Bromiley, and Carl F. Henry, eds., *Wycliffe Dictionary of Theology* (Peabody, Mass.: Hendrickson Publishers, 1960), s.v. "Atonement," 71–78.

18. *Wycliffe Dictionary of Theology*, s.v. "Atonement," 72.

19. *Wycliffe Dictionary of Theology*, s.v. "Atonement," 72.

20. *Wycliffe Dictionary of Theology*, s.v. "Atonement," 72.

21. *Wycliffe Dictionary of Theology*, s.v. "Atonement," 72.

22. *Wycliffe Dictionary of Theology*, s.v. "Atonement," 73.

23. *Wycliffe Dictionary of Theology*, s.v. "Atonement," 73.

24. Joel B. Green and Mark D. Baker, *Recovering the Scandal of the Cross: Atonement in New Testament and Contemporary Contexts* (Downers Grove, Ill.: InterVarsity Press, 2000), 22.

25. *Wycliffe Dictionary of Theology*, s.v. "Atonement," 74.

26. *Wycliffe Dictionary of Theology*, s.v. "Atonement," 74.

27. Weaver, *Nonviolent Atonement*, 16.

28. Green and Baker, *Recovering the Scandal of the Cross*, 142–43.

29. Snyder, *Protestant Ethic and Punishment.*

30. Weaver, *Nonviolent Atonement*, 2–3.

31. Green and Baker, *Recovering the Scandal of the Cross*, 23–24.

32. See Weaver, "Narrative Christus Victor: The Revisioning of Atonement," in *Nonviolent Atonement*, 12–69.

33. Green and Baker, *Recovering the Scandal of the Cross*, 97.

34. Talmud, *Sanhedrin* 42b³ (Gemara), note 30, par. 4.

35. Talmud, *Sanhedrin* 42b³ (Gemara), note 30, par. 4.

CHAPTER EIGHT

1. *Talmud Reference Guide*, par. 5, 261.

2. Talmud, *Sanhedrin* 2a³.

3. Talmud, *Sanhedrin* 2a².

4. See Moses Mielziner, *Introduction to the Talmud* (New York: Bloch Publishing, 1968).

5. Maimonides, "Sanhedrin," chap. 1, par. 3, 5.

6. Maimonides, "Sanhedrin," chap. 1, par. 3, 6.

7. Maimonides, "Sanhedrin," chap. 1, par. 10, 7.

8. Maimonides, "Sanhedrin," chap. 1, par. 3, 6.

9. Talmud, *Sanhedrin* 2a³⁻⁴.

10. Num. 14:27.

11. Talmud, *Sanhedrin* 2a⁴.

12. Exod. 23:2.

13. Talmud, *Sanhedrin* 2a⁴.

14. Talmud, *Sanhedrin* 2a⁴.

15. Talmud, *Sanhedrin* 17a³.

16. Maimonides, "Sanhedrin," chap. 9, pars.1–2, 28–29.

17. Maimonides, "Sanhedrin," chap. 10, par. 2, 30.

18. Maimonides, "Sanhedrin," chap. 4, par. 1, 13.

19. Maimonides, "Sanhedrin," chap. 3, par. 7, 11.

20. Maimonides, "Sanhedrin", chap. 11, par. 11, 41.

21. Maimonides, "Sanhedrin," chap. 14, par. 13, 41.

22. Nancy Gibbs, "Thou Shalt Be Removed: Alabama's Ten Commandments Judge Is Tossed from Office. Did He Want This All Along?" *Time Magazine*, November 24, 2003.

23. Maimonides, "Sanhedrin," chap. 14, par. 13, 41.

24. Rabbi Joseph Telushkin, *Biblical Literacy: The Most Important People, Events, and Ideas of the Hebrew Bible* (New York: William Morrow, 1997), 250.

CHAPTER NINE

1. *Ethics and Halakhah*, 157–58.

2. See *Dictionary of the Jewish Religion*, s.v. "Penal Law," 524; and *Essential Talmud*, 169–70.

3. *Ethics and Halakhah*, 164–65.

4. *Ethics and Halakhah*, 165.

5. Maimonides, "Sanhedrin," chap. 14, par. 1, 39.

6. Maimonides, "Sanhedrin," chap. 14, par. 2, 39.

7. *Ethics and Halakhah*, 161.

8. *Ethics and Halakhah*, 162.

9. *Tosefta Sanhedrin* 9:10, 228.

10. James Strong, *A Concise Dictionary of the Words in the Greek New Testament: With Their Renderings in the Authorized English Language Version*, in *The Complete Word Study New Testament with Greek Parallel (King James Version)*, Spiros Zodhiates, comp. and ed. (Iowa Falls: World Bible Publishers, 1992).

11. Hanks, *Christian Arguments*, 49.

12. Zodhiates, *The Complete Word Study New Testament*.

13. Donald G. Mathews, "'We Who Own Slaves Honor God's Law,'" in *Religion in the Old South*, Martin E. Marty, ed. (Chicago: University of Chicago Press, 1977), 136–84.

14. Eugene D. Genovese, *A Consuming Fire: The Fall of the Confederacy in the Mind of the White Christian South* (Athens, Ga.: University of Georgia Press, 1998), 3–4.

15. Neil Elliot, "The Canonical Betrayal of the Apostle: Paul and Slavery," in *Liberating Paul: The Justice of God and the Politics of the Apostle* (Maryknoll, N.Y.: Orbis Books, 1994), 32–40.

16. Elliot, *Liberating Paul*, 13.

17. Elliot, *Liberating Paul*, 14.

18. For example, see Matthew Henry, *Commentary on the Whole Bible* (Grand Rapids, Mich.: Zondervan, 1960), 1788, interpreting Romans 13:1–6 as follows: "The apostle therefore shows that obedience to civil magistrates is one of the laws of Christ, whose religion helps to make people good subjects."

19. Elliot, *Liberating Paul*, 223.

20. James Hastings, ed., *Encyclopedia of Religion and Ethics* (New York: Charles Scribner's Sons, 1955), s.v. "Slavery (Christian)."

21. Elliot, *Liberating Paul*, 225.

CHAPTER TEN

1. *Ethics and Halakhah*, 157.

2. *Ethics and Halakhah*, 161.

3. Talmud, *Sanhedrin* 41a[5] (Gemara), note 35.

4. *Ethics and Halakhah*, 161.

5. *Furman v. Georgia*, 2758 (Justice Brennan), 2763 (Justice White), and 2783 (Justice Marshall). Marshall's opinion also indicates that other nations have acknowledged this, 2783.

6. Sister Helen Prejean, *Dead Man Walking: An Eyewitness Account of the Death Penalty in the United States* (New York: Vintage Books, 1994), 110.

7. Prejean, *Dead Man Walking*, 110.

8. Dr. Lewis J. West, "Psychiatric Reflections on the Death Penalty," in Mackey, *Voices against Death*, 293.

9. West, "Psychiatric Reflections," 293.

10. DPIC *What's New* (August 6, 2002), citing *Issues Direct.com*, August 6, 2002.

11. The four studies are: John Sorenson, Robert Wrinkle, Victoria Brewer, and James Marquart, "Capital Punishment and Deterrence: Examining the Effect of Executions on Murder in Texas," 45 *Crime and Delinquency* 481–93 (1999); William Bailey, "Deterrence, Brutalization, and the Death Penalty: Another Examination of Oklahoma's Return to Capital Punishment," 36 *Criminology* 711–33 (1998); Ernie Thompson, "Effects of an Execution

on Homicides in California," 3 *Homicide Studies* 129–150 (1999); and Keith Harries and Derral Cheatwood, *The Geography of Execution: The Capital Punishment Quagmire in America* (Lanham, Md.: Rowman and Littlefield, 1997). For a summary of these studies, see *DPIC Deterrence.*

12. *DPIC Law Enforcement.*

13. *DPIC Law Enforcement,* quoting Willie L. Williams, police chief, Los Angeles, Calif., in text at note 4, citing R. Abramson, "Emphasis on Values Is Needed to Stem Crime, Williams Says," *Los Angeles Times,* April 27, 1992, B1.

14. Excerpted from *Law Enforcement Statement on Capital Punishment,* signed by various heads of law enforcement agencies, district attorneys, and law enforcement affiliated organizations in the United States, reproduced in *DPIC Law Enforcement.*

15. *DPIC Law Enforcement,* quoting Frank Friel, former head of Organized Crime Homicide Task Force, Philadelphia, in text at note 2, citing press release, DPIC, October 27, 1992.

16. *DPIC Law Enforcement,* quoting Robert M. Morgenthau, district attorney, Manhattan, N.Y. in text at note 3, citing R. Morgenthau, "What Prosecutors Won't Tell You," *New York Times,* February 7, 1995, A25.

17. U.S. Department of Justice, Federal Bureau of Investigation, *Uniform Crime Reports: Crime in the United States* 2000 (October 2001); available at http://www.fbi.gov/ucr/00 cius.htm.

18. U.S. Department of Justice, Federal Bureau of Investigation, *Uniform Crime Reports: Crime in the United States* 2001 (October 2002); available at http://www.fbi.gov/ucr/01cius. htm.

19. U.S. Department of Justice, Federal Bureau of Investigation, *Uniform Crime Reports January–December* 2002, by Robert S. Mueller III, director (Washington, D.C.: June 16, 2003); available at http://www.fbi.gov/ucr/cius_02/02prelimannual.pdf.

20. U.S. Department of Justice, Federal Bureau of Investigation, "Law Enforcement Officers Killed and Assaulted," in *FBI Uniform Crime Reports (1998),* available at *DPIC Deterrence.*

21. *DPIC Deterrence,* "States without the Death Penalty Have Better Record on Homicide Rates," citing *New York Times,* September 22, 2000.

CHAPTER TWELVE

1. *Tosefta Sanhedrin* 5:5, 213.

2. *Tosefta Sanhedrin* 5:2, 211–12.

3. *Everyman's Talmud,* 307.

4. Maimonides, "Evidence," chap. 10, par. 1, 102.

5. Maimonides, "Evidence," chap. 15, par. 1, 115.

6. *Everyman's Talmud,* 308.

7. *Everyman's Talmud,* 308.

8. Talmud, *Sanhedrin* 27b².

9. Maimonides, "Evidence," chap. 13, par. 15, 112.

10. *Tosefta Sanhedrin* 6:6, 216.

11. Steven Davidoff, "A Comparative Study of the Jewish and the United States Constitutional Law of Capital Punishment," 3 *ILSA Journal of International and Comparative Law* 1 (fall 1996) 93, 102.

12. Talmud, *Kethuboth* 27b¹.

13. *Tosefta Sanhedrin* 9:4, 226.

14. *Essential Talmud,* 167–68.

15. Maimonides, "Sanhedrin," chap. 18, par. 6, 53.

16. Thomas A. Horkan Jr., "'Tis Not the Season for This," *Florida Catholic*, December 2, 1999.

17. See DPIC *Executing the Innocent: 1997*, and DPIC *Cases of Innocence*.

18. See DPIC *Executing the Innocent: 1997*, and DPIC *Cases of Innocence*. See also Sydney P. Freedberg, "Freed from Death Row: Florida Leads the Nation in Wrongful Death Sentences with 20. What Has Become of the Survivors?"; "Yes, I'm Angry . . . Yes, I'm Bitter. I'm Frustrated"; "We'd Rather Have Died Than to Stay in That Place for Something We Didn't Do"; "I Had Nothing . . . the World I Left No Longer Existed"; "We Don't Look Back"; "The Stigma Is Always There"; "The 13 Other Survivors and Their Stories," *St. Petersburg Times*, July 4, 1999; all available at http://www.sptimes.com/Archive/070499/State.shtml.

19. Ken Armstrong and Maurice Possley, "Verdict Dishonor," *Chicago Tribune*, January 10, 1999; available at http://www.chicagotribune.com/news/specials.

20. Meg Laughlin, "Federal Court to Revisit 35-Year-Old Murder Case," *Miami Herald*, July 8, 2001; "1984 Murder Trial Revisited," *Miami Herald*, July 10, 2001; "Death Row Inmate Closer to New Trial after Judge's Ruling: Man in Prison for 22 Years," *Miami Herald*, December 31, 2002.

21. Series: "Death Penalty in Illinois," *Chicago Tribune*, November 14–18, 1999; available at http://www.chicagotribune.com/news/specials.

22. Ken Armstrong and Steve Mills, "Death Row Justice Derailed," *Chicago Tribune*, November 14, 1999; Ken Armstrong and Steve Mills, "Inept Defenses Cloud Verdict," *Chicago Tribune*, November 15, 1999; Steve Mills and Ken Armstrong, "The Jailhouse Informant," *Chicago Tribune*, November 16, 1999; Steve Mills and Ken Armstrong, "A Tortured Path to Death Row," *Chicago Tribune*, November 17, 1999; and Steve Mills and Ken Armstrong, "Convicted by a Hair," *Chicago Tribune*, November 18, 1999.

23. Steve Mills and Ken Armstrong, "The Jailhouse Informant," *Chicago Tribune*, November 16, 1999.

24. Raymond Bonner, "Death Row Inmate Is Freed after DNA Test Clears Him," *New York Times*, August 24, 2001.

25. *State ex. rel. Joseph Amrine Petitioner v. Donald P. Roper, Superintendent, Potosi Correctional Center, Respondent*, Slip Opinion, Missouri Supreme Court, SC84656 (April 29, 2003). The facts recounted in this and the next paragraphs are taken from the statement of facts in the opinion of the Missouri Supreme Court.

26. See *State ex. rel. Joseph Amrine*, dissenting opinion of Judge Duane Benton, citing *Amrine v. Bowersox*, 128 F.3d 1222 (U.S. Court of Appeals for the Eighth Circuit, en banc, 1997), 1224.

27. See *State ex. rel. Joseph Amrine*, dissenting opinion of Judge Duane Benton, citing *Amrine v. Bowersox*, 128 F.3d 1222 (U.S. Court of Appeals for the Eighth Circuit, en banc, 1997), 1229.

28. Series: "Cops and Confessions," *Chicago Tribune*, December 16, 2001–January 6, 2002; available at http://www.chicagotribune.com/news/specials.

29. Ken Armstrong, Steve Mills, and Maurice Possley, "Coercive and Illegal Tactics Torpedo Scores of Cook County Murder Cases," *Chicago Tribune*, December 16, 2001.

30. Armstrong, Mills, and Possley, "Coercive and Illegal Tactics"; Maurice Possley, Steve Mills, and Ken Armstrong, "Veteran Detective's Murder Case Unravels," *Chicago Tribune*, December 17, 2001; Ken Armstrong, Steve Mills, and Maurice Possley, "Illegal Arrests Yield False Confessions," *Chicago Tribune*, December 17, 2001; Ken Armstrong, Maurice Possley, and Steve Mills, "Officers Ignore Laws Set Up to Guard Kids," *Chicago Tribune*, December 18, 2001; Steve Mills, Maurice Possley, and Ken Armstrong, "When Jail Is No Alibi in Murders," *Chicago Tribune*, December 19, 2001.

31. Armstrong, Mills, and Possley, "Coercive and Illegal Tactics."

32. Armstrong, Mills, and Possley, "Coercive and Illegal Tactics."

33. Armstrong, Possley, and Mills, "Officers Ignore Laws Set Up to Guard Kids."

34. Garry Mitchell (AP), "Prosecutors Drop Baby Murder Case against Mentally Retarded Man," *Florida Times-Union*, January 10, 2003.

35. Series: "Spotlight on False Confessions," *Miami Herald*, December 22–24, 2002; available at http://www.miami.com/mld/miamiherald/news/state.

36. Wanda J. DeMarzo and Daniel de Vise, "Zealous Grilling by Police Tainted 38 Murder Cases," *Miami Herald*, December 22, 2002; "Police Ignored Defects in Cases," *Miami Herald*, December 23, 2002.

37. DeMarzo and de Vise, "Zealous Grilling by Police."

38. DeMarzo and de Vise, "Police Ignored Defects."

39. DeMarzo and de Vise, "Police Ignored Defects."

40. DeMarzo and de Vise, "Police Ignored Defects."

41. Associated Press, "Innocent Man: I Confessed to Murder under Electric Chair Threat," *Miami Herald*, October 3, 2003.

42. Mills, Possley, and Armstrong, "When Jail Is No Alibi."

43. Mills, Possley, and Armstrong, "When Jail Is No Alibi."

44. *Michael G. Bruno v. State of Florida*, 807 So.2d 55 (Florida Supreme Court, 2001).

45. *Bruno v. State*.

46. "When Believing Isn't Seeing," editorial, *Chicago Tribune*, September 30, 2002.

47. "When Believing Isn't Seeing."

48. Helen O'Neill, "The Perfect Witness," *Washington Post*, March 4, 2001, F01.

CHAPTER THIRTEEN

1. *Essential Talmud*, 167.

2. *Everyman's Talmud*, 308.

3. *Tosefta Sanhedrin* 8:3, 222–23.

4. *Everyman's Talmud*, 310–11.

5. Talmud, *Sanhedrin* 32b³ (Gemara).

6. Talmud, *Sanhedrin* 32b³ (Gemara) referring to R' Shimon Ben Eliezer.

7. Talmud, *Sanhedrin* 32b³ (Gemara), note 25, citing *Rashi*.

8. Talmud, *Sanhedrin* 32b³ (Gemara), note 25, citing *Rambam*.

9. Talmud, *Sanhedrin* 78b³–79a¹.

10. *Essential Talmud*, 168.

11. *Tosefta Sanhedrin* 11:1–4. 232–33.

12. *Tosefta Sanhedrin* 11:1, 232.

13. *Tosefta Sanhedrin* 11:5, 232–33.

14. Talmud, *Sanhedrin* 40a¹.

15. Talmud, *Sanhedrin* 40a¹, note 2, citing *Rashi*.

16. Talmud, *Sanhedrin* 40a¹.

17. Talmud, *Sanhedrin* 40a¹, note 13.

18. Talmud, *Sanhedrin* 40a².

19. Francis X. Clines, "Work by Expert Witness Is Now on Trial," *New York Times*, September 5, 2001.

20. Belinda Luscombe, "When the Evidence Lies: Joyce Gilchrist Helped Send Dozens to Death Row. The Forensic Scientist's Errors Are Putting Capital Punishment under a Microscope," *Time Magazine*, May 21, 2001, 38.

21. Associated Press, "Chemist's Testimony Refuted 1 Year after Man's Execution," *Florida Times-Union*, August 30, 2001.

22. *DPIC New Voices*, citing *Knight Ridder Tribune–Tallahassee Democrat*, June 15, 2003.

23. Sydney P. Freedberg, "Good Cop, Bad Cop: Special Report: Fallout from an FBI Scandal," *St. Petersburg Times*, March 4, 2001; also available at http://www.sptimes.com/News/030401/Worldandnation/Good_cop__bad_cop_.shtml.

24. Freedberg, "Good Cop, Bad Cop."

25. Other details in the case of James Duckett are discussed in chapter 14.

26. Freedberg, "Good Cop, Bad Cop."

27. Freedberg, "Good Cop, Bad Cop."

28. Freedberg, "Good Cop, Bad Cop."

29. Mills and Armstrong, "Convicted by a Hair."

30. *McCutchen v. State.*

31. Irene Merker Rosenberg and Yale L. Rosenberg, "Guilt: Henry Friendly Meets the MaHaRal of Prague," 90 *Michigan Law Review* 3 (December 1991), 604, 610.

32. Rosenberg and Rosenberg, "Guilt."

33. The discussion in the balance of this chapter summarizes and quotes liberally from *DPIC Executing the Innocent: 1997*.

34. *Model Penal Code (Proposed Official Draft 1962)*, American Law Institute.

35. *Gregg v. Georgia*, 428 U.S. 153 (1976), 193.

36. *DPIC New Voices*, citing *Oklahoman*, June 23, 2001.

CHAPTER FOURTEEN

1. Talmud, *Sanhedrin* 42b[1].

2. Talmud, *Sanhedrin* 42b[1], note 2, citing *Rambam Commentary* and *Chidushei HaRan*.

3. Talmud, *Sanhedrin* 42b[1] at note 5, citing *Rashi*.

4. Talmud, *Sanhedrin* 42b[1] at note 7, citing *Rashi*.

5. Talmud, *Sanhedrin* 42b[1] at note 8, citing *Rambam, Hil,* and *Sanhedrin* 13:1.

6. Talmud, *Sanhedrin* 42b[1] at note 9, citing *Rashi*.

7. Talmud, *Sanhedrin* 42b[1–2] (Gemara) note 13, citing *Rambam, Hil,* and *Sanhedrin* 12:3.

8. Talmud, *Sanhedrin* 42b[1–2] (Gemara) note 15, citing *Rambam, Hil,* and *Sanhedrin* 12:3.

9. Talmud, *Sanhedrin* 43a[4] (Gemara) note 32, citing *Rambam, Hil,* and *Sanhedrin* 13:1.

10. Talmud, *Sanhedrin* 43a[4].

11. Talmud, *Sanhedrin* 43a[4], note 34.

12. Talmud, *Sanhedrin* 43a[4], note 35.

13. Talmud, *Sanhedrin* 43a[4–5] (Gemara).

14. Rosenberg and Rosenberg, "Guilt," 616.

15. *DPIC Executing the Innocent: 1997*, 2.

16. Taylor Bright, "Guilty Until Proven Innocent? Four Men Are Proof That Not Everyone Sent to Death Row Should Be There," *Birmingham Post-Herald*, December 14, 2001; available at http://www.postherald.com/justice.shtml.

17. Bright, "Guilty Until Proven Innocent."

18. The procedural laws on this point are so convoluted and contradictory that professional legal practitioners in this area disagree as to whether the time period allowing for newly discovered evidence of innocence is one year or two years. The rule cited provides for one year, but the time doesn't start to run until counsel is appointed.

19. *West's Florida Statutes*, "Rules of Criminal Procedure," Rule 3.851(d).

20. Texas Code of Criminal Procedure, art. 11.071, Procedure in Death Penalty Case, which provides in relevant part at sec. 4(a):

An application for a writ of habeas corpus, returnable to the court of criminal appeals, must be filed in the convicting court not later than the 180th day after the date the convicting court appoints counsel. *Texas Criminal Procedure—Code and Rules*, art. 11.071 sec. 4(a) (St. Paul: West, 2002).

21. Maria Glod and Steven Ginsberg, "Va. Delays Change on Evidence Rule: Crime Panel Wants Legislators to Decide Deadline for Seeking New Trial," *Washington Post*, January 9, 2003, B1.

22. Glod and Ginsberg, "Va. Delays Change."

23. Glod and Ginsberg, "Va. Delays Change."

24. Texas Code of Criminal Procedure, art. 11.071, Procedure in Death Penalty Case, which provides in relevant part at sec. 5(a):

[A] court may not consider the merits of or grant relief . . . unless the application contains sufficient specific facts establishing that:

(1) the current claims and issues have not been *and could not have been presented previously* in a timely initial application . . . because the factual or legal basis for the claim was unavailable . . . ;

(2) by a preponderance of the evidence, *but for a violation of the United States Constitution* no rational juror could have found the applicant guilty beyond a reasonable doubt; or

(3) by clear and convincing evidence, *but for a violation of the United States Constitution* no rational juror would have answered in the state's favor [concerning the factual grounds for a death penalty]. (italics and bracketed language mine)

Texas Criminal Procedure—Code and Rules, art. 11.071 sec. 5(a).

25. Florida Statutes, sec. 837.021, Perjury by Contradictory Statements, which provides in relevant part:

Whosoever, in one or more official proceedings that relate to the prosecution of a capital felony, willfully makes two or more material statements under oath which contradict each other, commits a felony of the second degree. *West's Florida Statutes Annotated*, sec. 837.021(2).

26. *West's Florida Statutes Annotated*, sec. 837.021(3)(c).

27. Associated Press, "Witnesses in Death Row Release Plead Guilty to Perjury," *Tampa Tribune*, November 5, 2003.

28. For a complete history of the case of James Duckett, see Jeanne Bragg, *The Truth Shall Set Him Free: A True Story of Murder, Lies, and a Police Officer's Conviction of Convenience* (Kearney, Nebr.: Morris Publishing, 2001).

29. *Defendant's Post-Hearing Memorandum, State of Florida v. Duckett*, Case Nos. 87–1347CF and 88–0262CF, Cir. Ct. Fifth Judicial Circuit, Lake County, Fla., 6–7.

30. *Defendant's Post-Hearing Memorandum, State of Florida v. Duckett*, 7.

31. Sherri M. Owens, Rich McCay, and Jason Garcia, "Girl's Convicted Killer Seeks Freedom," *Orlando Sentinel*, September 14, 2003.

32. *SCHR 1996 Act*, 1.

33. *SCHR 1996 Act*, 1.

34. *SCHR 1996 Act*, 1.

35. This portion of the discussion quotes liberally from *DPIC Executing the Innocent: 1997, DPIC Cases of Innocence*, and *DPIC Freed from Death Row*.

36. Sydney P. Freedberg, "Bush Rejects Idea of Death Penalty Ban," *St. Petersburg Times*, February 15, 2000; available at http://www.sptimes.com/News/021500/State/Bush_rejects_idea_of_.shtml.

37. Based upon figures provided in *DPIC Cases of Innocence*.

38. Sydney P. Freedberg, "Bush to Ex-Justice: Name Names: Gerald Kogan Says

Some Innocent People Have Been Executed. The Governor Says Identify Them," *St. Petersburg Times*, February 29, 2000; available at http://www.sptimes.com/News/022900/State/Bush_to_ex_justice__N.shtml.

39. Sydney P. Freedberg, "DNA Testing Denied to Inmates Seeking Justice: Several Florida Prosecutors Are Blocking the Requests, Mostly on Procedural Grounds," *St. Petersburg Times*, June 21, 1999.

40. Associated Press, "Inmate Wins DNA Request," *Miami Herald*, August 29, 2001.

41. Bill Rankin, "DNA May Reopen '75 Massacre Case," *Atlanta Constitution*, January 15, 2003.

42. Susan Clary, "DNA Results Won't Set Zeigler Free," *Orlando Sentinel*, June 6, 2002.

43. For a complete history of this case, see Phillip Finch, *Fatal Flaw: A True Story of Malice and Murder in a Small Southern Town* (New York: Villard Books, 1992).

44. *Supplemental and Amended Petition for Writ of Habeas Corpus, Zeigler v. Singletary, et al.*, Case Nos. 82–1034-Civ-J-20 and 86–333-Civ-J-20, USDC Mid Dist Fla., 18–21.

45. *Motion to Limit Presentation of Evidence to Subjects Directly Related to the DNA Test Results Supporting Zeigler's Instant Postconviction Motion, or for Clarification of Court's Order Granting Evidentiary Hearing Dated August 11, 2003, Zeigler v. State of Florida*, Case Nos. CR-76–1076, CR 76–1082, CR 88–5355, and CR 88–5356 (Ninth Cir. Ct. Fla.).

46. Anthony Colarossi, "Murder Case Appeal Relies on DNA," *Orlando Sentinel*, January 26, 2003.

47. Mark D. Killians, "Court Sets Procedures for Postconviction DNA Testing," *Florida Bar News*, November 1, 2001, 13.

48. *Herrera v. Collins*, 506 U.S. 390 (1993) (denying retrial petition based on innocence claim).

49. *Herrera v. Collins*, 446 (denying retrial petition based on innocence claim), ruled "federal habeas courts sit to ensure that individuals are not imprisoned in violation of the Constitution—not to correct errors of fact"), (Blackmun, J., dissenting).

50. *Coleman v. Thompson*, 501 U.S. 722 (1991).

51. Samuel R. Gross, *The Risks of Death: Why Erroneous Convictions Are Common in Capital Cases*, 44 *Buffalo Law Review* 469 (1996), 499.

52. *Carriger v. Stewart*, 95 F.3d 755, 759–60 (U.S. Court of Appeals for the Ninth Circuit, 1996) (rehearing en banc granted, 106 F.3d 1415 [1997]).

53. *Carriger v. Stewart*.

54. *Carriger v. Stewart*.

55. *DPIC What's New* (February 11, 2003), citing *Kansas City Star*, February 8, 2003.

56. *DPIC What's New* (May 5, 2003), citing *Herald Sun*, April 29, 2003.

57. *DPIC Report 2003*, 4.

58. This portion of the discussion summarizes and quotes liberally from *DPIC Executing the Innocent: 1997*.

59. See *DPIC Killing for Votes*.

60. *DPIC Executing the Innocent: 1997*, text accompanying note 8, citing E. M. McCann, "Opposing Capital Punishment: A Prosecutor's Perspective," 79 *Marquette Law Review* 649, 667 (1996).

61. *SCHR Judges and Politics*, text following note 83.

62. *DPIC Executing the Innocent: 1997*, text accompanying note 9, citing L. Yackle, "A Primer on the New Habeas Corpus Statute," 44 *Buffalo Law Review* 381, 391–92 (1996) (standards for presenting a second habeas petition considerably more rigid than before).

63. Gross, "The Risks of Death," 475 ff.

64. This portion of the discussion summarizes and quotes liberally from *DPIC Executing the Innocent: 1997*.

65. DPIC *Executing the Innocent:* 1997, text accompanying note 55, citing E. Connors et al., "Convicted by Juries, Exonerated by Science: Case Studies in the Use of DNA Evidence to Establish Innocence after Trial," *U.S. Dept. of Justice Research Report,* June 1996, 33, 44.

66. DPIC *Executing the Innocent:* 1997, text accompanying note 56, citing E. Connors et al., "Convicted by Juries, Exonerated by Science: Case Studies in the Use of DNA Evidence to Establish Innocence after Trial," *U.S. Dept. of Justice Research Report,* June 1996, xviii–ix.

67. DPIC *Executing the Innocent:* 1997, text accompanying note 53, citing "Capital Punishment 1995," *Bureau of Justice Statistics* (1996), appendix table 1 (5,580 sentenced to death through the end of 1995, with approximately 300 new death sentences per year).

68. M. Radelet, H. Bedau, and C. Putnam, *In Spite of Innocence: Erroneous Convictions In Capital Cases* (Boston: Northeastern University Press, 1992), 17.

69. "Revisit Death Penalty," editorial, *Orlando Sentinel,* August 19, 2001.

70. DPIC *Innocence* (updated to June 20, 2004); for a list of the people released from death row for innocence, see DPIC *Freed from Death Row;* for specific information about each case, see, DPIC *Executing the Innocent:* 1997, and DPIC *Cases of Innocence.*

71. DPIC *Freed from Death Row* (updated to June 20, 2004).

72. DPIC *Freed from Death Row* (updated to June 20, 2004).

73. James S. Liebman, Jeffrey Fagan, and Valerie West, "A Broken System: Error Rates in Capital Cases, 1973–1995," *The Justice Project: Campaign for Criminal Justice Reform* (New York: Columbia Law School, 2000), 2; available at http://justice.policy.net/jpreport/index.html.

74. James S. Liebman, Jeffrey Fagan, and Valerie West, *A Broken System, Part 2: Why There Is So Much Error in Capital Cases, and What Can Be Done about It* (New York: Columbia Law School Publications, 2002); available at http://www.law.columbia.edu/brokensystem 2/index2.html.

75. "Practice Does Not Make Perfect," editorial, *New York Times,* February 23, 2002, quoting Senator Patrick Leahy.

76. DPIC *New Voices,* citing Justice Harrison, concurring in part and dissenting in part, in *People* v. *Bull,* November 10, 1998.

77. Associated Press, "Justice Questions Guilt of Executed," *Gainesville Sun,* December 24, 1998.

78. DPIC *New Voices,* citing Gerald Kogan, former chief justice of the Florida Supreme Court (speech, Amnesty International Southern Regional Conference, Orlando, Fla., October 23, 1999); speech available in its entirety on-line at DPIC *New Voices.*

79. DPIC *New Voices,* citing *Fort Worth Star-Telegram,* July 24, 2001.

80. DPIC *New Voices,* citing *Arizona Republic,* October 11, 2001.

81. DPIC *New Voices,* citing Michael Posner, federal trial judge, "Life, Death, and Uncertainty," *Boston Globe,* July 8, 2001.

82. *U.S. v. Alan Quinones et al.,* S3 00 Cr. 761 (JSR) *Opinion and Order,* July 1, 2002 (U.S. District Court for So. District of N.Y.), 2; text of opinion available at DPIC *New Voices,* July 2002.

83. *U.S. v. Quinones,* 17–18.

84. *U.S. v. Quinones,* 31.

85. Charles Lane, "Judge Says Executions Violate Constitution," *Washington Post,* July 2, 2002, A01.

86. "Justice Has Doubts about Death Penalty: Justice O'Conner Says 'The System May Well Be Allowing Some Innocent Defendants to Be Executed,'" *St. Petersburg Times,* July, 4, 2001; available at http://www.sptimes.com/News/070401/Worldandnation/Justice _has_doubts_ab.shtml.

87. *DPIC New Voices*, citing *NebraskaStatePaper.com*, October 19, 2001.

88. *SCHR Casualties and Costs*, 6.

89. *DPIC New Voices*, citing "Innocent on Death Row," *Washington Post*, April 4, 2000.

CHAPTER FIFTEEN

1. *Tosefta Sanhedrin* 14:17, 246.

2. *Everyman's Talmud*, 309.

3. Talmud, *Sanhedrin* 40a¹.

4. Talmud, *Sanhedrin* 43a⁴⁻⁵ (Gemara).

5. Talmud, *Sanhedrin* 43a⁵ (Gemara), note 36.

6. Talmud, *Sanhedrin* 32b³ (Gemara), note 26.

7. Talmud, *Sanhedrin* 32b³ (Gemara).

8. Talmud, *Sanhedrin* 32b⁴ (Gemara).

9. Talmud, *Sanhedrin* 32b⁴ (Gemara), note 31, citing *Rashi*.

10. *Essential Talmud*, 171.

11. Rudolph, "Misguided Reliance," 455.

12. Armstrong and Possley, "Verdict Dishonor."

13. *DPIC New Voices*, citing *Houston Chronicle*, June 24, 2003.

14. Bennett L. Gershman, "The New Prosecutors," 53 *University of Pittsburgh Law Review* 393 (1992), 393.

15. *The Center for Public Integrity*, 910 17th Street, NW, Seventh Floor, Washington, D.C. 20006; phone: 202-466-1300; fax: 202-466-1101; Website: http://www.public integrity.org/dtaweb/home.asp.

16. Steve Weinberg, "Breaking the Rules: Who Suffers When a Prosecutor Is Cited for Misconduct?" (Washington, D.C.: Center for Public Integrity), June 26, 2003; available at http://www.publicintegrity.org/pm.

17. Armstrong and Possley, "Verdict Dishonor."

18. Armstrong and Possley, "Verdict Dishonor."

19. Armstrong and Possley, "Verdict Dishonor."

20. Armstrong and Possley, "Verdict Dishonor."

21. Armstrong and Possley, "Verdict Dishonor."

22. Bennett L. Gershman, *Prosecutorial Misconduct*, 2d ed. (St. Paul, Minn.: West Group, 2001), vii.

23. *SCHR Counsel for the Poor*, text accompanying notes 212–13. "Today, it is unusual to see a capital case in which one or more issues presented in federal habeas corpus review is not found to be procedurally barred." Ibid.

24. *SCHR Counsel for the Poor*, text accompanying note 214.

25. *DPIC What's New* (September 28, 2001), citing *New York Times*, August 30, 2001, and *Morning Call*, August 28, 2001.

26. Douglas Holt and Steve Mills, "Double Murder Case Unravels: Once Two Days Away from Execution, Inmate May Go Free after Another Man Implicates Himself in Two Murders," *Chicago Tribune*, February 4, 1999.

27. The youth "received complete immunity for testifying" and "acknowledged that the prosecutor told him not to disclose the deal to anyone, even if asked." Gershman, "The New Prosecutors," 451, note 347.

28. Gershman, "The New Prosecutors," 451.

29. *DPIC What's New* (August 31, 2001), citing *Oklahoman*, August 14, 2001.

30. This portion of the discussion summarizes and quotes liberally from Taylor

Bright, "Love Letters Almost Fatal," *Birmingham Post-Herald*, December 14, 2001; available at http://www.postherald.com/justice.shtml.

31. Armstrong and Possley, "Verdict Dishonor."

32. Gershman, "The New Prosecutors," 451–52.

33. Armstrong and Possley, "Verdict Dishonor."

34. The term "suborning of perjury" means to secretly induce another to commit perjury.

35. Gershman, "The New Prosecutors," 452.

36. "Court: Prosecutors' Misconduct Too Frequent," *Fort Walton Daily News* (Fla.), April 2, 1999.

37. *Walter Ruiz v. State of Florida*, 743 So.2d 1 (Florida Supreme Court, 1999).

38. Sydney Freedberg, "DNA Clears Inmate Too Late: The FBI Clears Death-Row Inmate of Rape and Murder 10½ Months after Cancer Killed Him," *St. Petersburg Times*, December 15, 2000; available at http://www.sptimes.com/News/121500/State/DNA _clears_inmate_too.shtml.

39. Freedberg, "DNA Clears Inmate."

40. Freedberg, "DNA Clears Inmate."

41. Associated Press, "Two Broward Detectives Cleared in Death Row Perjury Case," *Florida Times-Union*, July 6, 2001.

42. "Law Hinders Weeding Out Bad Cops," editorial, *Miami Herald*, July 15, 2001.

43. Sandy Strickland, "Death Row to Freedom: Man Adjusts after 7-Year Prison Stretch," *Florida Times-Union*, July 17, 1999.

44. As of this writing, twenty-three inmates have come off Florida's death row exonerated by significant evidence of innocence. William Kelley, who is expected to be released soon, would be number twenty-four.

45. Sydney P. Freedberg, "Ex-Death Row Inmate Gets Walking Papers," *St. Petersburg Times*, March 17, 2000; available at http://www.sptimes.com/News/031700/State/Ex_death _row_inmate_g.shtml.

46. Sydney P. Freedberg, "Murder Witness Admits He Lied," *St. Petersburg Times*, November 28, 2001; available at http://www.sptimes.com/News/112801/State/Murder _witness_admits.shtml.

47. Freedberg, "Murder Witness Lied."

48. Meg Laughlin, "Judge Grants Inmate New Trial," *Miami Herald*, September 20, 2002.

49. Laughlin, "Federal Court to Revisit Case," and "1984 Murder Trial Revisited."

50. Laughlin, "Judge Grants Inmate New Trial."

51. Meg Laughlin, "State Blocks Death Row Inmate's Release One Day Before Deadline," *Miami Herald*, January 29, 2003.

52. Laughlin, "State Blocks Inmate's Release."

53. Associated Press, "Witnesses Plead Guilty to Perjury."

54. "Man on Death Row Gets New Trial: The Man Was Convicted 15 Years Ago of Raping and Killing a 17-Year-Old Prostitute. Police Withheld a Crucial Crime Report," *St. Petersburg Times*, November 3, 2001; available at http://www.sptimes.com/News/110301/ TampaBay/Man_on_death_row_gets.shtml.

55. *DPIC Cases of Innocence.*

56. David Karp, "Freed after Years on Death Row: A Man Convicted of a 1986 Murder Is Released; the State Says It Lacks Enough Evidence to Retry Him," *St. Petersburg Times*, January 24, 2003.

57. New York's legislative body reinstated the death penalty in September 1995.

58. Gershman, "The New Prosecutors," 452–53.

59. Paula Christian, "Prosecutor, under Scrutiny, Quits," *Tampa Tribune*, May 23, 2001.

60. Christian, "Prosecutor Quits."

61. Paula Christian, "Aisenberg Prosecutor Removed from Post," *Tampa Tribune*, July 20, 2001.

62. Christian, "Aisenberg Prosecutor Removed."

63. Christian, "Aisenberg Prosecutor Removed."

64. Paula Christian, "Aisenberg Prosecutor Moved," *Tampa Tribune*, August 1, 2001.

65. "Florida Briefs: Prosecutor Reassigned after Case Bungled," *Florida Times-Union*, July 31, 2002, A-3.

66. Graham Brink, "Officers' Discipline Is 'Slap on the Wrist,'" *St. Petersburg Times*, August 3, 2002; available at http://www.sptimes.com/2002/08/03/TampaBay/Officers_discipline_.shtml.

67. Brink, "Officers' Slap on the Wrist."

68. Bill Moushey and Bob Martinson, "Win at All Costs: Government Misconduct in the Name of Expedient Justice," *Pittsburgh Post-Gazette*, November 22, 1998; available at http://www.post-gazette.com/win.

69. Bill Moushey and Bob Martinson, "Win at All Costs: Out of Control," *Pittsburgh Post-Gazette*, November 22, 1998, available at http://www.post-gazette.com/win/day1_1a.asp.

70. Gershman, "The New Prosecutors," 453.

71. Moushey and Martinson, "Win at All Costs: Out of Control."

72. Gershman, "The New Prosecutors," 454.

CHAPTER SIXTEEN

1. *Talmud Reference Guide*, par. 2, 252.

2. *Ancient Hebrews*, sec. 50, 84–86.

3. *Ancient Hebrews*, sec. 46, 80–81.

4. *Ancient Hebrews*, sec. 48, 81.

5. *Talmud Reference Guide*, par. 2, 263.

6. *Talmud Reference Guide*, par. 7, 243.

7. Maimonides, "Evidence," chap. 9, pars. 9–10, 101.

8. *DPIC Juveniles*.

9. Richard Burr and Mandy Welch, "Killing Kids Who Kill: Desecrating the Sanctuary of Childhood," 29 *St. Mary's Law Journal* 4 (1998), 929, 931.

10. *DPIC Juveniles*, citing Victor L. Streib, *The Juvenile Death Penalty Today: Death Sentences and Executions for Juvenile Crimes (2003)* (Ada, Ohio: Claude W. Pettit College of Law, Ohio Northern University, 2003); available at http://www.law.onu.edu/faculty/streib/JuvDeathSept2003.htm (last updated October 6, 2003).

11. This portion of the discussion summarizes and quotes liberally from *DPIC Minimum Ages*.

12. Indiana became the sixteenth state to forbid the death penalty for those who were under eighteen years of age at the time of their crime. Gov. Frank O'Bannon signed the law that also requires judges to follow juries' unanimous sentencing recommendations. *DPIC Juvenile Executions*, citing *Associated Press*, March 26, 2002. South Dakota and Wyoming became the eighteenth and nineteenth states to ban execution of those who were under eighteen years of age when they committed their crimes. *DPIC Juvenile Executions* citing *Associated Press*, March 4, 2004.

13. Minimum age required by Missouri Supreme Court, August 2003.

14. Minimum age required by Washington Supreme Court.

15. Minimum age required by Florida Constitution per Florida Supreme Court.

16. (*) indicates minimum age required by U.S. Constitution per U.S. Supreme Court in *Thompson v. Oklahoma*, 487 U.S. 815 (1988).

17. This portion of the discussion summarizes and quotes liberally from DPIC *Juvenile Executions*.

18. This portion of the discussion summarizes and quotes liberally from DPIC *Juveniles*.

19. DPIC *Juveniles*.

20. Juveniles on death row in the Bible Belt (2003): Tex. 28, Ala. 13, La. 7, N.C. 5, Miss. 5, Fla. 2, Ga. 2, S.C. 2, Ky. 1, Va. 1: subtotal of 66; outside the Bible Belt: Ariz. 5, Pa. 3, Nev. 1: subtotal of 9; total: 75.

21. This portion of the discussion summarizes and quotes liberally from DPIC *Juveniles*.

22. DPIC *Juveniles: Recent Developments in the Juvenile Death Penalty*, citing *St. Louis Post-Dispatch*, August 26, 2003.

23. DPIC *Juveniles: Recent Developments in the Juvenile Death Penalty*, citing *Daily Oklahoman*, December 1, 1998.

24. DPIC *Juveniles: Recent Developments in the Juvenile Death Penalty*, citing *Associated Press*, August 15, 2001.

25. DPIC *Juveniles: Recent Developments in the Juvenile Death Penalty*, citing *New York Times*, February 26, 2002.

26. *Allen v. State*, 636 So.2d 494 (Florida Supreme Court, 1994).

27. *Brennan v. State*, 754 So.2d 1 (Florida Supreme Court 1999).

28. Jo Becker, "Court Raises Execution Age to 17: Florida Becomes the 16th State to Prohibit Execution of 16-Year-Old Defendants after the State Supreme Court Ruling," *St. Petersburg Times*, July 9, 1999; available at http://www.sptimes.com/News/70999/State/Court_raises_executio.shtml.

29. DPIC *What's New* (March 28, 2004), citing Orlando Sentinel, March 8, 2004; and *Associated Press*, "Lawmaker's Efforts Fails to Raise Minimum Age for Death Penalty," April 1, 2004.

30. NAMI, "Criminal Justice and Forensic Issues," chap. 9 in *Policy Platform* (Arlington, Va.: NAMI: The Nation's Voice on Mental Illness, 2001); available at http://www.nami.org/update/platform/criminal.htm.

31. NAMI, "The Criminalization of Mental Illness: The Criminalization Trend Is Worse than Ever," in *Advocacy: Public Policy and Legal: Where We Stand* (Arlington, Va.: NAMI: The Nation's Voice on Mental Illness, 2002); available at http://www.nami.org/update/unitedcriminal.html.

32. Human Rights Watch, *Ill-equipped: U.S. Prisons and Offenders with Mental Illness* (New York: Human Rights Watch, 2003), 19.

33. HRW, *Ill-equipped*, 20.

34. HRW, *Ill-equipped*, 18.

35. Adam C. Smith, "Care of Mentally Ill Prisoners Questioned: For the One in Nine Who Is Severely Ill, Prison Can Lead to Violence, Abuse, and Even Death, Experts Say," *St. Petersburg Times*, September 28, 1999; available at http://www.sptimes.com/News/92899/State/Care_of_mentally_ill_.shtml.

36. Erica Goode, "Minorities' Care for Mental Ills Is Called Inferior," *New York Times*, August 27, 2001.

37. Jo Becker, "Lawmaker: Crucify Inmate. Fed Up with the Delays Keeping a Killer Who Thinks He's Jesus Christ out of the Electric Chair, State Rep. Howard Futch Makes

a Suggestion," *St. Petersburg Times*, October 7, 1999; available at http://www.sptimes.com/News/100799/State/Lawmaker__Crucify_inm.shtml.

38. Catherine Forbes, letter to the editor, *Orlando Sentinel*, June 20, 2000.

39. Jo Becker, "Lawmaker: Crucify Inmate."

40. Jo Becker, "A Glimpse at Mental Illness," *St. Petersburg Times*, March 14, 2000; available at http://www.sptimes.com/News/031400/State/A_glimpse_at_mental_i.shtml.

41. Curtis Krueger, "State Mental Hospital Shuts Down," *St. Petersburg Times*, February 9, 2002; available at http://www.sptimes.com/2002/02/09/State/State_mental_hospital.shtml.

42. "Time for Humanitarian Intervention: The Imminent Execution of Larry Robison," Amnesty International Canada, July 14, 1999; available at http://www.amnesty.ca/library/1999/amr51107.htm

43. "No Rush to Judgment," *Amnesty Action*, fall 1999, 10.

44. In Texas, a death penalty case costs the state an average of about $2.3 million. C. Hoppe, "Executions Cost Texas Millions," *Dallas Morning News*, March 8, 1992, 1A.

45. *Dallas Morning News*, editorial, November 20, 2000.

46. *Atkins v. Virginia*, 536 U.S. 304 (2002).

47. *Atkins v. Virginia*, 11.

48. *Atkins v. Virginia*, 16.

49. *Atkins v. Virginia*, 13–14.

50. Brendan Farrington (AP), "DNA Clears Retarded Inmate," *Miami Herald*, June 16, 2001.

51. "Man to Be Freed after 22 Years: Judge Orders the Release of a Retarded Inmate in the Face of DNA Evidence and Doubts," *St. Petersburg Times*, June 16, 2001; available at http://www.sptimes.com/News/061601/State/Man_to_be_freed_after.shtml.

52. *Atkins v. Virginia*, note 8, 8.

53. *DPIC Mental Retardation*.

54. Gardner C. Hanks, *Capital Punishment and the Bible* (Scottdale, Pa.: Herald Press, 2002), 123.

55. *DPIC Mental Retardation*.

56. "A Life Sentence on Death Row," editorial, *Miami Herald*, August 5, 2001.

57. Julie Hauserman, "Law Bans Execution of Retarded: Governor Jeb Bush Signs a Measure That Will Let Experts Evaluate Defendants. If Found to Be Mentally Retarded, They Won't Face the Death Penalty," *St. Petersburg Times*, June 13, 2001; available at http://www.sptimes.com/News/061301/State/Law_bans_execution_of.shtml.

58. Jo Becker, "Group Ponders Death Penalty: A Task Force Discusses Whether the State Should Execute Mentally Retarded Inmates," *St. Petersburg Times*, January 29, 2000.

59. Source: Marty Moore, a lawyer for (then) state of Florida attorney general Bob Butterworth, as quoted in Associated Press, "Debate over IQ, Executions: Panel Considers Retardation Ban," *Florida Times-Union*, January 29, 2000, B-6.

60. Jackie Halifax (AP), "Court Considers Ban on Execution of Mentally Retarded," *Tampa Tribune*, August 25, 2003.

61. Halifax, "Court Considers Ban."

CHAPTER SEVENTEEN

1. *Ancient Hebrews*, note 95, 50.

2. Hanks, *Christian Arguments*, 37.

3. *Furman v. Georgia*, 238.

4. *SCHR Counsel for the Poor*, text accompanying note 4.

5. *SCHR Counsel for the Poor*, text accompanying note 46.

6. *SCHR Counsel for the Poor*, text accompanying note 10.

7. *SCHR Counsel for the Poor*, text accompanying note 41.

8. *SCHR Counsel for the Poor*, text accompanying note 48.

9. *SCHR Counsel for the Poor*, text accompanying note 75.

10. *SCHR Counsel for the Poor*, text accompanying notes 51–56.

11. *SCHR Counsel for the Poor*, text immediately following note 56.

12. *SCHR Counsel for the Poor*, text accompanying note 101.

13. Series: "Death Penalty in America," *Chicago Tribune*, June 11–12, 2000, and December 17–18, 2000; available at http://www.chicagotribune.com/news/specials.

14. Steve Mills, Ken Armstrong, and Douglas Holt, "Flawed Trials Lead to Death Chamber: Bush Confident in System Rife with Problems," *Chicago Tribune*, June 11, 2000; Ken Armstrong and Steve Mills, "Gatekeeper Court Keeps Gates Shut: Justices Prove Reluctant to Nullify Cases," *Chicago Tribune*, June 12, 2000; Steve Mills, Maurice Possley, and Ken Armstrong, "3 Cases Weaken under Scrutiny," *Chicago Tribune*, December 17, 2000; Steve Mills, "Questions of Innocence: Legal Roadblocks Thwart New Evidence on Appeal," *Chicago Tribune*, December 18, 2000.

15. Mills, Armstrong, and Holt, "Flawed Trials Lead to Death."

16. Mills, Armstrong, and Holt, "Flawed Trials Lead to Death."

17. Mills, Armstrong, and Holt, "Flawed Trials Lead to Death."

18. Mills, Armstrong, and Holt, "Flawed Trials Lead to Death."

19. "Special Report: Tennessee Death Penalty," *Tennessean*, July 22–29, 2001; available at http://tennessean.com/special/dp.

20. John Shiffman, "Troubled Lawyers Still Allowed to Work Death Cases," *Tennessean*, July 26, 2001; available at http://tennessean.com/special/dp/archives/01/04/06918869.shtml?Element_ID = 6918869.

21. Shiffman, "Troubled Lawyers Work Death Cases."

22. Shiffman, "Troubled Lawyers Work Death Cases."

23. Shiffman, "Troubled Lawyers Work Death Cases."

24. Shiffman, "Troubled Lawyers Work Death Cases."

25. Common Sense Foundation, P.O. Box 10808, Raleigh, N.C. 27605-0808, phone: 919-821-9270; fax: 919-821-3669; website: http://www.common-sense.org/.

26. Frances Ferris, *One in Six Death Row Inmates Defended at Trial by Lawyers Disciplined by State Bar* (Raleigh, N.C.: Common Sense Foundation, 2002).

27. "Special Reports: Death Penalty: Uncertain Justice," *Seattle Post-Intelligencer*, August 6–8, 2001; available at http://seattlep-i.nwsource.com/specials/deathpenalty.

28. Lise Olsen, "Life and Death in Lawyers' Hands," *Seattle Post-Intelligencer*, August 6, 2001; available at http://seattlepi.nwsource.com/local/33820_defense06.shtml.

29. Olsen, "Life and Death in Lawyers' Hands."

30. Olsen, "Life and Death in Lawyers' Hands."

31. Series: "Execution of Justice," *Birmingham Post-Herald*, December 14, 2001: Jeb Phillips, "Talladega: Death Row Country: Is Fairness Missing from the State's Use of Capital Punishment?"; *Birmingham Post-Herald*, December 14, 2001; Taylor Bright, "Guilty Until Proven Innocent?"; Taylor Bright, "Love Letters Almost Fatal," Taylor Bright "Fighting for Another Chance," *Birmingham Post-Herald*, December 14, 2001; Jeb Phillips, "Does Race Decide Who Dies? Some Say Color of Defendant, Victim Plays Significant Role," *Birmingham Post-Herald*, December 14, 2001; Jeb Phillips, "Justice at 50 Cents an Hour: Defending Death Row Case Drove Lawyer into Bankruptcy," *Birmingham Post-Herald*, December 14, 2001; Jeb Phillips, "Some Face Death without Attorney," *Birmingham Post-Herald*, December 14, 2001; available at http://www.postherald.com/justice.shtml.

32. Bright "Fighting for Another Chance."

33. Phillips, "Justice at 50 Cents an Hour."

34. Phillips, "Some Face Death without Attorney."

35. *SCHR Casualties and Costs*, 4.

36. Cathleen Burnett, *Justice Denied: Clemency Appeals in Death Penalty Cases* (Boston: Northeastern University Press, 2002), note 18, 222.

37. Burnett, *Justice Denied*, note 20, 222–23.

38. *SCHR Counsel for the Poor*, at note 80.

39. Marcia Cole, "Suit: Death Defense Is a Sham," 21 *National Law Journal* 17, December 21, 1998, A1.

40. Cole, "Death Defense Is a Sham," A14.

41. *Affidavit of Robert L. Spangenberg*, Exhibit C to *Petition in Florida Supreme Court* Cases Nos. 92,026 and 82,322, par. 6.

42. *Affidavit of Robert L. Spangenberg*, par. 33.

43. Lesley Clark, "Death Penalty Office Targeted," *Miami Herald*, January 22, 2003.

44. Brent Kallestad (AP), "Crist Backs Death Row Plan," *Miami Herald*, January 30, 2003.

45. Joe Follick, "State-funded Counsel for Death Row Reviewed," *Tampa Tribune*, March 28, 2003.

46. Jan Pudlow, "The Pros and Cons of Privatizing the Death Penalty," *Florida Bar News*, March 1, 2003, 7.

47. Mike Salinero and Joe Follick, "Tallahassee 2-Step Begins," *Tampa Tribune*, November 27, 2001; Abraham J. Bonowitz, "Florida Cannot Afford the Death Penalty," *Fort Lauderdale Sun-Sentinel*, May 19, 2003.

48. Susan Spencer-Wendel, "Death Row Appeals Office Closing," *Palm Beach Post*, June 2, 2003.

49. Rich Tucker, "Legal Defense Group Faces Another Fight for Survival," *Florida Times-Union*, April 13, 2003.

50. "Death Appeals Not Quite Dead," *Daily Business Review* (Miami, Fla.), May 20, 2003.

51. *SCHR Counsel for the Poor*, text accompanying notes 212–14.

CHAPTER EIGHTEEN

1. *Talmud Reference Guide*, par. 6, 243, citing Talmud, *Kiddushin* 4:1.

2. There were some distinctions in the method of capital punishment to be applied depending upon one's category of lineage, but not as to whether the death penalty applied.

3. Hanks, *Christian Arguments*, 37–38.

4. This discussion summarizes and quotes liberally from DPIC *Race of the Executed*.

5. DPIC *Race of the Executed*.

6. This discussion summarizes and quotes liberally from DPIC *Black and White*.

7. DPIC *Black and White*, text accompanying note 16, U.S. General Accounting Office, *Report to Senate and House Committees on the Judiciary, Death Penalty Sentencing: Research Indicates Pattern of Racial Disparities, February 1990* (Washington, D.C.: U.S. General Accounting Office, 1990), 5 (referred to in this work as GAO Report).

8. DPIC *Black and White*, text accompanying note 17, citing D. Baldus et al., "Reflections on the 'Inevitability' of Racial Discrimination in Capital Sentencing and the 'Impossibility' of Its Prevention, Detection, and Correction," 51 *Washington and Lee Law Review* 359 (1994), 365.

9. *DPIC Black and White*, text accompanying note 21, citing D. Baldus and G. Woodworth, *Race Discrimination in America's Capital Punishment System Since Furman v. Georgia* (1972); *The Evidence of Race Disparities and the Record of Our Courts and Legislatures in Addressing This Issue* (1997) (report prepared for the American Bar Association).

10. The study of racial disparities in Georgia was the basis for the most important case brought before the U.S. Supreme Court on the issue of race and the death penalty, *McCleskey v. Kemp*. For their work in what has become known as the "Baldus study," these researchers were awarded the Harry Kalven Prize for distinguished scholarship by the Law and Society Association.

11. *DPIC Black and White*, text accompanying note 21, citing Baldus and Woodworth, *Race Discrimination in America's Capital Punishment System*.

12. Samuel R. Gross and Robert Mauro, *Death and Discrimination: Racial Disparities in Capital Sentencing* (Boston: Northeastern University Press, 1989), 151.

13. Gross and Mauro, *Death and Discrimination*, 172.

14. *Essential Talmud*, 155.

15. Stuart Banner, *The Death Penalty: An American History* (Cambridge: Harvard University Press, 2002), 6.

16. Banner, *Death Penalty History*, 57.

17. Banner, *Death Penalty History*, 7.

18. Friedman, *Crime and Punishment*, 44.

19. Friedman, *Crime and Punishment*, 90.

20. Friedman, *Crime and Punishment*, 90.

21. Friedman, *Crime and Punishment*, 93.

22. Friedman, *Crime and Punishment*, 91–92.

23. Banner, *Death Penalty History*, 112–13.

24. *SCHR Racial Discrimination*, text accompanying note 31.

25. Banner, *Death Penalty History*, 112–13.

26. Banner, *Death Penalty History*, 112–13.

27. Banner, *Death Penalty History*, 113.

28. Banner, *Death Penalty History*, 142.

29. Banner, *Death Penalty History*, 137.

30. Banner, *Death Penalty History*, 137.

31. Banner, *Death Penalty History*, 228.

32. *SCHR Judicial Independence*, text accompanying notes 2–7.

33. Friedman, *Crime and Punishment*, 95.

34. Banner, *Death Penalty History*, 229.

35. *SCHR Racial Discrimination*, text accompanying note 32.

36. Banner, *Death Penalty History*, 230.

37. John D. Bessler, *Kiss of Death: America's Love Affair with the Death Penalty* (Boston: Northeastern University Press, 2003), 80.

38. *SCHR Racial Discrimination*, text accompanying note 29.

39. Banner, *Death Penalty History*, 243–44.

40. *SCHR Judicial Independence*.

41. *SCHR Judicial Independence*, text accompanying notes 61–67.

42. *SCHR Judicial Independence*, text accompanying notes 68–80.

43. In the spring of 1998, the Commonwealth of Kentucky passed the Racial Justice Act and Governor Paul Patton signed it into law. The Kentucky Racial Justice Act reads, in pertinent part, as follows:

"An act relating to the fair and reliable imposition of capital sentences. Be it enacted by the General Assembly of the Commonwealth of Kentucky:

Section 1. A New Section of KRS Chapter 532 Is Created to Read as Follows:

(1) No person shall be subject to or given a sentence of death that was sought on the basis of race.

(2) A finding that race was the basis of the decision to seek a death sentence may be established if the court finds that race was a significant factor in decisions to seek the sentence of death in the Commonwealth at the time the death sentence was sought.

(3) Evidence relevant to establish a finding that race was the basis of the decision to seek a death sentence may include statistical evidence or other evidence, or both, that death sentences were sought significantly more frequently:

(a) Upon persons of one race than upon persons of another race; or

(b) As punishment for capital offenses against persons of one race than as punishment for capital offenses against persons of another race.

(4) The defendant shall state with particularity how the evidence supports a claim that racial considerations played a significant part in the decision to seek the death sentence in his or her case. The claim shall be raised by the defendant at the pre-trial conference. The court shall schedule a hearing on the claim and shall prescribe a time for the submission of evidence by both parties. If the court finds that race was the basis of the decision to seek the death sentence, the court shall order that a death sentence shall not be sought.

(5) The defendant has the burden of proving by clear and convincing evidence that race was the basis of the decision to seek the death penalty. The Commonwealth may offer evidence in rebuttal of the claims or evidence of the defendant." *Source:* Death Penalty Information Center, Washington, D.C.

44. *SCHR Racial Discrimination*, text accompanying note 159.

45. *SCHR Racial Discrimination*, text accompanying notes 14–15.

46. *SCHR Racial Discrimination*, text accompanying note 26.

47. Michael Graczyk (AP), "For First Time in Decades, Texas Executes White Man for Killing Black; Critics Say System Biased," September 20, 2003.

48. *SCHR Racial Discrimination*, text accompanying note 11.

49. *SCHR Racial Discrimination*, text accompanying note 13.

50. Clauses 1 and 2 are from Sydney P. Freedberg and William Yardley, "The Race Issue: Governor Bush Forms a Task Force to Study the Role of Race in Capital Sentencing," *St. Petersburg Times*, January 7, 2000.

51. Samuel R. Gross and Robert Mauro, "Patterns of Death: An Analysis of Racial Disparities in Capital Sentencing and Homicide Victimization," 37 *Stanford Law Review* 27, 78, 96 (1984); Gross and Mauro, *Death and Discrimination*, 65–66.

52. Freedberg, "The Race Issue."

53. The racial breakdown of the 364 men on Florida's death row is as follows: white = 230 (63.2 percent); black = 124 (34.1 percent); other = 10 (2.7 percent). *Source:* State of Florida, Florida Department of Corrections, *Corrections Offender Network—Death Row Roster* (updated as of Apirl 20, 2004); available at http://www.dc.state.fl.us/activeinmates/death rowroster.asp.

54. Jeb Phillips, "Talladega: Death Row Country."

55. Jeb Phillips, "Does Race Decide Who Dies?"

56. Equal Justice Initiative of Alabama, 643 South Perry Street, Montgomery, Ala. 36104; phone: 334-269-1803; fax: 334-269-1806; e-mail: contact_us@eji.org; website: http://www.eji.org.

57. *SCHR Racial Discrimination*, text accompanying notes 46–47.

58. *SCHR Racial Discrimination*, text accompanying note 118.

59. *SCHR Vengeance.*

60. *SCHR Vengeance*, 5.

61. *SCHR Vengeance*, 5–6.

62. *SCHR Vengeance*, 4–5.

63. *SCHR Vengeance*, 10.

64. As used in this sentence, "racial animus" means intentional racial discrimination.

65. Susan Levine and Lori Montgomery, "Large Racial Disparity Found by Study of Md. Death Penalty," *Washington Post*, January 8, 2003, A01.

66. Lori Montgomery, "Steele Seeks New Study of Death Penalty Cases: Finding of Bias against Blacks in Prosecutions Concerns Lieutenant Governor," *Washington Post*, January 26, 2003, C01.

67. *DPIC What's New* (November 15, 2003), citing report of Washington Death Penalty Assistance Center (May 2003).

68. Dan Eggen, "Ashcroft Aggressively Pursues Death Penalty," *Washington Post*, July 1, 2002, A01.

69. *SCHR Racial Discrimination*, text accompanying notes 81–87.

70. Scott D. Makar, letters to editor, *Florida Times-Union*, February 8, 2000.

71. *SCHR Racial Discrimination*, text accompanying notes 230–38.

72. *SCHR Racial Discrimination*, text accompanying notes 232–33.

73. *McCleskey v. Kemp*, 481 U.S. 279 (1987), 292.

74. *DPIC Black and White*, text accompanying note 28.

75. *SCHR Racial Discrimination*, text accompanying notes 243–44.

76. *SCHR Twenty-first Century*, text accompanying notes 59–78.

CHAPTER NINETEEN

1. *Talmud Reference Guide*, par. 5, 261.

2. Maimonides, "Sanhedrin," chap. 1, par. 1, 1.

3. Talmud, *Sanhedrin* 2a³.

4. Talmud, *Sanhedrin* 2a².

5. *Tosefta Sanhedrin* 7:5, 219.

6. Maimonides, "Sanhedrin," chap. 2, par. 3, 8.

7. *Essential Talmud*, 165.

8. Hanks, *Christian Arguments*, 39.

9. Maimonides, *Book of Judges*, "Sanhedrin," chap. 10, par. 1, 29.

10. Maimonides, *Book of Judges*, "Sanhedrin," chap. 2, par. 7, 8.

11. Maimonides, *Book of Judges*, "Sanhedrin," chap. 2, par. 7, 8–9.

12. Maimonides, *Book of Judges*, "Sanhedrin," chap. 3, par. 8, 12.

13. Maimonides, *Book of Judges*, "Sanhedrin," chap. 3, par. 8, 12.

14. Maimonides, *Book of Judges*, "Sanhedrin," chap. 3, par. 10, 12.

15. Maimonides, *Book of Judges*, "Sanhedrin," chap. 3, par. 9, 12.

16. *Ancient Hebrews*, sec. 57, 92–95.

17. *DPIC Killing for Votes*, note 1, citing U.S. Supreme Court Justice Paul Stevens, "Address to the Opening Assembly," *American Bar Association Annual Meeting*, August 3, 1996, 12.

18. *SCHR Judicial Independence*, text accompanying notes 172–73.

19. William Glaberson, "States Take Steps to Rein in Excesses of Judicial Politicking," *New York Times*, June 15, 2001.

20. Mike Schneider (AP), "Cash Flow into Judges' Campaigns Swelling," *Florida Times-Union*, July 28, 2003, B-4.

21. *DPIC Killing for Votes*, text accompanying note 2, citing R. Marcus, "Justice White Criticizes Judicial Elections," *Washington Post*, August 11, 1987, A5.

22. Justice Robert H. Jackson, as quoted in *SCHR Fairness*, text accompanying note 92.

23. *SCHR Casualties and Costs*, 2.

24. *SCHR Judges and Politics*, text accompanying notes 169–70.

25. *DPIC Killing for Votes*, 2.

26. *SCHR Judges and Politics*, text following note 189.

27. *DPIC Killing for Votes*, iii.

28. *Harris v. Alabama*, 115 S.Ct. 1031 (1995), 1039–40 (Justice John Paul Stevens, dissenting).

29. *Ring v. Arizona*, 536 U.S. 2428 (2002).

30. "Four States have hybrid systems, in which the jury renders an advisory verdict but the judge makes the ultimate sentencing determinations" (*Ring v. Arizona*, at note 6).

31. As of this writing there is a conflict between U.S. circuit courts of appeal on this issue. Consequently, the issue is ripe for a determination by the U.S. Supreme Court.

32. *DPIC Killing for Votes.*

33. *DPIC Killing for Votes*, text accompanying notes 45–46.

34. *DPIC Killing for Votes*, text accompanying note 61, citing *Appellant's Brief, Missouri v. Kinder*, No. 75082 (Missouri Supreme Court, 1996); complete text of press release is on file with the DPIC.

35. *DPIC Killing for Votes*, 19–20; copies of campaign advertisement are on file with the DPIC.

36. *SCHR Judges and Politics*, text accompanying note 99.

37. *SCHR Judges and Politics*, text following note 83.

38. *DPIC Killing for Votes*, text accompanying note 85.

39. *DPIC Killing for Votes*, text accompanying note 86, citing B. Newton, "A Case Study in Systemic Unfairness: The Texas Death Penalty, 1973–1994," 1 *Texas Forum on Civil Liberties and Civil Rights* 1, 18 (1994).

40. *DPIC Killing for Votes*, text accompanying note 87, citing J. Zuniga, "Death Row Inmate Gets a New Trial," *Houston Chronicle*, November 16, 1994.

41. *DPIC Killing for Votes*, text accompanying note 88, citing "A Conviction for Murder Set Aside," *New York Times*, November 20, 1994. Judge Hoyt was unanimously upheld by the U.S. Court of Appeals for the Fifth Circuit, *Guerra v. Johnson*, No. 95–20443 (July 30, 1996).

42. *SCHR Judges and Politics*, text accompanying note 151.

43. *Texas Lawyer* is the weekly newspaper of the legal profession in the state of Texas.

44. *SCHR Fairness*, text accompanying notes 75–82.

45. *DPIC What's New* (June 20, 2001), citing *New York Times*, June 16, 2001.

46. *SCHR Political Attacks.*

47. *SCHR Political Attacks*, text accompanying notes 44–46.

48. *SCHR Political Attacks*, text accompanying notes 47–49.

49. *SCHR Political Attacks*, text accompanying note 50.

50. *SCHR Fairness*, text accompanying notes 71–74.

51. *DPIC What's New* (March 17, 2000), citing *Orange County Register*, March 1, 2000.

52. *SCHR Fairness*, text accompanying note 70.

53. *DPIC Killing for Votes*, text accompanying note 4, citing "Penny White Deserves Seat on High Court," editorial, *Tennessean*, July 21, 1996.

54. *DPIC Killing for Votes*, text accompanying note 5, citing J. Woods, "Judge Raps Critics, Vows to Survive," *Nashville Banner*, July 15, 1996, A1.

55. *SCHR Fairness*, text accompanying notes 67–68.

56. *SCHR Fairness*, text accompanying note 58.

57. *SCHR Casualties and Costs*, 5.

58. Jo Becker and William Yardley, "Bush Backs Off Firm Limit to Death Row Appeals: The Deal with Legislative Leaders Is Made on the Eve of the Opening of a Special Session on the Death Penalty," *St. Petersburg Times*, January 5, 2000, available at http://www.sptimes.com/News/010500/news_pf/State/Bush_backs_off_firm el.shtml.

59. Jayne Hustead, "Death Row Conviction Overturned," *Vero Beach Press Journal*, July 5, 2003.

60. Hustead, "Conviction Overturned."

61. See Lesley Clark, "DNA Law Facing Tough Battle: Lawmakers Want to Narrow Scope," *Miami Herald*, August 27, 2001; and "For Justice, Get It Right," editorial, *Miami Herald*, August 28, 2001.

62. Section 1 of Florida's postconviction DNA testing statute reads in pertinent part as follows:

"(a) *A person who has been tried and found guilty* of committing a crime and has been sentenced by a court established by the laws of this state may petition that court to order the examination of physical evidence collected at the time of the investigation of the crime for which he or she has been sentenced which may contain DNA (deoxyribonucleic acid) and which would exonerate that person or mitigate the sentence that person received." (italics mine) *West's Florida Statutes*, sec. 925.11 (1)(a).

63. *West's Florida Statutes*, "Rules of Criminal Procedure," Rule 3.853.

64. Jo Becker, "Justices Leery of Appeal Changes: State Supreme Court Justices Have Plenty of Questions for Lawmakers, Who Were Defending a New Law to Limit Death Row Appeals," *St. Petersburg Times*, March 15, 2000; available at http://www.sptimes.com/News/031500/State/Justices_leery_of_app.shtml.

65. David Wasson, "Death Penalty Decision Bitter for Bush, GOP," *Tampa Tribune*, April 15, 2000.

66. Lucy Morgan, "Lawyers, Judges Fight Bills That Dilute Control: The President of the Florida Bar Argues That Dumping the Current Court System Would Set the State Back 100 Years," *St. Petersburg Times*, March 15, 2001; available at http://www.sptimes.com/News/031501/State/Lawyers__judges_fight.shtml.

67. Wasson, "Decision Bitter for Bush."

68. Jo Becker, "Measure to Weaken Judiciary Advances," *St. Petersburg Times*, March 16, 2000; available at http://www.sptimes.com/News/031500/State/Justices_leery_of_app.shtml.

69. Daniel Ruth, "The Plan to Turn Florida's Supreme Court into a PAC," editorial, *Tampa Tribune*, August 31, 2001.

70. Jo Becker, "Measure to Weaken Judiciary."

71. Glaberson, "States Rein in Excesses."

72. *SCHR Judges and Politics*, text accompanying note 210.

73. *DPIC Killing for Votes*, text accompanying note 18, citing N. Lewis, "G.O.P. to Challenge Judicial Nominees Who Oppose Death Penalty," *New York Times*, October 15, 1993.

74. *DPIC Killing for Votes*, text accompanying note 19.

75. *SCHR Political Attacks*, text accompanying note 51.

76. *SCHR Political Attacks*, text accompanying note 88.

77. *SCHR Judges and Politics*, text accompanying note 162.

78. *SCHR Political Attacks*, text accompanying notes 37–38.

79. *SCHR Political Attacks*, text accompanying notes 41–43 and note 43.

80. *SCHR Casualties and Costs*, 6.

81. *SCHR Judges and Politics*, text following note 212.

82. States with clemency powers residing in the governor: Alabama, California, Colorado, Kansas, Kentucky, New Jersey, New Mexico, New York, North Carolina, Oregon, South Carolina, Virginia, Washington, and Wyoming. *Source: DPIC Clemency*.

83. States where governor must have recommendation of clemency from board or advisory group: Arizona, Delaware, Florida (Florida's governor must have recommendation of board, on which he or she sits), Indiana, Louisiana, Montana, Oklahoma, Pennsylvania, and Texas. *Source: DPIC Clemency*.

84. States where governor has clemency power after nonbinding recommendation of clemency from board or advisory group: Arkansas, Illinois, Maryland, Mississippi, Missouri, New Hampshire, Ohio, South Dakota, and Tennessee. *Source: DPIC Clemency*.

85. States where board or advisory group makes the determination: Connecticut, Georgia, and Idaho. *Source: DPIC Clemency*.

86. States where governor sits on clemency board which makes the determination: Nebraska, Nevada, and Utah. *Source: DPIC Clemency*.

87. *DPIC Clemency*.

88. *DPIC Clemency*.

89. *DPIC Killing for Votes*, text accompanying note 74, citing Prejean, *Dead Man Walking*, 171.

90. *DPIC Killing for Votes*, text accompanying note 75, citing D. Rose, "Dead Man Stalking," *Observer Review* (London), April 21, 1996.

91. Randolph Pendleton, "Clemency Rarely Given in Florida," *Florida Times-Union*, June 24, 2000.

92. "Delaying an Execution: Governor Takes Heat for Decision," editorial, *Miami Herald*, December 9, 2002.

93. *State v. Makwanyane and M Mchunu*, Constitutional Court of the Republic of South Africa (Case No. CCT/3/94).

94. *State v. Makwanyane*, 80.

95. Governor George H. Ryan Sr., *Report of the Governor's Commission on Capital Punishment*, April 15, 2002, 1.

96. Ryan, *Report of Commission*, 1.

97. "The Future of Capital Punishment," editorial, *Chicago Tribune*, October 3, 2002.

98. Ryan, *Report of Commission*, 1.

99. Ryan, *Report of Commission*, 2.

100. *Chicago Tribune*, "The Future of Capital Punishment."

101. Governor George H. Ryan Sr., "Clemency for Illinois Death Row Inmates" (speech, Northwestern University College of Law, Chicago, Ill., January 11, 2003).

102. Steve Mills and Maurice Possley, "Decision Day for 156 Inmates: Ryan Poised to Make History after 3 Years of Debate on Death Penalty," *Chicago Tribune*, January 12, 2003.

103. "Ryan Pardons 4: Men Say They Were Tortured by Chicago Police," *Chicago Tribune*, January 10, 2003.

104. Associated Press, "Ryan Defends Death Row Decisions on Winfrey Show," *Chicago Tribune*, January 15, 2003.

105. Steve Mills and Christi Parsons, "The System Has Failed," *Chicago Tribune*, January 11, 2003.

106. Maurice Possley and Steve Mills, "Clemency for All: Ryan Commutes 164 Death Sentences to Life in Prison without Parole," *Chicago Tribune*, January 12, 2003.

107. Ryan, clemency speech, Northwestern University College of Law.

108. Nicole Ziegler Dizon (AP), "Death Penalty Opponents Hope Clemency Move

Leads to Wider Change; Supporters Question Motive," *Florida Times-Union*, January 12, 2003.

109. Dizon, "Death Penalty Opponents."

110. Wes Allison, "State Death Penalty Review? Not in Fla.," *St. Petersburg Times*, January 14, 2003; available at http://www.sptimes.com/2003/01/14/State/State_death_penalty_r.shtml.

111. "Mistakes on Death Row: Fairness Is Compromised," editorial, *Miami Herald*, January 15, 2003.

CHAPTER TWENTY

1. Matt Helms, "Now, the Healing Can Begin: Man Is Found Guilty of 4 Claw-Hammer Murders after Home Break-In," *Detroit Free Press*, October 19, 1999, 1A.

2. Helms, "Healing Can Begin."

3. Talmud, *Sanhedrin* 33b' (Gemara).

4. Talmud, *Sanhedrin* 33b' (Gemara).

5. Talmud, *Sanhedrin* 33b' (Gemara), note 3, citing *Rashi*.

6. Talmud, *Sanhedrin* 33b' (Gemara).

7. Talmud, *Sanhedrin* 33b' (Gemara), note 4, citing *Aruch LaNer*.

8. *DPIC New Voices*, citing "Nebraska Prosecutor Decides to 'End Suffering' by Not Seeking Death Penalty," *Lincoln Journal Star*, September 8, 2001.

9. Kathleen Dillon, letters to the editor, *Florida Times-Union*, January 24, 2003.

10. Robert Renny Cushing and Susannah Sheffer, *Dignity Denied: The Experience of Murder Victims' Family Members Who Oppose the Death Penalty*. 2d printing (Cambridge, Mass.: Murder Victims' Families for Reconciliation, 2002). For information, contact Murder Victims' Families for Reconciliation (MVFR), 2161 Massachusetts Avenue, Cambridge, Mass. 02140; phone: 617-868-0007; fax 617-354-2832; website: www.mvfr.org.

11. Cushing and Sheffer, *Dignity Denied*, 4.

12. Cushing and Sheffer, *Dignity Denied*, 9.

13. Cushing and Sheffer, *Dignity Denied*, 11.

14. Cushing and Sheffer, *Dignity Denied*, 11.

15. Cushing and Sheffer, *Dignity Denied*, 11.

16. Cushing and Sheffer, *Dignity Denied*, 12, note 2, citing *State of Nebraska ex rel. Gus Lamm and Audrey Lamm v. Nebraska Board of Pardons et al.*, 620 NW 2d 763 (Nebraska District Court).

17. Cushing and Sheffer, *Dignity Denied*, 14–15.

18. Cushing and Sheffer, *Dignity Denied*, 16.

19. Cushing and Sheffer, *Dignity Denied*, 18.

20. Cushing and Sheffer, *Dignity Denied*, 19–20.

21. Cushing and Sheffer, *Dignity Denied*, 20.

22. Cushing and Sheffer, *Dignity Denied*, 29.

23. Ryan, clemency speech, Northwestern University College of Law.

24. Helms, "Healing Can Begin."

25. Ryan, clemency speech, Northwestern University College of Law.

26. Ryan, clemency speech, Northwestern University College of Law.

27. Paul Pinkham, "Grief's Journey," *Florida Times-Union*, November 9, 2003, A1.

28. Gerald Kogan, former chief justice of the Florida Supreme Court, "Personal Experiences with the Death Penalty" (speech, St. Thomas More Society of Catholic Lawyers, Co-Cathedral of St. Thomas More, Tallahassee, Fla., October 10, 2003).

29. Jackie Halifax (AP), "Victims of Death Row Inmates Support, Oppose Executions, Second of a Series," *Tampa Tribune*, July 5, 2003.

30. *DPIC New Voices*, citing *Silverton Appeal Tribune*, March 12, 2003.

31. Johnnie Cabrera, "Forgiving the Unforgivable," *Family Circle*, August 6, 2002, 160.

32. Cabrera, "Forgiving."

33. Davidoff, "A Comparative Study," 111.

34. John Keilman, David Heinzmann, Shia Kapos, and Maurice Possley, "Relatives of Victims Feel Cheated," *Chicago Tribune*, January 12, 2003.

35. *DPIC What's New* (August 7, 2003), citing *Baltimore Sun*, July 26, 2003.

CHAPTER TWENTY-TWO

1. "DNA Exoneration Changes Former Detective's Mind about Capital Punishment," *Ft. Lauderdale Sun-Sentinel*, June 2, 2001.

2. *DPIC New Voices*, citing Associated Press, July 15, 2002.

3. *DPIC New Voices*, citing *Fort Worth Star-Telegram*, July 24, 2001.

4. Ryan, clemency speech, Northwestern University College of Law.

5. Kari Lydersen, "Death Penalty Foes See Progress in Illinois," *Washington Post*, March 11, 2002, A2.

6. *DPIC New Voices*, citing *Catholics against Capital Punishment: News Notes*, November 26, 2001.

7. Brooke A. Masters, "Pat Robertson Seeks Moratorium on U.S. Executions," *Washington Post*, April 8, 2000. Reverend Pat Robertson was speaking at the Symposium on Religion and the Death Penalty, College of William and Mary.

8. *Talmud Reference Guide*, par. 5, 204.

9. *Talmud Reference Guide*, par. 5, 204.

10. Talmud, *Sanhedrin* 81b[3].

11. *DPIC LWOP*.

12. *DPIC LWOP*.

13. Snyder, *Protestant Ethic and Punishment*, 112–17.

14. Snyder, *Protestant Ethic and Punishment*, 112–17.

15. *Essential Talmud*, 155.

16. Snyder, "Jesus and Me: The Individualization of Redemptive Grace," in *Protestant Ethic and Punishment*, 55–73.

17. Christopher D. Marshall, *Beyond Retribution: A New Testament Vision for Justice, Crime, and Punishment* (Grand Rapids, Mich.: Wm. B. Eerdmans, 2001), 16–31.

18. 2 Sam. 11–12.

19. Acts 9:4–6.

20. Mathews, "We Who Own Slaves," 136.

21. Mathews, "We Who Own Slaves," 136.

22. Genovese, *A Consuming Fire*, 5–6.

23. Genovese, *A Consuming Fire*, 8–9.

24. Genovese, *A Consuming Fire*, 9.

25. Genovese, *A Consuming Fire*, 5.

BIBLIOGRAPHY

Ahlstrom, Sydney E. *A Religious History of the American People*. New Haven, Conn.: Yale University Press, 1972.

Allison, Wes. "State Death Penalty Review? Not in Fla." *St. Petersburg Times*, January 14, 2003. Available at http://www.sptimes.com/2003/01/14/State/State_death_penalty_r.shtml.

Amnesty International. "No Rush to Judgment." *Amnesty Action*, fall 1999.

Amnesty International Canada. "Time for Humanitarian Intervention: The Imminent Execution of Larry Robison. July 14, 1999. Available at http://www.amnesty.ca/library/1999/amr51107.htm.

Armstrong, Ken, and Steve Mills, "Death Row Justice Derailed." *Chicago Tribune*, November 14, 1999.

———. "Gatekeeper Court Keeps Gates Shut: Justices Prove Reluctant to Nullify Cases." *Chicago Tribune*, June 12, 2000.

———. "Inept Defenses Cloud Verdict." *Chicago Tribune*, November 15, 1999.

———, and Maurice Possley. "Coercive and Illegal Tactics Torpedo Scores of Cook County Murder Cases." *Chicago Tribune*, December 16, 2001.

———. "Illegal Arrests Yield False Confessions." *Chicago Tribune*, December 17, 2001.

Armstrong, Ken, and Maurice Possley. "Verdict Dishonor." *Chicago Tribune*, January 10, 1999. Available at http://www.chicagotribune.com/news/specials.

———, and Steve Mills. "Officers Ignore Laws Set Up to Guard Kids." *Chicago Tribune*, December 18, 2001.

Associated Press. "Chemist's Testimony Refuted 1 Year after Man's Execution." *Florida Times-Union*, August 30, 2001.

———. "Death Sentence Tossed over Reliance on Bible." *Florida Times-Union*, May 25, 2003.

———. "Debate over IQ, Executions: Panel Considers Retardation Ban." *Florida Times-Union*, January 29, 2000.

———. "Inmate Wins DNA Request." *Miami Herald*, August 29, 2001.

———. "Innocent Man: I Confessed to Murder under Electric Chair Threat." *Miami Herald*, October 3, 2003.

———. "Justice Questions Guilt of Executed." *Gainesville Sun*, December 24, 1998.

———. "Lawmaker's Efforts Fails to Raise Minimum Age for Death Penalty," April 1, 2004.

———. "Ryan Defends Death Row Decisions on Winfrey Show." *Chicago Tribune*, January 15, 2003.

———. "Two Broward Detectives Cleared in Death Row Perjury Case." *Florida Times-Union*, July 6, 2001.

————. "Witnesses in Death Row Release Plead Guilty to Perjury." *Tampa Tribune*, November 5, 2003.

Bahnsen, Greg L. *Theonomy in Christian Ethics*. Nutley, N.J.: Craig Press, 1977.

Baldus, David C., Charles A. Pulaski Jr., and George Woodworth. "Arbitrariness and Discrimination in the Administration of the Death Penalty: A Challenge to State Supreme Courts." 15 *Stetson Law Review* 2 (1986).

Banner, Stuart. *The Death Penalty: An American History*. Cambridge: Harvard University Press, 2002.

Becker, Jo. "Court Raises Execution Age to 17: Florida Becomes the 16th State to Prohibit Execution of 16-Year-Old Defendants after the State Supreme Court Ruling." *St. Petersburg Times*, July 9, 1999. Available at http://www.sptimes.com/News/70999/State/Court_raises_executio.shtml.

————. "A Glimpse at Mental Illness." *St. Petersburg Times*, March 14, 2000. Available at http://www.sptimes.com/News/031400/State/A_glimpse_at_mental_i.shtml.

————. "Group Ponders Death Penalty: A Task Force Discusses Whether the State Should Execute Mentally Retarded Inmates." *St. Petersburg Times*, January 29, 2000.

————. "Justices Leery of Appeal Changes: State Supreme Court Justices Have Plenty of Questions for Lawmakers, Who Were Defending a New Law to Limit Death Row Appeals." *St. Petersburg Times*, March 15, 2000. Available at http://www.sptimes.com/News/031500/State/Justices_leery_of_app.shtml.

————. "Lawmaker: Crucify Inmate. Fed Up with the Delays Keeping a Killer Who Thinks He's Jesus Christ out of the Electric Chair, State Rep. Howard Futch Makes a Suggestion." *St. Petersburg Times*, October 7, 1999. Available at http://www.sptimes.com/News/100799/State/Lawmaker__Crucify_inm.shtml.

————. "Measure to Weaken Judiciary Advances." *St. Petersburg Times*, March 16, 2000. Available at http://www.sptimes.com/News/031500/State/Justices_leery_of_app.shtml.

————, and William Yardley, "Bush Backs Off Firm Limit to Death Row Appeals: The Deal with Legislative Leaders Is Made on the Eve of the Opening of a Special Session on the Death Penalty." *St. Petersburg Times*, January 5, 2000. Available at http://www.sptimes.com/News/010500/news_pf/State/Bush_backs_off_firm_l.shtml.

Berg, Thomas C. "Religious Conservatives and the Death Penalty." 9 *William and Mary Bill of Rights Journal* 31 (December 2000).

Bessler, John D. *Kiss of Death: America's Love Affair with the Death Penalty*. Boston: Northeastern University Press, 2003.

Birmingham Post-Herald. Series: "Execution of Justice." December 14, 2001. Available at http://www.postherald.com/justice.shtml.

Blume, John H., and Sheri Lynn Johnson. "Limiting Religious Arguments in Capital Cases." Paper presented at A Call for Reckoning: A Conference Reader on Religion and the Death Penalty, sponsored by Pew Forum on

Religious and Public Life, University of Chicago Divinity School, Chicago, Ill., January 25, 2002.

Bonhoeffer, Dietrich. *The Cost of Discipleship*, rev. ed. New York: Macmillan, 1959.

Bonner, Raymond. "Death Row Inmate Is Freed after DNA Test Clears Him." *New York Times*, August 24, 2001.

Bonowitz, Abraham J. "Florida Cannot Afford the Death Penalty." *Fort Lauderdale Sun-Sentinel*, May 19, 2003.

Bowden, Henry Warner. *Dictionary of American Religious Biography*. Westport, Conn.: Greenwood Press, 1977.

Bragg, Jeanne. *The Truth Shall Set Him Free: A True Story of Murder, Lies, and a Police Officer's Conviction of Convenience*. Kearney, Nebr.: Morris Publishing, 2001.

Bright, Stephen B. "Can Judicial Independence Be Attained in the South? Overcoming History, Elections, and Misperceptions about the Role of the Judiciary." 14 *Georgia State University Law Review* 817 (July 1998), also available at http://www.schr.org/center.

———. "Counsel for the Poor: The Death Penalty: Not for the Worst Crime but for the Worst Lawyer." 103 *Yale Law Journal* 1835 (1994), also available at http://www.schr.org/center.

———. "The Death Penalty: Casualties and Costs of the War on Crime." Lecture, the City Club of Cleveland, November 7, 1997, also available at http://www.schr.org/center.

———. "Discrimination, Death, and Denial: The Tolerance of Racial Discrimination in the Infliction of the Death Penalty." 35 *Santa Clara Law Review* 433 (1995), also available at http://www.schr.org/center.

———. "Is Fairness Irrelevant? The Evisceration of Federal Habeas Corpus Review and Limits on the Ability of State Courts to Protect Fundamental Rights." 54 *Washington and Lee Law Review* 1 (winter 1997), also available at http://www.schr.org/center.

———. "Political Attacks on the Judiciary: Can Justice Be Done amid Efforts to Intimidate and Remove Judges from Office for Unpopular Decisions?" 72 *New York University Law Review*, 308 (May 1997), also available at http://www.schr.org/center.

———. *A Preference for Vengeance: The Death Penalty and the Treatment of Prisoners in Georgia—A Report on Human Rights Violations in Georgia*. Atlanta: SCHR, 1996, also available at http://www.schr.org/center.

———. *Restrictions on Federal Review of Death Sentences Passed by Congress in 1996*. Atlanta: SCHR, 1997, also available at http://www.schr.org/center.

———. "Will the Death Penalty Remain Alive in the Twenty-first Century? International Norms, Discrimination, Arbitrariness, and the Risk of Executing the Innocent." 1 *Wisconsin Law Review* 1 (2001), also available at http://www.schr.org/center.

———, and Patrick J. Keenan, "Judges and the Politics of Death: Deciding between the Bill of Rights and the Next Election in Capital Cases." 73 *Boston University Law Review* 759 (May 1995), also available at http://www.schr.org/center.

Bright, Taylor. "Fighting for Another Chance." *Birmingham Post-Herald*, December 14, 2001.

———. "Guilty Until Proven Innocent? Four Men Are Proof That Not Everyone Sent to Death Row Should Be There." *Birmingham Post-Herald*, December 14, 2001.

———. "Love Letters Almost Fatal" *Birmingham Post-Herald*, December 14, 2001.

Brink, Graham. "Officers' Discipline Is 'Slap on the Wrist.'" *St. Petersburg Times*, August 3, 2002. Available at http://www.sptimes.com/2002/08/03/Tampa Bay/Officers__discipline_.shtml.

Burnett, Cathleen. *Justice Denied: Clemency Appeals in Death Penalty Cases*. Boston: Northeastern University Press, 2002.

Burr, Richard, and Mandy Welch. "Killing Kids Who Kill: Desecrating the Sanctuary of Childhood." 29 *St. Mary's Law Journal* 4 (1998).

Cabrera, Johnnie. "Forgiving the Unforgivable." *Family Circle*, August 6, 2002.

Camp, Ken. "Christian Life Commission Endorses Moratorium on Death Penalty." *Baptist Standard*, January 14, 2003.

Chicago Tribune. "The Future of Capital Punishment." Editorial. October 3, 2002. Available at http://www.chicagotribune.com/news/specials.

———. "Ryan Pardons 4: Men Say They Were Tortured by Chicago Police." January 10, 2003.

———. Series: "Death Penalty in Illinois." November 14–18, 1999. Available at http://www.chicagotribune.com/news/specials.

———. Series: "Cops and Confessions." December 16, 2001–January 6, 2002. Available at http://www.chicagotribune.com/news/specials.

———. Series: "Death Penalty in America." June 11–12, 2000, and December 17–18, 2000. Available at http://www.chicagotribune.com/news/specials.

———. "When Believing Isn't Seeing." Editorial. September 30, 2002. Available at http://www.chicagotribune.com/news/specials.

Childress James F., and John Macquarrie, eds. *The Westminster Dictionary of Christian Ethics*. Philadelphia: Westminster Press, 1986.

Christian, Paula. "Aisenberg Prosecutor Moved." *Tampa Tribune*, August 1, 2001.

———. "Aisenberg Prosecutor Removed from Post." *Tampa Tribune*, July 20, 2001.

———. "Prosecutor, under Scrutiny, Quits." *Tampa Tribune*, May 23, 2001.

Clark, Lesley. "Death Penalty Office Targeted." *Miami Herald*, January 22, 2003.

———. "DNA Law Facing Tough Battle: Lawmakers Want to Narrow Scope." *Miami Herald*, August 27, 2001.

Clary, Susan. "DNA Results Won't Set Zeigler Free." *Orlando Sentinel*, June 6, 2002.

Clines, Francis X. "Work by Expert Witness Is Now on Trial." *New York Times*, September 5, 2001.

Cohen, Abraham. *Everyman's Talmud: The Major Teachings of the Rabbinical Sages*. New York: Schocken Books, 1949.

Colarossi, Anthony. "Murder Case Appeal Relies on DNA." *Orlando Sentinel*, January 26, 2003.

Cole, Marcia. "Suit: Death Defense Is a Sham." 21 *National Law Journal* 17, December 21, 1998.

Crüsemann, Frank. *The Torah: Theology and Social History of Old Testament Law*. Minneapolis: Fortress Press, 1996.

Cushing, Robert Renny, and Susannah Sheffer. *Dignity Denied: The Experience of Murder Victims' Family Members Who Oppose the Death Penalty*. 2d printing. Cambridge, Mass.: Murder Victims' Families for Reconciliation, 2002. Available at http://www.mvfr.org/.

Daily Business Review (Miami, Fla.). "Death Appeals Not Quite Dead." May 20, 2003.

Dallas Morning News. Editorial. November 20, 2000.

Davey, Monica, and Steve Mills. "Ryan Issues Blanket Clemency." *Chicago Tribune*, January 11, 2003.

Davidoff, Steven. "A Comparative Study of the Jewish and the United States Constitutional Law of Capital Punishment." 3 *ILSA Journal of International and Comparative Law* 1 (fall 1996).

DeMarzo, Wanda J., and Daniel de Vise. "Police Ignored Defects in Cases." *Miami Herald*, December 23, 2002.

———. "Zealous Grilling by Police Tainted 38 Murder Cases." *Miami Herald*, December 22, 2002.

Dieter, Richard C. *Cases of Innocence: 1973–Present*. Washington, D.C.: DPIC, 2004 (continuously updated), http://www.deathpenaltyinfo.org.

———. *Clemency: Clemency Process by State* (Washington, D.C.: DPIC, 2004 (continuously updated), http://www.deathpenaltyinfo.org.

———. *The Death Penalty in Black and White: Who Lives—Who Dies—Who Decides: New Studies on Racism in Capital Punishment*. Washington, D.C.: DPIC, 1998, also available at http://www.deathpenaltyinfo.org.

———. *The Death Penalty in 2000: Year End Report*. Washington, D.C.: DPIC, 2000, also available at http://www.deathpenaltyinfo.org.

———. *The Death Penalty in 2001: Year End Report*. Washington, D.C.: DPIC, 2001, also available at http://www.deathpenaltyinfo.org.

———. *The Death Penalty in 2002: Year End Report*. Washington, D.C.: DPIC, 2002, also available at http://www.deathpenaltyinfo.org.

———. *The Death Penalty in 2003: Year End Report*. Washington, D.C.: DPIC, 2003, also available at http://www.deathpenaltyinfo.org.

———. *Execution of Juvenile Offenders*. Washington, D.C.: DPIC, 2004 (continuously updated), http://www.deathpenaltyinfo.org.

———. *Facts about Deterrence and the Death Penalty*. Washington, D.C.: DPIC, 2004 (continuously updated), http://www.deathpenaltyinfo.org.

———. *Freed from Death Row*. Washington, D.C.: DPIC, 2004 (continuously updated), http://www.deathpenaltyinfo.org.

———. *Federal Death Penalty of the U.S. Government*. Washington, D.C.: DPIC, 2004 (continuously updated), http://www.deathpenaltyinfo.org.

———. *Innocence and the Death Penalty*. Washington, D.C.: DPIC, 2004 (continuously updated), http://www.deathpenaltyinfo.org.

———. *Innocence and the Death Penalty: The Increasing Danger of Executing the Innocent*.

Washington, D.C.: DPIC, 1997, also available at http://www.deathpenal
tyinfo.org.

————. *Juveniles and the Death Penalty.* Washington, D.C.: DPIC, 2004 (continuously updated), http://www.deathpenaltyinfo.org.

————. *Killing for Votes: The Dangers of Politicizing the Death Penalty Process.* Washington, D.C.: DPIC, 1996, also available at http://www.deathpenalty
info.org.

————. *Life without Parole.* Washington, D.C.: DPIC, 2004 (continuously updated), http://www.deathpenaltyinfo.org.

————. *Mental Retardation and the Death Penalty.* Washington, D.C.: DPIC, 2004
(continuously updated), http://www.deathpenaltyinfo.org.

————. *Minimum Death Penalty Ages By American Jurisdiction.* Washington, D.C.:
DPIC, 2004 (continuously updated), http://www.deathpenaltyinfo.org.

————. *New Voices, Articles, and Statements on the Death Penalty.* Washington, D.C.:
DPIC, 2004 (continuously updated), http://www.deathpenaltyinfo.org.

————. *On the Front Line: Law Enforcement Views on the Death Penalty.* Washington,
D.C.: DPIC, 1995, also available at http://www.deathpenaltyinfo.org.

————. *Race of Defendants Executed Since 1976.* Washington, D.C.: DPIC, 2004,
(continuously updated), http://www.deathpenaltyinfo.org. (Last updated
as used herein with execution in Virginia on March 31, 2004.)

————. *Summaries of Recent Poll Findings.* Washington, D.C.: DPIC, 2004 (continuously updated), http://www.deathpenaltyinfo.org.

————. *What's New.* Washington, D.C.: DPIC, 1998–2004 (continuously updated), http://www.deathpenaltyinfo.org.

Duffy, Brian C. "Barring Foul Blows: An Argument for a Per Se Reversible-Error
Rule for Prosecutors' Use of Religious Arguments in the Sentencing Phase
of Capital Cases." *50 Vanderbilt Law Review* 1335 (1997).

Eggen, Dan. "Ashcroft Aggressively Pursues Death Penalty." *Washington Post,* July
1, 2002.

Elliot, Neil. "The Canonical Betrayal of the Apostle: Paul and Slavery." Chap. 2
in *Liberating Paul: The Justice of God and the Politics of the Apostle.* Maryknoll,
N.Y.: Orbis Books, 1994.

Epstein, I., ed. *Hebrew–English Edition of the Babylonian Talmud.* Translated by Samuel
Daiches and Israel W. Slotki. London: Soncino, 1971.

Farrington, Brendan (AP). "DNA Clears Retarded Inmate." *Miami Herald,* June 16,
2001.

Ferris, Frances. "One in Six Death Row Inmates Defended at Trial by Lawyers
Disciplined by State Bar." Raleigh, N.C.: Common Sense Foundation,
2002.

Finch, Phillip. *Fatal Flaw: A True Story of Malice and Murder in a Small Southern Town.*
New York: Villard Books, 1992.

Fins, Deborah. *Death Row U.S.A., Winter 2004, A Quarterly Report by the Criminal
Justice Project of the NAACP Legal Defense and Education Fund, Inc.* New York:
NAACP Legal Defense Fund, 2004 (updated quarterly), available at
http://www.deathpenaltyinfo.org/DEATHROWUSArecent.pdf.

Florida Times-Union. "Florida Briefs: Prosecutor Reassigned after Case Bungled." July 31, 2002.

Follick, Joe. "State-funded Counsel for Death Row Reviewed." *Tampa Tribune,* March 28, 2003.

Fort Lauderdale Sun-Sentinel. "DNA Exoneration Changes Former Detective's Mind about Capital Punishment." June 2, 2001.

Fort Walton Daily News (Fla.). "Court: Prosecutors' Misconduct Too Frequent." April 2, 1999.

Freedberg, Sydney P. "Bush Rejects Idea of Death Penalty Ban." *St. Petersburg Times,* February 15, 2000. Available at http://www.sptimes.com/News/021500/State/Bush_rejects_idea_of_.shtml.

———. "Bush to Ex-Justice: Name Names: Gerald Kogan Says Some Innocent People Have Been Executed. The Governor Says Identify Them." *St. Petersburg Times,* February 29, 2000. Available at http://www.sptimes.com/News/022900/State/Bush_to_ex_justice__N.shtml.

———. "DNA Clears Inmate Too Late: The FBI Clears Death-Row Inmate of Rape and Murder 10½ Months after Cancer Killed Him." *St. Petersburg Times,* December 15, 2000. Available at http://www.sptimes.com/News/121500/State/DNA_clears_inmate_too.shtml.

———. "DNA Testing Denied to Inmates Seeking Justice: Several Florida Prosecutors Are Blocking the Requests, Mostly on Procedural Grounds." *St. Petersburg Times,* June 21, 1999.

———. "Ex-Death Row Inmate Gets Walking Papers." *St. Petersburg Times,* March 17, 2000. Available at http://www.sptimes.com/News/031700/State/Ex_death_row_inmate_g.shtml.

———. "Freed from Death Row: Florida Leads the Nation in Wrongful Death Sentences with 20. What Has Become of the Survivors?" *St. Petersburg Times,* July 4, 1999. Available at http://www.sptimes.com/Archive/070499/State.shtml.

———. "Good Cop, Bad Cop: Special Report: Fallout from an FBI Scandal." *St. Petersburg Times,* March 4, 2001. Available at http://www.sptimes.com/News/030401/Worldandnation/Good_cop__bad_cop_.shtml.

———. "Murder Witness Admits He Lied." *St. Petersburg Times,* November 28, 2001. Available at http://www.sptimes.com/News/112801/State/Murder_witness_admits.shtml.

———, and William Yardley. "The Race Issue: Governor Bush Forms a Task Force to Study the Role of Race in Capital Sentencing." *St. Petersburg Times,* January 7, 2000.

Friedman, Lawrence M. *Crime and Punishment in American History.* New York: Basic Books, 1993.

Genovese, Eugene D. *A Consuming Fire: The Fall of the Confederacy in the Mind of the White Christian South.* Athens, Ga.: University of Georgia Press, 1998.

Gershman, Bennett L. "The New Prosecutors." *53 University of Pittsburgh Law Review* 393 (1992).

———. *Prosecutorial Misconduct.* 2d ed. St. Paul. West Group, 2001.

Gibbs, Nancy. "Thou Shalt Be Removed: Alabama's Ten Commandments Judge

Is Tossed from Office. Did He Want This All Along?" *Time Magazine*, November 24, 2003.

Glaberson, William. "States Take Steps to Rein in Excesses of Judicial Politicking." *New York Times*, June 15, 2001.

Glod, Maria, and Steven Ginsberg. "Va. Delays Change on Evidence Rule: Crime Panel Wants Legislators to Decide Deadline for Seeking New Trial." *Washington Post*, January 9, 2003.

Goldenberg, David M. *The Curse of Ham: Race and Slavery in Early Judaism, Christianity and Islam*. Princeton: Princeton University Press, 2003.

Goldwurm, Hersch, ed. *Talmud Bavli: Tractate Kiddushin*. ArtScroll Series, Schottenstein Edition. Brooklyn: Mesorah Publications, 1993.

———, ed., *Talmud Bavli: Tractate Makkoth*. ArtScroll Series, Schottenstein Edition. Brooklyn: Mesorah Publications, 1993.

———, ed., *Talmud Bavli: Tractate Sanhedrin*. ArtScroll Series, Schottenstein Edition. Brooklyn: Mesorah Publications, 1993.

Goode, Erica. "Minorities' Care for Mental Ills Is Called Inferior." *New York Times*, August 27, 2001.

Graczyk, Michael. "For First Time in Decades, Texas Executes White Man for Killing Black; Critics Say System Biased." Associated Press, September 20, 2003.

Green, Joel B., and Mark D. Baker. *Recovering the Scandal of the Cross: Atonement in New Testament and Contemporary Contexts*. Downers Grove, Ill.: InterVarsity Press, 2000.

Gross, Samuel R. *The Risks of Death: Why Erroneous Convictions Are Common in Capital Cases*, 44 Buffalo Law Review 469 (1996).

———, and Robert Mauro. *Death and Discrimination: Racial Disparities in Capital Sentencing*. Boston: Northeastern University Press, 1989.

———. "Patterns of Death: An Analysis of Racial Disparities in Capital Sentencing and Homicide Victimization." 37 *Stanford Law Review* 27 (1984).

Halifax, Jackie (AP). "Court Considers Ban on Execution of Mentally Retarded." *Tampa Tribune*, August 25, 2003.

———. "Victims of Death Row Inmates Support, Oppose Executions, Second of a Series." *Tampa Tribune*, July 5, 2003.

Hanks, Gardner C. *Against the Death Penalty: Christian and Secular Arguments against Capital Punishment*. Scottdale, Pa.: Herald, 1997.

———. *Capital Punishment and the Bible*. Scottdale, Pa.: Herald Press, 2002.

Harrison, Everett F., Geoffrey W. Bromiley, and Carl F. Henry, eds. *Wycliffe Dictionary of Theology*. Peabody, Mass.: Hendrickson Publishers, 1960.

Hastings, James, ed. *Encyclopedia of Religion and Ethics*. New York: Charles Scribner's Sons, 1955.

Hauserman, Julie. "Law Bans Execution of Retarded: Governor Jeb Bush Signs a Measure That Will Let Experts Evaluate Defendants. If Found to Be Mentally Retarded, They Won't Face the Death Penalty." *St. Petersburg Times*, June 13, 2001. Available at http://www.sptimes.com/News/061301/State/Law_bans_execution_of.shtml.

Helms, Matt. "Now, the Healing Can Begin: Man Is Found Guilty of 4 Claw-

Hammer Murders after Home Break-In." *Detroit Free Press*, October 19, 1999.

Henry, Matthew. *Commentary on the Whole Bible*. Grand Rapids, Mich.: Zondervan, 1960.

Herring, Basil F. *Jewish Ethics and Halakhah for Our Time: Sources and Commentary*. New York: KTAV Publishing and Yeshiva University Press, 1984.

Hershman, Abraham M., trans. *The Code of Maimonides (Book Fourteen): The Book of Judges*. New Haven, Conn.: Yale University Press, 1949.

Holt, Douglas, and Steve Mills. "Double Murder Case Unravels: Once Two Days Away from Execution, Inmate May Go Free after Another Man Implicates Himself in Two Murders." *Chicago Tribune*, February 4, 1999.

Hoppe, C. "Executions Cost Texas Millions." *Dallas Morning News*, March 8, 1992.

Horkan, Thomas A., Jr. "'Tis Not the Season for This." *Florida Catholic*, December 2, 1999.

Human Rights Watch. *Ill-equipped: U.S. Prisons and Offenders with Mental Illness*. New York: Human Rights Watch, 2003.

Hustead, Jayne. "Death Row Conviction Overturned." *Vero Beach Press Journal*, July 5, 2003.

Kallestad, Brent (AP). "Crist Backs Death Row Plan." *Miami Herald*, January 30, 2003.

Karp, David. "Freed after Years on Death Row: A Man Convicted of a 1986 Murder Is Released; the State Says It Lacks Enough Evidence to Retry Him." *St. Petersburg Times*, January 24, 2003.

Keilman, John, David Heinzmann, Shia Kapos, and Maurice Possley. "Relatives of Victims Feel Cheated." *Chicago Tribune*, January 12, 2003.

Killians, Mark D. "Court Sets Procedures for Postconviction DNA Testing." *Florida Bar News*, November 1, 2001.

Kogan, Gerald, former chief justice of the Florida Supreme Court. "Personal Experiences with the Death Penalty." Speech, St. Thomas More Society of Catholic Lawyers, Co-Cathedral of St. Thomas More, Tallahassee, Fla., October 10, 2003.

Kotlowitz, Alex. "In the Face of Death." *New York Times Magazine*, July 6, 2003, 34.

Krueger, Curtis. "State Mental Hospital Shuts Down." *St. Petersburg Times*, February 9, 2002. Available at http://www.sptimes.com/2002/02/09/State/State _mental_hospital.shtml.

Lane, Charles. "Judge Says Executions Violate Constitution." *Washington Post*, July 2, 2002.

Laughlin, Meg. "Death Row Inmate Closer to New Trial after Judge's Ruling: Man in Prison for 22 Years." *Miami Herald*, December 31, 2002.

———. "Federal Court to Revisit 35-Year Old Murder Case." *Miami Herald*, July 8, 2001.

———. "Judge Grants Inmate New Trial." *Miami Herald*, September 20, 2002.

———. "State Blocks Death Row Inmate's Release One Day Before Deadline." *Miami Herald*, January 29, 2003.

————. "1984 Murder Trial Revisited." *Miami Herald*, July 10, 2001.

Levine, Susan, and Lori Montgomery. "Large Racial Disparity Found by Study of Md. Death Penalty." *Washington Post*, January 8, 2003.

Liebman, James S., Jeffrey Fagan, and Valerie West. "A Broken System: Error Rates in Capital Cases, 1973–1995." *The Justice Project: Campaign for Criminal Justice Reform*. New York: Columbia Law School, 2000. Available at http://justice.policy.net/jpreport/index.html.

————. *A Broken System, Part 2: Why There Is So Much Error in Capital Cases, and What Can Be Done about It*. New York: Columbia Law School Publications, 2002. Available at http://www.law.columbia.edu/brokensystem2/index2.html.

Luscombe, Belinda. "When the Evidence Lies: Joyce Gilchrist Helped Send Dozens to Death Row. The Forensic Scientist's Errors Are Putting Capital Punishment under a Microscope." *Time Magazine*, May 21, 2001.

Lydersen, Kari. "Death Penalty Foes See Progress in Illinois." *Washington Post*, March 11, 2002.

Mackey, Philip English, ed. *Voices against Death: American Opposition to Capital Punishment, 1787–1975*. New York: Burt Franklin, 1976.

Marshall, Christopher D. *Beyond Retribution: A New Testament Vision for Justice, Crime, and Punishment*. Grand Rapids, Mich.: Wm. B. Eerdmans, 2001.

Masters, Brooke A. "Pat Robertson Seeks Moratorium on U.S. Executions." *Washington Post*, April 8, 2000.

Mathews, Donald G. "'We Who Own Slaves Honor God's Law.'" Chap. 4 in *Religion in the Old South*. Edited by Martin E. Marty. Chicago: University of Chicago Press, 1977.

McKenzie, John L. *Dictionary of the Bible*. New York: Collier Books/Macmillan, 1965.

Megivern, James J. *The Death Penalty: An Historical and Theological Survey*. Mahwah, N.J.: Paulist Press, 1997.

Mello, Michael A. "Florida: The Buckle of the Death Belt." Chap. 1 in *Dead Wrong: A Death Row Lawyer Speaks Out against Capital Punishment*. Madison, Wis.: University of Wisconsin Press, 1997.

Mendelsohn, S. *The Criminal Jurisprudence of the Ancient Hebrews: Compiled from the Talmud and Other Rabbinical Writings, and Compared with Roman and English Penal Jurisprudence*. 2d ed. New York: Hermon Press, 1968.

Merker Rosenberg, Irene, and Yale L. Rosenberg. "Guilt: Henry Friendly Meets the MaHaRal of Prague." 90 *Michigan Law Review* 604 (December 1991).

————. "Lone Star Liberal Musings: 'Eye for Eye' and the Death Penalty." 1998 *Utah Law Review* 505.

Miami Herald. "Delaying an Execution: Governor Takes Heat for Decision." Editorial. December 9, 2002.

————. "For Justice, Get It Right." Editorial. August 28, 2001.

————. "Law Hinders Weeding Out Bad Cops." Editorial. July 15, 2001.

————. "A Life Sentence on Death Row." Editorial. August 5, 2001.

————. "Mistakes on Death Row: Fairness Is Compromised." Editorial. January 15, 2003.

———. Series: "Spotlight on False Confessions." December 22–24, 2002. Available at http://www.miami.com/mld/miamiherald/news/state.

Mielziner, Moses. *Introduction to the Talmud.* New York: Bloch Publishing, 1968.

Mills, Steve. "Questions of Innocence: Legal Roadblocks Thwart New Evidence on Appeal." *Chicago Tribune,* December 18, 2000.

———, and Ken Armstrong. "Convicted by a Hair." *Chicago Tribune,* November 18, 1999.

———. "The Jailhouse Informant." *Chicago Tribune,* November 16, 1999.

———. "A Tortured Path to Death Row." *Chicago Tribune,* November 17, 1999.

———, and Douglas Holt. "Flawed Trials Lead to Death Chamber: Bush Confident in System Rife with Problems." *Chicago Tribune,* June 11, 2000.

Mills, Steve, and Christi Parsons. "The System Has Failed." *Chicago Tribune,* January 11, 2003.

Mills, Steve, and Maurice Possley. "Decision Day for 156 Inmates: Ryan Poised to Make History after 3 Years of Debate on Death Penalty." *Chicago Tribune,* January 12, 2003.

———, and Ken Armstrong. "3 Cases Weaken under Scrutiny." *Chicago Tribune,* December 17, 2000.

———. "When Jail Is No Alibi in Murders." *Chicago Tribune,* December 19, 2001.

Mitchell, Garry (AP). "Prosecutors Drop Baby Murder Case against Mentally Retarded Man." *Florida Times-Union,* January 10, 2003.

Montgomery, Lori. "Steele Seeks New Study of Death Penalty Cases: Finding of Bias against Blacks in Prosecutions Concerns Lieutenant Governor." *Washington Post,* January 26, 2003.

Morgan, Lucy. "Lawyers, Judges Fight Bills That Dilute Control: The President of the Florida Bar Argues That Dumping the Current Court System Would Set the State Back 100 Years." *St. Petersburg Times,* March 15, 2001. Available at http://www.sptimes.com/News/031501/State/Lawyers__jud ges_fight.shtml.

Moushey, Bill, and Bob Martinson. "Win at All Costs: Government Misconduct in the Name of Expedient Justice." *Pittsburgh Post-Gazette,* November 22, 1998. Available at http://www.post-gazette.com/win.

———. "Win at All Costs: Out of Control." *Pittsburgh-Post Gazette,* November 22, 1998. Available at http://www.post-gazette.com/win/day1_1a.asp.

NAMI. "Criminal Justice and Forensic Issues." Chap. 9 in *Policy Platform.* Arlington, Va.: NAMI: The Nation's Voice on Mental Illness, 2001. Available at http://www.nami.org/update/platform/criminal.htm.

———. "The Criminalization of Mental Illness: The Criminalization Trend Is Worse than Ever." In *Advocacy: Public Policy and Legal: Where We Stand.* Arlington, Va.: NAMI: The Nation's Voice on Mental Illness, 2002. Available at http://www.nami.org/update/unitedcriminal.html.

National Conference of Catholic Bishops/United States Catholic Conference. *To End the Death Penalty: A Report of the National Jewish/Catholic Consultation.* Washington, D.C: NCCB/USCC, 1999.

Neusner, Jacob. *The Tosefta Translated from the Hebrew, Fourth Division NEZIQIN (The Order of Damages).* New York: KTAV Publishing, 1981.

New York Times. "Practice Does Not Make Perfect." Editorial. February 23, 2002.

Olsen, Lise. "Life and Death in Lawyers' Hands." *Seattle Post-Intelligencer,* August 6, 2001. Available at http://seattlepi.nwsource.com/local/33820_defense 06.shtml.

O'Neill, Helen. "The Perfect Witness." *Washington Post,* March 4, 2001.

Orlando Sentinel. "Revisit Death Penalty." Editorial. August 19, 2001.

Owens, Sherri M., Rich McCay, and Jason Garcia. "Girl's Convicted Killer Seeks Freedom." *Orlando Sentinel,* September 14, 2003.

Pendleton, Randolph. "Clemency Rarely Given in Florida." *Florida Times-Union,* June 24, 2000.

Phillips, Jeb. "Does Race Decide Who Dies? Some Say Color of Defendant, Victim Plays Significant Role." *Birmingham Post-Herald,* December 14, 2001.

————. "Justice at 50 Cents an Hour: Defending Death Row Case Drove Lawyer into Bankruptcy." *Birmingham Post-Herald,* December 14, 2001.

————. "Some Face Death without Attorney." *Birmingham Post-Herald,* December 14, 2001.

————. "Talladega: Death Row Country: Is Fairness Missing from the State's Use of Capital Punishment?" *Birmingham Post-Herald,* December 14, 2001.

Pinkham, Paul. "Grief's Journey." *Florida Times-Union,* November 9, 2003.

Possley, Maurice, and Steve Mills. "Clemency for All: Ryan Commutes 164 Death Sentences to Life in Prison without Parole." *Chicago Tribune,* January 12, 2003.

————, and Ken Armstrong. "Veteran Detective's Murder Case Unravels." *Chicago Tribune,* December 17, 2001.

Prejean, Sr. Helen. *Dead Man Walking: An Eyewitness Account of the Death Penalty in the United States.* New York: Vintage Books, 1994.

Pudlow, Jan. "The Pros and Cons of Privatizing the Death Penalty." *Florida Bar News,* March 1, 2003.

Radelet, Michael L. "Recent Developments in the Death Penalty in Florida." Paper presented at Life over Death: Capital Litigators Training Conference, Florida Public Defender Association, Orlando, Fla., September 7, 2001. Available (updated through December 21, 2001) at http://www .fadp.org/pad/aresearch.html.

————, H. Bedau, and C. Putnam. *In Spite of Innocence: Erroneous Convictions in Capital Cases.* Boston: Northeastern University Press, 1992.

————, and Glenn L. Pierce. "Choosing Who Will Die: Race and the Death Penalty in Florida." 43 *Florida Law Review* 1 (1991).

Rankin, Bill. "DNA May Reopen '75 Massacre Case." *Atlanta Constitution,* January 15, 2003.

Rudolph, Daniel A. "The Misguided Reliance in American Jurisprudence on Jewish Law to Support the Moral Legitimacy of Capital Punishment. 33 *American Criminal Law Review* 437 (1996).

Ruth, Daniel. "The Plan to Turn Florida's Supreme Court into a PAC." Editorial. *Tampa Tribune,* August 31, 2001.

Ryan, Governor George H., Sr. "Clemency for Illinois Death Row Inmates."

Speech, Northwestern University College of Law, Chicago, Ill., January 11, 2003.

———. *Report of the Governor's Commission on Capital Punishment.* April 15, 2002.

St. Petersburg Times. "Justice Has Doubts about Death Penalty: Justice O'Conner Says 'The System May Well Be Allowing Some Innocent Defendants to Be Executed.'" July 4, 2001. Available at http://www.sptimes.com/News/070401/Worldandnation/Justice_has_doubts_ab.shtml.

———. "Man on Death Row Gets New Trial: The Man Was Convicted 15 Years Ago of Raping and Killing a 17-Year-Old Prostitute. Police Withheld a Crucial Crime Report." November 3, 2001. Available at http://www.sptimes.com/News/110301/TampaBay/Man_on_death_row_gets.shtml.

———. "Man to Be Freed after 22 Years: Judge Orders the Release of a Retarded Inmate in the Face of DNA Evidence and Doubts." June 16, 2001. Available at http://www.sptimes.com/News/061601/State/Man_to_be_freed_after.shtml.

Salinero, Mike, and Joe Follick. "Tallahassee 2-Step Begins." *Tampa Tribune,* November 27, 2001.

Schneider, Mike (AP). "Cash Flow into Judges' Campaigns Swelling." *Florida Times-Union,* July 28, 2003.

Seattle Post-Intelligencer. "Special Reports: Death Penalty: Uncertain Justice." August 6–8, 2001. Available at http://seattlep-i.nwsource.com/specials/death penalty.

Shiffman, John. "Troubled Lawyers Still Allowed to Work Death Cases." *Tennessean,* July 26, 2001. Available at http://tennessean.com/special/dp/archives/01/04/06918869.shtml?Element_ID=6918869.

Smedes, Lewis B. *Mere Morality: What God Expects from Ordinary People.* Grand Rapids, Mich.: Wm. B. Eerdmans, 1983.

Smith, Adam C. "Care of Mentally Ill Prisoners Questioned: For the One in Nine Who Is Severely Ill, Prison Can Lead to Violence, Abuse, and Even Death, Experts Say." *St. Petersburg Times,* September 28, 1999. Available at http://www.sptimes.com/News/92899/State/Care_of_mentally_ill_.shtml.

Snyder, T. Richard. *The Protestant Ethic and the Spirit of Punishment.* Grand Rapids, Mich.: Wm. B. Eerdmans, 2001.

Spencer-Wendel, Susan. "Death Row Appeals Office Closing." *Palm Beach Post,* June 2, 2003.

State of Florida Department of Corrections, *Corrections Offender Network—Death Row Roster,* updated as of April 20, 2004. Available at http://www.dc.state.fl.us/activeinmates/deathrowroster.asp.

Steffen, Lloyd. *Executing Justice: The Moral Meaning of the Death Penalty.* Cleveland, Ohio: Pilgrim Press, 1998.

Steinsaltz, Adin. *The Essential Talmud.* Translated by Chaya Galai. New York: Basic Books, 1965.

———. *The Talmud; The Steinsaltz Edition: A Reference Guide.* New York: Random House, 1989.

Stewart, Malcolm. "Enactment of the Florida Death Penalty Statute, 1972: History and Analysis." 16 *Nova Law Review* 1299 (1992).

Streib, Victor L. *The Juvenile Death Penalty Today: Death Sentences and Executions for Juvenile Crimes* (2003). Ada, Ohio: Claude W. Pettit College of Law, Ohio Northern University, 2003, available at http://www.law.onu.edu/faculty/streib/JuvDeathSept2003.htm (last updated October 6, 2003).

Strickland, Sandy. "Death Row to Freedom: Man Adjusts after 7-Year Prison Stretch." *Florida Times-Union*, July 17, 1999.

Strong, James. *A Concise Dictionary of the Words in the Greek New Testament: With Their Renderings in the Authorized English Language Version*, in *The Complete Word Study New Testament with Greek Parallel (King James Version)*. Compiled and edited by Spiros Zodhiates. Iowa Falls: World Bible Publishers, 1992.

Telushkin, Joseph. *Biblical Literacy: The Most Important People, Events, and Ideas of the Hebrew Bible*. New York: William Morrow, 1997.

Tennessean. "Special Report: Tennessee Death Penalty." July 22–29, 2001. Available at http://tennessean.com/special/dp.

Tucker, Rich. "Legal Defense Group Faces Another Fight for Survival." *Florida Times-Union*, April 13, 2003.

U.S. Census Bureau. "Resident Population Estimates of the United States by Sex, Race, and Hispanic Origin: April 1, 1990 to July 1, 1999, with Short-Term Projection to November 1, 2000." http://www.census.gov/population/estimates/nation/intfile3-1.txt.

U.S Department of Justice, Federal Bureau of Investigation. *Uniform Crime Reports: Crime in the United States 2000*. Washington, D.C.: October 2001. http://www.fbi.gov/ucr/00cius.htm.

U.S Department of Justice, Federal Bureau of Investigation. *Uniform Crime Reports: Crime in the United States 2001*. Washington, D.C.: October 2002. http://www.fbi.gov/ucr/01cius.htm.

U.S. Department of Justice, Federal Bureau of Investigation. *Uniform Crime Reports January–December 2002*, by Robert S. Mueller III, director. Washington, D.C.: June 16, 2003. http://www.fbi.gov/ucr/cius_02/02prelimannual.pdf.

U.S. General Accounting Office, *Report to Senate and House Committees on the Judiciary, Death Penalty Sentencing: Research Indicates Pattern of Racial Disparities (February 1990)*. Washington, D.C.: U.S. General Accounting Office, 1990.

Von Drehle, David. *Among the Lowest of the Dead: Inside Death Row*. New York: Fawcett Crest, 1995.

Wasson, David. "Death Penalty Decision Bitter for Bush, GOP." *Tampa Tribune*, April 15, 2000.

Weaver, J. Denny. *The Nonviolent Atonement*. Grand Rapids, Mich.: Wm. B. Eerdmans, 2001.

Weinberg, Steve. "Breaking the Rules: Who Suffers When a Prosecutor Is Cited for Misconduct?" Washington, D.C.: Center for Public Integrity, June 26, 2003. Available at http://www.publicintegrity.org/pm.

Werblowsky, R. J. Zwi, and Geoffrey Wigoder, eds. *The Oxford Dictionary of the Jewish Religion*. New York: Oxford University Press, 1997.

West, Lewis J. "Psychiatric Reflections on the Death Penalty." Chap. 25 in *Voices against Death: American Opposition to Capital Punishment, 1787–1975.* Edited by Philip English Mackey. New York: Burt Franklin, 1976.

West Group. *Texas Criminal Procedure—Code and Rules, 2002 ed. (West's Texas Statutes and Codes).* St. Paul: West, 2002.

——. *West's Florida Statutes Annotated (Annotated Statute & Code Series).* St. Paul: West, a Thomson business, 2002.

——. *West's Reported Cases.* St. Paul: West, a Thomson business, 1957–2003.

Wright, Christopher J. H. *Walking in the Ways of the Lord: The Ethical Authority of the Old Testament.* Downers Grove, Ill.: InterVarsity Press, 1995.

Zampaglione, Arturo. "Non è merito del papa se o'Dell è ancora vivo." *La Repubblica* (Rome, Italy), December 19, 1996.

Ziegler Dizon, Nicole (AP). "Death Penalty Opponents Hope Clemency Move Leads to Wider Change; Supporters Question Motive." *Florida Times-Union,* January 12, 2003.

Zodhiates, Spiros, comp. and ed. *The Complete Word Study New Testament with Greek Parallel (King James Version).* Iowa Falls: World Bible Publishers, 1992.

Zorea, Aharon W. *In the Image of God: A Christian Response to Capital Punishment.* Lanham, Md.: University Press of America, 2000.

Zucconi, Vittorio. "O'Dell torna a sperare: La Corte Suprema ferma Il boia a poche ore dall'esecuzione." *La Repubblica* (Rome, Italy), December 18, 1996.

CASES CITED

U.S. Supreme Court

Wilkerson v. Utah, 99 U.S. 130 (1879).
In re Kemmler, 136 U.S. 436 (1890).
Trop v. Dulles, 78 U.S. 590 (1958).
Furman v. Georgia, 92 S.Ct. 2726 (1972).
Proffitt v. Florida, 428 U.S. 242 (1976).
Gregg v. Georgia, 428 U.S. 153 (1976).
Lockett v. Ohio, 98 S.Ct. 2954 (1978).
McCleskey v. Kemp, 481 U.S. 279 (1987).
Thompson v. Oklahoma, 487 U.S. 815 (1988).
Penry v. Lynaugh, 109 S.Ct. 2934 (1989).
Stanford v. Kentucky, 109 S.Ct. 2969 (1989).
Walton v. Arizona, 110 S.Ct. 3047 (1990).
Coleman v. Thompson, 501 U.S. 722 (1991).
Herrera v. Collins, 506 U.S. 390 (1993).
Callins v. Collins, 114 S.Ct. 1127 (1994).
Harris v. Alabama, 115 S.Ct. 1031 (1995).
Atkins v. Virginia, 536 U.S. 304 (2002).
Ring v. Arizona, 536 U.S. 2428 (2002).

Federal Appeals Court

Carriger v. Stewart, 95 F.3d 755. (U.S. Court of Appeals for the Ninth Circuit, 1996).

Federal District Court

U.S. v. Alan Quinones et al., S3 00 Cr. 761 (JSR) (U.S. District Court for So. District of N.Y., July 1, 2002).

Florida Supreme Court

McCutchen v. State, 96 So.2d 152 (Florida Supreme Court, 1957).
State v. Dixon, 283 So.2d 1 (Florida Supreme Court, 1973).

Walter Ruiz v. State of Florida, 743 So.2d 1 (Florida Supreme Court, 1999).
Allen v. State, 636 So.2d 494 (Florida Supreme Court, 1994).
Brennan v. State, 754 So.2d 1 (Florida Supreme Court 1999).
Michael G. Bruno v. State of Florida, 807 So.2d 55 (Florida Supreme Court, 2001).

Missouri Supreme Court

State ex. rel. Joseph Amrine Petitioner v. Donald P. Roper, Superintendent, Potosi Correctional Center, Respondent, Slip Opinion, SC84656 (Missouri Supreme Court, April 29, 2003).

Foreign Courts

State v. Makwanyane and M Mchunu, Case No. CCT/3/94 (Constitutional Court of the Republic of South Africa).

PERMISSIONS

Permission is gratefully acknowledged, as follows, for permission to print the excerpted text from each of the following.

Scriptures

Reprinted from *TANAKH: The Holy Scriptures,* © 1985 by The Jewish Publication Society, with the permission of the publisher, The Jewish Publication Society. (Signified by TNK.)

Scripture taken from *The Holy Bible, King James Version,* © 1990 by Thomas Nelson, Inc., used courtesy of Thomas Nelson, Inc. (Signified by AV.)

Scripture verses taken from the HOLY BIBLE, NEW INTERNATIONAL VERSION, copyright © 1973, 1978, 1984, by International Bible Society. Used by permission of Zondervan Bible Publishers. (Signified by NIV.)

Materials Involving Talmud

Excerpts from Rabbi Hersch Goldwurm, ed., *Talmud Bavli: Tractate Sanhedrin,* ArtScroll® Series, Schottenstein Edition (Brooklyn: Mesorah Publications, 1993), reproduced from the ArtScroll® Schottenstein Edition of the Talmud with permission of the copyright holders, ArtScroll®/Mesorah Publications, Ltd.

Excerpts from Jacob Neusner, *The Tosefta Translated from the Hebrew, Fourth Division NEZIQIN (The Order of Damages),* © 1981 KTAV Publishing. Reprinted with permission. All rights reserved.

Excerpts from Basil F. Herring, *Jewish Ethics and Halakhah for Our Time: Sources and Commentary,* © 1984 KTAV Publishing and Yeshiva University Press. Reprinted with permission. All rights reserved.

Excerpts from Rabbi Adin Steinsaltz, *The Essential Talmud,* translated from the Hebrew by Chaya Galai (Basic Books, USA, 1965), and *The Talmud; The Steinsaltz Edition: A Reference Guide* (Random House, New York, 1989), © 1989 by The Israel Institute for Talmudic Publications and Milta Books. Reprinted with permission. All rights reserved.

Excerpts from S. Mendelsohn, LL.D, *The Criminal Jurisprudence of the Ancient Hebrews: Compiled from the Talmud and Other Rabbinical Writings, and Compared with Roman and English Penal Jurisprudence*—2nd Edition, © 1968 Hermon Press. By permission of the publisher, Sepher-Hermon Press. All rights reserved.

Legal and Scholarly Books

Excerpts reprinted by permission of the publisher from *The Death Penalty: An American History* by Stuart Banner, pp. 6, 7, 57, 112–13, 137, 142, 228–30, 243–44, Cambridge, Mass.: Harvard University Press, Copyright © 2002 by the President and Fellows of Harvard College.

Excerpts from *A Consuming Fire: The Fall of the Confederacy in the Mind of the White Christian South,* by Eugene D. Genovese. Copyright © 1998 by the University of Georgia Press. Reprinted by permission of the University of Georgia Press.

Excerpts from *Crime and Punishment in American History* (paper) by Friedman, Lawrence M. Copyright © 1994 by Perseus Books Group. Reproduced with permission of Perseus Books Group in the format Textbook via Copyright Clearance Center.

Excerpts from Bennett L. Gershman, *Prosecutorial Misconduct, 2nd Edition,* © 2001 West Group; West's® Florida Statutes Annotated (Annotated Statute & Code Series) © 2003 West, a Thomson business; Texas Criminal Procedure—Code and Rules, 2002 ed. (West's® Texas Statutes and Codes) © 2002 West; and West Reported Cases, © 1957–2003 West, a Thomson business; are reprinted with permission. All rights reserved.

Legal Articles and Speeches by Stephen B. Bright, Esq., Southern Center for Human Rights, Atlanta, Georgia

Excerpts from Stephen B. Bright, "Counsel for the Poor: The Death Penalty: Not for the Worst Crime but for the Worst Lawyer," reprinted by permission of The Yale Law Journal Company and William S. Hein Company from The Yale Law Journal, Vol. 103, pages 1835–83 and of Stephen B. Bright. All rights reserved.

Excerpts from Stephen B. Bright, "Is Fairness Irrelevant?: The

Evisceration of Federal Habeas Corpus Review and Limits on the Ability of State Courts to Protect Fundamental Rights," 54 *Washington and Lee Law Review* 1 (1997), reprinted with permission. All rights reserved.

Excerpts from Stephen B. Bright, "Discrimination, Death, and Denial: The Tolerance of Racial Discrimination in the Infliction of the Death Penalty," 35 *Santa Clara Law Review* 433 (1995), reprinted with the permission of the Santa Clara Law Review and Stephen B. Bright, and first appeared in 35 *Santa Clara Law Review* 433 (1995).

Excerpts from Stephen B. Bright, "Will the Death Penalty Remain Alive in the Twenty-first Century? International Norms, Discrimination, Arbitrariness, and the Risk of Executing the Innocent," 1 *Wisconsin Law Review* 1, Copyright © 2001 by the Board of Regents of the University of Wisconsin System; Reprinted by permission of the Wisconsin Law Review and Stephen B. Bright. All rights reserved.

Excerpts from Stephen B. Bright, "Political Attacks on the Judiciary: Can Justice Be Done amid Efforts to Intimidate and Remove Judges from Office for Unpopular Decisions?" 72 *New York University Law Review*, 308 (May 1997), reprinted with permission. All rights reserved.

Excerpts from Stephen B. Bright, "Can Judicial Independence Be Attained in the South? Overcoming History, Elections, and Misperceptions about the Role of the Judiciary," reprinted with permission. This work was originally published with the *Georgia State University Law Review*. The original text can be found at 14 *Georgia State University Law Review* 817 (July 1998). All rights reserved.

Stephen B. Bright and Patrick J. Keenan, "Judges and the Politics of Death: Deciding between the Bill of Rights and the Next Election in Capital Cases," 73 *Boston University Law Review* 759 (May 1995), reprinted with permission. All rights reserved.

Excerpts from Steven B. Bright, *Restrictions on Federal Review of Death Sentences Passed by Congress in 1996* (Atlanta: SCHR, 1997), reprinted with permission. All rights reserved.

Excerpts from Stephen B. Bright, "The Death Penalty: Casualties and Costs of the War on Crime" (lecture, City Club of Cleve-

Excerpts from Stephen B. Bright, *A Preference for Vengeance: The Death Penalty and the Treatment of Prisoners in Georgia—A Report on Human Rights Violations In Georgia* (Atlanta: SCHR, 1996), reprinted with permission. All rights reserved.

Materials Produced by Richard Dieter, Esq., Death Penalty Information Center, Washington, D.C.

Excerpts from: Richard Dieter, *The Death Penalty in 2003: Year End Report,* © 2003 Death Penalty Information Center; *The Death Penalty in 2002: Year End Report,* © 2002 Death Penalty Information Center; *The Death Penalty in 2001: Year End Report,* © 2001 Death Penalty Information Center; *The Death Penalty in 2000: Year End Report,* © 2000 Death Penalty Information Center; *The Death Penalty in Black and White: Who Lives–Who Dies–Who Decides: New Studies on Racism in Capital Punishment,* © 1998 Death Penalty Information Center; *Innocence and the Death Penalty: The Increasing Danger of Executing the Innocent,* Richard C. Dieter, © 1997 Death Penalty Information Center; *Killing for Votes: The Dangers of Politicizing the Death Penalty Process,* © 1996 Death Penalty Information Center; *Cases of Innocence: 1973–Present* (DPIC, Washington, D.C., © 2004 Death Penalty Information Center); *Clemency: Clemency Process by State* © 2004 Death Penalty Information Center; *Federal Death Penalty of the U.S. Government* (DPIC, Washington, D.C., © 2004 Death Penalty Information Center); *Freed from Death Row,* © 2004 Death Penalty Information Center; *Innocence and the Death Penalty,* © 2004 Death Penalty Information Center; *Execution of Juvenile Offenders,* © 2004 Death Penalty Information Center; *Juveniles and the Death Penalty,* © 2004 Death Penalty Information Center, incorporating Victor L. Streib, *The Juvenile Death Penalty Today: Death Sentences and Executions for Juvenile Crimes,* (2003) (Ada, Ohio: Claude W. Pettit College of Law, Ohio Northern University, 2003); *On the Front Line: Law Enforcement Views on the Death Penalty,* © 1995 Death Penalty Information Center; *Life without Parole* © 2004 Death Penalty Information Center; *Mental Retardation and the Death Penalty,* © 2004 Death Penalty Information Center; *Minimum Death Penalty Ages by American Jurisdiction,* © 2004 Death Penalty Information Center; *Summaries*

Other Periodicals

Churches and Nonprofit Organizations

Excerpts from *To End the Death Penalty: A Report of the National Jewish/Catholic Consultation* (National Conference of Catholic Bishops/United States Catholic Conference, Washington, D.C.), © 1999 USCCB, reprinted with permission. All rights reserved.

Excerpts Robert Renny Cushing and Susannah Sheffer, *Dignity Denied: The Experience of Murder Victims' Family Members Who Oppose the Death Penalty*, 2ⁿᵈ printing, © 2002 Murder Victims' Families for Reconciliation, reprinted with permission. All rights reserved.

Excerpts from Frances Ferris, *One in Six Death Row Inmates Defended at Trial by Lawyers Disciplined by State Bar*, © 2002 Common Sense Foundation, reprinted with permission. All rights reserved.

Excerpts from Steve Weinberg, "Breaking the Rules: Who Suffers When a Prosecutor Is Cited for Misconduct?" © 2003 Center for Public Integrity, reprinted with permission. All rights reserved.

Excerpts from NAMI: The Nation's Voice on Mental Illness, "Criminal Justice and Forensic Issues," chap. 9 in *Policy Platform*, © 2001 NAMI: The Nation's Voice on Mental Illness; and "The Criminalization of Mental Illness: The Criminalization Trend Is Worse than Ever," in *Advocacy: Public Policy and Legal: Where We Stand* © 2002 NAMI: The Nation's Voice on Mental Illness, reprinted with permission. All rights reserved.

Speeches

Excerpts from Governor George H. Ryan Sr., "Clemency for Illinois Death Row Inmates" (speech, Northwestern University College of Law, Chicago, Ill., January 11, 2003), used with permission.

INDEX OF SCRIPTURES CITED

INDEX